THE TRAVELERS' GUIDE TO

ASIAN

CUSTOMS & MANNERS

By the same authors

The Travelers' Guide to African Customs and Manners
The Travelers' Guide to European Customs and Manners
The Travelers' Guide to Latin American Customs and Manners
*The Travelers' Guide to Middle Eastern and North African Customs
and Manners*

THE TRAVELERS' GUIDE TO

ASIAN

CUSTOMS & MANNERS

How to converse, dine, tip, drive, bargain,
dress, make friends, and conduct business
while in Asia

Elizabeth Devine
and
Nancy L. Braganti

ST. MARTIN'S GRIFFIN ✹ NEW YORK

First Revised Edition: December 1998

10 9 8 7 6 5 4 3 2 1

To Connie, Jim, Joanie, Cheryl, Frank, and Daniel, the best of friends;
to Dick, Pat, Bill, and La, the best of siblings;
to Harry, the best of traveling companions and a *raconteur extraordinaire*;
with thanks for the good times, the moral support, the affection,
and, most of all, the laughter.

E.D.

With gratitude to
Betsy, for sleepovers, "pochons," and *listening;*
Cate and Nash, for physical and spiritual nourishment;
Jane, for stitching new patches on old quilts;
Joan F., for finding, fixing, and "foreign" jaunts;
Lanie, for making wise choices for Stowaways and empowering the shipwrecked;
My husband, Fausto, my best fellow traveler, for leading me off the beaten path;
My daughter, Tanya, for laughter, "kitsies," and "Tales of the City."

N.L.B.

CONTENTS

ACKNOWLEDGMENTS

We wish to thank the following for their help in preparing this book: Barbara Allen, Lorraine and Stephen Armitage, Ris Azehari, Terry Bagley, Geneviève Baroux, Béatrice Bastiani, Joël Bellassen, Sushila Bhagat, Kanin Boonsuwan, Bruce Bowman, Beverly Brenner, Vichai Chaicharoen, Sharon Chan, Neil and Phoebe Chen, Teming Chen, Tom and Dorothy Chin, Rita Christiensen, Walt Chu, Tom Clark, the Complete Traveller bookstore in New York City, Bob and Rose Cooper, Cora Costaldi, Anni Crofut, Dr. Kathie Culhane-Pera, Jeanette DeHaan, Riet Dekleermaeker, Louise Delagran, Judith de Rubini, William J. Devine, M. Ajith Dissanayake, Lisa Dobrusin, Katy Dolhun, Krishna Dudani, Victor Eugene Dyer III, Eastern Travel and Trade of Hingham, MA, Lois Fischer, Joan Fontanilla, Theodore Foss, Marion Freedman, Henry C. Fung, Juliet Garcia, Helen Giss, Marcia Goldstick, Ellen Gould, Lynn Grebstad, Clyde Haberman, Julie Harrington, Robert and Nancy Hefner, James L. Hill, Catherine Hindman, Robert Holmes, Harry M. Hughes, Imad Husain, Wilfred Jamison, Japan Club Tours, Nusrat Javeed, Briareus Jayewardene, J. E. Jesudason, Rita Kakar, Ahmed Khaled, Kam-Fun Lam, Patricia Lee, Pei-Fang Lee, Yung Ven Lee, Kevin Leong, Allen and Adina Linden, Paulette Litz, Li Xiaobo, William Lyons, Norma Mahmood, Mao Quing, Meghan McCloskey, Mary Jo McConnell, Ginny Mellinger, Jim Meek, Dr. Min Lu, Ross Monnox, Nighat Mosin, Karin Muller, Robert and Sudha Newman, Anita Nesiah, Joanne O'Keefe, Patricia Parker, Hans Pittinger, Helaine Pryor, Danny Quah, Qi Chong, Lucivic P. Quicho, Mirella and Pietro Rampazzo, Ninette Ravji, Diana Reynolds, Janet Rutherfurd, Lark Schulze, Urs and Elizabeth Sieber, Donna and Eddy Subegdjo, Sun Jie, Shigemichi and Judy Takata, Junji Takeuchi, Charlotte Tannheimer, Binod Thapa, Nora Thapa, Yen Thi Tran, Nancy Turner, Monica Veneziano, Lesley Moore Vossen, Grazia Walker, Thomas Webb, Ann Williams, Richard Winslow, Yoshio Yamada. And special thanks to Anne Savarese for her encouragement, advice, and patience.

INTRODUCTION

"I've a feeling we're not in Kansas anymore." So says the bewildered Dorothy to her little dog, Toto, when she first sees the Land of Oz. Her response is very like that of a Westerner arriving in an Asian country such as Japan, China, or Thailand for the first time. Once beyond the airport (where signs are often in English), the first realization is that you can't read anything—except signs for the ubiquitous fast-food restaurants.

Hard on the heels of finding yourself an illiterate comes the realization that people do things differently—*very* differently. While bookstores in Europe and North America stock plenty of guides about places to see and religious monuments to visit, no one—until *The Travelers' Guide to Asian Customs and Manners*—has told you how to behave in Asian countries, where people are very conscious of the accepted ways of greeting, conversing, etc.

In this book, we let you know what to expect and what is expected of you. It's comforting to know the correct ways to greet, converse, bargain, use the telephone, eat, and do business in a foreign country and culture.

In revising the text, we have verified that much of the information from the first edition is still accurate, and we have noted the many changes in Asian customs and manners since the first edition. We found that—with Western TV programs available via satellite and CNN almost everywhere— Asians are much more familiar with the ways of the West than they were even ten or twelve years ago. We also found that most Asian countries tenaciously hold to customs and manners that have served them well over the centuries.

For convenience, we have arranged the Asian countries alphabetically, with a supplement on two major nations in the South Pacific—Australia and New Zealand. For quick reference we have divided the information into a series of topics:

Greetings: Be conscious that forms of greetings differ widely. In Japan, bow your head slightly, but in India, incline your head with hands together (as though in prayer).

Priorities in greeting are very important. In Europe and North America, it is customary to greet the host first. In most Asian countries, however, it is essential to greet the oldest person in the group first.

Conversation: Some topics can start you off on the right foot (when in doubt, try a sincere compliment about the country), while others may be construed as insults. Many Westerners know Thailand only through the hit musical *The King and I* and think it a natural subject to bring up. Thais, however, have long felt that the musical held one of their national heroes up to ridicule.

People who have traveled in Europe, where personal questions are verboten, may be astonished to find that Asians often ask very personal questions on the briefest acquaintance. Someone with whom you have struck up a conversation in a restaurant may ask, "How old are you?" or "How much money do you make?"

In all countries, resist the temptation to share your favorite jokes. Humor doesn't travel well.

Telephones: We try to take the mystery out of public telephones and warn not to expect the sort of phone service often available in the United States, Canada, and Europe. In some countries you will find phone booths in the usual public places, while in others you must depend on the goodwill of shopkeepers to let you use their phone for local calls.

Although some hotels impose surcharges on long-distance or overseas calls, the extra cost may be worthwhile to avoid the wear and tear on your nerves that making calls from a post office usually entails. If you do use the post office phones, bring reading material—*War and Peace* should do—because the waits for calls to go through are interminable.

In Public: Gestures that are acceptable in Western countries can offend in Asia. Westerners are, by and large, given to touching other people. In Japan, that's a major error in behavior. And one way we show approval of a child is with a pat on the head. That's a terrible mistake in Asia, where the head is regarded as the repository of the soul. Another problem could rise with the usual acceptance, in North America and Western Europe, of public displays of affection between the sexes; in China, such displays outrage the culture's moral values.

Some travelers miss the comfort of letters from home because their mail is misfiled. If you aren't sure where you'll be staying, you can have mail sent to you c/o American Express (if you hold their credit card or use their travelers' checks) or at *Poste Restante* at post offices in major cities. Be aware, however, that there may be confusion as to which is your first and which your family name. Advise your correspondents to underline your last name, and, when you pick up mail, ask if there is any filed under your first name.

A problem for (relatively) affluent Westerners in Asia is whether to give to beggars. If you give to one, you may be deluged by masses of beggars. If your conscience bothers you about the poverty you're observing, make a contribution to an organization—e.g., a health clinic in a rural area.

In this section, we have also covered one of the great bugbears of travel: where the public toilets are, what they are called, and how you can tell the men's from the women's.

For many people, one of the pleasures of a trip to Asia is shopping, but Westerners aren't often attuned to the usual method of shopping in Asia—bargaining. We've tried to give some pointers on how you can obtain the best price, whatever you're buying.

If you're having clothes made for you, start the process as soon as you arrive to allow time for two or three fittings. Beware of accepting a tailor's offer to have a garment ready in 24 hours. Often the fit isn't correct, the quality of the workmanship isn't high, and the finishing details may be neglected.

Some travelers like to buy fabric, such as silk, to have made into a garment later in their home country. In some countries, fabric is sold by the yard—36 inches. In others, it is sold by the meter—39.37 inches.

Be aware that ready-made clothes are prepared for the smaller Asian figure and that size systems may vary from country to country. Large department stores will usually have charts enabling you to decide which size is appropriate for you. Make a note of it, in case you find yourself in a small shop where no one speaks English.

Women's sizes larger than U.S. 12 (U.K. 10) will probably not be available in ready-made clothes. For larger sizes, ask at your hotel or the tourist office about factory-outlet shops for exports—or indulge in the luxury of having a dress or blouse custom-made. A warning for those who plan to look for bargains in Asia. In recent years, prices have skyrocketed. For example, in Tokyo, in May 1998, shaving cream cost $20 per can.

Finally, we have dealt with the subject of exercise, specifically jogging. Many Westerners have taken up fitness with a vengeance in the last few years, and jogging has become one of the most popular forms of exercise. We'll tell you when to jog (in most places it's best to jog very early in the morning, before the oppressive heat takes over), where to jog, and what to wear.

Swimmers should try to stay at one of the many hotels with pools. If your hotel doesn't have a pool, ask if guests are accorded pool privileges at a nearby hotel.

In response to the Western fitness craze, some newer hotels have health clubs with pools, workout rooms, and, in some cases, indoor jogging tracks.

Dress: You can't offend by being conservative. While many travelers often favor bright colors, a colorful outfit might make you feel out of place in Japan, where muted colors are the rule.

In some countries, it is both a compliment and a pleasant experience to wear native dress. For example, men will probably find the *barong* shirt worn in the Philippines both comfortable and attractive.

Visitors from the West are usually unprepared for the heat and humidity they encounter in much of Asia. Although synthetic fabrics are a convenience, they are murderously hot. Stick to natural fabrics. (*Note:* Men shouldn't pack seersucker suits—seersucker is a synthetic fabric.)

Meals: What you'll eat and when. Eating in Asia can be as much or as little an adventure as you want it to be. In Hong Kong, you can eat at McDonald's, you can sample food from every province of China, or you can retreat to the cuisine of Europe at most of the large hotels.

While many of us travel to Asia in search of culinary adventures, we often want to confine them to lunch and dinner. It's therefore a comfort to know that most large hotels offer Western-style breakfasts. But one day at least try *congee*, the Chinese rice gruel that's the standard breakfast fare in many Asian countries. It's filling, mild, and good.

Visitors to Asia often fear the embarrassment of coping with chopsticks. Remember the old joke: A traveler needing directions stops a New Yorker and asks, "How do you get to Carnegie Hall?" The New Yorker's response is "Practice, practice." That's good advice for using chopsticks as well. Go to a Chinese restaurant in your local area, order a meal to take out, and ask for chopsticks. Practice using them at home. Clean them after the meal, and practice picking up small objects with them. The major mistake that most people make is holding the chopsticks too close to the bottom. Hold them half to three-quarters of the way up, and you'll find them much easier to manipulate.

Asians are accustomed to foreigners asking for fork and spoon, but they will be pleased if you use chopsticks. (You will never need a knife, because the ingredients are always cut into small pieces.)

We cannot stress too strongly the need to exercise caution with food and water. NEVER drink water unless you see it being poured from a bottle or know that it has been boiled. Even places where you might expect the water to be safe might not be. One traveler was staying at a deluxe hotel in Thailand. She went to lunch in the hotel's plush European-style dining room and thought surely the water served there would be safe to drink. She spent the next ten days paying for that mistake.

It's also important to avoid raw vegetables (good-bye, salads) and fruit that you can't peel. And in countries such as India and Pakistan, order milk products—including yogurt—only in restaurants where you can feel sure that standards of hygiene are high.

Tempting as the sights and smells of food from street vendors may be, never buy or eat anything from street stalls. On a hot day, the fruit juices or the ice cream may look appealing, but succumbing to that temptation could prove disastrous.

We finish this section with information on some of the specialties you'll probably want to try, and some few—such as tangerine-flavored ox penis, a Chinese dish—that you may want to avoid.

Hotels: The hotels frequented by Western visitors offer accommodations that range from acceptable to almost incredibly luxurious.

Another option in countries such as Japan and Korea is to stay in the inns native to those nations. In Japan, staying at a *ryokan*—where the visitor senses the serenity derived from the effort to harmonize the inn with its natural surroundings—is really a short course in Japanese culture.

Or consider reliving the days of the Raj by renting a houseboat in northern India.

Tipping: It's hard to get used to tip-free societies, but that's what many countries in Asia are. Not only is tipping usually not expected, but, in some cases, it is regarded as an insult. Some may remember when U.S. President Ronald Reagan, on a trip to China, tried to tip a shopkeeper, who then chased him down the street to return the money.

As a general rule of thumb: people in hotels, restaurants, etc., frequented by tourists are much more likely to be acquainted with the Western custom of tipping than those outside such areas.

Private Homes: Most Asians are very, very hospitable, and while Westerners probably won't be invited to spend the night in a home because of space limitations, they may well be asked to come for a visit. Spending some time in a private home in the populous Asian countries will teach you a genuine lesson in making the maximum use of space. After learning that the Japanese fold up their bedding, store it in cupboards, and then use the room for other purposes, one traveler we know considered restructuring her home in Boston.

Business: One of the major reasons for the strong interest in Asia has been business opportunities there, and planes to Tokyo, Hong Kong, and Singapore are filling with people eager to cash in on the markets there.

We begin this section with some nuts and bolts: first, the hours that banks, offices, and shops in each country are open (make special note of Muslim areas where Friday is the Sabbath). We've also given information on the currency of each country and the denominations in which it comes. A common mistake when dealing with foreign currency is to stuff a supply in your wallet without looking at it and then panic when you have to use it. When you get your first supply of a country's currency, sit down and familiarize yourself with the bills and coins and identify them with approximate equivalents in your own currency.

There is also advice on which credit cards are accepted and where. In general, you can use plastic money in areas frequented by tourists, but if you're striking into non-tourist areas, bring a supply of cash. Major credit cards—American Express, Visa (Barclaycard in England), MasterCard (Access in England), and Diners Club—are accepted in the same places you would find them accepted at home.

Under "Business Practices," we've given advice on how to have the best chance of making your business trip profitable. Be prepared for a high value to be placed on personal relationships before business relationships. Your first meeting may simply be a "get acquainted" session—sometimes over a meal—and may involve very little, if any, actual discussion of business.

In countries other than Japan and the Philippines, it's best not to use a favorite Western business method—doing business by telephone. Most Asians don't like the practice, and problems with phone service make it impractical.

Remember that, though business in the West often tends to favor youth, a company starting to do business in Asia would be well advised to send a delegation headed by someone at least fifty years old, because of the great value Asians place on age and experience.

Some important phone numbers for business include the U.S. Department of Commerce, Asia Business Center, will fax information to you on a variety of topics for many countries. The telephone number for the hotline menu is 1-800-USA-TRAD. For a directory of American Chambers of Commerce overseas, call (202) 659-6000. The Trade Information Center, an arm of the U.S. Department of Commerce, provides information on sources of international financing and promotion, trade leads, trade events and activities, documentation and licensing requirements (phone 1-800-872-8723, fax (202) 482-4473). The Overseas Private Investment Corporation has a telephone InfoLine (202) 336-8799, which offers brief recorded program descriptions and takes request for printed information; a FactsLine (202) 336-8700 takes requests for documents and reports to be faxed.

Other business advice applicable to all of Asia: Never use jargon or slang, because people will not understand it. Avoid using jargon from sports— e.g., "ballpark figure."

Asians usually adhere to an agenda. They do not like surprises.

Don't push people to make immediate decisions. Asians need time to discuss matters among themselves first.

Don't expect people to ask questions in a group setting. They will do so in a one-on-one meeting.

Bring an adapter or batteries for any appliances you plan to use, since Asian countries' current is 220 volts. When one traveler went to purchase an adapter for her laptop computer, she was told that she would be better off using a battery, since computers could become damaged by the adapter/ current.

Holidays: Tourists often want to plan a trip around a certain festival— the Chinese New Year or Hong Kong's famous Dragon Boat Festival— while people doing business may wish to avoid such celebrations because businesses are usually closed.

Whether you are an includer or an avoider, it's important to check with the tourist office, embassy, or consulate of the country you plan to visit, since many, many holidays and festivals are determined by the lunar calendar—and thus the dates change each year.

The holidays we have included for each country are the national holidays, celebrated throughout the country. There are, however, countless local festivals, religious celebrations, etc., which are holidays in the area where they are celebrated. Be sure to check with the country's tourist office to learn about such holidays. On national holidays, expect to find all banks, businesses, and stores closed. (If you become desperate for food or drink, remember that hotel restaurants and bars are usually open on holidays.)

Transportation: The quality and quantity of transportation vary widely in Asia. Probably the most felicitous public transportation in the world is the Star Ferry, which connects Kowloon and Hong Kong islands and offers a spectacular view of the harbor. On the other hand, buses in most urban areas are crowded and hot almost beyond description. Getting around is best accomplished by taxi or by hiring a car and driver.

In this section we have also given information on the types of accommodations available on trains.

Whatever method of transportation you choose, always have your destination and the name of your hotel written down in the local language, so that you can show it to taxi drivers or to other people if you are lost.

Legal Matters, Safety, and Health: This section specifies the items you can bring in and take out of a particular country. Be especially conscious of those countries from which it is illegal to remove religious images. Violations of such rules are taken *very* seriously.

In addition, there are two important items to be considered when planning a trip to Asia. The first is health. To insure a healthy trip, U.S. travelers should call the Centers for Disease Control in Atlanta, Georgia— (404) 639-3311—to learn about required immunizations and about any special health problems you may encounter. The hotline number for up-to-date worldwide health information is (404) 332-4565. If you have access to a fax machine, the information can be faxed to you. Or you can call the office of the U.S. Public Health Service Quarantine Station nearest you:

Chicago—(312) 686-2150; Honolulu—(808) 541-2552; Los Angeles—(213) 215-2365; Miami—(305) 526-2910; New York—(718) 917-1685; San Francisco—(415) 876-2872; Seattle—(206) 442-4519.

Canadians should write or call for the brochure "Travel and Health," which gives information about health precautions to take when traveling outside Canada. Address: Health and Welfare Canada, 5th Floor, Brooke Claxton Building, Tunney's Pasture, Ottawa K1A OK9. Phone: (613) 957-2991.

British travelers should ask their travel agents about health conditions, since the agents are updated frequently by the Department of Health and Social Security. Travelers may also telephone the Department at (01) 407-5522 to ask for "Public Inquiries" (to learn of any updated health forecasts) and to request a copy of their booklet, "Protect Your Health Abroad." Australians should call the health department in Sydney at 239-3000.

To avoid illness on your trip or as an unpleasant souvenir on your return home, read about appropriate precautions and about recognizing symptoms of potentially serious diseases in *International Travel and Health 1996* available from W.H.O. Publications Center, c/o Boyd Printing, 49 Sheridan Avenue, Albany, NY 12210; (518) 436-9686.

To avoid malaria, a serious problem in some countries, take the following precautions: Use a prophylactic drug (ask your physician about starting a regime of antimalarial drugs before leaving home), use mosquito repellant, wear long-sleeved clothing, use a mosquito net on your bed, and avoid wearing perfume at night, as it can attract mosquitoes.

Always keep your prescription drugs in their original containers. Don't, for example, take them out to put them in moisture-proof pill boxes. When you enter an Asian country, you could be suspected of attempting to smuggle drugs into the country. Remember, also, that drugs available over the counter in Asian countries may be available only by prescription in your home country. Bringing such medicine (even something as seemingly innocent as cough medicine) with you when you come home may subject you to arrest.

The second item of concern may be the many political conflicts that have erupted in various Asian countries. To find out if you're at risk, call the Citizen's Emergency Center for the U.S. Department of State at (202) 647-5225. For the same information, Canadians should call Canadian Travel Advisory at 800-267-6788, British Travel Service is at 037-500-900, and Australian Travel Advisory is available at 06-261-2093.

As soon as you've decided to go to Asia and know which countries you'll be visiting, check with embassies, consulates, or a travel agency to learn visa requirements for those countries. (Requirements change frequently.)

We mention that, in several countries, people will approach you and ask to practice their English. Make your own decision about this. If someone approaches you in a restaurant or bar and asks to practice English, be cautious. One Australian visitor to Bangkok agreed to such a request in the cocktail lounge of one of the city's best hotels. His drink was drugged, and his car was stolen. (His life was saved only because the thieves underestimated the amount of the drug that would be needed to kill him.)

As a precaution, keep copies of your passport, credit cards, airline tickets, and travelers' checks in a separate, secure place in case the originals are lost or stolen. A passport copy is not a legal document, but it will be easier to replace your passport if you lose it.

A Few Words for Women: Don't drink or dine late in the day with a male business associate. To exit gracefully, say that you're tired or have an early morning appointment.

Asian men view foreign businesswomen of Asian heritage as having less authority than Caucasian women. Such women will have to be assertive—always with dignity—to command respect. At meetings, it's a good idea for such women to speak English and bring a translator so that Asian counterparts are aware of their managerial position.

In many countries, we've recommended that if you're traveling in the countryside, a long skirt instead of pants is cooler and makes it easier to "use the field" if there are no public bathrooms available.

Key Phrases: There's no doubt that communicating with an Asian who doesn't speak English is difficult. Several languages, such as Thai, are tonal, and the tone determines the meaning of the word. A few phrases, however, can ease things. In using the key phrases, pay special attention to the pronunciation, since, in most cases, you are unlikely to see the words written in the Roman alphabet. If possible, learn the words for numbers in the language of the country you're visiting. Despite the problems in verbal communication, you'll be amazed at what a few gestures can accomplish.

Note: If we have had to choose between different advice on behavior in certain situations, we have selected the more conservative option, since you can rarely err by being "too polite," whereas you can by being too informal.

GENERAL TIPS ON ASIAN TRAVEL

Prepare, prepare, prepare. Read whatever you can about the countries you are going to visit. Whether traveling for business or pleasure, you will please people if you know something of the history and culture of their country. Any encyclopedia will have a brief summary of the country's past; for a really comprehensive view, try the *Insight Guides* (APA Productions, Prentice-Hall, New Jersey; Harrap, London; Lansdowne Press, New South Wales), which devote a whole book to each country. They're a bit pricey (about $15 or £10 each) and probably too heavy to take along, but they are superb background reading.

To understand any Asian country is impossible without some knowledge of the religions that are such a dominant force in the history, customs, and cultures of the countries (just as a knowledge of Christianity greatly enhances a visit to most European countries). Watching people in Japan pull giant ropes before and after they pray is more interesting when you know that the first pull summons the spirits and the second sends them back. It will be well worth the effort to visit used bookstores or your library to find a copy of Huston Smith's *The Religions of Man* (published by Harper and Row). Since the book is now out of print, finding it may take some hunting, but reading it will add immeasurably to your understanding of Asia. It's written for the layperson and is filled with fascinating and easily understandable information about the religions of the world.

Some other tips:

• Learn to refer to the area as Asia and to the people as Asians. Don't call it the Far East, since that name is a reminder of the colonial domination of Britain, when the expression meant "far from London." Also avoid the terms "Orient," "Orientals," and "Asiatic."

• If your travel habits have been formed in European cities, consider a major change in travel practices (a lesson the authors learned the hard way). The best way to see London or Paris is to put on your walking shoes and tour the cities on foot. That's a good way to get heat stroke in Singapore. It wasn't easy to get up the nerve to hire a car and driver for a half day, but it isn't really that expensive and it makes all the difference between discomfort and enjoyment. (If you can, get an English-speaking driver; he'll probably also function as a guide.) Your hotel can easily arrange such transportation for you.

• Don't judge. Because things are different doesn't make them either better or worse. Be especially careful not to compare the way something is done in your country to the way it's done in Asia. One traveler offended a Thai by commenting that traffic in her hometown of Chicago was certainly controlled better than the traffic in Bangkok. Also note that in many Asian countries driving is on the left, as in Britain. North Americans sometimes find this pattern confusing and say that driving is on the "wrong" side of the road. Don't use such an expression. Roads don't have right and wrong sides; they simply have different sides.

• Ask questions—and listen to the answers. There are few people who don't love to be interviewed—in a non-pushy way—and fewer still who aren't closet restaurant critics or tour guides. An almost sure way to make friends is to ask advice about things to see and places to eat. Sometimes you don't even have to ask for help. One traveler was trying to order a meal in a small hotel about 100 miles from Tokyo. A Japanese woman saw her despair at being unable to communicate. She rescued the traveler by recommending what turned out to be an excellent meal and then invited the tourist to visit her home in Kobe.

• Be prepared for total strangers—especially schoolchildren—to approach and greet you. The approach of a stranger in New York's Central Park is a signal to flee, but people in Asia are not only very friendly but also very eager to practice their English (and Westerners are pretty easy to pick out). People may even ask you to be photographed with them, especially if you are a blonde female, a real oddity in Asia.

• Keep your sense of humor. It's a valuable asset for any travel. In retrospect, travel tragedies have a way of turning into great dinner-party anecdotes. If a situation is really bothersome, try to pretend you're an observer, not a participant. It's one way to see the funny side.

Packing List: This isn't intended as a comprehensive packing list but simply advice on some items you should consider packing. Common sense will dictate many many of the supplies you bring. If you're sticking to cities, such as Singapore and Hong Kong, you can count on being able to get aspirin, shampoo, and ordinary toiletries (an exception: cities in China, which may/may not have supplies you need). If you're venturing into rural areas, you would be well advised to bring anything you might need. A specific brand of shampoo, headache remedy, etc., might not be available easily, so if you're accustomed to one brand, best bring it.

Medical Supplies: Be sure to bring a more than adequate supply of any prescription drugs (in their original containers) you may be taking. If you run out, you could be in trouble, since drugs are known by different names in different countries. A good bet is to ask your physician to provide you with a detailed list—with generic names—of all prescription drugs you are taking, plus duplicate prescriptions for these items. Always pack your medication in your carry-on bag for safety.

If you wear glasses, bring an extra pair as well as a copy of your prescription.

Besides any medication you may be taking, bring an antidiarrhea medication and a broad-spectrum antibiotic to combat bacterial infection. You'll need a prescription for both.

Other items to consider bringing: Aspirin or your favorite headache/fever remedy, an antacid, a laxative, a motion-sickness remedy, insect repellant, lotion for insect bites, sunscreen, a cream to relieve sunburn, an antibiotic ointment for cuts, Band-Aids, a mentholated decongestant, cough medicine, a remedy for muscle pains, and salt pills to combat heat exhaustion—especially in summer. Women may wish to include remedies for menstrual cramps and vaginal yeast infections. It's also wise to bring a thermometer.

Toiletries: Shampoo, deodorant, toothbrush and toothpaste, soap powder or liquid for washing clothes, a portable clothesline that can be strung over a bathtub, a shower cap (most first-class hotels furnish plastic shower caps), tissues (always carry some, as public washrooms do not have toilet paper), and moist towelettes.

Supplies: A flashlight with batteries and a hair dryer (if you're about to buy a new one, choose one that works on both 110 and 220 volts; if not, bring the one you have and ask for a converter at your hotel—most hotels have an ample supply of converters).

As Glinda, the Good Witch, helped Dorothy maneuver through the mysteries of Oz, we hope to enhance your travels to Asia—because you'll be familiar with the customs and manners.

Bon voyage.

ELIZABETH DEVINE
NANCY L. BRAGANTI

CHINA

Until recently, China, home to a quarter of the world's population, was a vast mystery to most Westerners. Many of us knew little about China beyond the suspect information derived from old Rita Hayworth movies. In the mid-1970s all that changed, when relations between the Western countries and China were normalized.

Travelers discovered an ancient and awesome civilization. Who invented paper? Who probably invented pasta? Who developed methods of constructing houses that would sway in an earthquake but not collapse?

However, since the events of spring 1989, in Beijing, many travelers who could choose whether or not to travel to China have changed their plans. Many people have felt a moral conflict about whether to spend their travel funds in support of China's government.

In response to this dilemma, the respected travel writer Simon Winchester wrote, "The kind of travel that takes one to the China of the Chinese people is admirable and to be encouraged; the kind that most tour companies organize that takes one to the China of the present Chinese government, is, for the time being, less morally justifiable."

GREETINGS

• Remember that in Chinese names, the family names always comes first (e.g., in the name Chen Hua, Chen is the family name). Refer to persons as "Mr.," "Mrs.," or "Miss" with the family name (Mr. Chen, Miss Chen, etc.). If you know a person's title—e.g., Doctor, Professor, Mayor, Officer (for a government official)—use it. Only family members or close friends use first names. Keep in mind that women don't take their husbands' family names when they marry; they keep their own family names.

• Don't use official titles in social conversation. Use "Mr.," "Mrs.," or "Miss."

• When you visit communes, theaters, factories, or schools, people may clap in greeting. Clap in return.

• In cities such as Beijing or Shanghai, and in business situations, expect the Western greeting of a handshake. Wait for Chinese to extend a hand first, as not everyone uses this gesture.

• Note that relatives are called by their relationship to you; i.e., second-aunt-older-than-my-father. They will tell you what to call them.

• Be aware that the Chinese use nicknames with each other; i.e., they add the prefix *xiao*, meaning "small," for short or young people, and *lao* for older people. As a Westerner, don't use these terms of endearment unless you are a very close friend.

• Don't kiss when saying "hello" or "good-bye," even with close relatives.

CONVERSATION

• Expect the Chinese to ask the following questions in the following order:

1. Where are you from?
2. How old are you?

3. Are you married?
4. How much money do you make?

If you decide to answer number 4, explain how much such items as rent, food, and clothing cost in your home country.

• Don't be surprised if a Chinese person stands very close to you when conversing—much closer than you are probably used to. Personal space is less important to the Chinese than it is to most Westerners.

• Good conversation topics include personal questions, such as those above; sights you've seen and sights the Chinese would advise you to see; Chinese culture; where to buy things; life in Western countries.

• Avoid talking about sex, or asking what people think of their government.

• Don't joke about sex, politics, or government leaders—either Chinese or foreign.

• Expect shock if you as a foreigner criticize your own government.

• Don't refer to the country as "Mainland China," "Red China," or "Communist China." Call it the "People's Republic of China." Refer to Taiwan as the "Province of Taiwan" never the "Republic of China."

TELEPHONES

• Be aware that only about 30 percent of Chinese people have private telephones.

• Make local calls from public pay phones or from privately owned booths. You'll find one on almost every street corner. You can make long-distance domestic calls from the phone booths, but not international calls.

• For international calls, go to a telecommunications office. You will usually find one in or near the main post office. They are open 24 hours a day. After you pay a deposit, you will be directed to a booth. When you have finished your call, the cost will be calculated, and you pay at the desk. The minimum charge is for three minutes.

• In cities, consider buying a phone card, available in denominations of 20, 50, 100, and 200 *yuan*. You will be charged by the minute. Phones that take these cards are located in hotel lobbies or telecommunications buildings. Buy the cards in hotels, some shops, and post offices. You can use phone cards only in the province in which you purchased them.

• Look for telegraph offices and post offices that offer fax and Telex services.

• Note that most large hotels offer telephone, fax, and Telex services. You needn't be a guest to use them. However, be prepared for a very high surcharge on international calls from hotels.

• If you need police, dial 110. For a fire emergency, dial 119. For an ambulance, dial 120.

• Expect people to answer the phone by saying *"Wei, wei"* (pronounced "way, way"—the equivalent of "hello" when answering the phone).

IN PUBLIC

• Never back-slap or hug. The Chinese are not demonstrative and will not understand such behavior.

• Avoid violating the strict Chinese moral code by flirting or making displays of affection.

• Don't be offended if Chinese stare at you. It is their natural curiosity about Western appearance and clothing.

• Realize that there is almost no concept of privacy. People may grab things such as books, letters, etc., from you to get a closer look at them.

• Pulling your earlobe gently between thumb and index finger signals excellence.

• Don't be surprised to see people frequently spitting on the street.

• Be prepared to be bombarded by Chinese people wanting to ask you questions and to practice English.

• In making plans, keep in mind that cities other than Shanghai, Canton, and Beijing close down very early. Stores close at 6:00 P.M., it's hard to find a place open for dinner after 7:00 P.M., and the last bus usually leaves around 8:30 or 9:00 P.M.

• For directions or other information, look for students, who are usually well informed. Ask questions in a way that doesn't imply a specific answer, because the Chinese will tell you what they think you want to hear. Don't say, for example, "Is the museum in the next street?" The Chinese will say "Yes," which may not be true. Asking "Where is the museum?" is more likely to produce an accurate answer.

• In the countryside, ask questions (about directions, etc.) of men. Women probably won't know the answers.

• Be aware that women never

smoke, except at banquets and parties. (You may see older women, who don't care what others say, smoke.) If you're a businesswoman or the wife of a businessman, don't smoke except at banquets and parties. Smoking in private is acceptable.

• If you smoke, offer your cigarettes to others in your group. Chinese don't usually offer women cigarettes unless they've seen them smoking.

• Pack plenty of reading material, since there isn't much to do at night, and restaurants may close very early.

• If you need a public bathroom, go into a hotel; their bathrooms are usually fine. In restaurants, they are marginal. Bring your own toilet paper, because none is furnished. Public restrooms in parks, museums, and temples are usually only porcelain bowls imbedded in the ground or floor. Be prepared to squat. In some places, you'll find low partitions without doors between the holes, but in other places you won't.

• Throw toilet paper in a wastebasket next to the toilet. Don't toss it in the toilet, or the whole system may become clogged.

• Before you photograph anyone at close range, ask permission. Be aware that people may be upset if you take an instant-image picture of a group and then give the print to just one individual, or if you take a picture of one person and keep it for yourself.

• Don't photograph police sta-

tions, military institutions, cultural performances (with a flash), and in certain museums. Don't take pictures emphasizing poverty; authorities are distressed by such pictures.

• Don't photograph from airplanes or at airports. If one member of a group takes pictures at an airport, the entire group may have their film confiscated.

Shopping: Be aware that some shops and streets display signs in *pinyin*—a Romanizing of Chinese characters.

• Feel free to bargain in markets. Try bargaining in shops. In large stores, where prices are marked, don't bargain.

• Be prepared for people to stare at you or even follow you if you shop at local stores. Most tourists shop at Friendship Stores, which are only for tourists. Those watching you are merely curious. Just smile.

Exercise: Men and women should feel free to jog or to join the groups doing *taiji* in the parks. Many people exercise at 5:30 A.M. before going to work. Shorts are acceptable for exercising.

DRESS

• Jeans are acceptable informal wear for both men and women.

• To be treated with respect by the Chinese, always dress neatly—no torn jeans or shirts. Western men who wear shorts or go shirtless will be stared at.

• For business or dinners out, women should wear a suit (skirt or pants), skirt and blouse, or a dress.

• For summer business meetings, men don't need a jacket or tie, but they should wear a suit or jacket and tie in winter.

• To summer banquets, men should wear a jacket, but will usually be able to remove it during the meal. (Take your lead from your host.) For both business meetings and summer banquets, an alternative is a safari suit with short sleeves; it appears more formal than shirt and slacks.

• Formal dress for men is suit and tie. Women should wear a dressy outfit—high heels and evening gown—to a formal reception given by a foreign diplomat.

• If going to the opera, circus, or theater, wear ordinary dress as the Chinese do. In rural areas, the floor will be mud. For discos and clubs, dress up, as the Chinese do.

• When visiting a mosque in a Muslim area, women should wear long sleeves and either a skirt that covers them to the ankles or pants. In the countryside, women can wear short-sleeved shirts.

• Note that people do wear bikinis, but nudity is unacceptable.

• Both men and women should bring rubber-soled shoes (e.g., sneakers, tennis shoes) for visiting factories and farms, where you're likely to encounter dirty floors and mud.

MEALS

Hours and Foods

• Keep in mind that during the week, Chinese eat their main meal at night; on weekends the main meal is eaten at noon.

Breakfast (zau san): 6:00 or 7:00 A.M. to 7:00 or 8:00 A.M. Typical dishes are cakes and bread, a rice gruel (zhou), dumplings, rice, pickles, salted or "1000-year-old" eggs, and tea. In large hotels, a Western-style breakfast is available.

• "Thousand-year-old" eggs are usually duck eggs coated with lime, ashes, and mud and placed in a jar to ripen for three to four months. The egg white becomes firm and the yolk becomes green. Besides breakfast, they are served as an hors d'oeuvre.

Lunch (wu san): noon or 12:30 P.M. to 1:00 or 1:30 P.M. A typical meal for guests would be an omelette with stir-fried vegetables, and soup.

Dinner (wan san): 6:00 or 7:00 P.M. to 7:00 or 8:00 P.M. A typical meal consists of four meat or fish dishes, two vegetable dishes, one soup, and boiled rice—for example: cooked meat with turnips; diced chicken cubes in yellow bean sauce; quick-fried sliced lamb with spring onions; stirred shrimp; cabbage; cold mixed cucumbers; beancurd and sliced meat soup; plain steamed rice.

• If you are invited to a meal, expect not a typical meal but a feast. You might be served a cold plate (such as tofu—bean-curd—salad and 1000-year-old eggs), steamed fish, sweet-and-sour fish, a meat dish, and an egg dish. During the meal you'll drink beer; after the meal, tea. At an ordinary meal in a home or restaurant, all dishes may be served at the same time or in sequence; at a banquet, courses will be served in sequence.

• Should you be invited to a birthday dinner, expect hand-made noodles *(lie mien)* to be featured—vermicelli is a symbol of longevity and is served to ensure long life.

• Express special appreciation if you are served shark's-fin or bird's-nest soup. They are banquet-style dishes conveying honor and respect. The nests for bird's-nest soup are made by sea swallows that nest in the South China Sea. The swallows gather and eat fish and then regurgitate them to form a nest. The nests are simmered for an hour until they shred. Then they are cooked with chicken stock, ham, and chicken to make a translucent soup.

• Be prepared for Chinese food in China to be hotter and spicier than the Chinese food usually served in the West.

Beverages: Maotai is a colorless alcohol, made from sorghum and wheat germ and then aged; it is very potent and used only for toasts at banquets. Visitors have variously described its taste as "like gasoline," "white firewater," or "like bad gin or vodka."

• For a drink less potent than *maotai,* choose *Shao xing,* a red rice wine served warm and sometimes available at banquets.

• Try local beer, the best brands being Beijing and Tsing Tao (beer is usually served warm).

• Note that white wine is rarely served chilled. If you enjoy chilled wine, buy some at a store, ask the hotel's room attendant to chill it for you, then take it to the restaurant with you.

• Realize that although coffee is

served in major hotels, its quality is not good. Bring your own instant coffee and milk powder if you wish. You'll find boiled water in a carafe in your hotel room. It may have cooled slightly, but it is usually hot enough for acceptable coffee or tea.

• Don't drink tap water anywhere. A second carafe in your hotel room will hold water that has been boiled and chilled. Use this for drinking, brushing teeth, etc.

• Be aware that tea is served only before and after a meal. Soup is the main liquid drunk during the meal. Sugar and cream are never used. If you visit someone, tea will be served, accompanied by cakes, nuts, dried fruits, or watermelon seeds.

• At meals, drink mineral water, lemonade (if it's bottled), or green tea. Other drinks commonly available are Coca-Cola, Sprite, and a lychee-flavored carbonated drink. Fresh yogurt, in a container that resembles a small milk bottle, is sipped through a straw.

• Buy foreign alcoholic beverages at major hotels.

Table Manners

• Expect to eat at a round table with dishes in the center.

• Be prepared for the table to be set with a soup bowl, several pairs of chopsticks to take food from serving plates to individual bowls, a wine cup, a rice dish, and a dish for shells and bones. There will be no serving spoons.

• Expect the host and hostess to use longer chopsticks in order to reach special pieces of food and place them on guests' plates. Children use shorter chopsticks, as befits their social position.

• When using chopsticks, remember that one chopstick (the lower one) remains stationary, while the top one moves. The lower chopstick rests on the ring finger, with the thumb on top of it. Hold the top chopstick as you would a pencil—resting against the thumb and manipulated by the second and third fingers. Hold the chopsticks half to three-quarters of the way up, because they will be easier to manipulate.

• Try not to drop your chopsticks. It's considered bad luck.

• To show that you have finished, place your chopsticks across the top of your bowl.

• Use the porcelain spoon for soup. The Chinese prefer porcelain because it doesn't absorb heat as metal does.

• Don't be surprised to hear your Chinese table companions making a sucking noise when eating hot soup and noodles; it's meant to cool them.

• If you don't like the food served to you, leave it untouched.

• At a banquet, expect to be served rice in an individual bowl by a waiter. In a home, your hostess will serve the rice.

• Don't pass serving dishes around. Reach for food with your chopsticks. It's perfectly acceptable to reach in front of others to get to the serving dishes. You may either take small amounts of food from the serving bowl and eat them, or you may first transfer one dish at a time from the serving dish to the rice on your plate. Don't pick through items in the serving dish to find something you like. Take what's close to you on the dish.

• Eat one dish at a time. The Chinese believe that each dish has its own unique flavor and should not be mixed with others.

• Never touch food with your fingers, eat with your fingers, or lick your fingers. Only children eat that way.

• As a guest, don't drink wine until the host invites you to.

• To eat steamed rolls with chopsticks, hold the roll with your chopsticks and take small bites.

• To eat rice, bring the bowl to your mouth and shovel the rice in with chopsticks.

• To eat shrimp with the shells left on, point the meaty end toward the back of your mouth and bite down on the shell near the tail. Then take little bites to squeeze the meat out.

• To eat the whole fish that is often served with bone in, and head, tail, and fins, break off bits of the fish with your chopsticks. Cooking will have made the fish very soft, so you should have no problem.

• Be prepared for meat and fish dishes to have many small bones. To remove them from your mouth, use your chopsticks (not an easy feat). It is rude to remove them with your hands. (When eating a meat dish, be careful—so you will avoid losing a filling or a tooth.)

• Expect food to be shared. People will often pick out a choice morsel to give to you, the guest. The choice morsels may include the lips and eyes of a fish. It's rude to refuse such an offer.

• If you don't want more tea, leave some in your cup. Every time it is empty, it will be refilled.

• If you are guest of honor at a formal meal, plan to sit with your back facing north. The host will sit with his back facing south. At the beginning of the meal people fight to avoid the seat of honor. Finally the guest of honor is pushed into the seat by the host. (As a Western visitor, don't feel obliged to play this game if you are guest of honor.) People then sit at random. The host will move around the table and drink to the health of each person. Then he will point his chopsticks at the cold dishes on the table as a signal to start eating. Rise slightly and, with chopsticks, take morsels of food from the bowls in the center of the table. Starting with lighter foods, main dishes are served in courses.

• Don't worry about leaving a little vegetable or meat on your plate, but never leave rice. It's considered the "sweat of fellow man."

• If you are entertained at a banquet, expect three glasses at your place setting: one for beer or soda, one for sweet wine, and one for *maotai*, the sorghum-based liquor used for making toasts.

• At banquets, expect a good deal of toasting. The host begins the toasting (frequently to the friendship of China and your country). Toasts and wine-drinking continue all evening, with the appearance of the main course the signal for a round of toasts. It's acceptable to toast with a soft drink.

• Prepare a short speech. Don't be surprised to be called on to sing a song (in your language).

• Don't be surprised if the appearance of the main course also signals a round of the "finger game": two players fling out a varying number of fingers and shout guesses as to how many fingers are displayed. The loser must drink.

• At a banquet, eat one course at a time.

• Expect the banquet meal to contain the five tastes basic to Chinese cuisine: acid, hot, bitter, sweet, and salt. Dishes also alternate between crisp and tender, and dry and thick sauces. A typical banquet might begin with dried fruits and nuts, followed by cold plates and stir-fried dishes; next will be a dessert, such as a pudding, to clear the palate for the more exotic dishes, such as Peking duck; then for variety—and again to clear the palate—there will be two soups, followed by a whole fish. The last dish will be rice.

• Note that fruit is symbolic: the orange is for happiness, the pomegranate for fertility, the apple for peace, the peach for longevity, and the pear for prosperity.

• If you are the guest of honor at a banquet, leave before the hosts. The serving of fruit signals the end of the meal. Wait ten minutes after tea is served and towels have been passed, then leave.

• Should you be invited to two banquets in the same evening, attend the first, having wine and a few courses there. Then leave for the second party. The traditional banquet lasts about 1½ hours—usually from about 7:30 to 9:00 P.M.

Places to Eat

• Remember that there are no names for particular kinds of restaurants. If you don't speak Chinese, look for a place where you can point to what you want. Either point to what another diner is having or a dish that is being prepared. (In many places, the food is cooked in view of diners.)

• Note that most restaurants have tanks of live fish, eel, snakes, frogs, and river shrimp. Either go to the tank and make your choice, or order from your waiter or waitress.

• Look for inexpensive restaurants on the second floor of some noodle and dumpling shops. They serve meat and vegetable dishes.

• Restaurant hours: Breakfast from 5:30 or 6:00 A.M. to 8:00 A.M. Lunch from 11:00 A.M. to 3:00 P.M., and dinner from 4:30 P.M. to 10:00 P.M. or even midnight.

• In Western-style hotels, meals are usually served all day and through the evening. You will be assigned a table. Breakfast is Western style, unless you request a Chinese breakfast a day in advance. Such a breakfast will be prepared only for a group of eight to ten. Chinese cuisine is served at lunch and dinner. Most beverages, including beer, are included in the price of the meal. If you have dietary restrictions, the hotel kitchen will prepare special meals for you.

• Arrive shortly after the restaurant opens for a meal; if you go later, it will be out of everything. In the South there are street stalls that stay open later; however, you should never buy food from street vendors because the risk of food poisoning and even hepatitis is just too great.

• Be aware that most good restaurants have an elegant section for tourists and an ordinary dining room for Chinese. Foreigners are usually permitted to eat in the dining room for Chinese, although the staff will make a strenuous effort to direct you to the dining room for tourists. Use your discretion as to whether to persist in your request to use the dining room for Chinese.

• Prepare for a shock if you eat at one of the restaurants frequented by local people. People toss chicken bones on the floor and spit freely. In this type of restaurant, ask for some boiling water to clean the chopsticks. Such a request is not rude.

• In larger cities, eat in a hotel to avoid the hassle of eating in a restaurant (people don't speak English, you won't be able to read the menu,

and conditions are very crowded). Another advantage of hotel dining rooms is that the food in them is often better and cheaper than in other places.

• If you're on a tour and wish to eat somewhere other than your hotel, get a group together and go to the desk at your hotel. Give your price range, mention one or two special dishes you would like to have (leaving the rest of the meal to the restaurant manager), and the hotel will make the arrangements. (Be sure to make reservations and requests for special dishes at least a day in advance.)

• Seat yourself in restaurants. Expect to share a table with others (in fact, you'll practically be sitting on someone else's lap because there is so little room), and don't be surprised if your group has to split up to find seats. There are usually round tables for six to eight. Grab a chair and try to find a space. If you can't find a seat, stand behind someone who is finishing. It isn't considered rude.

• If you see a man handing out tickets, that's a sign to pay before you eat. This is common in small restaurants where local people eat, not in better restaurants or hotel dining rooms.

• If you want your pot of tea refilled, take the lid off your cup, or turn it over to signal the waiter or waitress.

• Be aware that your bill may be up to ten percent higher than that of Chinese patrons because they have ration tickets that foreigners don't have.

• Realize that restaurant bills are never shared. Usually the person who invited the group or the most senior person pays. Don't try to pay your share. You'll merely embarrass yourself.

• Arriving at a restaurant, women may notice that there are only men there. In China, men go out in groups, while women stay home with the children. You have no cause to worry; the men won't bother you.

• Don't expect waiters or waitresses to speak English.

• To call the waitress, say, *"Xiao jie"* (shao jee-eh) Though it's rare to have a waiter, if you do, address him as *"Xian sheng"* (sheeyan sheng).

• In restaurants for Westerners, ask for a spoon and fork, if you wish. In smaller restaurants, only chopsticks are available. People often bring their own chopsticks, since soap is not used for washing dishes. You would be wise to take a cue from the Chinese and buy yourself a set of personal chopsticks to use during your visit to China.

• Don't expect to linger and chat after a restaurant meal. People leave immediately after finishing.

Specialties

• In Canton, be sure to try *dim sum*, a light and inexpensive meal, usually available only during the daytime and traditionally served in teahouses. *Dim sum* (which means

"little heart") refers to food that comes in small portions on equally small plates. *Dim sum* are served in bamboo basket steamers. A typical selection of savories: *shiu mai* (steamed meat dumplings), *har gau* (steamed shrimp dumplings), *gwor mai gai* (rice with chicken or pork, steamed in a lotus leaf), *chueng fun* (steamed rice-flour rolls with roast pork, minced beef, or shrimp), *char siu pan* (steamed rolls with chicken), and *pai gwat* (steamed spareribs in red-pepper sauce). Dishes are left on the table until it's time to add up the bill. The waiter counts the dishes to determine the charge.

• Other Canton specialties are *tíao ren jí ding* (diced chicken with walnuts), *gú láo ròu* (sweet-and-sour pork), *kè jía niàng dòu fū* (Cantonese stuffed bean curd).

• You may want to avoid tangerine-flavored ox penis, called *gou qi niu bian tang* in Mandarin and *gau gei ngauh bin tong* in Cantonese.

• Typical dishes from Shanghai are *zhǐ bāo jī* (paper-wrapped chicken), *táng cù pái gú* (sweet-and-sour spareribs), *xī hu cù yú* (West Lakefish), *qié zhi mīng kīa* (prawns with tomato sauce).

• From Szechuan cooking, sample *gōng bǎo jī dīng* (chicken with peanuts), *zhāng chā yā* (camphor- and tea-smoked duck), *yú xīang rou sǐ* (stir-fried pork in hot sauces), *xīa rēn gúo bā* (sizzling rice with shrimp), *má pó doù fū* (Ma Po's bean curd), and *yú xīang qíe zi* (eggplant Szechuan-style).

• Note that Szechuan food, prepared with a great deal of red chili, can be very hot. If you want your food milder, ask for *bu la* (boo lah) or *ching hung* (ching hoong). These terms mean "not spicy."

• From Northern China, try *běi jing kǎo ya*, roast Peking duck, the region's most famous specialty. Platters of duck meat and crispy skin, thin pancakes, a dish of *hoi sin* sauce, and scallion "brushes" are put in the center of the table. Put a pancake on your plate, dip a scallion in the sauce and brush it on the pancake, place the scallion in the center of the pancake with a piece of duck meat and a piece of skin. Fold the pancake over its contents and tuck in the ends so that you can pick it up with your fingers and eat it. The next course is a soup made of celery cabbage cooked in a stock made from the duck carcass. Sometimes you have to ask for the soup, since some restaurants try to cut corners with foreigners by not serving it.

• Other specialties of Northern China are *shuàn yāng roù* (rinsed mutton in hotpot), *méng gǔ kǎo rou* (Mongolian barbecue), and *tang cù quán yú* (fried whole fish with sweet-and-sour sauce).

HOTELS

• If you are going to be in the country on May 1 or October 1 (both major national holidays), reserve your room well in advance; otherwise, you may not be able to find a room.

• Be patient when dealing with members of the hotel staff. They are usually young boys and girls studying foreign languages. If you are aggressive, they will be very negative. If, for example, there are no towels in your room, keep asking for them—gently. Never raise your voice.

• Look for a service counter on your floor. Most hotels have them. There you can make international phone calls, order drinks, or give your laundry to be washed.

• Book hotels on your own or through CITS (China International Travel Service). In Chinese, it's called "*Luxingshe*" (Lushingsher). In addition to arranging for hotels, they can book train tickets, cars to meet you at your next stopover, and plane tickets. CITS offices are located in most tourist towns, usually in the largest hotels.

• Note that there are CITS offices in cities outside Beijing. You can make advance reservations through CITS, but you usually can't choose your hotel. You may be assigned a hotel that is far out of town and may be charged a fee to have someone meet you; however, don't be surprised if the person doesn't show up. If no one comes, try to find a taxi, or use public transportation. Outside Beijing, you can book a hotel room on your own—by phone, cable, or Telex—but it takes a long time.

• Remember that most large hotels have Telex and fax facilities.

• Don't try to stay in the very inexpensive, dingy hotels where Chinese stay. Oftentimes, many strangers are put into one room.

• Be aware that bathrooms may be shared (except in Western-style hotels), and there may be hot water only during certain hours.

• In a small hotel, expect to sleep on a hard cot, under a coverlet like an eiderdown. Expect sheets and pillows in hotels that cater to Westerners; some small hotels will also have them.

• If you are traveling independently and are staying in small hotels, use the large Western-style hotels for the amenities they offer; i.e., use the toilets in their bathrooms, the money-changing services, and their postal services. No one will bother you.

• If you are expecting a phone call either from within China or from abroad, try to be sure that the caller knows your room number. Operators often have difficulty understanding foreign names. Another option is to tell the operator that you are expecting a call, and write down your room number and name (both first and last name, underlining your last name).

• Most hotels have an attendant on every floor to prevent stealing and to learn if anyone is bringing a Chinese person back to her/his room, a practice which is forbidden. Be aware that the floor attendants have keys and have a habit of coming into the room without knocking.

• Be prepared for less-than-adequate lighting in your room. For reading, bring along a battery-operated light that clips on to the book. If you can wrap it securely, bring a high-wattage bulb.

• Use the laundry service in large hotels. It's fast and inexpensive.

• If you want to store luggage, ask at your hotel. You will probably be allowed to store it there. Be aware, however, that the luggage will be inspected thoroughly, and there may be a time limit.

TIPPING

• Be aware that tipping is not common in most restaurants or hotels, but you are expected to tip in better hotels. Part of the ritual is that any tip will be rejected initially.

• As a substitute for a tip, try giving American cigarettes, books, or cassette tapes to tour guides, hotel attendants, or people who have been helpful in negotiating a business agreement.

PRIVATE HOMES

• Feel free to drop in on people if you know them. If they have a telephone, call in advance.

• Realize that it would be unu-

sual to be invited to a Chinese home, but it would not be illegal for Chinese to entertain you. People are embarrassed by their cramped living quarters. They will likely invite you to a restaurant for a meal.

• Should you be staying with a family for the first time, try not to be intrusive. For example, don't go into the kitchen; knowing that you come from abroad, people may be embarrassed by the low standard of equipment.

• Especially in homes of poorer people, don't be effusive in your admiration of any object; the people may feel obliged to give it to you.

• In new apartments, expect to find Western-style beds. In older apartments, or in the countryside, the bed may simply have a mat on it.

• In new apartments, be prepared for the bathroom facilities (toilet and showers) to be Western style. In an old apartment, the toilet will be a hole in the floor with the shower above it.

• Offer to pay for local phone calls.

• Remember that most people do not have the special service needed for making overseas calls, because it is too expensive. If necessary, you can make a collect call (if you speak English or French so that you can reach and deal with the international operator). Chinese cannot make collect calls from their homes.

• If you know people well, offer to help with chores.

Gifts: If people you are visiting have asked you to bring English-language books or magazines, be discreet in giving them because your friends could get in trouble if the material is considered anti-Communist.

• To a school, give English-language textbooks, picture books from your country, the L. L. Bean catalogue, or any similar catalogues or novels in English (if you know the people speak or read English).

• If you are visiting relatives in China, be assured that you may give them substantial gifts—household appliances such as a TV, a radio, or a camera. People also appreciate Western-style clothing, coins, and postage stamps from your country, or canned goods, especially if you bring foods that are rationed.

• Other popular gifts include barrettes and combs; cigarette lighters; T-shirts with writing in English (e.g., the Boston Symphony Orchestra—the Chinese remember their visit to the country).

• If you are invited to a home, bring fruit, candy, or cookies. Especially welcome are imported wine or imported beer. If there are children, bring them a small gift. (There are many toy stores in China.)

• For younger people, give a gift with an American designer label, such as Reebok.

• Note that it's a custom to give gifts in groups of two.

• Expect people to refuse a gift several times out of politeness. Keep insisting that the person take it. Follow this practice if someone offers you a gift.

MONEY AND BUSINESS

Hours

• Realize that all of China is in one time zone, so that 10:00 A.M. in one area may be bright and sunny, while in another the same time may be dawn—or even dark. Therefore, the start of the workday may be 9:00 A.M. in one part of the country and much later in another part.

• Times below are approximate.

Government and Business Offices: Monday through Friday, 8:30 A.M. to 5:30 P.M.

Bank of China: Monday through Friday, 9:00 A.M. to 5:00 P.M.

Shops: 9:00 A.M. to 8:00 P.M., daily, including holidays.

Money

• Note that the monetary unit is the *renminbi* (RMB), which means "People's currency." The basic unit is the *yuan*, which is divided into ten *jiao* and 100 *fen*. Coins are 1, 2, and 5 *fen*. (There are also small slips of paper for these amounts.) Banknotes are 1, 2, and 5 *jiao* and 2, 5, 10, 20, 50, and 100 *yuan*.

• Remember that in speech, *yuan* are often referred to as *kuai* (kooaye).

• Realize that you will very rarely see *fen* or a 1 *yuan* brass coin.

• Expect American Express, Visa, Barclaycard, MasterCard, Access, and Diners Club credit cards to be accepted at hotels, the larger Friendship Stores, and antique shops. Expect to pay a four percent commission to the shop, restaurant, or hotel when using the card. Most restaurants require payment in cash, as do places at which airplane tickets are sold.

• Keep a large supply of cash on hand, since shopkeepers may tell you that their credit card machine is broken.

• Change travelers' checks at some Friendship Stores, Bank of China branches, some of the large department stores, and hotels for foreigners.

• As a foreigner or an Overseas Chinese, expect to pay more for airfares and entry fees to museums and other tourist sites.

• Spend any RMB before you leave China. You won't be able to exchange them for Western currency.

Business Practices

• Remember that to do business in China, you must have an invitation. Several of China's foreign trade corporations have representatives in North America and Europe. In the United States, start by getting advice from U.S. experts (not the Chinese representatives) at the U.S. Department of Commerce, the Bureau of East/West Trade, the U.S.– China Trade Council, or the Office of East/West Consumer Affairs (People's Republic of China Division), all in Washington, D.C. In Canada, contact the Canada–China Trade Council in Toronto or the PRC Embassy in Ottawa. There is also a PRC Consular Office in Vancouver. In Europe, check with the PRC Embassy in your country to learn the details of gaining an invitation to do business in China.

• Realize that you are at a disadvantage if you are with a small company and that you have an edge if you are with a large, well-known foreign company, since the Chinese generally prefer to deal with the largest foreign firms.

• Plan to travel to China several times before any arrangement is made final. It's best not to make return reservations for each trip. Wait to see how long negotiations last.

• Once you've decided to visit China, schedule meetings at least one to two weeks in advance.

• Avoid suggesting an appointment between noon and 2:30 or 3:00 P.M., because most people use that time for a lunch break.

• Don't plan business trips during the Chinese Lunar New Year (whose date varies according to the lunar calendar). Many businesses close for a week before and a week after that festival.

• Hire a local representative or a consultant on overseas transactions, so that you maintain a presence for your company in China. To find a reputable person, contact your embassy or consulate or the Chamber of Commerce in China.

• Realize that it is *very* important to verify that the government agency with which you are dealing is the appropriate one. Seek advice from your embassy, consulate, or from the Chamber of Commerce.

• Note that most towns and some neighborhoods in large cities have a Commerce Office. Some employees are very helpful; others are not. If you are involved in some sort of commercial dispute—for example, you did not receive what you ordered—contact that office.

• Before leaving, be sure to familiarize yourself with the artistic, creative, political, and historical background of China. The Chinese are very proud of their past and will be impressed that you have taken the time to learn about their culture. They are often hurt that Western visitors know so little of their ancient and important culture.

• Also bone up on your competitors and the specific details of their products. Expect searching questions from the Chinese as to your product versus those of your competitors.

• Because men and women get equal pay for equal work in China, women have as good a chance as negotiators in business as men have.

• Men should be aware that women in China have important positions in international trade and should be very careful not to speak or behave in a sexist/chauvinist manner. It will only hamper negotiations.

• Look for business service centers, which offer typing and photocopying services, off the lobbies of large hotels. You don't have to be a guest at the hotel to use them.

• Bring business cards. The Chinese have begun to use them. Have one side printed in Chinese. The printing can be done in Hong Kong or at your hotel, if you're staying at one often used by businesspeople. It may take four to five days to get the cards.

• Remember that punctuality is *very* important for foreigners, but the Chinese will probably be late.

• When you receive someone's business card, remember that the first name on the card is the family name. When doing business and meeting someone for the first time, address the person by professional title plus family name.

• When entering a business meeting with a group, come in led by the highest-ranking person in your group. At the end of the meeting, leave before the Chinese.

• Expect most of the conversation to be between the senior Chinese and the senior foreign team members. If other members of your group interrupt, the Chinese will be shocked. Suggest to subordinate members of your own team that they raise hands if they wish to speak.

• Note that business meetings often begin with innocuous conversations about a neutral topic, such as the weather. The Chinese may ask blunt personal questions, so be prepared. Tea is usually served at the beginning of a meeting.

• When you deal with Chinese organizations, be prepared for them to supply an interpreter. Be sure to use short, simple sentences, and pause to make sure your exact words are understood. Avoid slang or Western business "jargon" (especially figures of speech derived from sports). If possible, bring your own interpreter. A professional translator will help you to understand the nuances of the discussion.

• In preparing your proposal, make it objective and factual, telling why you and your firm are the best choice. Don't exaggerate your ability to deliver, because the Chinese check such claims. When you arrive in China, have at least 20 copies of the proposal available for distribution to the organization and its factories.

• Prepare to present your material to many different groups at different levels. It's difficult to identify the person who makes the actual decision, so it's important to treat everyone with equal respect.

• Use color photographs for your collateral materials because colors have great significance to the Chinese. Don't use maps showing Hong Kong as British or Taiwan as independent. Do not use red ink when writing or on your diagrams for lettering; it is considered bad luck.

• Show patience and tolerance for the Chinese method of doing business, which is to develop and then maintain a relationship. It may take years to develop a good relationship of cooperation between your foreign firm and the Chinese bureaucracy.

• Try to phrase questions so that they do not require "Yes" or "No" answers. Don't ask, "Can you deliver one thousand of the toys we ordered by November 1?" Ask "When can you deliver one thousand of the toys we ordered?" Chinese do not like to say "No" and may avoid the issue, or say "Yes," whether they mean it or not in order to avoid offending you.

• Remember also that the Chinese in the South make no important decisions without first consulting the stars for a lucky day and an auspicious hour.

• Expect the Chinese to be excellent hosts, a quality that may lead you to believe that they think of you as someone special. This is usually not so; the hospitality is part of their negotiating strategy.

• Be prepared for the Chinese to take notes during meetings. You may wish to do so also. Don't, however, try to use a tape recorder, as they are usually not allowed.

• Expect the Chinese to drive a hard bargain on prices. Sometimes, when you think you have reached an agreement on financial terms, they will want to reopen the issue of prices.

• Listen for clues as to when to end a meeting. The Chinese usually finish work by 4:00 P.M. and may say something such as, "You must be in a hurry," or "You must be tired." Regard such a statement as an invitation to leave.

• Avoid telling the Chinese businesspeople the date of your departure, because they may wait until the last minute to force you to accept their offer. Say that you're planning to stay as long as it takes to finish the deal.

• To impress someone and show respect, defer to her/him when getting into a car, choosing a seat, or going through a doorway.

Business Gifts: Give illustrated books about your section of your country, music, a subscription to a magazine, pens, notepads, or calendars. Other good gifts are imported whiskey, brandy, or chocolates. Don't give a clock, as the word for clock sounds like the word for funeral, and don't bring food, as Chinese tastes are very different. If appropriate, wrap the gifts, preferably in red, a lucky color. (Don't use white; it's the color for funerals.)

• Give gifts to everyone who is involved in a transaction or who is present at an event. Make sure the quality of the gift reflects the person's rank.

Business Entertainment: Be aware that business lunches have become more popular with the in-

crease in international-style hotels, but as a foreign businessperson, you will be treated to at least one evening banquet. You may receive the invitation only the day before—or up to a week in advance. If at all possible, reciprocate for the banquet on the same trip; if not, be sure to do so on your next trip. Always allow the Chinese to issue the first invitation.

• In making the guest list for your banquet, include everyone with whom you have dealt. It's difficult to figure out who is really making the decisions, so don't risk excluding the most important person. Include both Chinese and Western wives.

• Ask your interpreter, the Chinese interpreter, or your hotel information clerk to arrange your banquet. Specify the menu; always reciprocate with the same price per person as the Chinese spent at your banquet. Tell the restaurant manager what was served at the banquet hosted by the Chinese and say that you would like dishes in the same price range. Invite your guests several days in advance, and make your reservations at least one day in advance. Arrive half an hour before your guests; they will arrive precisely on time. Most dinners start between 6:30 and 7:00 P.M. and last for about two hours. Restaurants usually close by 9:30 or 10:00 P.M.

• Note that toasting customs are the same at business and social banquets (see "Table Manners").

• Don't initiate a discussion of business during the meal; business conversation while eating is not customary.

Note: For advice regarding business greetings, dress, gifts, or table manners, see the appropriate sections earlier in this chapter.

HOLIDAYS AND SPECIAL OCCASIONS

• Below are national holidays, on which banks, offices, and stores will usually be closed. Many regions and towns have festivals which are holidays in that area. Check with the tourist office for dates of local festivals.

Holidays: New Year's Day (January 1), Chinese Lunar New Year and Spring Festival (late January/early February), International Working Women's Day (March 8), Labor Day (May 1), Youth Day (May 4), Children's Day (June 1), founding of the Communist Party of China (July 1), People's Liberation Army Day (August 1), National Day (October 1), celebrating the founding of the People's Republic of China in 1949.

• Remember that many Chinese holidays are celebrated according to the lunar calendar. For example, the Chinese New Year falls on the first day of the First Moon (usually in early February). The Chinese year is divided into 12 months of 29 and 30 days, with an extra month added every three years. Thus the lunar year is 354 days. There are no names for days of the weeks or month. Monday is Day One, Tuesday Day Two, etc., as January is the first month and February the second month, etc. The Chinese count by the moon and may say that a certain holiday comes on the fifth day of the Fifth Moon.

• If you are in the country during the Chinese Lunar New Year, look for parades in the cities. There are no spectators—everyone marches in the parade. In the country there are plowing ceremonies and offerings to the gods of spring and husbandry. If you wish to join the spirit of the celebration, wear new clothes, especially new shoes. It's bad luck to step on the ground in old shoes on New Year's Day. Note that people clean their homes thoroughly, put red lacquer on the front door to keep the evil spirits away, and on New Year's Eve seal all doors. The following morning they break the seals and spend the day in worship of their ancestors. (Businesses and shops will be closed for one week during the celebration.)

TRANSPORTATION

Public Transportation

• Realize that there are extensive subway systems in Beijing and Shanghai, with trains running from 5:30 A.M. to 10:30 P.M. Platform signs are in Chinese and Pinyin (Romanized Chinese characters). Purchase tickets from the ticket office at the top of the stairs above the platform. There is a single fare, regardless of distance. Hand the ticket, which will be a slip of paper, to the attendant before stepping onto the platform. Consider purchasing several tickets at a time to avoid queues. Tickets are not dated, so you can use them whenever you want. Stops are announced on an intercom in both Chinese and English.

• If you take a bus, prepare for extremely crowded conditions. When you get on, state your destination and the ticket taker will collect your fare. If you have language problems, have someone write your stop in Chinese characters, and show it to the fare collector while holding out a handful of change. The conductor will take the correct amount (fares are based on distance traveled), and, since you are a foreigner, will probably signal you when the bus arrives at your stop.

• Recall that the last bus usually leaves at around 8:30 or 9:00 P.M. in smaller communities, somewhat later in large cities. In Beijing or Shanghai, most buses run until midnight.

• Hail taxis on the street in large cities. Look for them also at train stations, or ask the hotel staff or staff at restaurants and shops to help you find one. Since taxi drivers don't usually speak English, have the person who finds the taxi tell the driver your destination and whether you want the driver to wait. (Waiting time is relatively inexpensive.) The driver will give you tickets with numbers stating the fare. Be sure to have change, as drivers often don't.

• Note that some taxis have meters and some don't. If there are meters, they are rarely turned on.

• Realize that in some Chinese cities, such as Beijing, there are minibuses holding 16 people; they go along specific routes. The driver will stop at any place you want along the route.

• In most towns, expect to find bus stations for overland travel in the main areas of town. On trips lasting several days, you will find simple restaurants and hotels near the bus station. Many buses have numbered seats which can be reserved in advance. In tourist areas, you'll often find buses with air-conditioning.

• Remember that for long-distance travel, there are private and government buses, the latter being safer. Many have blaring loudspeakers; avoid sitting near them. Anticipate *very* slow progress. For night travel, sleeper buses have reclining seats or two-tiered bunks. For medium-length trips, look for private minibuses. They are usually cramped, and there may an extra charge for heavy luggage.

• Book a bus ticket in advance at the bus station or through some hotels and travel agents.

• Wait until you get to China to buy train tickets. They cost only half as much in the country as outside. You will, however, pay 70 percent more than Chinese, because there is a different standard for natives and foreigners.

• Buy train tickets at least one day in advance at CITS, at the ticket offices at town centers, or at your hotel. There is no such thing as a round-trip ticket. In general, routes are circuitous, and train trips are long and exhausting.

• Look for the special ticket counters for foreigners at railway stations.

• Note that there are basically two classes of train travel: "soft" is equivalent to first class and is the way most tourists travel; "hard" is economy class, the way ordinary Chinese must travel. For daytime trips, take soft seating, which is ar-ranged much the same as the seating on a Western train. For overnight trips, soft sleepers offer compartments, each with four berths. There are no curtains across the bunks and no segregation by sex, so an upper berth will allow at least a little privacy. You can change under the covers, but people usually make an effort to look away from anyone who is changing. (In the summer you might want to trade privacy for comfort, since most trains don't have air conditioning, and the upper berth can become very hot.) Sometimes, for an extra charge, you can have a four-berth compartment to yourself.

• Hard berth, which costs about the same as soft seating, allows you to lie down on a long trip. In hard berth, the car is open and lined on both sides with three levels of berths, which fold up. If you choose this class, try for the middle berth, since the top one is hot and the bottom one has no privacy and is the one on which people sit during the day. Hard seating is extremely uncomfortable, with smoky cars and people spitting on the floor. People often put newspapers on the floor and sleep under the seats. If you want to travel hard class, you'll have to make your own arrangements, which can be tedious and time-consuming, since CITS puts foreign visitors into soft class only.

• Don't be surprised to be wak-ened at 5:00 or 6:00 A.M. by a public-address system blasting martial music and announcements.

Most of the announcements exhort you not to be rude to your fellow passengers and prescribe a series of exercises to get you going. You can join the many who jump off at stops to do calisthenics, but be alert, because stops are often short, and the train may leave with little or no notice.

• Try to get a compartment in the middle of the train. It isn't as noisy or bumpy as in other areas.

• If you are sleeping on a train, take a small bag with toiletries and other essentials with you. Luggage is usually stored either at one end of the car or in an overhead rack, so it may be difficult to reach to take out a toothbrush, face cloth, etc.

• Expect train compartments to be comfortable, with pillows and towels provided. Under the table with a lamp will be a thermos of hot water for tea. Ask the cabin attendant for tea bags; there is a small fee. Every compartment has a fan, but it's turned off at night—even during the hot summer months.

• Keep your ticket to show when you get off the train.

• If you have bought a "hard seat" ticket and decide that you want a "hard berth," pay on the spot.

• If you have brought food onto the train, share it, and expect Chinese people to offer you their food.

• Expect to find dining cars only on long-distance trains. The food varies in quality.

• The waiter will bring you a menu at your seat (in soft class) about an hour before the meal is to be served, and you order in advance. You will be called when your meal is ready. If you want your drinks chilled, tell the waiter when you order.

Driving

• Be aware that Beijing and Shanghai are in the early stages of providing car rental service. The service is bureaucratic and, at this point, experimental. You'll need an International Driver's License, which can be applied for, in the U.S., at post offices. Regulations permit you to drive *only* within the city limits. Alternatively, you can hire a car and driver. If you are staying at a Western-style hotel, ask the doorman to recommend a driver to you. Get him or one of the hotel's English-speaking employees to tell the driver where you want to go and in what order. As insurance, carry a copy of your itinerary in Chinese. If the service has been good, tip the driver 10 to 20 *yuan* for half a day.

• As an alternative to a car, consider renting a bicycle (or buying a bicycle and reselling it). Rentals cost one to two *yuan* per day. Leave your passport or a deposit of 100 *yuan*. Be sure to check out lights, brakes, and tires before you accept the bike. If traffic gets heavy, walk it. Be careful at street corners and traffic lights, as drivers make sudden turns. If you want to stop somewhere, look for a bicycle parking lot. Pay the attendant when you park your bike.

LEGAL MATTERS, SAFETY, AND HEALTH

• At Customs, fill out a form listing your valuables—radio, watch, calculator, camera, etc. Keep this form, and turn it in when you leave the country. Make sure that you take all declared items out of the country with you; otherwise, you will have to pay an import duty. (If you bring in such items as radios or calculators and give them as gifts, you'll have to pay this duty.) You must also fill out a currency form, declaring all the money you have with you. Keep this form and present it whenever you change money.

• Don't bring in any reading material, videos, or tapes that might be considered morally or politically harmful to the Chinese people. They may be confiscated.

• Don't bring in any books portraying the Dalai Lama.

• Don't be surprised if authorities keep your passport for some time. It must be stamped by the Public Security Bureau. You'll have to work out something with them so you can use the passport to change money.

• Don't bring Chinese currency into the country or try to take it out of the country.

• Don't try to buy anything with foreign currency. It is illegal.

• If you buy an antique unofficially from a Chinese person, remember that you are risking a confrontation with Customs authorities and a possible jail term. If the antiques have a red wax seal of approval showing that they have been purchased from an authorized dealer, you're safe. If you buy an antique from a store outside the chain of state stores, take it to an office of the Bureau of Cultural Relics, which you can find at some Friendship Stores. They have the authority to give the red wax state seal to your package. *Note:* No items more than 180 years old may be exported.

• Don't try to take articles of historical value out of the country. It is forbidden.

• Realize that your luggage will be X-rayed at the airport when you leave.

• Be very cautious with purses or wallets. Pickpockets and bag snatchers may be a problem in stations and on crowded buses, especially in Guangzhou, where there are many migrant workers seeking employment.

• Contact the Public Security Bureau (the police) for missing property, travel passes, or visa extensions. The officers on the street wear blue or white uniforms with gold emblems on their hats.

• Don't expect a Chinese person to lead you to a police station. They don't want to be seen with a foreigner, and they try to avoid the bureaucracy whenever they can.

• Don't forget that smoking is now banned on subways and buses, and in theaters and stores.

• Follow the advice given to Chinese women in Beijing—do not go out after 9:30 at night. There is street crime outside the center of large cities.

Health: Although standard medicines and antibiotics are available, bring an ample supply of any prescription drugs you're taking. Women can buy tampons and sanitary napkins in supermarkets and department stores (not pharmacies).

It's best to bring your own toiletries. For example, though toothpaste is available, the taste is strange to a Western palate. Bring extra moisturizer, because some areas of China are very dry.

• Don't drink tap water. Buy bottled water, and make sure it's sealed.

• Don't eat fruit or vegetables that cannot be peeled.

• Don't eat popsicles (called "ice lollies").

• Never eat ice cream bought from a street vendor.

• Bring with you items that may be unavailable. All travelers should bring tissues, toilet paper, and cellophane or transparent tape (since Chinese envelopes don't have glue). Either bring or buy as soon as you arrive a small cup, preferably one made of plastic. If you get tea from a vendor, it's safer to use your own cup.

KEY PHRASES

A note on language: If you're visiting relatives, expect them to speak a dialect. For traveling around China, it's most practical to learn the Beijing dialect—*pu tung hua*—which is understood all over China. Note that the more of the language you learn, the cheaper your expenses will be.

Chinese is a tonal language. Often one word means many different things, depending on the tone.

Some common pronunciations: q=ch; x=sh; zh=j; c=ts; i=ee; ai=eye; ong=oong; eng=ung; ian=yen.

If you learn nothing else before going to China, learn to read numbers.

English	*Pinyin*	*Pronunciation*
Hello	Nǐ hǎo	Knee how
Good morning	Zǎo shàng hǎo	Tzaow shang how
Good evening	Wǎn shàng hǎo	Wahn shang how
Good night	Wǎn àn	Wahn ahn
Good-bye	Zaì jìan	Dzye jee-en
Please	Qǐng	Ching
Thank you	Xiè xiè	Shee-yeh shee-yeh
You're welcome	Bù xiè	Boo shee-yeh
Excuse me	Duì bū qǐ	Doo-oi boo chee
I don't understand	Wǒ bù dǒng	Wah boo dong
I don't speak Chinese	Wǒ bù hui shuō zhōng wén	Wah boo hway shwo jung wen
Does anyone speak English?	Shéi huì shūo yiñg wén?	Shay hway shwo ying wen?

HONG KONG

Imagine the largest shopping mall you've ever seen. Then double it. Then triple that. Because it's so large, divide it in two—why not with a scenic harbor. Shopping makes one hungry, so dot the mall with some of the world's great restaurants. Shopping leads to fatigue, so throw in a few of the world's greatest hotels. Shopping produces lots of money, so you'll need several banks. Put this shopping mall in a location that will make it one of the world's commercial centers. *Voilà!* Hong Kong. Economists are still debating the effect on Hong Kong's commercial status of its return to Chinese control. As of this writing, nothing has really changed. Hong Kong's export and import controls are separate from China. It is a separate customs territory and maintains autonomy in trade. The Hong Kong dollar is freely convertible. It continues to be an open, pluralistic society with an independent judiciary and freedom of speech, press, and assembly.

If you feel up to a little more imagining, take a short ferry ride to a former Portuguese colony, now a paradise for gamblers—Macao. (Below we have indicated special customs for Macao, where appropriate.)

GREETINGS

TELEPHONES

• Greet family members in order of age, beginning with the oldest.

• Expect older people to clasp their own hands, shake them a bit, and nod (not bow as the Japanese do).

• Shake hands with members of both sexes.

• Use titles (e.g., Professor Yu). The Chinese are conscious of professional status and prize titles.

• Note that Chinese names are listed with family name first, then the given name. However, some people who are Westernized list the family name last. Ask the person to whom you're speaking how he/she would like to be addressed.

• Remember that most married women keep their birth name. Address them as "Madam" plus that surname.

• Do not kiss anyone in greeting. Even close friends don't kiss.

• At a party, introduce yourself or wait to be introduced, as you prefer. There are no strict rules.

• Look for English-language telephone directories for both residences and business, as well as Yellow Pages.

• Realize that there aren't many public phones, because everyone in Hong Kong seems to have a cellular phone. Look for public telephones in hotels, convenience stores, ferry terminals, MTR (subway) stations, and post offices.

• For convenience, consider renting a cellular phone. You can use them everywhere, even on the MTR.

• Note that there is no charge for local calls made on most telephones available in shops and hotels. Both businesses and private homes are charged a flat rate per month for local calls.

• Public phones are painted red or pink. Deposit Hong Kong $1 and dial. There is no time limit.

• Be aware that pay phones usually have a slot for HK $2, but the phones don't give change. You can make a second call if you press the "FC" (Follow-on call) button before you hang up.

• Remember that phone numbers

have five to eight digits plus an area code: 5 is for Hong Kong Island, 3 for Kowloon, and 12 for the New Territories.
• Note that long-distance calls can be made from homes or at Hong Kong Telecom.
• Look for IDD (International Direct Dialing) telephones. Using them is the least expensive way to make overseas calls. To avoid using a huge number of HK $5 coins, buy a phone card, which you can purchase in a variety of denominations. Telephones that accept these cards are found in shops, on the street, or in Hong Kong Telecom offices. "Duet" phones accept both coins and phone cards.
• Don't mistake regular phone cards for the "Hello Phonecard." The "Hello Phonecard" can be used to call from *any* phone, including a coin phone or a phone in a private home. Buy one at Hong Kong Telecom. Be sure to use the special code you need to dial before using one. The regular phone card can be used only in special card phones.
• To send a fax, go to any Hong Kong Telecom office. You can also send faxes from most hotels and youth hostels.
• Remember that the number for emergencies is 999.
Macao: Note that local calls are free from hotels. At a local pay phone, local calls cost M $1 for five minutes. All pay phones have international direct dialing capabilities. Call collect, use a phone card, or your credit card. You can buy tele-

phone cards at the CTM telephone office. Special phones accept these cards.

CONVERSATION

• Good topics for conversation include best *dim sum* restaurants, travel, food, family, hobbies, or the area you're from. Women enjoy discussing clothes, the latest fashions, and jewelry.
• Avoid: personal questions regarding family or salary, the political situation in China, and the future of Hong Kong under Chinese control. Also avoid unpleasant topics such as disasters and death.
• Though you should avoid asking personal questions, be prepared for people to ask you personal questions.
• Be sure to keep your voice modulated. Don't ever lapse into shouting or screaming. The Chinese do not react favorably to raised voices.

IN PUBLIC

• Don't be surprised to be referred to as a European, even if you are from North America. The Chinese lump all Western nationalities together under that term (just as Westerners usually do not differentiate among different types of Chinese).

• Be sure to show respect for older people—hold doors for them; greet them first; never contradict them openly; do not sit down until they invite you to do so. If you want to photograph an older person, ask first. Most will agree, but some do object.

• Never be loud or conspicuous in public; be reserved and tactful. Women must be especially careful never to appear aggressive. Be especially careful to avoid flashing money.

• Don't be demonstrative or physically familiar (i.e., throwing your arm around someone's shoulder or kissing hello or good-bye). The Chinese are very modest, both personally and sexually. Expect them to be reserved in expressing what they are thinking and planning, where they're going and what they're doing. Expect people to stand very close to you, however, when they are conversing with you.

• Don't be surprised to see members of the same sex holding hands.

• To beckon someone, turn your palm down and wave your fingers. Note that waving good-bye, Western style, often means "Come here."

• Never gesture with your fist up in the air. It's obscene.

• Don't wink; it's impolite.

• When seated, place your hands in your lap.

• Women may feel free to cross their legs—either at the knees or the ankles.

• Since a Buddhist priest must never touch women, women should be careful not to brush against any monk.

• Give sincere compliments, but expect them to be denied. If someone pays you a compliment, shrug it off. Don't say, "Thank you."

• Don't be upset if someone in mourning rejects your invitation—even to a small gathering. He or she would be guilty of "infecting" the gathering.

• Note that road signs, bus stop signs, and signs in banks are in both English and Chinese.

• Don't photograph customs and immigrations procedures at the airport, airport police, ferry terminals, or overland border crossings. You'll see signs at these places advising you that photographing them is illegal.

• Look for public bathrooms in

hotels, bars, transportation terminals, some fast-food outlets, and some large department stores. There are toilets in malls, but they're for employees only and are kept locked.

• Often public toilets on the street are marked "W.C." To distinguish the men's from the women's room, watch who goes in where. Take some toilet paper, which you will find outside the toilets, before you go in. Toilets are frequently holes in the floor, although in Western-style hotels you will find Western-style facilities. Leave HK$1 as a tip.

Shopping: Before going to Hong Kong, check the prices at home on items you plan to buy. Cameras and other electronic items may cost about the same in both places.

• Spend one day canvassing shops in Hong Kong, comparing the quality of items and prices. Most professional shoppers advise that you negotiate price only when you are ready to buy. Have in mind what you are willing to spend for the item. Start by offering 40 to 50 percent off the marked price, and bargain from there. Keep in mind that the merchant with whom you're bargaining has to make a living. If you're buying an item in quantity, ask for a special discount for the multiple purchase.

• Don't bargain in the elegant boutiques (such as those in the Peninsula and Regent hotels), in large department stores, or in silk factories (where the prices are wholesale). Feel free, however, to bargain in the finest jewelry shops.

• If you're an early riser, try to be the first customer of the day. It's good luck for a Chinese merchant to make a sale to the day's first customer, so you may get an especially good deal.

• If you're not happy with the price, leave the shop. The merchant will call you back and will usually lower the price.

• Ask for the price in U.S. dollars or your country's currency if dealing in Hong Kong currency is confusing to you. Most merchants can calculate that price quickly, and many are happy to accept payment in U.S. dollars.

• Offer to pay cash. That will bring a better price than paying by credit card. (Travelers' checks are treated the same as cash.)

• Don't assume that an item is a genuine stone (or a real gold bracelet) because it looks like one. Ask "What is that?" And let the merchant volunteer that it is a ruby (if indeed it is). He will not lie. The Hong Kong merchant naturally wants to make the sale—but he will make it honestly.

• Be aware that there's a difference between buying a one-of-a-kind art object and a piece of jewelry. If, for example, you see a painting but decide not to buy it on the spot and then return later to find it sold—it's gone forever (unlike a piece of jewelry, which can usually be duplicated). If you are seriously thinking of buying a painting, a vase, a screen, or some other *objet d'art*, ask the dealer for "first refusal" for a specific time period—24 or 48 hours. Leave your hotel and room number with him. If someone comes in and wants to purchase the object during the specified time period, he will call and ask you to make a decision. Should you decide before the time is up that you don't want the artwork, give the dealer the courtesy of a call.

• Be prepared for clerks to follow you around a store, even when you make it clear that you're just browsing. They work on commission and want to be sure of getting the sale. If the hovering bothers you, ask the clerk's name and say, "When I am ready to buy something, I will let you know" or "I will make sure that you get the sale."

• For any purchase, get a receipt in case a Customs officer doesn't believe your statement of the price.

Exercise: The best place for jogging is around the car-free two-mile loop at Victoria Peak on Hong Kong Island. If you can find an uncrowded area near your hotel, jog there. Men and women can wear shorts in hot weather and sweatshirts and sweatpants in cold.

Macao: Note that the gambling casinos, Macao's biggest attraction, are open 24 hours a day and are packed on weekends. Don't try to take photographs in a casino. Guards often check to see if you're carrying a hidden camera.

DRESS

• For business, men should wear suits and ties. Women should wear suits and should add to their prestige by carrying an attaché case.

• Women appearing in public places should not wear low-cut or revealing dresses or shorts. Men, however, may wear Bermuda shorts on the street. Both men and women may dress in good-quality jeans.

• For a meal in a home, a man should wear a shirt, tie, and blazer in the summer, and a shirt, tie, and sweater in the winter. Women should wear a skirt and blouse or a dress in muted colors and of good quality. These costumes are considered informal dress.

• If formal wear is required—tuxedos for men and long dresses for women—the invitation will so specify.

• Women may wear pants when visiting a temple, but should not wear a top that is sleeveless or décolleté or bares the shoulders. Men should dress in long pants—not shorts—and should be sure to roll down their shirt sleeves, if they are wearing long-sleeved shirts.

• Wear thongs (flip-flops) only in hotel rooms, in the corridor, at the beach, or at the pool. Some hotels and restaurants won't allow you in wearing them. Sandals, however, are acceptable.

• Bikinis are acceptable at the beach.

• Never wear white to a Chinese wedding—it's the color associated with death. (At Western-style marriage ceremonies, however, brides do wear white.)

MEALS

Hours and Foods

Breakfast: 6:00 to 7:30 A.M. The main dish is *congee,* a thick rice porridge, often containing pieces of chicken. Tea is, of course, the beverage. In large hotels, a Western-style breakfast is available.

Lunch: From noon to 1:00 P.M. *Dim sum* is the usual fare. (See under "Places to Eat" for more details.)

Dinner: The day's main meal begins between 6:30 and 7:00 P.M.

A typical dinner consists of soup, steamed cabbage with black mushrooms, a shredded beef dish, and steamed fish with broth. Rice will be a separate course. Popular desserts are melon or double-boiled milk (English custard).

• A formal meal will have twelve courses, beginning with a cold dish.

• The Hong Kong Chinese usually eat two meals a day, with snacks at noon and late at night.

TABLE MANNERS

• If you are the guest of honor, expect to be seated opposite the host.

• At your place setting, expect a small plate (to be used as your main plate), a very small saucer for dipping sauces, a bowl, chopsticks, a porcelain soup spoon, and toothpick holders. There probably won't be a napkin. If this is so, wipe your hands on the tablecloth (even in a restaurant). The messier your area of the table, the more you show that you have enjoyed the meal.

• Although forks and spoons are sometimes offered, learn to use chopsticks, if possible, rather than asking for silverware. Point the thin ends of chopsticks toward the food. The tips of the chopsticks should be even—at the same level. (If one slips while you're eating, tap the ends gently on the table so they will again be even.) Hold one chopstick between the joint of the thumb and the tip of the third (ring) finger.

This chopstick remains rigid. Hold the second chopstick between the tip of your thumb and the tips of the first and second fingers. Move this chopstick when you pick up food. Hold the chopsticks half to three-quarters of the way up. Such a grip makes them much easier to manipulate.

• Expect to be seated at a round table with a serving dish in the center. Choose a morsel from this dish with your chopsticks, and be sure to put it on your own plate before putting it in your mouth. Don't "fish around" in the serving dish. Take the item closest to you. You could also turn your chopsticks around and use the other, clean ends to pick items from the serving dish.

• Instead of the serving dish, there may be a lazy Susan in the center of the table with a porcelain spoon. Serve yourself with the spoon and then turn the lazy Susan to the next person.

• Don't expect appetizers or hors d'oeuvres before a Chinese dinner, since the meal itself consists of many courses.

• To eat rice, hold the rice bowl up against your lips and shovel the rice into your mouth with your chopsticks.

• Don't be embarrassed to slurp or belch (or to hear others do it). Both sounds are regarded as indications of satisfaction.

• Between courses, place your chopsticks on the chopstick rest next to your plate.

• Don't be surprised if people smoke between courses; if you can't decide whether you ought to, follow the lead of your host.

• Don't worry that people will press you to eat more and more; they won't. The Chinese will, however, be very pleased if you take at least a taste of everything offered. At a formal dinner, guests are expected to finish every course except the last, which is usually noodles or fried rice. If you finish this course, the hostess will think you are still hungry.

• Eat slowly. If you wolf down your food, people will think they didn't give you enough.

• To show that you're finished, hold your hand over your plate when someone offers more food.

• Expect to be offered ordinary cocktails such as gin-and-tonic before dinner. In simpler homes only tea will be served. With meals, men drink beer and women tea. The Chinese also drink a great deal of brandy during meals, and for celebrations (e.g., weddings) brandy and cognac will be the featured drinks. You may be offered a very potent wine called *Maotai*; it's like absinthe or schnapps and without any flavor. Go easy on *Maotai*; it packs a powerful punch.

• Exercise discretion when drinking at a business lunch or dinner. The Chinese think that Westerners drink too much.

• Don't suggest meeting for drinks (apart from a meal). The Chinese don't usually drink alcoholic beverages without eating.

• To use a toothpick as the Chinese do, cover your mouth with the hand not maneuvering the toothpick.

• Since meals are lengthy, don't linger after they are over.

• If you are invited to a meal by a Chinese—whether business or social—expect to be entertained in a restaurant, since so much work is involved in the preparations of the various courses and people would not want to lose face by not offering enough food. To be invited to a home is a very special honor.

• If you're on a business visit, expect to be invited to a banquet in honor of your visit. The invitation, which will be sent to your hotel room, may come one day or a few days before the banquet. The banquet, which will begin about 9:00 P.M. and end at 11:00 P.M., will be held at a restaurant, in a private room with a large round table. There will be another table with soda, wines, liquors, and bowls of fried walnuts (the host will serve drinks from it). There may also be a TV, which will be left on throughout the meal. You will be given a menu of the meal—probably in Chinese. A waiter will serve one dish at a time, changing the china between courses. Plan to leave as soon as the meal ends.

• Among the dishes that often appear at banquets are shark's-fin soup, corn chowder with crabmeat, roasted whole pigeon, chopped pigeon (which you fold in a lettuce leaf), Peking duck, steamed prawns (remove them from the shells with your fingers), steamed ginger fish (eating the head and gills is a great compliment to the Chinese, but don't feel obliged to do so), chicken with deep-fried seaweed, scallops steamed in the shell with sauce and scallions, and cellophane noodles.

• Tea will be served throughout the banquet. Sometimes toasting is done with tea. Hold the glass of tea in your right hand, and place your left hand under the glass. If the toasting is done with the potent *Maotai*, don't be surprised to see one Chinese delegate another to do his toasting for him, so he won't get drunk. At the end of the meal, everyone will be served very tiny cups of bitter tea. Take one sip, and then pour the rest onto the tray on which the cups were served. This signifies the bond that everyone shares after dining together.

Places to Eat

• Hong Kong is a paradise for lovers of Asian food. Chinese regional cooking is represented in Cantonese (the predominant type of Chinese restaurant), Szechuan, Shanghai, and Pekinese restaurants. Other Asian ethnic restaurants are also popular: Indian, Vietnamese, Japanese, Korean, and Filipino.

• For lunch, seek out a Cantonese *yum cha (dim sum)* restaurant. On several levels, there will be dining rooms with tables (no booths). Try to arrive no later than noon (*dim sum* restaurants are open from 11:00 A.M. to 2:00 P.M.), as the food will be fresh and there will be a large selection. Be advised that *dim sum* restaurants are usually full by 12:30 P.M. Try not to sit at the back of the restaurant, as it is difficult to attract the waiter's attention from there. Waiters push carts of dishes, most of them steamed—for example, shrimp dumplings, meat-filled steamed buns, vegetable-filled dumplings, and sweet cakes. If the *dim sum* is in covered bamboo baskets, lift the lids to see what is inside. Dishes will be left on the table so that the waiter can count them and determine your bill. Tea is usually free at *dim sum* restaurants. Invert the teapot lid, and the waiter will bring a refill.

• You will probably see noodle stalls on the side streets. Avoid them because you can't judge their hygienic standard.

• To save money on meals, try hotel and restaurant chains that offer set meals. And seek out restaurants at the back of bakeries, another source of economical meals. For a really quick meal, go to a fast-food counter serving hot dogs, hamburgers, and soft drinks. Usually you first buy a ticket from the cashier.

• Note that there are no restrictions on serving hours for restaurants in Hong Kong.

• Make reservations for lunch and dinner at better restaurants. The Information Desk at your hotel can book you a table.

• Menus are not posted outside Chinese restaurants, but inside most restaurants have at least one copy of the menu in English. Many small restaurants have ducks, chickens, pork, and other items displayed in the window. Waiters usually don't speak English, but you can point to what you want.

• Don't join strangers at their table.

• Expect knives and forks only in Western-style restaurants.

• If you're the guest of honor at a meal, expect to sit facing the door.

• In restaurants, expect to find bottles on the table containing vinegar, soy sauce, and sesame oil. Don't confuse the dark vinegar with soy sauce. Usually, a separate little dish for the sauces is available, so that you can dip the food into the sauce. There will be one dish per person. People like to mix the sauces.

• Realize that the Chinese order noodles just before the dessert. Keep this in mind if you're being entertained.

• Be aware that live seafood in tanks is price by the *tael* (a little more than an ounce). Ask beforehand what the price of an item will be, because fish can be extremely expensive.

• When tea is served, tap the table lightly with three fingers, a gesture that is a silent "Thank you."

• Don't eat raw fruits and vegetables that can't be peeled, and drink only bottled water.

• Call the waiter by waving your hand. (A vocal summons probably won't be heard because restaurants tend to be very noisy.)

• After dinner look for a tea cart to be brought to the table with many different kinds of teas in canisters. Choose the one you want; point, if the waiter doesn't speak English. Tea is served in round cups with covers. The waiter will pour hot water onto the tea leaves in your cup and then dump it out. (This is "washing the leaves.") Then he will add more water to make the tea you will drink. (Tea in restaurants is made in your cup, while in a home it is made in a pot.)

• Remember that the person who suggests the meal is the one who pays the bill. There is no such thing as Dutch treat in Hong Kong.

• To ask for the check, say *"My don"* (Cantonese for "Check"), or make a scribbling motion across your left palm. Only one bill will be presented for a group. The person who issued the invitation to the meal pays.

• Study your bill (or ask) to see if you need to leave a 10 percent tip. Most Chinese restaurants add on a service charge, but some of the more traditional, smaller places do not.

• If you visit a fast-food restaurant, expect to have an unusual drink, called a Fleecy, available. It contains red or green mung beans, pineapple, or some other fruit, and usually has milk or ice cream added. Sometimes it includes black grass jelly. It's safe to drink.

Macao: Expect to find both Chinese and Portuguese restaurants.

• Note that most people tend to eat early, about 7:00 or 7:30 P.M. If you arrive at a restaurant after 8:30 P.M., you may be too late to be served.

• Be sure to make reservations for weekends or holidays. It's a good idea to book in advance for all dinners. Have someone who speaks Portuguese or Cantonese telephone to make the reservation.

• Expect a pleasant surprise when you look at prices. Most restaurants cost much less than those in Hong Kong, and you'll also find Portuguese wines, brandies, and ports very inexpensive.

• Check your bill to see if a 10 percent service charge has been added. If not, leave 10 percent.

Specialties

• In Cantonese restaurants try *yu chi tong* (shark's-fin soup), *yen wo tahng* (bird's-nest soup), *ku lao ju* (sweet-and-sour pork), *t'ao jen chi ting* (diced chicken with walnuts, *siu ngoh* (roast goose with pickled plums), *paak ch'euk ha* (prawns boiled in the shell with chili sauce), *chin ha luk* (fried prawns in tomato sauce), *siu p'aai kwat* (roast pork ribs), *ch'a siu* (barbecued pork), *si yau kai* (steamed chicken in peanut oil with ginger). Cantonese food uses an abundance of rice and fresh vegetables. Food is parboiled, steamed, and quick-fried to retain natural juices and flavor (but it isn't greasy).

• Szechuan food, prepared with a great deal of red chili, can be very, very hot. If you want your food less spicy, ask for *bu la* (boo lah) or *ching hung* (ching hoong). For a treat, order *yim kuk kai* (chicken baked in salt and served with a sauce of peanut oil, salt, and ginger), *yim kuk chan kon* (salt-baked chicken livers), *chang cha ya* (camphor-and-tea-smoked duck), *yu hsiang jou szu* (stir-fried pork in hot sauces), *hsia jen kuo pa* (sizzling rice with shrimp), *ma po tou fu* (Ma Po's bean curd), and *yu hsiang ch'ieh tzu* (eggplant Szechuan-style).

• Shanghai cooking, with dishes richer than Cantonese, usually contains soy sauce and ginger. Specialties are *chih pao chi* (paper-wrapped chicken), *t'ang ts'u pai gu* (sweet-and-sour spareribs), *hsi hu ts'u yu* (West Lake fish), and *ch'ieh chih ming hsia* (prawns with tomato sauce).

• Northern China produces Peking-style cooking, often relying on deep-frying; Peking foods are drier in texture than other Chinese dishes. Rice is not commonly served in Peking restaurants, because wheat is more common in the north. Hand-made noodles and *pao* (a steamed bread) are popular wheat-based accompaniments to meals.

• Be sure to have *pei ching ya* (Peking duck), the area's most famous specialty. Traditionally, platters of duck meat and crispy skin, thin pancakes, a dish of *hoi sin* sauce, and scallion "brushes" are put in the center of the table. Put a pancake on your plate, dip the scallion in the sauce and brush it on the pancake, place the scallion in the center of the pancake with a piece of duck meat and a piece of skin. Fold the pancake over its contents and tuck in the ends so that you can pick it up with your fingers and eat it. The next course is a soup made of celery cabbage cooked in a stock made from the duck carcass. If the soup isn't brought, be sure to ask for it. Some restaurants try to take advantage of foreigners by not serving the soup.

• Also try *jiao zi* (ravioli stuffed with meat and served steamed or fried), *shuan yang jou* (rinsed mutton in hotpot), *meng ku kao pou* (Mongolian barbecue), *tang tsu chuan yu* (fried whole fish with sweet-and-sour sauce), and *basal* (a dessert of toffee-covered apples).

• Between November and March, Peking restaurants offer *shua yang jou*, Mongolian hotpot (also called Mongolian firepot). Thin slices of lamb or other meat are served raw. Cook them yourself in the chafing dish with the charcoal stove built in underneath. The bubbling broth therein is a soup stock with herbs and vegetables.

Macao: Food and its preparation have been influenced by Macao's years as a Portuguese colony and by the Portuguese colonies in Africa. The most famous dish is African chicken—charcoal-grilled chicken with spices and pepper, similar to India's *tandoori* chicken. Also try prawns *biri-biri* (spiced prawns), and fish, or chicken baked in garlic.

HOTELS

• If you arrive without a reservation, head for the Hong Kong Tourist Association desk at the airport, but be aware that they deal only with the more expensive hotels.

• If you stay in one of the top hotels (e.g., The Peninsula or The Regent), anticipate an unmatched level of service. There are room boys, with a station behind a curtain on each floor, who are responsible for about four rooms each. Shortly after you reach your room, one will wheel in a tray with tea and sweets and fruit. As soon as you leave your room, he will have a maid clean it; your towels will be changed every time you use them. If you leave your shoes out, he will have them polished. And he will deliver an English-language newspaper to your room each morning.

• For special assistance, see the concierge. He can arrange a trip for you to the People's Republic of China or can recommend shops and restaurants.

• If you need to change money when the banks are closed, check to see if your hotel has a 24-hour cashier's desk. The rate will be slightly higher than at a bank or a money-changer.

• Should you visit Hong Kong during their low season (end of June through August) and be staying at a less expensive hotel—or if you are planning a long stay—bargain for the room rate. Prices fluctuate with supply and demand.

• Be wary if you see an empty bar and a few stools at the entrance to a "hotel." It may be one of the many guesthouses for "amorous encounters." Most of them are located in the Wanchai District, Hong Kong's "red light district" (*The World of Suzie Wong*). If you ask for a room, you will be refused.

Macao: Reserve well in advance if you plan to stay on a weekend.

• Be aware that for some special occasions (e.g., the Grand Prix), you may have to pay for several nights, even if you only plan to stay one night.

• Look for the pitcher of boiled water provided by your hotel. Use that water for drinking, brushing teeth, etc. Never drink tap water.

TIPPING

PRIVATE HOMES

• Tipping isn't an industry in Hong Kong as in some other countries.

• You need not tip a cab driver, but many drivers round off the fare to the next highest Hong Kong dollar.

• Don't tip ushers or gas-station attendants.

• For small services, give a doorman Hong Kong $1.

• In almost all restaurants, the service charge is included. If not, leave 10 percent. If the service charge is included, it's still customary to leave an additional 5–10 percent.

• Give porters and bellboys HK$5 per bag. Give porters at the airport HK $2.

• Realize that the housekeeping staff at hotels do not expect a tip. If you use room service, give the waiter 5–10% if the service was good.

Macao: Some restaurants and most hotels add a 10 percent service charge, and all but the smallest guesthouses add a 5 percent "tourist tax."

• Make plans in advance for visiting. Don't drop in, since many women now work.

• Be prepared for apartments and homes to resemble Western-style homes. Beds, however, sometimes have a board covered with a padded quilt rather than a mattress.

• Don't praise excessively any particular item in the house, or the host will feel obliged to give it to you.

• Don't be surprised to hear parents call their sons by such unflattering names as "Pig" or "Dog." They are protecting them from the evil spirits; if they call them a flattering name, something bad might happen to them.

• Be aware that you would embarrass people by offering to help with the cleaning or cooking, since most families have servants.

• If you're staying with a family, expect the woman (if she doesn't work and has servants) to want to take you shopping and sightseeing. If you wish to go off by yourself, be very tactful when telling the family your plans.

• Offer to pay for long-distance calls made in a home, but not for local calls, since they are free with monthly service. Dial 003 (instead of 001—the usual prefix for an international call), and you'll reach an operator who will call you back to tell you the cost of the call you have made.

• Take a daily bath, if you wish, except during periods of water rationing. Advance notice of rationing will be given; during such periods water will be turned off for several hours each day.

Gifts: If invited to a meal, bring a bottle of brandy, a fruit basket, candy, or cookies.

• From Western countries, bring good chocolates, brandy, CDs or cassettes, or watercolor prints or placemats with scenes of your country.

• Children love to receive clothing from the U.S. (such as OshKosh overalls) and Europe; they also enjoy books in English.

• Keep in mind that well-mannered Chinese are supposed to refuse a gift the first few times it is offered. Keep insisting. If you're offered a gift, demur at first. If you accept too readily, you will be considered greedy.

• Present the gift with both hands. Don't expect the gift to be opened in your presence; a Chinese would consider that rude. If you receive a gift, open it in a private, too.

• Give things in pairs. That arrangement is considered auspicious.

• Don't give flowers, which connote funerals.

• Don't send white flowers to newlyweds, since white is the color of death and funerals.

• Don't send yellow flowers to friends, because you would be signaling that you wish to end the friendship.

• Never give a clock, because the word for *clock* in Chinese is similar to the word for *death*.

• Avoid giving a gift wrapped in blue paper, because blue is the color of mourning.

MONEY AND BUSINESS

Hours

Government and Business Offices: Monday through Friday, 9:00 or 9:30 A.M. to 5:00 or 5:30 P.M., with a lunch hour from 1:00 to 2:00 P.M. Some offices are open on Saturday from 9:00 A.M. to 1:00 P.M.

Banks: Monday through Friday, 9:30 A.M. to 4:00 P.M., and on Saturday, 9:00 A.M. to 1:00 P.M.

Shops: In the Central area, from 10:00 A.M. to 6:00 P.M. daily. In Wan Chai and Causeway Bay, from 10:00 A.M. to 9:30 P.M. daily. In Tsim Sha Tsui, from 10:00 A.M. to 9:00 P.M. daily. On Sundays or holidays, many only open from 1:00 to 5:00 P.M.

Macao: *Banks*, Monday through Saturday, 9:00 A.M. to 4:30 P.M. *Government Offices*, Monday through Thursday, 9:00 A.M. to 1:00 P.M. and 2:30 to 5:45 P.M. On Friday, until 5:30 P.M. *Businesses*, Monday through Friday, 9:00 A.M. to 1:00 P.M. and 2:00 P.M. to 5:30 P.M. Most are open on Saturday from 9:00 A.M. to 1:00 P.M.

Money

• Note that the unit of currency is the Hong Kong dollar, which is divided into 100 cents. Coins are available in 10, 20, and 50 cents, and HK$1, $2, and $5. Banknotes come in HK$10, $20, $50, $100, $500, and $1000. When people say "dollars," they almost always mean Hong Kong dollars; sometimes they will say "10 plus plus," meaning HK$10.

• Realize that your plastic money will be welcome in Hong Kong. American Express, Visa, Barclaycard, MasterCard, and Access are the most frequently accepted credit cards. You can use them in hotels, shops, and large restaurants. Some places accept travelers' checks. (Remember that some shops will give a discount if you pay in travelers' checks or cash rather than with a credit card.)

Macao: The currency is the *pa-taca*, which is divided into 100 *avos*, often called cents. Coins are 10, 20, and 50 *avos*, and 5 and 20 *patacas*. Banknotes are 5, 10, 50, 100, 500, and 1000 *patacas*.

• Don't bring *patacas* into Hong Kong. It will be difficult to change them.

Business Practices

• Realize that Hong Kong is the most Westernized and diverse area you will find in Asia. Business will be done at a faster pace than elsewhere on the continent.

• Be sure to make appointments well in advance—two to three months, if you're making them from outside Asia. The Chinese would not appreciate your dropping in, as nothing is improvised but is planned well in advance.

• Plan business trips in October, November, March, April, or May. Avoid the summer months, which are very warm and are the period when heavy tourist traffic occurs and many businessmen vacation. Steer clear of the two weeks before and after Christmas and the week before and after Easter. Check on the date of Chinese holidays and festivals, because they vary according to the lunar calendar.

• Make appointments by fax or telephone, and be sure to reconfirm just before you leave for Hong Kong. When you arrive in Hong Kong, reconfirm again, because appointments are sometimes changed at the last minute.

• Realize that many businesses close from noon until 2:00 P.M., and executives often take lengthy lunch hours. Don't try to schedule appointments during those hours.

• To have the best chance of doing business both successfully and quickly, arrange for an introduction before you arrive. Get in touch with Hong Kong trade offices in your country for help in finding contacts who will write a letter of introduction or introduce you in person.

• Try to choose someone age 50 or older to represent your company. Chinese are impressed by older people with experience.

• If possible, send your business proposal in advance. Then when you do arrive, prepare to explain the proposal and go over it very carefully.

• If you are traveling by taxi or car, allow plenty of time to get to an appointment; punctuality is *very* important and traffic is often congested.

• Consider renting two devices that will enable you to keep in touch: a cellular phone and a pager. They're very easy to come by.

• Bring business cards because almost every business appointment begins with an exchange of cards. Be sure that they include your position in your company. They can be printed in English. However, make a good impression by having the cards printed in Chinese on one side. Most hotels will assist with this service.

• When first meeting either a male or female, bow. If you know the person's rank is superior, bow lower and let him/her rise first. Always show great courtesy to those older than you and those senior in rank. Allow them to go through doors first and to be seated first.

• When meeting a group, be sure to introduce yourself to each person individually.

• Expect to be offered tea or coffee at the beginning of the meeting. Don't drink until your host has done so. Even if you don't want it, accept. Informal small talk will precede business discussions. Subjects may be your family, your itinerary, and general business trends in your country. People want to get to know you and your company well. Then the meeting will become formal and discussion will turn to the main business points.

• Note that many of the younger generation in business have studied abroad, speak English well, and are acquainted with sophisticated Western business techniques.

• Keep in mind that the Chinese respect Westerners as long as they don't try to take unfair advantage. Hong Kong businessmen prize their reputation for being very honest and very reputable.

• Anticipate lengthy negotiations. Meetings may go on for weeks or months and may require several trips to Hong Kong. The Chinese are tough bargainers, expert at stalling. Visiting foreign business people are usually at a disadvantage— experiencing jet lag, changes in diet and in routine. The Chinese have the upper hand and are in no hurry to complete a deal.

• Try to ensure that any group going to negotiate is made up of the same people on each trip. The Chinese like to deal with people they know. If someone new comes, be sure to explain where the person being replaced is, and allow the Chinese time to get to know the new person.

• Realize that there are special difficulties in dealing with small businesses, which are usually family-run. In such firms, business does not go outside the family unless absolutely necessary, and an individual member who deals with anyone outside the family is disowned.

• Be prepared for resistance to a new or untried idea. The Chinese respect tradition and wait until something new has been proven before trying it.

• Try to find out who the top man is in the group with which you are meeting. This is often difficult (partly because everyone dresses the same), so rely on hearsay, any information network you may have developed, or your own sixth sense.

• Note that "Yes" means only "I have heard you." It must be followed by a positive statement to really mean "Yes."

• If you are a college graduate or hold an advanced degree, especially one from a prestigious institution, let the Chinese know it. They have tremendous respect for education.

• Don't be surprised if it takes a long time to reach an agreement with Chinese businessmen. They are very wary and want to be sure that they know you.

• Remember that a man's word is his bond. In the past, written agreements were not necessary in Hong Kong, but the Chinese realize that Westerners insist on them. Be apologetic, however, about asking for a written contract.

• Note that, for the Chinese, courtesy has a higher priority than accuracy. They don't like explicit disagreement and may say what they think you want them to say in order to avoid conflict and disagreement at any cost.

• Never directly confront anyone with having made a mistake. Talk around the subject, allowing him/her to save face.

• Realize that the Chinese always maintain a calm exterior and dislike displays of annoyance or anger. Never show your anger or talk loudly, and don't talk with your hands.

• Never use obscenities.

• Avoid jargon and slang, especially figures of speech derived from sports. You won't be understood. ("Game plan" may be clear at business meetings in the United States or United Kingdom, but it will make no sense in Hong Kong.)

• Although red is usually associated with happiness, don't use red ink to write a note or a telephone message.

• If someone laughs at what seems an inappropriate time, realize that laughter is often a sign of anger or embarrassment.

• When using an interpreter, explain your goal beforehand (e.g., "At this meeting I want Mr. Yu to agree to study our blueprints"). Also indicate whether you want exact quotes or a free translation.

• If you're setting up a branch office for your company in Hong Kong, or establishing a new business, be sure to consult a *feng shui* (pronounced "fung soy") man, a religious man who will tell you which day to move in, which position your desk should be in, and, depending on the year you were born (year of the dog, rat, snake, etc.), what symbol to place in your office. Ask for the name of a *feng shui* man at Chinese businesses and engage the best and most expensive. The Chinese are very superstitious and blame bad spirits if things go wrong. The *feng shui* man will probably advise you to ensure good luck by opening at the time of the new moon.

• Avoid blue in packaging or printing. Use red, gold, and green, favorite colors of the Chinese. If you're asked to change the color of a product, heed the advice.

• Bring promotional literature, catalogs, and instructions for using products in English. It's helpful if you also bring instructions for use in Chinese or in self-explanatory symbols.

• Western women should know that it will be easy for them to conduct business in Hong Kong, since local women are very visible in the workplace.

Business Entertaining: Be aware that business is often conducted over meals, more often lunch than dinner. Never refuse a lunch or dinner invitation if at all possible. If you must refuse, suggest an alternate time.

• If you're dealing with Chinese, expect business entertaining to be in a restaurant. In the Western community, business entertainment is often at home. Most entertaining, done before and after a deal is made, is primarily for men. Even though Western wives will be invited, Chinese wives probably will not attend. If the host is the top man in the company, he may bring his wife. If wives are in the party, the occasion will be entirely social, and no business will be discussed.

• If you wish to host a banquet (to get a business relationship off to a good start or to celebrate an agreement that's about to be finalized), make arrangements several days in advance. As a courtesy, invite Hong Kong wives, though they may choose not to attend. As host, choose the menu and plan the seating and any other details (e.g., you may wish to have flowers for any women who are coming).

• Be sure to reciprocate with a dinner for any Chinese group that hosts a dinner for you.

• An alternative is to entertain at the restaurant in one of the fine Western-style hotels (e.g., The Peninsula or The Regent). To be entertained there is a boost to businessmen's egos and gives them face. It's not necessary to entertain in a private dining room (more widely available in Japanese and Chinese restaurants than in hotel restaurants) because the Chinese enjoy others seeing that they are being entertained.

Business Gifts: Realize that the Chinese are fond of prestige items, so bring a bottle of imported liquor, cigarettes, or chocolates from abroad.

Note: For advice regarding business greetings, dress, or table manners, see the appropriate sections earlier in this chapter.

HOLIDAYS AND SPECIAL OCCASIONS

• Expect to find banks, offices, and most shops closed on the holidays listed below. Check with the tourist office for specific dates since some holidays are based on the lunar calendar.

Holidays: New Year's Day (January 1), Chinese New Year (three to four days long, usually in February, but the date varies according to the lunar calendar), Ching Ming Festival (106th day after the winter solstice), Easter Weekend (including Good Friday and Easter Monday), Queen's Birthday (April 21), Dragon Boat (*Tuen Ng*) Festival (in the spring; date varies), the first weekday in July and the first Monday in August (bank holidays), the Mid-Autumn Festival, also called the Moon Festival (on the 15th day of the eighth month of the lunar calendar; date varies in a two- to three-week period in September/October), Chung Yeung Festival (observed on the ninth day of the ninth month of the year), Christmas Day (December 25), and Boxing Day (December 26).

• Note that on one day of the Chinese New Year celebration, people don't go out. It's considered bad luck. If you're invited to visit a friend during the New Year celebration, give money to the children (and servants) in the house in special red envelopes obtainable in bookstores. If you're a good friend of the family give HK$10, if a casual friend HK$1. Food is a good gift for the whole family: a canned ham, dried duck, or mandarin oranges. Dress up for visits to families.

• Be aware that traditional Chinese close their businesses for two weeks at the Chinese New Year, while more modern Chinese close for just three days.

• Ching Ming marks the beginning of spring. If you are invited to an observation, expect a visit to the family's ancestral graves, where offerings are made to honor the ancestors, possibly followed by a picnic at the gravesites. It's not a solemn occasion, but a time of happy communion with ancestors.

• To a celebration of the Mid-Autumn Festival, bring gifts of wine, fruit, or mooncakes, and join in the moongazing.

Macao: Most Hong Kong holidays are observed here plus the following additional days: Anniversary of the 1974 Portuguese Revolution (April 25), Labor Day (May 1), Feast of Our Lady of Fatima (May 13), Camoes and Portugal Communities Day (June 10), Feast of St. John the Baptist (June 24), Feast of Kuan Tai (June, date varies), Confucius Day (September, date varies) Portuguese Republic Day (October 5), Portuguese Independence Day (December 1), Feast of the Immaculate Conception (December 8), Winter Solstice Day (December 22), and Christmas (December 24 and 25).

TRANSPORTATION

Public Transportation

• For trams, be aware that cost is the same no matter how far you go. Have exact change. Enter from the rear and leave from the front. As you leave, put your fare into a box near the driver. Destinations are marked in English on the front of the car. Have your own destination written in Chinese and ask someone to tell you at which stop to get off. Avoid trams during the rush hours, when 100 people—more than the 48 the two decks comfortably hold—will be jammed in.

• Note that bus stops have signs saying "All Buses Stop Here." That's not true. Under the sign is a list of buses that actually do make the stop. Look for the destination written on the front in English. Bus fare is determined by distance traveled. Look for a chart (in English) that will list fares. Be sure to have exact change. If there is no ticket seller on the bus, deposit the exact change into a box as you get on. Have your destination written in Chinese characters. Drivers rarely speak English, but someone on the bus usually does and will help you. Ring the bell when you want to get off.

• Hail a minibus on the street. There is a standard fare for each route, but it may vary according to the time of day or the weather. Look for an indication of the destination on the front of these cream-colored buses with red stripes. The final destination is written in Chinese and English on a sign at the front, but the English is in very small print. They are most expensive late at night and on holidays. They will pick you up and drop you anywhere along their route. Be aware that most drivers don't speak English. There is no standing room on minibuses.

• Note that subways, called the MTR (Mass Transit Railway), are modern, quick, and clean. Destinations are displayed in both Chinese and English. Fares are based on distance. Get a ticket (actually a magnetic plastic card about the size of a credit card) by putting money into an automatic machine. If you need change, there are machines that give it. At the turnstiles controlling access to the trains, put your ticket into the slot, which will stamp and return it. Keep your ticket. When you leave the train, insert it into the turnstile at the exit. If you haven't paid the correct fare, the gate won't open. If this happens go to the Excess Fare Office and pay the difference. There are many exits at each stop. To find the one you want, ask

at the Information Office; show a card with your destination written in Chinese. Smoking, eating, or drinking are not permitted in the stations or on the trains. There are strict fines for violating those rules.

• To go from Hong Kong Island to Kowloon, consider taking the Star Ferry, which links the two. (Area residents suggest that you take the ferry if you have time—the trip is only about 7 minutes—and the subway if you are in a rush). The ferry runs every 5 minutes between 6:00 A.M. and 2:00 A.M. Buy a token for either first class (the upper deck) or second class (the lower deck) before boarding. (The ferry is very inexpensive, and the difference in cost between first and second class is minimal.) Don't smoke on the ferry. If you miss the last ferry, look for a *walla-walla*, a small motorboat, which will take you across the harbor. On Hong Kong Island, find walla-wallas at the Queen's Pier, to the east of the Star Ferry concourse. On Kowloon, they are located at the Kowloon Public Pier, to the left of the Star Ferry as you face the water.

• Hail taxis on the street, go to a taxi stand, or order one by phone. To signal to a taxi that you want to cross the harbor, make a dipping motion with your hand. Crooking your index finger means that you want to go to Kowloon. They have meters, which are used (not ignored, as in some other countries). If you are going from Kowloon to Hong Kong, or vice versa, be aware that there is a toll for the cross-harbor tunnel. The fare doesn't register on the meter, but you will be expected to pay the surcharge *both ways*. Most drivers can take you to well-known places; if your destination is out of the way, have its name and directions to it written in Chinese. Remember that traffic in the morning and evening rush hours (before 9:00 A.M., and between 4:00 and 7:00 P.M.) is extremely congested. Be sure to allow extra time—as much as 30 minutes—to arrive at your destination.

• Look for rickshaws only in central Hong Kong and Kowloon. They are only used by tourists, principally for taking photos. Bargain for your fare.

• Take trains to the New Territories. Choose first class (with airplane-like seats) or second class. Trains depart every 3 to 5 minutes and take just 30 minutes to travel from Kowloon to the Chinese border.

• Realize that it takes extra time to get anywhere on Sunday, since everyone in Hong Kong sets off for another place on that day.

Driving

• If you're going to make any trips by car, hire a car and driver. Although rental cars are available, it's best to let someone else deal with Hong Kong's traffic.

• Be aware that you can rent a car if you're over eighteen, but you must have an International Driver's License.

• Driving is on the left, as in Britain.

• Wear a seat belt if you're in the front seat, as the law requires it, and be sure that any children under four are in a car seat.

• Be wary of bicyclists. They usually pay no attention to traffic regulations.

Macao: To reach Macao, take a jetfoil, hydrofoil, or ferry from Hong Kong. The jetfoil trip takes 50 minutes, the hydrofoil 75 minutes, and the ferry 3 hours. From May to September, there is always the risk of typhoons. If a typhoon seems likely, hydrofoils do not run.

• Note that buses are air-conditioned. Ask for the bus schedule and the routes at the Tourist Information Office. There is one fare, regardless of distance. You need exact change in either Macao or Hong Kong currency.

• Be aware that some taxi drivers will try to bargain, even though taxis are metered. If that happens, find another taxi. Many taxi drivers speak English. It's a good idea, however, to have a hotel clerk write down your destination in Chinese because place names are different in Portuguese and Chinese.

• You can also travel by pedicab, a rickshaw for two people, propelled by a bicycle. Bargain for the fare in advance.

LEGAL MATTERS, SAFETY, AND HEALTH

• Bring in to Hong Kong and take out as much currency as you want. There are no restrictions.

• Don't bring firearms into the country.

• Change a minimum amount of money at the airport when you arrive, since the moneychangers in the city give a better rate.

• Don't worry about personal safety on the streets. Mugging of foreigners is almost unheard of. There are pickpockets in the crowded shopping areas, however. Women should hold purses and bags close to them and men should not carry wallets in back pockets.

• Women should take taxis after dark.

• Even though the Chinese are inveterate gamblers, don't expect to find legal casinos in Hong Kong. The only legal gambling is at the horse races controlled by the Royal Hong Kong Jockey Club. Macao, a short ferry ride from Hong Kong, does have legal gambling. On weekends, it is usually packed with people from Hong Kong.

• If you need a policeman, look for one with a red patch on his sleeve; he speaks English.

• Never try to bribe a policeman. If you are stopped by one for any reason, be polite and act penitent. Otherwise, you may suffer a more severe penalty. Don't get angry and talk fast, as this makes the police—whose ability to understand English varies widely—very uncomfortable.

Health: Drugs and patent medicines are widely available as are toiletries, sanitary napkins, and tampons.

• Never buy ice cream from a street vendor.

KEY PHRASES

A note on language: English is the official language of Hong Kong, and most business affairs are conducted in it. Cantonese is the second language and is widely spoken in urban areas.

English	*Cantonese*	*Pronunciation*
Good morning	Jóu Sahn	Joe-sun
Good afternoon	N'ang	N-on
Good night	Jóu Táu	Joe-tow (as in cow)
Mr./Sir	Sin Sang	Seen-sahng
Mrs./Madam	Tai Tai	Tie tie
Miss	Síu Jeh	See-oo-jeh-eh
Yes	Haih	High
No	Mhaih	Mm-high
Please	Ching Néih	Ching-nay
Thank you	Dò Jeh	Doh-jeh
Good-bye	Joi Gin	Joy-geen
Excuse me	Deui Mjyuh	Duh-ee m jyu
I don't understand.	Mming Baak	Mm ming-bahk

INDIA

We asked some travelers what had made them determined to visit India. One said, "It was reading Paul Scott's *The Raj Quartet*." Another said, "It was Ben Kingsley as Gandhi." A third sheepishly admitted, "It was the picture of the Taj Mahal on my grandma's cookie tin." Whatever the reason, the vast subcontinent has mesmerized travelers for centuries.

We discovered there a true melting pot—of cultures, of ethnic groups, of religions, of cuisines. We discovered the spellbinding art of the Moghul emperors. We learned more about Buddhism and Hinduism, two of the world's oldest religions, both born and nurtured in India. Vicariously, we lived through the love-and-hate relationship of Britain and India, and the agony of their separation. Mostly we discovered the truth of one writer's comment, "Love it or hate it you can never ignore India. . . . Nothing is ever quite the way you expect it be."

GREETINGS

• Hold palms together at chin level and nod (never bow) your head, and say *"Namaste"* (nah-mahs-táy) or *"Namaskar"* (nah-mahs-cár). Do this for "Good morning," "Good afternoon," or "Good evening." To Muslims say *"Salaam al-eikum"* (Sah-laȟm ah-lay-kúhm). The greeting to Sikhs is *"Sat Sri Akal"* (Saȟt shŕee ah-káhl). *Ji* is used following a name as a sign of respect, e.g., Gandhi-*ji*.

• Note that it is sometimes difficult to select the correct greeting, since it isn't easy to tell Hindus from Muslims from Sikhs—with so many people in Western dress. One clue is in names: many Muslims have as part of their name "Muhammed," "Ali," "Khan," or "Hussein." Muslim women have "Jan" or "Begum" at the end of their name. Common Hindu names are "Krishna," "Gopal" "Vijay," "Rajendra," and

"Prakash." Religious Sikhs can be identified by the turbans that they wear and by the steel arm bracelet on the right wrist.

• Men shouldn't be surprised if an Indian man shakes hands with them instead of using the traditional greeting. Women should not expect an Indian man to shake hands, but an Indian woman will. If the meeting takes place in a Westernized setting, however, men and women do shake hands.

• In major cities, men usually shake hands, while women use the more traditional greeting. A Western man introduced to a man—especially a Muslim—should shake hands when greeting and departing. When introduced to an Indian woman, or to a man and a woman, he should say *"Namaste."*

• Don't use first names unless you know someone very well. Use "Mr.," "Mrs.," or "Miss."

• Use titles such as "Professor" and "Doctor," and use "Sir" or "Madam" with a superior.

• Be aware that garlands of flowers are used for formal occasions, such as the opening of buildings, the reception of a distinguished visitor, or at the end of a concert. The garlands are draped around the neck of the honored person. If you are "garlanded," wear the flowers for a few minutes, then remove the garland and give it to someone else or else hold on to it. *Never* leave it behind, except at the foot of a statue in a temple.

• Note that a Hindu may greet a man by adding *"sahib"* ("sir" or "master") to the name (Mr. Jones-*sahib*) and a woman by adding *"ji"* (Miss Jones-*ji*) as a sign of respect.

• Don't hug a person of the opposite sex in greeting. Only people of the same sex hug one another. Cross-gender touching (shaking hands, hugging, or kissing) is rare, except among very Westernized Indians. Women sometimes hug when meeting a woman for the first time and very often on a second meeting.

• Feel free to approach a group at a party and introduce yourself.

• Carry business cards with you, because Indians usually exchange them, even at social occasions such as receptions and parties. The cards can help enable Indians to understand and remember Western names and visitors to understand Indian names.

CONVERSATION

• Good topics include food and restaurants; movies; family; children; schools. Ask advice on sights to visit.

• Note that women enjoy discussing clothes. They are pleased to talk about saris and sari textiles.

• Avoid: politics; weather (Indians get tired of hearing foreigners complain about the heat); sex; salaries; poverty; beggars; famines; snake charmers; and widow-burning, called *sati*, a practice that has been banned by the government.

• Do not ask questions about caste unless you know the person you're talking to very well.

• Never criticize anything you see in India, no matter how much it bothers you.

TELEPHONES

IN PUBLIC

• Note that there are few public telephones. A local call costs between 1 and 5 rupees, depending on where you make the call. A phone at a deluxe hotel will cost 5 rupees. Use either a coin or a token purchased at the reception desk. To use a public phone, dial the number, and deposit the coin when your party answers. At the end of 3 minutes, you can deposit more money, with a limit of 6 minutes.

• Realize that it's easier to make phone calls from your hotel, but the cost is frequently high.

• Keep in mind that people who don't have a telephone may give you a "PP" number. The term stands for "Particular Person," a neighbor who will call your party to the phone.

• Use telephone credit cards in most hotels, or call collect from a hotel or a private home.

• To make a long-distance call, go to the post office or to an STD (Standard Trunk Dialing—for long-distance and overseas calls) office where you place a call with a clerk, go into a booth, if there is one, and pay for your call when you've finished.

• When visiting a temple, remove your shoes and step *over* the threshold. People move through the temple to do *puja* (worship), laying offerings on the statues of the gods of their choosing or receiving a blessing—sometimes a mark on the forehead. It's customary to leave a small amount of money for the priest after receiving a blessing.

• Hindu custom dictates that women not go into temples if they are menstruating.

• Be alert for signs indicating that non-Hindus may not visit the inner sanctum of the temple and may see only its outer precincts. If there is no sign, ask a priest.

• If you are visiting a temple and are offered a portion of sweet or fresh coconut or banana, it's *prasad*, offered to the gods, sacred food. Since it's a great honor to be offered it, never refuse it. Accept it—and eat it. If you don't want it, take it and give it to someone else.

• Don't forget that men and women sit in separate areas in Muslim mosques.

• Avoid public displays of affection. Hugging close friends of the same sex is acceptable. So is kissing children.

• Maintain a distance of about an arm's length with members of the opposite sex.

• Never put your hand on an adult's head. Indians believe that the head is the most sacred part of the body, and one should not take a chance of hurting it—even by touching. Since the feet are the least sacred part of the body, one should never sit so that the soles of one's feet are facing another person—e.g., feet on the desk, facing someone else.

• Don't whistle.

• Don't eat on the street. It's rude.

• Note that Indians often point with the chin or, in some communities, with the eyes.

• Beckon with palm turned down, flexing fingers rapidly a few times.

• In the south of India, shaking the head from side to side means "yes."

• To accept something, or when eating, always use your right hand. In India, the left hand is used for cleaning after using the toilet.

• Be aware that an Indian grasping his/her ears is conveying repentance or indicating sincerity.

• Apologize if your feet or shoes touch someone, especially an elderly person.

• Don't be surprised if all the In-dians you meet—even in the most casual way—ask for your address in your own country. They want to be accepted as a friend, even for a short time (e.g., the length of a bus trip). They don't want the address to come to visit you. Don't refuse. If you don't want to give your correct address, give a vague one.

• If you become acquainted with Indians, expect them to give you a nickname indicating some family relationship; e.g., "auntie." Old women are called "mother," and old men "father." Indians try to fit everyone into a slot associated with a family relationship. If you refuse this overture, the Indians will be very hurt. Children will call adults who are acquainted with their parents "auntie" or "uncle," as a sign of respect. The name usually precedes the title—e.g., "Mary Auntie," or "Jim Un-cle."

• Never predict bad fortune openly or associate a person with death in any way; e.g., "He looks like death warmed over." It is equivalent to putting a curse on the person.

• Don't praise children's looks or state of health. Both Hindus and Muslims fear this will invite the evil eye.

• Phrase questions carefully. In-dians often say "Yes" in order to avoid upsetting a person.

• To avoid the enormous bu-reaucracy of everyday life, ask at your hotel for someone who will run errands, stand in line for tickets, etc., for a small fee.

• Be advised that it's not a good idea to walk—even short distances. You will be besieged by beggars. Take taxis whenever you leave your hotel.

• If you wish, give money to beggars, especially children and lepers. However, try to do it from a vehicle—car, taxi, or auto-rickshaw—to avoid being besieged.

• When walking by a temple, don't be surprised if someone puts a religious thread bracelet on your arm. Give the person a few rupees.

• To mail a package, prepare it in advance. It must be sewn up in linen and all seams sealed with sealing wax, which must be pressed with a seal—a non-Indian coin can be used. Get a tailor to prepare the package, or, at larger post offices, look for the people outside who will do this task, or ask for help at your hotel.

• If you have letters sent to you at American Express or at *poste restante*, tell your correspondents to underline your last name. When picking up mail, check to see if letters have been filed under your first name by mistake.

• Don't expect change to be counted out, as it is in most Western countries. At certain places, such as the post office, you'll be handed a fistful of change. If you wait, you'll probably be handed more.

• Before photographing the in-side of sacred temples, be sure to get permission.

• Note that there is a fee to take photographs in India's many wildlife sanctuaries.

• Always ask permission before photographing people. Lower-class people are especially sensitive, suspicious as to why they are being photographed.

• Never photograph airports, railways and railway stations, big bridges, or a military area. It's good taste *not* to photograph Muslim women, women bathing, cremations, slums, or beggars.

• Expect to find Western-style toilets only in better hotels and restaurants. Indian trains usually have both Indian-style and Western-style toilets. In many public bathrooms, toilets are simply basins in the floor. You have to squat and then pull the flush. There is always a bucket of water, which people use instead of toilet paper. Bring toilet paper or tissues with you, if you don't want to use the water. These public bathrooms are found in hotels, restaurants, train stations, bus stations, and some shops. There is usually a picture on the door to indicate which bathroom is for which sex. In some places, there may be a row of stalls with Indian-style "squat" toilets and one that is Western-style.

Shopping: Bargain everywhere except in government craft emporiums, government textile shops, pharmacies, bookstores, or Western-style grocery stores.

• Expect especially spirited bargaining with shoeshine boys, vendors, taxi drivers, and rickshaw drivers.

• Be aware that store owners will often tell you that they are offering a good price because you are their first customer of the day. They are not always telling the truth.

• Even if a price is written on an object, ask the price. Then offer half and bargain from there. Indians want to make a good deal, but they won't try to cheat you. Decide what you are willing to spend for an item. Make this your last offer in a bargaining session. Then start for the door. If the shop owner is willing to sell at your price, he will stop you and agree. However, if you make it out the door, it probably means that he will not agree to your price.

• Don't feel you have to pretend not to be interested in an item (as in the Middle East); it's okay to show a strong interest.

• Buy large and expensive items, such as rugs or jewelry, only from reputable dealers recommended by Indian acquaintances or hotels.

Exercising: If you jog, do so early because of the heat. Stick to areas near hotels and residential areas where Westerners live. Women should not jog alone and should always wear long pants. Men can wear shorts.

DRESS

• As a Westerner, feel free to wear anything, as long as it isn't very revealing (e.g., extremely tight jeans, low-cut blouses). It is *extremely* important for women to keep their legs covered as much as possible by wearing longish skirts or pants. Shorts are never acceptable, except at beach resorts.

• When visiting temples, women should be covered—short or long sleeves and a long skirt or pants. Women should not wear sleeveless dresses or blouses. They need not cover their face or head. Men should wear long pants and a short-sleeved shirt.

• For business, note that office wear is usually informal: shirt, tie, and slacks.

• For an informal evening, men should wear a bush shirt and trousers, and for formal evenings a suit.

• In northern India, men should wear a jacket in the winter, even during daytime.

• In the North, both young and older women may wear *salwar kameez* (baggy pants, a long tunic, and a long scarf) in informal settings.

• To a dinner party, women can wear a dress, skirt and blouse, or slacks. Indian women will wear saris. Men should wear shirts and trousers.

• Western women should feel free to wear saris, but be aware that they are difficult to put on—they consist of one six-foot-long piece of material, tucked into a slip, pleated, and worn over a very short blouse. The sari tends to pull out of the slip, and the shawl part tends to fall. If you want to try wearing a sari (and Indians are almost always delighted when Westerners wear Indian clothing), ask the help of an Indian woman, an acquaintance, a hotel chambermaid, or even a shopkeeper. They are usually happy to help arranging to have the blouse and slip made and to demonstrate how to wear the sari. (Fabrics from the North differ from those in the South.) *Salwar Kameez* can be bought ready-made and are cool and offer the covering that Indian custom requires.

• Western women should wear conservative (i.e., not revealing) clothing *unless* they want to get felt in crowded places or bumped into "accidentally" on the street. They may get propositioned in situations when they thought they were just having a chat. (Physical attacks, however, are very rare.) Being with a male Indian friend is a sure way of avoiding such unpleasantness.

• Women should note that in non-tourist areas, clothing that isn't conservative (e.g., very short skirts) will attract a crowd of spectators.

• Be sure to wear a hat. It is essential protection against the sun. Men should not, however, wear turbans because they will look strange.

• Realize that in temples it may be offensive if you wear leather shoes or belts or carry leather handbags, since cows are sacred.

MEALS

Hours and Foods

Breakfast: 6:00 to 8:00 A.M. In the North, people eat *paratha* (fried *chappati*, a whole-wheat bread), sweets, and fruit; they drink tea with milk and sugar, or *lassi* (a yogurt shake). In the South, coffee is served with *idlis* (rice and lentil dumplings) or *dosas* (rice and lentil pancakes) accompanied by coconut chutney and *sambhar* (lentil soup). Large hotels offer Western-style breakfasts.

Lunch: 12:00 P.M. to 2:00 P.M. It consists of *chappati*, meat, and fish or egg curry. Water is served with the meal.

• Between 4:00 and 5:00 P.M., Indians break for tea and biscuits.

Dinner: 8:30 to 10:00 or 11:00 P.M. Dishes are similar to lunch. Typical might be lentil curry, three different vegetable curries, rice, and yogurt. Drinks are tepid water with the meal and tea after the meal. Other drinks that sometimes accompany meals are milk or coconut milk.

• If you are offered water, ask if it is boiled water. If it isn't, refuse it. Bottled water is now available almost everywhere in India and is usually reliable. Travelers should *always* drink bottled water, even in good hotels, and they should carry a bottle of water with them on day trips. Coca-Cola is now readily available, as are Fanta and plain soda water. When you purchase bottled water, make *sure* that the seal is firm. After finishing, crush the bottle and throw it away so that it cannot be refilled with tap water.

• An elegant meal will include rice or Indian bread, *dahl* (lentils), two or three vegetable dishes, or, if the hosts are not vegetarian, fish curry and meat curry. Condiments accompany the main dishes: chutneys, green chilies, and chopped coriander leaves.

• In the North, tea is the prevalent drink, always prepared with milk and sugar. It is served at any time of the day. In the South, the drink is strong coffee, always with milk and sugar, served at any time of the day.

• In many homes, people do not drink alcoholic beverages. And there are several states in which you can drink alcohol only in your hotel room.

• Note that alcohol is prohibited in several of India's states. You can get an All-India Liquor Permit when you get your visa. It allows you to buy, possess, transport, and drink bottled liquor while traveling in places where prohibition is enforced. Ask about further specifics of the permit when you get it.

• A rule of thumb about dairy products: Feel free to drink milk and eat yogurt in better-class restaurants and hotel restaurants; standards of cleanliness there are high. But don't drink the milk or eat the yogurt in family-style or small restaurants, where the sanitary practices are suspect.

Table Manners

• If an Indian invites you to a meal, expect to be entertained at home. They regard it as insulting to guests and to one's wife to go to a restaurant. Tell your host in advance if you can't (or don't want to) eat a certain food or spicy foods. Use the excuse that you have a stomach problem.

• If invited to dinner in a home, arrive 15 to 30 minutes late. Indians sometimes arrive as much as an hour late.

• Have a snack before you go to dinner at an Indian's home. If you are invited for 8:00 P.M., you probably won't sit down to dinner until about 11:00 P.M.

• In very Westernized homes, expect to be offered beer or whiskey before dinner. Peanuts or *papadum* (crisp, flat bread) will also be served.

• Don't be upset if the sexes are segregated at a meal, although the custom is now more common in the country than in urban areas. Even when the sexes eat together, men usually talk to men and women to women.

• If you're invited to a traditional home, expect to eat on a floor mat or low wooden seat. In more modern homes, tables are used.

• As a guest, anticipate being the first to be seated, but there is no place of honor.

• In a traditional home, look for a table set with *thalis*—round, shallow, silver trays used for special occasions. (For every day, Indians use brass trays.) On the *thalis* will be a number of small matching bowls containing meat, fish, chicken, lentils, raw vegetables, and rice or bread. There will be metal tumblers for water. The more modern people in cities use Western-style china.

• If you are invited to a meal of celebration in a small town, don't be surprised if the food is served on banana leaves, with earthenware bowls. The leaves will be thrown out at the end of the meal.

• Even in Westernized homes, always go into the washroom and wash your hands before and after eating.

• Expect guests and men to be served first, then children and women. To show graciousness, the cook eats last. Always wait to be served; never serve yourself.

• Note that Muslims like everyone to partake of food together—as in eating from the same plate. If you don't feel comfortable, refuse.

• Remember that to Indians food and religion are interwoven. Since food comes from God, the giving of food is a spiritual act. Even an unexpected guest must take some refreshment. Don't refuse an offer of food in an Indian home.

• Take small portions at first, because your hosts will push you to take more, sometimes even if you have refused. You won't offend anyone by leaving some on your plate.

• Hope to be offered a fork. Otherwise, eat as the Indians do—with your hands. (They believe eating with the hands allows one to get the "feel" of the food.) There will be serving spoons for gravies, yogurt, and rice. In the North, take whatever bread is offered—e.g., *chappatis.* Break it into bits, and with each bit, scoop up the vegetables or curries. In the South, mix rice with curry to form a small ball, and eat that. (This is a difficult art for Westerners to master. Watch others at the table, and try to imitate them.) As you can see, eating Indian-style takes practice.

• Remember that you *must* eat with your right hand, even if you are left-handed. The left hand is considered unclean, as it is used for cleaning after using the toilet.

• If you are eating with your hands, note that in the North, food should not come beyond the second joint on your finger, while in the South, the whole hand is plunged in. (If you are wearing long sleeves, be sure to roll them up.)

• Never touch a common dish with your fingers or with a utensil you have used. If you do, the family may stop eating from that dish, though nothing will be said. Always use serving spoons.

• Never pop a finger into cooking food for a quick taste.

• Use the left hand to pass things since the right hand will be sticky from eating.

• Don't worry if you find dishes too spicy and can't eat them. Your host will understand. (To Indians, one of the advantages of spicy curries is that they promote the perspiration needed to cool the body in temperatures that can climb to 115 degrees Fahrenheit.)

• If your mouth burns from a hot curry, eat yogurt, tomatoes, or fruit. They will reduce the heat better than water.

• Note that the religion of the family with which you are dining will determine the menu. Muslims in India usually don't eat beef but rather lamb or mutton (which can mean sheep or goat). Hindus never eat beef and usually eat no meat, including chicken. Some may eat fish. Many don't eat eggs. Jains (a sect of Hinduism) don't eat meat or root vegetables.

• Never offer another person food from your plate—even husband to wife. As soon as you receive your food it becomes "polluted," so you should not share it with anyone. To do so is a major social insult.

• In the North, everyday desserts are *kheer* (made of milk, rice, and nuts) and *firni* (similar to *kheer* but thicker and more custard-like). In other areas, expect desserts only on festive occasions. Sometimes sweets come with a thin layer of edible silver (looking as though someone didn't get all the aluminum foil off the dish). Don't peel it off—it's edible (and a delicacy).

• At the end of the meal, prepare to chew *paan*, folded betel leaves stuffed with spices such as saffron, cardamom, cloves, anise, and fennel. It's considered a digestive and an astringent. It turns saliva red, so don't think that you are bleeding.

• When drinking from a communal container (probably in a Muslim home), don't touch it with your lips. This isn't easy.

• Even though Indians may not say "Please" or "Thank you," you should say, "Thank you for a lovely evening." You must return the meal to show that you value the relationship, so be sure to invite your hosts to a meal.

• Leave *immediately* after dinner, e.g., midnight, if you sat down to dinner at 11:00.

Places to Eat

• Pop into a coffeehouse for coffee, soft drinks, sandwiches, or Indian snacks: *samosas* (deep-fried dough filled with meat or vegetables) or *bhajia* (vegetables dipped in chickpea flour and fried). Some coffeehouses also serve tea.

• Snackbars offer mango juice, fresh orange juice, *lassi* (an ice and yogurt drink), *Campa Kola* (a Coca-Cola–like drink), and all kinds of sweets. It's best to avoid the fruit juices, since the machines used to make them are often very dirty.

• Both snackbars and coffeehouses are easy to identify, since they are called by their English names.

• A *mithaiwala* is a pastry vendor. In addition to pastries to take out, vendors serve milkshakes, juices, tea, and pastries to be eaten in their shops.

• *Chaiki dukaan* are teahouses, serving tea, *lassi*, biscuits, and salty snacks.

• *Dhabba* are roadside restaurants, offering rough Indian food, which is often very spicy but is sometimes good. It's best to avoid eating food from these stands. If you are desperately hungry, get a *tandoori* chicken, which will be well cooked. Never eat salads, vegetables, or raw fruits there.

• Note that there are very few bars in India and, except for those in hotels, they tend to be sleazy.

• Remember that the word "hotel" often means only a restaurant.

• For a good meal at a modest price, try the buffet lunch in one of the larger hotels, but go easy on such extras as soft drinks, because they are extremely expensive.

• Don't look for menus to be posted in restaurant windows. It's not the usual practice.

• If a restaurant is full, you may ask a party with space at their table if you can share the table.

• To summon the waiter, beckon Western-style, though Indians snap their fingers or hiss.

• Note that many well-known restaurants provide food that is not too spicy for non-Indian palates. Say "mild" to the waiter when ordering. In Western-style hotels, the food served will be mild. You don't even have to ask.

• In many Indian restaurants, expect the food to be prepared out front, so you can see what is going on.

• To taste a variety of dishes, ask if it is possible to order half portions. This is usually acceptable in small restaurants.

• Don't eat pork, ham, or salami, because you can pick up parasites if the meat is not cooked well enough.

• Avoid freshwater fish. During the monsoon season torrential rains wash the land, and everything slides into the river. If you aren't sure that the fish came from salt water, don't eat it.

• Note that the beef served in India is water buffalo, not much appreciated by the Western palate.

• Stick to dishes with lamb, mutton, chicken, or salt water fish.

• Ask for a "tray tea": Western tea, milk, and sugar served separately. A tea called *chai* can be made by simmering Assam tea leaves in water and milk with sugar and spices, or by making a milk/sugar/ spice concentrate that is mixed with brewed Assam tea.

• Expect beer to be available only in Western-style restaurants.

• Foreign women should not feel embarrassed to dine alone. Indians expect it; however, Indian women don't do the same.

Specialties

• Throughout India, look for *Mullagatanni*, better known as Mulligatawny soup, a rich broth flavored with onions and spices, to which cream, milk, or peanut butter is added; *channe* (chickpeas in tamarind sauce); and *samosas* (pastries with potato or meat filling).

• In east India, where rice is the mainstay of the meal, try *machher jhol*, a curry of rice, vegetables, and fish; *malai* curry, with prawns and coconut; and *loochi*, the east India name for *poori*—a dough of flour, water, and ghee, which is deep-fried and puffs up.

• Madras and south India offer many special dishes: *sambar* (a lentil purée cooked with vegetable and spices); *appam* (a rice and coconut pancake fermented with toddy and baked in a clay pot); *cochin* (a prawn curry with turmeric and coriander); *raita* (a yogurt mixture with fruits, vegetables, or seasonings that provides a contrast to the spicy main dishes); and *payasam* (a sweet made from milk and cereals).

• In Andhra Pradesh, the northernmost southern state, sample *ka-*

bobs; *pulao* (rice pilaf); *biryanis* (mild rice dishes); *haleem* (pounded wheat with meat and fried onion rings); and *nahari* (sheep trotters and spice, stewed over a slow charcoal fire) eaten with *kulchas* (hot bread cakes).

• In Delhi and the North, expect the accent to be on lamb, poultry, clarified butter (called *ghee*), spices, and milk. One of the area's best-known specialties is *tandoori*, a mild dish of chicken, marinated in yogurt and spices, baked in a special charcoal oven, and served with yogurt, raw onion, radish salad, and *naan*, an unleavened, flat bread. Other regional dishes are *korma*, lamb curry with cashew nuts; *pulao*, spiced saffron rice with meats, garnished with chopped, boiled eggs; marinated kabobs on skewers; *rogan josh*, aromatic lamb curry cooked in *ghee*, ginger, coriander seed, red chilies, and other spices; *dahl*, lentils of many varieties, eaten at almost every meal; *mattar pannir* (a homemade cheese with peas); *lassi*, a yogurt drink; and *nimbu pani*, a fresh lime drink.

• The North offers many breads: *naan*, crisp on the outside and spongy inside; *paratha*, unleavened bread, made from wheat flour and pan fried; *poori*, soft, unleavened, wholewheat bread, which is deep fried; *chappati*, an unleavened whole wheat bread, baked on the griddle; *pappad,* made of unleavened, seasoned lentil flour and served crisped.

• Bombay and the West offer *khaman dhokla*, a salty, steamed cake made from chickpea flour; *dhansak*, lamb or chicken cooked with curried lentils and served with rice; *khadi*, yogurt and fried puffs flavored with ginger, chilies, bay leaves, and finely chopped vegetables; *khicheri*, a plain dish of rice and lentils; *min vela curry*, a mixed fish curry with spices, tamarind, and coconut; and *Bombay halwa*, a sweetmeat made of finely ground wheat, milk, sugar, butter, and pistachio nuts—it is gummy in consistency and served cut into squares.

• In Goa, try *chorissu*, a spicy sausage like the Portuguese chorizo; *vindaloo*, meat marinated in vinegar; *sarpatel*, pig's liver in a hot, spicy sauce; and the plentiful seafood, such as shrimp, oysters, crab, and lobster.

HOTELS

• Reserve well in advance for the Western-style hotels in major cities; they have air-conditioning and private baths. Five-star hotels have business centers with phones, computers, and fax machines.

• Check the Indian government ratings of hotels; there are offices in all cities. It's best to stay in three- to five-star hotels.

• Note that the Indian government operates tourist bungalows, which are clean and safe. They must adhere to certain standards. There are none in remote areas of the country, however.

• Be sure to see the room you've reserved before registering for it. Be sure that the door locks securely.

• Keep in mind that if you buy drinks in a hotel, you'll pay 100 percent duty. Alternatively you can bring duty-free liquor and serve it in your room.

• In Indian hotels that are lower than first class, try to find and recognize *one* room servant and tip him consistently. Learn his name, and ask for him. Otherwise—especially in Bombay—you will constantly be besieged by servants who will want to carry even small items (e.g., your purse) to get a tip.

• Bring a towel with you if you're staying in small hotels, as they may not furnish them.

• Pay your hotel bill either in cash (rupees) or with a major credit card. If you are paying in cash, have with you the receipt you received when you changed your foreign money into rupees. The hotel clerk may ask to see this to make sure that you haven't changed money on the black market.

4 hours and 80 rupees for a full day.

• Don't offer money to poor people who do something for you out of friendship or kindness. Sometimes it's difficult to know which is the case. As a rule of thumb: usually someone who approaches you and offers help wants a tip.

TIPPING

• Remember that tipping in India is a way of getting things accomplished. If you know you're going to be using a service repeatedly, tipping will ensure better service.

• Tip porters 10 rupees per bag. In a five-star hotel, tip the porter 30 rupees.

• Leave 15 percent in a restaurant, unless a service charge is included in the check, in which case tipping is optional.

• Give taxi drivers 10 percent of the fare as a tip.

• If you stay in a private home, tip servants 20–30 rupees per day. It's acceptable to hand them the money.

• Don't tip ushers or gas station attendants.

• Tip railway coolies who carry your bags about 10 rupees per bag. The fee can usually be negotiated, depending on the weight of the bags.

• If you hire a car and driver, tip the driver 50–100 rupees per day.

• Tip local guides 40 rupees for

PRIVATE HOMES

• Note that the customary time for visiting is between 5:00 and 8:00 P.M. Unless you know someone well, arrange the time of your visit in advance. It's rude to drop in on someone other than a good friend.

• If you're invited to stay in an Indian home, be aware that being a guest in India is a full-time job. People will want to talk to you a great deal and show you around. They'll be insulted if you want to sightsee on your own.

• Outside many homes, especially in the South, expect to see *rangoli*, intricate designs made of white or colored rice flour. Since they symbolize prosperity, be careful not to step on them.

• Before entering a home, ask if you should remove your shoes, the custom in traditional Indian homes. Even if shoes are worn in the house, they are never worn in the kitchen or in the *puja* room (the worship room).

• In traditional homes, expect to sit cross-legged on a cushion on the floor and to eat on little raised tables while sitting on a mat on the floor.

• If you see religious pictures or statues and want to make your hosts happy, hold your palms together in front of your face while looking at the objects. It's rude to stare at pictures or statues without holding your hands in prayer. (To make this gesture is not an expression of belief in the religion; it is a courtesy.)

• Expect to be entertained in the living room. Don't wander into other rooms in the house.

• In a traditional Indian home, never enter the kitchen.

• Treat servants with respect (not as you've seen them treated in countless films about India). To order them around brusquely or to shout at them is to offend your hosts.

• In a Muslim home, when invited to have tea or coffee, refuse the first time.

• Foreign husbands may bring their wives when visiting an orthodox Muslim home, though orthodox Muslim women cannot be seen by men outside their families.

• If you are visiting a traditional home, don't be surprised if the wife does not sit down while male guests are present. When both men and women are present, the men usually congregate in one part of the room or house and women in another. Western women can stay with the men if they wish.

• If there are no servants, women guests should make the gesture of offering to help, but men should not. If there are servants, don't offer to help.

• When leaving a Hindu home, women shouldn't be surprised if the oldest woman of the house paints a red or black dot (a *bindi*) on her forehead, puts scent on her hands, and offers betel leaves with turmeric and betel nuts. This small ceremony is to wish a woman prosperity.

• Don't leave a home in a group of three, an inauspicious number. Two people should leave, and the third follow a few seconds later.

• If you are staying with a family, feel free to take a daily bath. Your hosts will be surprised if you don't.

• Note that if you stay at an Indian home more than one night, your hosts will give you a small gift when you leave (a gesture showing that they hope you will return).

Gifts: When invited to a meal, bring flowers, or a box of sweets and pastry or fruit.

• When you pay a visit in the afternoon or evening, bring flowers, which are symbols of prosperity. Marigolds, roses, and jasmine are very popular. Women like to string flowers and put them in their hair. Don't, however, give frangipani blossoms; they are used for funerals.

• When you give money, give odd denominations of 21, 51, or 101 rupees.

• When traveling by train, bring postcards of your region at home to give to fellow travelers; however, don't bring beach scenes with pictures of women in bathing suits.

• For close friends, bring calculators, radios, blenders, toasters, jeans for children, shirts, or liquor. Westernized people enjoy Scotch, but don't bring alcoholic beverages unless you are sure that the recipients drink.

• Other popular gifts include speciality items from your area, such as patchwork quilts or picture books; Western clothing; appliances; suitcases. Cosmetics—especially those from France—are valued by women.

• Another welcome gift is an expensive wall calendar. Indians enjoy them because they can be used for a year and then thrown away. Pictures on the walls often get mildewed during the monsoon season, so don't bring objects to hang on a wall.

• Bring electric watches, calculators, or chocolates for children.

• Don't give Muslims gifts of toy dogs or pictures of dogs, since dogs are considered unclean.

• Don't wrap gifts in black or white, colors considered unlucky.

• However kind house servants are to you, give them only money, not a gift. Giving them a present is to equate them with the family, an insulting action.

• If you receive a gift, do not open it in the presence of the giver. Put it aside.

MONEY AND BUSINESS

Note: As of May 1998, trade with India is illegal. Check newspapers (especially those with business orientation) to learn when/if the embargo is lifted.

Hours

Bank hours: 10:00 A.M. to 2:00 P.M., Monday through Friday, and 10:00 A.M. to noon on Saturdays.

Government and Business Offices: 10:00 A.M. to 1:00 P.M. and 2:00 to 5:00 P.M., Monday through Friday. (Some are open Saturday mornings, and others are open on alternate Saturday mornings.)

Shops: 10:00 A.M. to 5:00 P.M., Monday through Saturday. In Delhi, shops are open on different days, depending on which market they are in. Check at your hotel to find a market and its hours.

Money

• Remember that the rupee is divided into 100 *paise*. (Abbreviation for the singular is *Re*, for the plural *Rs*). Coins are 1, 2, 3, 5, 10, 25, 50 *paise* and *Re* 1. Banknotes are *Re* 1, *Rs* 2, 5, 10, 20, 50, 100, and 1000. Note that the rupee was once divided into 16 *annas*, and prices may be quoted in *annas*; 4 *annas* = 25 *paise* or a quarter rupee, and 8 *annas* = 50 *paise* or half a rupee. Because of inflation, *paise* are rarely used, and the use of *annas* is even more infrequent.

• Realize that major credit cards—American Express, Visa, Barclaycard, MasterCard, Access, Diners Club—are accepted at most hotels, large restaurants, and large shops. Travelers' checks must be changed into rupees at a Bank of India. There are branches everywhere, including hotels.

• Be aware that it can take several hours to cash travelers' checks in small towns. Try to deal with large banks in large cities. Don't accept large denomination notes, because they will be difficult to change, and don't accept damaged or torn notes, because merchants will refuse them, especially in small towns.

• Keep a supply of small change. Very often taxi drivers and vendors will say that they don't have change.

Business Practices

• Plan business trips between December and March. Before leaving, check with the Government of India Tourist Office, the Indian Embassy, or a nearby Indian Consulate for the schedule of religious holidays during the period that you plan to be in India. There are hundreds of holidays in various regions, and business is not conducted during that time. Avoid traveling in India during the *Dussehra-Diwali* period, usually in October or November. Dates vary from year to year, so consult the tourist office, embassy, or consulate. Another time to avoid is the monsoon season—June, July, and August—because transportation becomes difficult to impossible.

• If you plan to do business in Delhi, try to arrange an appointment with the commercial attache of your country. He/she can often put you in touch with officials in the government as well as relevant people in the private sector.

• Be sure to telephone as soon as you arrive in a city to confirm all your appointments.

• Make appointments at least one month in advance. Fax service may be a problem because of the unreliable Indian telephone service. Try to have a schedule flexible enough to allow for extra days in India, because people sometimes don't appear for a meeting.

• Note that executives prefer late-morning or early-afternoon appointments, so try to schedule meetings between 11:00 A.M. and 4:00 P.M. (Lunch is usually taken from 1:00 to 2:00 P.M.) Don't be surprised if Indian businesspeople are somewhat vague in commitment, since they don't like to be pressed for exact times.

• Be aware that Indians are impressed by punctuality but will often not be on time themselves. Try to keep your schedule loose to accommodate delays.

• Bring business cards. It's acceptable to have them printed in English.

• In nearly every city, expect to find private fax and computer services available. They may be less expensive than those in your hotel, but the latter often provides better service. Keep in mind that some fax facilities charge even for an unsuccessful transmission. Be sure to ask the policy before sending a fax.

• Recognize that most company executives are very Westernized. They have often studied in England, dress in Western style, and follow Western behavior.

• Expect to be offered sweet, milky tea, no matter what time of day your meeting occurs. If you don't want to drink a great deal (i.e., 10 cups), drink very slowly or ask for something else, such as a soft drink. Never say "No" to the offer of a drink. If food, such as sweets, is pressed on you and you don't care for it, just leave it.

• Be prepared to answer many personal questions. When you meet someone for business the first time, you'll be asked about yourself, your family, whether you like sports, and what your hobbies are. You are expected to ask your Indian hosts the same questions. Show special interest in your host's children, and bring pictures of your own family. Don't begin a business discussion without these preliminaries.

• Expect to be overwhelmed by hospitality. Westerners sometimes have a problem in avoiding the many invitations. Never directly refuse an invitation, but don't make an explicit commitment unless you genuinely want to accept. If someone says, "Come to my house and meet my children," respond, "I certainly will," but don't commit yourself to a time and date. Then you need not go, because there's no obligation unless you have named a specific time. Never merely say "No."

• Realize that business will be conducted at a very slow pace, and dealings won't be concluded quickly. After they present and discuss a proposal, Indians don't conclude an agreement at once. Expect additional discussion about the contract as a whole or individual clauses in it.

• Be aware that there are both male and female secretaries. Men usually work in government offices and women in private business.

• Always take notes during meetings in order to have a good reference at a later time for any verbal agreements made.

• Don't be surprised if people wander in and out of your meetings. For example, clerks may appear with files or letters that need attention. Keep calm and don't show any resentment about the interruptions.

• Recall that Indians do not like to say "No," and they may avoid a negative response by stalling. Be patient, but have a realistic idea of how long you're willing to wait. If there are constant delays, you may have to accept that the Indian businesspeople aren't interested in your project.

• If you are in a position where "No" would be your response, avoid using that direct negative. Saying "I'll try" is as good as a refusal.

• Keep in mind that all decisions are made at the top. While middle managers do have input and are usually able to meet with you more readily, they will not be making the final decision.

• A Western man doing business with an Indian woman should wait for her to offer her hand in greeting. If she greets with the *Namaste* greeting, he should do the same.

• Note that foreign women who represent large companies, or who have senior titles, will have the most credibility.

• If you are giving a speech and are offered a flower garland (a sign of respect and affection), accept it, but remove it from your neck at once to show humility.

Business Entertaining: If you plan to entertain at a meal, note that business lunches are more popular than dinners.

• Expect business to be done informally—e.g., during a tennis game, or during lunch or dinner. Accept any invitation, if at all possible. You will build trust by attending informal gatherings.

• If you are hosting a business meal, remember that Hindus don't eat beef, and Muslims don't eat pork. Also check to see if your guests are vegetarian.

• Women should not feel awkward about entertaining Indian businessmen. They will usually offer to pay for the dinner but will not prevent the woman from picking up the check.

Note: For advice regarding business greetings, dress, or table manners, see the appropriate sections earlier in this chapter.

HOLIDAYS AND SPECIAL OCCASIONS

• Expect banks, offices, and most shops to be closed on the holidays listed below. Some towns and regions have festivals, which are holidays in the area. Check with the tourist office for dates of local festivals.

Holidays: Republic Day (January 26); Holi, celebrating the destruction of the evil demon Holika (February/March); Mahavira Jayanti, a major Jain (a Hindu sect that will never hurt a living creature— including insects) festival, marking the birth of Mahavira (March/April); Ramanavami, celebrating the birth of Rama, an incarnation of Vishnu, the preserver (March/April); Good Friday (March/April); Buddha Purnima, celebrating Buddha's birth, enlightenment, and reaching nirvana (May/June); Independence Day, the anniversary of independence from Britain (August 15); Janmashtami, the anniversary of the death of Krishna, another reincarnation of Vishnu (August); Dussehra, a 10-day commemoration of Rama's victory over Ravana, the demon king (September/October); Gandhi Jayanti, a solemn celebration of Gandhi's birth (October 2); Diwali, the happiest Hindu festival, celebrating the struggle between good and evil in the epic *Ramayana* and marked by the lighting of oil lamps to guide Rama home from his exile (October/November); Govardhana Puja, a Hindu festival dedicated to the cow (November); Nanak Jayanti, the birthday of Guru Nanak, founder of the Sikh religion (November 16); Christmas (December 25).

• Note that most of the holidays above follow the lunar calendar.

Check with the Indian tourist office before leaving either to include or avoid certain holidays. In addition to the holidays above, there are many, many regional holidays.

• Be aware that the first day of Diwali is the first day of the commercial year.

• To please friends, send cards to them for Diwali.

• Keep a raincoat handy during the spring festival of Holi. People shower passersby with colored liquid. Also, expect people to wear yellow, symbolizing spring, and green, symbolizing green earth, and to fast until noon.

• Remember that there are several Muslim holidays, whose dates vary greatly from year to year: Ramadan, lasting 30 days with dawn to dusk fasts; Idu'l-Fitr, celebrating the end of Ramadan; Id-Uz-Zuha, commemorating Abraham's sacrifice; Muharram, a 10-day festival honoring the martyrdom of Imam Hussein, Mohammed's grandson.

TRANSPORTATION

Public Transportation

• Don't look for subways except in Calcutta, where 5 miles of subway opened in 1985. Fare is based on distance traveled.

• If you get on a bus toward the beginning of the route, don't expect the driver to have change. You'll be given a receipt for the change owed to you. Keep this receipt and ask for your change at the end of the trip.

• On other buses, the conductor will come around and collect the fare. Be sure to keep the ticket you receive until the end of the ride.

• Be aware that buses in large cities are *very, very* crowded. It's better to use auto-rickshaws. Bombay's bus service is probably best: service is frequent, the buses are double-decker, and people wait in line, which they don't often do in other areas.

• Remember that in northern India, city buses have special sections for women, but buses in the South do not.

• If you want a taxi, hail one on the street. It's usually quicker than calling one. Some taxis are in good condition; others have torn seats and are noisy. Either type will probably get you to your destination.

• Most taxis have meters. If the driver says that the meter is "broken," say that you're going to take another taxi. Often, the meter will miraculously work. Many taxis have "fare adjustment" cards, since the meter prices may be outdated. Ask at information desks at the airport or in hotels beforehand to get an idea of what the fare should be.

• At major airports, remember that you can prepay for your taxi ride to your hotel. Pay at a booth, where you will be given a receipt to give to the driver. What you've paid does not include a tip nor a ride to another location if you have a problem at your hotel.

• Be aware that in Delhi you can't hail a taxi; you must phone for one. You can, however, hail auto-rickshaws.

• An alternative to taxis and buses is the auto-rickshaw, which uses a motorcycle engine. The driver is in the front and there are seats for two people in the rear. They are about half the price of taxis and are often faster than taxis because the drivers are much more aggressive than taxi drivers.

• In small towns, look for a cycle-rickshaw, a three-wheel bicycle with seats for two passengers behind the driver.

• Note that there are two classes

of trains—first and second—with several "subclasses" under each. Air-conditioned first-class is available on some trains. Regular first class is comfortable but often dusty and hot. Second-class reserved guarantees you a seat. Second-class unreserved guarantees you only an opportunity to jam yourself into the train in any way possible. People often enter through the windows, and you're lucky to get a luggage rack to lie down on.

• Try to get a mail or express train that runs on a broad-gauge track (There are three gauges.) If possible, avoid taking passenger trains; on them the trips are almost interminable.

• For overnight trips, take a first- or second-class sleeper. In first-class, expect compartments with two to four sleepers and sometimes a toilet. The sleeping berths fold up to make a sitting compartment during the daytime. Second-class sleepers have two or three tiers. Although it sounds contradictory, the three-tier is more likely to lead to a decent night's sleep, since the two-tier has a row of seats below the berths, and people are getting on and off all night.

• Don't be surprised if train travel in the monsoon season—June through September—is difficult. Trains can be greatly affected by high rivers and floods.

• When taking any class above the lowest, be sure to reserve your seat well in advance. Reservations can be made up to six months in advance. You can reserve at a railroad station, through a travel agent, or at the Ministry of Railways in New Delhi. If you reserve through a local travel agent, he/she may need to borrow your passport.

• If you book yourself, go to the Tourist Information section of the Railway Central Reservations Office. You will get a voucher to take to an adjacent ticket counter, where you actually pay for the ticket. Before getting in line to arrange for your sleeper, fill out a sleeper reservation form, which you will find in the boxes around the reservation hall. Your ticket will indicate your compartment and berth seat number.

• Be aware that there are tourist quotas on most trains. If there are no more sleepers, check with the tourist office, or ask the stationmaster if any VIP quotas are available. He may be willing to give you such a seat at the last minute.

• Women can ask if the train has special cars for women. Many Indian trains do. They are called *purdah*, or ladies' cars. It is one way to avoid nighttime hassles. On the other hand, such cars attract bandits.

• Look for first- and second-class waiting rooms in train stations. You must have a first-class ticket to use the first-class waiting room.

• If you just need information, people will be tolerant if you jump the queue, but don't do it to buy a ticket.

• If you will be traveling often by train, buy the *Trains at a Glance* timetable, available at railway station newsstands. It covers the faster trains on all the main routes.

• Allow plenty of time before departure to find your seat. Sleeper and seat numbers are displayed on lists posted on the platform and outside each carriage, along with passengers' names.

• Expect to be besieged by food and drink sellers at each stop.

• Women traveling alone should take precautions: wear Indian dress; be careful not to act provocatively; make friends with Indian women or families on trains; sit next to women on trains or other public transport.

Driving

• Be conscious that driving is on the left, as in Japan, Hong Kong, and Britain.

• If at all possible, hire drivers; don't drive yourself.

• If you're hiring a car for the day, ask the driver to come an hour earlier than you want to leave, since drivers tend to be late.

• If you drive, drive slowly and *very* cautiously. There are cyclists, buses, trucks, rickshaws, camels, cows, goats, pigs, elephants, dogs— and countless pedestrians. At night, watch for ox carts and cars without lights on.

• Be aware that vehicles have the right of way over pedestrians, and larger vehicles have right of way over smaller ones.

• If you are involved in an accident with a person or a cow, don't stop. Drive to the nearest police station (they are marked in English) and report the accident. If you stop, witnesses may become physically violent.

LEGAL MATTERS, SAFETY, AND HEALTH

• Don't bring Indian currency into the country or try to take it out.

• If you bring more than $1000 into the country, be sure to fill out a Customs declaration form.

• Don't bring guns or pornography into India.

• Be prepared to declare radios, cameras, and other electronic equipment on a special form; Customs will check to make sure that you take those items out with you when you leave the country.

• Change all money at banks or other authorized agencies. Keep receipts of exchange so that you can reconvert unspent rupees back into your own currency at the end of your trip.

• Never try to bribe police.

• Be aware that the police can be

very arbitrary. In case of a small theft, it's better to forget it than to go to the police. Report any significant theft to the police so that you can have a statement for your insurance company. It's very unlikely that you will recover the stolen goods. To minimize the possible loss of money, never carry more than $200 in cash; use travelers' checks.

•Remember that drinking is prohibited in Gujarat, Tamil Nadu, and Bihar. Others states may have days when no liquor is sold. An All-India Liquor Permit may be obtained from a government tourist office. It allows you to buy, transport, and drink liquor in the states where prohibition is enforced. Get the permit when you get your visa, or ask at a tourist office after you arrive in India. Also ask what conditions apply to the permit.

Health: Bring tissues, since toilet paper is difficult to obtain outside large cities. Soap, toothpaste, and toiletries are readily available. Tampons are more difficult to find than sanitary napkins, so women who use tampons should bring a supply.

•Note the cautions on milk products in the section on "Meals."

•Never buy ice cream from a street vendor.

KEY PHRASES

English	Hindi	Pronunciation
Good morning, afternoon, evening, night	Namaste	Nah-mahs-táy
Sir, Mr.	Sahib, Shri, Ji*	Saab, Shree, Jee
Madam, Mrs.	Shrimati, Ji*	Shree-máh-tee, Jee
Miss	Kumari, Ji*	Koo-máh-tee, Jee
Please	Not applicable	
Thank you	Shukriya	Shoe-kree-yá
You're welcome	Koi baat nahi	Kó-ee báht neh-hée
Yes	Haji	Háh-jee
No	Ji nahi	Jée neh-hée
Excuse me	Maaf kijiye	Máhf kee-jee-yáy
Good-bye	Namaste	Nah-mahs-táy

I don't understand	Mai nahi samajhta hu (masc.)	Máy neh-hée sah-máhj-tah hóo
	Mai nahi samajhti hu (fem.)	Máy neh-hée sah-máhj-tee hóo
I don't speak Hindi	Mai Hindi nahi bol sakta hu (masc.)	Máy Hín-dee neh-hée bol sáhk-tah hóo
	Mai Hindi nahi bol sakti hu (fem.)	Máy Hín-dee neh-hée bol sáhk-tee hóo
Does anyone speak English?	Yaha par koi angrezi boita hai?	Yah-háh par kóee ahn-gráy-zee bói-teh heh

*Sahib goes after the name, as does ji (e.g., Pandey-sahib; Pandey-ji), but shri, shrimati, and kumari go before the name, as a title in English.

INDONESIA

Of Indonesia's 13,000 islands straddling the equator, Westerners usually recognize the names of only a few—Java, Bali, and Sumatra. Although commerce is centered in Jakarta on the largely Muslim island of Java, most travelers agree that the lure of Indonesia is Bali, which practices a form of Hinduism. As early as the sixteenth century, a ship's crew landed at Bali and was so entranced that they couldn't be persuaded to leave until two years later.

Modern travelers echo the sailors' view. English writer Geoffrey Gorer commented that he went to Bali "half unwillingly, for I expected a complete 'bali-hoo'; picturesque and fake to a Hollywood standard; I left wholly unwillingly, convinced that I had seen the nearest approach to Utopia that I was ever likely to see."

We have given customs that apply to Indonesia as a whole, and then special customs of Bali and Java.

GREETINGS

• Note that people usually shake hands only when introduced for the first time. On other occasions, it isn't customary to shake hands. Shake hands very lightly, and state your name on first meeting someone. If someone touches her/his heart while shaking hands, that indicates that the greeting is especially heartfelt.

• Shake hands when someone leaves on or returns from a long journey.

• Remember that titles are important, and many are based on kinship. Call an older man *bapak* (báh-pahk), which means "father"; it is sometimes shortened to *pak* (pahk). You can use the title without the person's name. Call an older woman *ibu* (ée-boo) or *bu* (boo), which means "mother." If you know a person's title—e.g., Doctor, Professor, Engineer—use it.

• At a party, expect to be introduced individually. Don't be surprised if your host and other guests make welcoming speeches—and call upon you to give a speech as well. Say that you're happy to be at the party and to have met everyone, and thank the host for the invitation.

CONVERSATION

• Note that families are a major subject of conversation. Questions that many visitors may regard as personal (e.g., your marital status, your children) are often brought up, even on short acquaintance. Even if you strike up a conversation with strangers in a bar or restaurant, they will probably ask personal questions immediately.

• Good topics of conversation are food and the beauties of Indonesia. Feel free to ask the same personal questions the Indonesians ask you.

• Good subjects of conversation include politics in Western countries, the weather, the seasons, the Indonesian person's neighborhood—Indonesian neighborhoods are very close-knit communities.

• Expect prices to be another frequent topic of conversation.

• Avoid discussing political issues, both local and national, Socialism, the events of 1965 (when

Sukarno was deposed), and the relations of Indonesia with foreign governments. Also avoid the subjects of the country's bureaucracy and its human rights record.

Java: Don't discuss religion. Never say that you are an atheist (if you are), because people equate atheism and Communism. Sex is also taboo as a subject of conversation. Avoid any discussion of material goods—questions such as, "Do you have a car?"

TELEPHONES

• In major cities and towns, look for public telephones—coin phones and card phones—in hotels, on street corners, and in shopping centers. Public telephones are blue and take 50 and 100 *rupiah* coins. A beep will signal that you must deposit more money or be cut off.

• To buy a phone card, which is available in different denominations, go to a bookshop, money changer, supermarket, or *wartel*. (Telecommunications agencies, either Telkom, government run, or privately run are called *wartels*.) The card is called a Kartu Telepon.

• If you need to make a local call and can't find a booth, ask in a restaurant if you may use the phone. Some with phones will allow you to make local calls.

• Note that there are no public phones in small villages.

• Realize that only rarely can you make a direct dial international call from any type of public telephone. However, there are some Home Country Direct phones, located in some airports, luxury hotels, and some Telkom offices. Pressing a button will get you through to an operator in your country, who can then assist you in reversing charges. You could also go to a Telkom office or a luxury hotel, but the hotel will levy a huge surcharge.

• Look for Telkom offices in most towns and cities. They may be open 24 hours and may offer fax as well as Telex services. A Telkom office is the least expensive place to make long-distance, international, and collect calls.

• Note that the emergency number for police is 110, for fire 113, and for an ambulance 118.

Java: Expect most private homes in Jakarta to have phones, but be aware that there aren't any pay phones in the countryside, and most people do not have telephones.

IN PUBLIC

• Realize that the right thumb extended with the other fingers in a fist means "Please, you go first."

• Never hold hands, kiss, or show affection to a member of the opposite sex in public.

• Realize that Indonesians are very physical and may touch your arm while speaking to you or guiding you.

• To show respect to an elderly or high-ranking person, use both hands when giving them an object.

• Never let your feet be higher than another person's head.

• Don't sit with the soles of your feet pointing at anyone (e.g., feet on the table).

• Don't be surprised to see people spitting a red fluid or having red teeth. People in villages chew betel nut, which causes this coloring.

• Women should not sit with their legs apart, even when wearing pants.

• Don't beckon with a single finger. Signal with the whole hand down, palm open, bringing your hand toward you.

• Never use your left hand to take or give money, to signal a waiter, or to pass food.

• Don't stand with hands on hips while talking to someone.

• Don't touch anyone's head. It is considered the seat of the soul and is sacred.

• If you're seeking directions, ask at least three people. Indonesians want to be helpful and may give you incorrect directions rather than admit that they don't know.

• Remember that Indonesians tend to be late. If you arrange a meeting for a certain hour, repeat the time over and over to emphasize it, or invite them for 7:00 if you want them to come at 7:30.

• Don't photograph people in public bathing areas or people dressed informally at home.

• Don't photograph airports, bridges, railway terminals, stations, seaports, or military bases.

• Note that there are two types of bathrooms. A *kamar mandi* (kah-maĥr maĥn-dee) is for bathing and for urinating on the floor. Take water from the tub, pour it onto the floor, and wash it down the drain. A *kamar kecil* (kah-maĥr kay-chíll) has a hole in the floor. You'll find Western-type toilets only in large hotels. Note that there is no toilet paper in bathrooms. Bring your own. Put toilet paper in a wastebasket you'll find near the toilet; if you put it in the toilet, the toilet will become clogged.

• Realize that another word for a

room with a toilet is W.C. (wee-cee). The women's room is the *perempuan*, and the men's room is the *laki-laki*, or *pria*.

Shopping: Remember that since you're a Westerner, merchants will assume that you have a lot of money. If you bargain, you may lose status. Be aware, however, that if you don't see prices, they aren't fixed. Even if there are prices, it's all right to ask for a discount.

• Beware of people who offer to help you find articles you want. They often get a commission from a shop to direct you there—or they expect a tip from you.

• On leaving a store, always acknowledge the people there by saying *"Mari"* (mah-ree), which means "I take leave of you," or "Excuse me."

Exercise: Joggers often use the beaches in the early morning. By 8:00 A.M., the heat is oppressive. Wear a bathing suit or shorts. In inland villages, people will think it strange if you jog.

Bali: Prepare to bargain everywhere. Ask the price, offer half, and negotiate from there. If someone pressures you to buy an item you don't want, offer a ridiculously low price. (However, keep in mind that if the merchant accepts your offer, you're obliged to buy.)

• Don't be surprised if people ask for money if you want to photograph them.

• If you want to photograph at temple festivals or dance perform-ances, be sure that you don't interfere with the festivities. If you are discreet, you will find the Balinese relaxed in front of the camera.

• When visiting a temple, be sure that your head is never higher than a priest's, that you move to the back or side when people kneel to pray, and that you don't climb on the walls. You can identify temple custodians because they wear white. Follow their instructions. There are some seats you must not use because they are reserved for the gods.

• Look for indications that you should remove shoes before entering the temple.

• To enter a temple, both men and women must have a sash around the waist. Use a scarf or buy a Balinese sash.

• Women should note that they are not supposed to enter a temple while menstruating.

• Don't sit with one foot resting on the other knee; it's regarded as rude.

Java: Don't be upset if people—especially children—stare at you. If you are Caucasian, in villages women may even want to touch you because they may never have seen a Caucasian before.

• Be aware that it's a virtue for Javanese *not* to say what they really mean. Someone who says "Yes" to you may not necessarily agree. You'll have to decide whether the remark is sincere.

• Never make loud noises in a temple.

• Remember that 90 percent of the Javanese are Muslims. In mosques, remove your shoes before entering, and don't pass in front of men or women praying.

DRESS

• For a business meeting, men should wear a white shirt, tie, and slacks. Because of the heat, jackets aren't necessary, except for meetings with government officials. Women should wear a dress or a skirt and a blouse with short sleeves (never a sleeveless dress or blouse).

• Wear shoes that are snug to your feet. Don't wear sandals that flap.

• Don't wear thongs (flip-flops), bathing suits, shorts, or strapless tops. (Shorts are consider low class and are worn only by little boys.)

• Note that Indonesian men wear very colorful shirts for evening. It's acceptable for visitors to do so also. Women should wear a lightweight dress or a skirt and blouse.

• It's acceptable for men to wear jeans, but it's usually too warm for

them to be comfortable. Women should never dress in tight jeans.

• Note that most Indonesian women wear dresses or skirts. Western women should be sure to dress modestly, since most Indonesians are Muslims. Avoid shorts, short skirts, and sleeveless blouses and dresses, except at the beach.

• Both sexes should take special care to dress appropriately when visiting temples or mosques—no shorts or revealing clothing.

• Remember that for dinners at home people dress casually because of the heat. Men should wear shirts and trousers and women skirts and blouses or dresses.

• For formal events—weddings, theater openings, etc.—men should wear suits (Indonesians don't wear tuxedos) and women long dresses or long skirts with tops.

• To please the people, wear something made of batik (the traditional cloth). Don't be surprised if people stop you on the street and compliment you on your outfit.

Bali: Don't wear your bathing suit when not at the beach. You might mistakenly wander into what seems an alley but is really a temple or the courtyard of a house.

• Remember that nude bathing is both illegal and impolite.

Java: For a first business meeting, men should wear a jacket, tie, shirt, and pants. For subsequent meetings, the jacket isn't necessary. If you wish to appear more formal, wear a long-sleeved shirt. For business, women should wear a dress or skirt and blouse with short sleeves (never sleeveless).

MEALS

Hours and Foods

Breakfast: 7:00 to 8:00 A.M. Usual fare is fried rice, oatmeal, and tea served with sugar.

Lunch: 12:30 to 1:30 P.M. The day's biggest meal, lunch usually consists of *krupuk* (shrimp or rice crackers); rice; chicken or beef in a sauce, *satay*, or fish; a salad of parboiled string beans, cabbage, and bean sprouts, served with a peanut sauce; fruit for dessert (eat it only if you can peel it). The meal will probably be accompanied by boiled water (which is safe to drink) and iced tea (which isn't).

Dinner: 7:00 P.M. Dinner is usually a light meal, made up of leftovers from lunch and, of course, rice.

• In Java, a *selamatan* is a meal to celebrate a special occasion: the opening of a store, a circumcision,

or the cutting of a child's hair for the first time. Prayers are offered, and then the meal begins: a huge rice cone with baked chicken, shredded sweet beef, chilies, and hardboiled eggs. Don't be surprised if people take their meal home to eat.

• Remember that rice is the main course in all meals. Any dish with the word *nasi* at its beginning means that it is served with rice. It's served in a strainer-like dish to keep the grains separate. Indonesian rice is dry, unlike the sticky rice served in Japan and China. Indonesians usually mix rice with other foods just before they eat it.

• Look for *sambal*, a very hot side dish made of hot chilies, shrimp paste, and lime juice. In homes, it's served separately because children don't eat hot, spicy food. Adults usually mix it in with their food. Be sure to mix *sambal* with a great deal of rice. Never eat it by itself because it is *extremely* hot. If your throat burns from eating *sambal*, eat bread, boiled rice, or cucumber for relief. Don't drink water as it will only spread the heat.

• Expect some unusual beverages: *bajigur*, which is made of coconut milk sweetened with palm sugar; *es pokat*, an avocado drink; and *tuak*, a palm wine. Coffee and tea are usually available. Indonesians usually don't like to drink alcoholic beverages, because they don't want to lose control.

• Be aware that water is always boiled and is usually served warm.

Indonesians believe that cold drinks affect health adversely. To be safe, drink only bottled water, called Aqua. If someone offers you water in a home, reply that you have a sensitive stomach and can only drink bottled water.

• Note that Western soft drinks, such as Coca-Cola, 7-Up, Fanta, and Sprite are available throughout Indonesia.

Java: Java is Muslim, so there is no drinking in homes, and no pork is served.

• Don't expect bread to be served with the meal. It is eaten as a dessert—with butter and sugar on it.

Table Manners

• If you're invited to dinner in a home, expect to sit in the living room, where there will be special guest chairs and a table. A servant or the children will bring out tea, coffee, or a cold drink; the drink will have a metal cover to keep out flies and dust. Drinks may be accompanied by fried bananas or sticky rice cakes. Don't drink before your host insists. To be truly elegant, don't drink until the host urges you several times. To be polite, leave a little of the beverage in your glass.

• Don't be surprised if men and women are seated separately. If a woman of high status is present, she may be seated with the men.

• At each place setting will be a large spoon and fork. A right-handed person should hold the fork in the left hand and the spoon in the right. Push food onto the spoon with the fork, and eat with the spoon. If you are left-handed, reverse the utensils.

• If you are in a situation where you must eat with your fingers, always use your right hand. The left hand is used for washing after going to the toilet. People don't use toilet paper—just the hand and water.

• Expect the table to be set with serving dishes and individual plates. From the serving dishes, help yourself to rice and three or four vegetable or meat dishes. Take small portions at first so that you can have at least two helpings of food. Having just one helping will offend your host.

• Be aware that there is little conversation at meals. Eating is considered a private act.

• When finished with your meal, cross the fork and spoon on your plate, with the fork—tines down—under the spoon.

• Be sure to leave a little food on your plate. Indonesians value restraining one's physical desires.

• Use your judgment about how late to stay after a meal. Your host will always urge you to stay longer. People with small children tend to go to bed early. The more educated classes like to stay up late and talk after a meal.

Bali: Beverages popular on Bali are tea, which is similar to Chinese tea; coffee, which is served Turkish style; and beer, which is seldom served chilled. Unusual drinks are *markisa*, a cordial (with alcohol) made from passionfruit, and *air jeruk*, an orange juice that you can order hot or cold. Drink the orange juice only if no water has been added.

• Remember that on Bali food is very spicy and often served cold. Rice is the main ingredient of each meal, and grated coconut is the main flavoring.

Java: Expect the male guest of honor to be seated next to the host and the female guest of honor next to the hostess. (Even though the Javanese are Muslims, men and women eat together.)

• Be aware that many people eat with their hands. More modern people use forks and spoons. Don't look for knives on the table. They aren't necessary because food is cut into very small pieces and is very tender because it has been cooked for hours in sauces.

• Note that the table setting includes napkins and finger bowls. In homes where people eat with their fingers, finger bowls are used throughout the meal.

• Eat only with the right hand. Muslims use the right hand for eating and the left hand for washing after going to the toilet.

• Be sure to *try* everything. It's better to try something and leave it on your plate if you don't like it than to refuse to sample it.

Places to Eat

• A *restoran* is an expensive restaurant.

• A *rumah makan* is a small native restaurant or stand. *Warung* are street stalls, sometimes with awnings and benches. Don't eat at such places; their health standards are usually poor.

• Be especially careful not to buy ice cream from a street vendor.

• Most major towns have Chinese restaurants, which are the safest places (in terms of cleanliness) to eat and the most like restaurants in Western countries. Chinese restaurants tend to be more expensive than Indonesian ones, but they have more varied menus.

• Note that most restaurants close at 11:00 P.M.

• Be aware that local people may pester a foreigner dining alone. They want to chat and practice their English.

• If a restaurant is crowded, feel free to ask others if you can join them at their table.

• To signal the waiter for the check, hold your left hand out flat and with your right hand pretend to write.

• Never whistle to summon the waiter, and don't say "Waiter" or "Waitress." Say "Sir," "Miss," or "Excuse me."

Java: A *restorahsee* is a restaurant. There are no cafés—just stands for soup, rice, coffee, and tea. It's unwise to eat food from the stands because the dishes may not be properly washed. Local people have developed resistance to bacteria. Foreigners don't have that resistance.

• Although there is no alcohol drinking at Muslim homes on Java, there are cocktail lounges in hotels and bars on the streets. Local bars are safe for men, but not for women.

• Don't expect to find bars outside Jakarta. In the countryside, you can buy beer at stands.

• Realize that menus are not posted outside restaurants.

• Expect menus in English in large hotels and restaurants in Jakarta.

• Expect to find the most varied cuisine—European, Mexican, Korean, Chinese, Thai, and Japanese—in Jakarta.

Specialties

• Try *satay* (sometimes spelled *sate*), the national dish: meat or poultry on skewers, marinated in soy sauce and oil, then grilled, and dipped in a sauce made of chili, spices, and peanuts. Other Indonesian dishes are *lontong* (rice wrapped in banana leaves and steamed); *soto ajam* (gingered chicken soup), often poured over rice; *opor ajam* (chicken and coconut milk).

Bali: Try *mee kuah* (noodle soup); *krupuk* (prawn crackers, often served as a side dish); *kare* (curry); *babi guling* (spit-roasted suckling pig); *befutu bebek* (duck roasted in banana leaves); *mee goreng* (fried noodles with vegetables or meat); *cap cai* (mixture of fried vegetables); *nasi goreng* (fried rice with shrimp, meat, and spices); *mie goreng* (fried wheat-flour noodles); *gado gado* (lightly cooked salad made of bean sprouts, potatoes, and cabbage with a peanut sauce).

• Popular side dishes are *rempeyek* (cookies made of peanuts) and *tempe* (fermented soybean cake).

HOTELS

• To stay at one of the country's best hotels, choose one built after 1980.

• Realize that there are seven categories of hotels ranging from family compounds to luxury hotels, the latter found only in Jakarta and Bali. Five-star hotels can be incredibly lush and offer all types of service. Middle-range hotels often come with a private bath. Budget hotels are spartan and have shared baths.

• Keep in mind that many hotels display their prices (often in U.S. dollars), but feel free to ask for a discount (especially at the most expensive hotels). Ask to see a printed price list, because sometimes different rooms have different prices. Many hotels have a range of rooms—some with air-conditioning and private baths while others may have ceiling fans and shared baths.

• Note that even the least expensive hotels are reasonably clean. Some may be very noisy with televisions blaring in the hallway. Bring earplugs.

• Be aware that Indonesians prefer rooms on the ground floor, so rooms on higher floors may be less expensive.

• Be prepared for hotels to have name changes. The government made a law that all tourist accommodations must have Indonesian names, a regulation that can lead to great confusion.

• Before registering for a room, check to be sure the windows and door can be securely locked. This is especially important in smaller hotels.

Bali: Consider staying at one of the family style hotels, called *losmens*. Most of these compounds have 10–12 rooms with verandahs with table and chairs outside. The rooms are usually used only for sleeping, cooking, and eating, as most activities take place outside. Sometimes bananas, coffee, and tea are included in the price of the room. You can't make reservations, but you will almost always find a room available.

TIPPING

• Tipping taxi drivers is optional. If you wish, give 200–300 *rupiahs,* regardless of the length of the journey.

• Tip porters at airports, railroad stations, and hotels 500 rupiahs per bag.

• At hotels, restaurants, and nightclubs, expect a 10 percent service charge to be included. If in doubt whether it's included, ask. If it isn't included leave 10 percent. In small Indonesian restaurants, don't tip.

• To washroom attendants and those who perform small services (e.g., someone who goes out to get you a drink or cigarettes), give 100 *rupiahs.*

Bali: Remember that tipping is not traditional.

• Give taxi drivers change if you wish; tipping cab drivers isn't compulsory.

Java: Note that the recent influx of foreigners has brought tipping to Java. It is not a long-standing custom, and outside of Jakarta there is no tipping.

PRIVATE HOMES

• Try to schedule visits between 4:00 and 6:00 P.M.—after siestas and before evening prayers (in Islamic areas). Although Indonesians drop in on one another, it's best to schedule visits in advance. You'll always be welcomed, however, as visitors are never turned away.

• To be polite, remove your shoes when entering a home. (Some people disregard this custom.) It's fine to go barefoot in the house.

• If you stay with a middle-class family, expect them to have servants. Besides taking care of your room, the servants will do your laundry.

• Don't worry about daily bathing; it's the custom here. Most homes have only cold water, but some middle-class homes have a heater hook-up.

• Remember that the toilet and the bathroom are usually separate rooms. The toilet has a hole in the floor. In the bathroom, you'll find a tub about three feet high called a *mandi*. Don't get into it. Stand *outside* the tub, and scoop water over yourself from the tap or tub with the scoop provided. (The tub is simply to hold water.)

Java: Be aware that in many homes there are servants who are treated as members of the family. Don't offend by offering to help them. In homes without servants, the hostess will be insulted if you offer to help. She may feel embarrassed that she has no servants.

• Expect food vendors to come door-to-door selling such items as *satay* and pastries. Most people don't go to restaurants but do buy from such vendors. If the meat is well cooked and there are no raw vegetables, such food is generally safe to eat.

• If you're staying with a family, always be dressed for breakfast. Never appear in your bathrobe.

Gifts: When invited to a meal, bring fruit (the most frequent gift), sweets, a tin of imported butter cookies, or coffee.

• If you visit a family, then leave for another town and return, *always* bring them a gift.

• Other gifts include fancy thermoses (everyone keeps a large thermos of boiled water on the kitchen table); blue jeans (if you know sizes); T-shirts; sweatshirts; spiral notebooks with a university logo; baseball caps; lipsticks; cigarettes.

• Don't expect people to open gifts when you present them. If you receive a gift, follow this custom, and put the gift aside.

Java: Don't try to bring cassette tapes to Java. Customs may confiscate them, because they're afraid they contain propaganda. If you want to give tapes, buy them in Java; they have many with rock and popular music and are extremely inexpensive.

• Don't give toy dogs or gifts with pictures of dogs, since Muslims consider them unclean.

MONEY AND BUSINESS

Hours

Banks: Most are open Monday through Friday from 8:00 A.M. to 3:00 or 4:00 P.M. In major cities, some open on Saturday morning, and others may open for limited hours on Saturday for foreign exchange.

Government Offices: Monday through Friday, 7:00 A.M. to 3:00 P.M.

Business Offices: Monday through Friday, 8:00 A.M. to 4:00 P.M., or 9:00 A.M. to 5:00 P.M., with a break in the middle of the day. Some offices are open on Saturday morning until noon.

Shops: Monday through Friday, 8:30 A.M. to 8:00 or 10:00 P.M., and Saturday, 8:30 A.M. to

12:30 P.M. Shops (except those run by Chinese) close for a siesta from about noon until 1:00 or 2:00 P.M. Sunday is a holiday, but some shops open for part of the day.

Money

• Note that the currency is the *rupiah,* pronounced "roo-pyah." The *rupiah* is made up to 100 *sen.* Coins are Rp 25, 50, and 100. Banknotes are Rp 100, 500, 1,000, 5,000, and 10,000.

• Note that you can generally use plastic money. American Express, Visa, Barclaycard, MasterCard, Access, Diners Club, and Carte Blanche are all accepted in larger hotels, restaurants, and shops. Exchange travelers' checks at hotels and banks. Very few shops will accept payment in travelers' checks.

• Always change money at banks or large hotels (which have the same rates as banks). Keep your exchange receipts so that you can reconvert your *rupiah* into foreign currency when you leave the country.

• Use only well-known travelers' checks; if a rural bank doesn't recognize the issuer, it may not cash the check.

• If you're going into the countryside, bring change with you from the city. In rural areas, small change is in short supply.

• If you plan to travel to remote areas of Indonesia, bring a good supply of *rupiah,* because you won't be able to change foreign money or travelers' checks.

Business Practices

• Don't feel obliged to make appointments in advance, except for visits to very large companies. Even company owners often receive visitors without an appointment. If you are traveling a long distance, however, it's wise to make an advance appointment.

• Schedule business trips to Indonesia between September and June. Most businessmen vacation during July and August. Check the dates of holidays before planning your trip, as most vary from year to year.

• Note that Muslims celebrate Ramadan, which lasts for a month. During that time people must not eat, drink, or smoke between sunrise and sunset. They do, however, continue to work. This may not be the best time to do business.

• Businesswomen should be assured that they will be accepted in Indonesia.

• Remember that personal contact is *very* important. There are no sales without face-to-face negotiation.

• Plan to spend a minimum of a week in negotiating the simplest agreement. Business dealings tend to be long, frustrating, and slow. To plan realistically, expect to make several trips to Indonesia over a period of months.

• Don't be surprised or upset if Indonesians are late for business appointments. Foreigners are expected to be punctual.

• Realize that Indonesians have a strong sense of social ranking. A senior Indonesian will often keep an Indonesian of lesser status waiting.

• Bring business cards. They should always be exchanged at a first meeting. The flashier your card the better. Use the initials for whatever degrees you may hold.

• Present the card with both hands with the print facing the person to whom you're giving it. When you receive a card, don't put it in your back pocket—hold it in your hand for a little while. Don't write on a business card, because Indonesians would regard you as defiling it.

• Although the atmosphere of most business meetings is informal, don't voice criticism at a group meeting. Criticism is always given in private.

• Realize that Indonesians feel very comfortable with pauses and silences. They are not rejecting you—they are just thinking.

• Don't be surprised if Indonesians laugh at inappropriate times (e.g., during a serious discussion). The laughter is a signal that they are anxious.

• Remember that Indonesians rarely say "No," because they consider it impolite to disagree. If a person says "Yes, but . . ." that is the same as saying "No." If you hear people sucking air through their teeth, that also signals "No."

• Realize that government officials may speak some English, but they prefer to hold meetings in Bahasa Indonesia, their native language. Hire an interpreter through your hotel. Some government officials may have English translators, but it's best to have your own.

• Have any official correspondence and official publication translated into Bahasa Indonesia.

• Whatever the provocation, remain calm. People who express anger are not trusted or respected.

• Note that you can send faxes and Telexes from Permutel and *wartel* offices (which are found in most major towns) and from major hotels.

Gifts: Be prepared for an exchange of gifts, whether dealing with people from government or the private sector. Good gifts are calculators, a book with photos of your region, or some item typical of your region of the country.

• Don't expect the recipient to open the gift in your presence. You should also observe this custom if you receive a gift.

Business Entertaining: Expect to be entertained by Indonesian businessmen. Be sure to reciprocate on the same trip.

• Feel free to arrive half an hour late for social engagements. Indonesians do.

• Note that if spouses are present, no business will be discussed.

• If you wish to entertain, host a buffet dinner. Indonesians feel most comfortable with this entertainment. Have the party from about 7:00 to 9:00 P.M., because people retire early. Be sure to escort the guest of honor to her/his car.

• If a businesswoman wishes to entertain, she should say, "It would give me pleasure to invite you to dinner," and then arrange payment beforehand by giving the maître d' her credit card.

Bali: Try to visit business or government offices between 8:00 and 11:30 A.M. People like to get work done early to avoid the heat of the afternoon.

Java: Note that you are expected to be punctual.

• Remember that business lunches are more popular than business dinners.

• A man shouldn't include a Javanese businessman's wife in an invitation to a meal unless his own wife is to attend. A businesswoman, however, should include a Javanese man's wife in an invitation.

HOLIDAYS AND SPECIAL OCCASIONS

• Expect businesses, banks, and most shops to be closed on the holidays listed below, which are national holidays. Villages and regions also have holidays when everything in the area will be closed. Check with the tourist office for dates of local festivals.

Holidays with fixed dates: New Year's Day (January 1); Independence Day (August 17); Christmas (December 25).

Holidays with variable dates: Christian holidays—Good Friday (March/April) and the Feast of the Ascension (40 days after Easter, usually April/May). Islamic holidays—Idul Adha, Muslim Day of Sacrifice (January); Maulid Nabi Muhammad, Mohammed's birthday (January/February); Mi'raj Nabi Muhammad, Night of the Ascension, celebrating Mohammed's ascent to heaven (August); Idul Fitr, two days celebrating the end of Ramadan (usually August/September). Buddhist holiday—Waicak Day, commemorating the Lord Buddha's birth, death, and enlightenment (May).

• Don't eat, drink, or smoke in public during the period of Ramadan, whose date varies every year.

Bali: Note that every village has its own festival, and almost every day is a festival somewhere. Buy a Balinese calendar when you arrive.

• Realize that Nyepi—the New Year according to the Balinese calendar—falls on the day after the new moon of the ninth month. On the day before Nyepi, wines and meats are placed on the ground at all crossroads for the evil spirits. People stay outside all night, using noisemakers to chase away the evil spirits. On New Year's Day itself, everyone stays home.

TRANSPORTATION

Public Transportation

• On all forms of public transportation, be very careful to protect yourself against pickpockets.

• Note that Jakarta has an extensive bus system with large buses, but—once again—guard against pickpockets.

• On Java and Bali, look for special shuttle buses in the main tourist areas. Primarily for foreigners, they connect the most popular destinations. They have fixed schedules and will pick up and drop off passengers at their hotels.

• For long-distance travel, consider taking an air-conditioned bus, as they are less cramped. To be more comfortable, buy two seats. The air-conditioned buses tend to be very cold, so be prepared. When you book your ticket, ask to be sure that the bus you're taking is air-conditioned.

• If taking a bus, pay a conductor—there's one in front and another in back. There's one fare for all destinations. Keep your ticket until you get off because inspectors occasionally check tickets.

• Don't be surprised when you are sitting on a crowded bus if standing passengers hand you their packages.

• For transportation more comfortable and frequent than the large buses, take one of the Colts, also called Oplets, which are minibuses traveling the major and secondary roads on Bali and Java. There are Colt stops all over. They cost only slightly more than regular buses, but the price is well worth the comfort and convenience.

• Hail taxis on the street, or get one at a hotel. The quality of most taxis is poor, and few have air conditioning. Taxis are metered only in Jakarta. If there is no meter, bargain with the driver over the price. Ask at your hotel what the correct fare should be. Even if there is a meter, you may have to pay extra on irregular routes.

• Ask the staff at your hotel or an Indonesian friend what the appropriate fare would be for various forms of public transportation, so you can avoid being overcharged.

• Keep in mind that all *registered* taxis, rental cars, and minibuses have yellow number plates.

• In Jakarta, be sure to lock the doors when you are in a taxi. Robberies have become common when taxis are stuck in traffic jams.

• Realize that taxi drivers may not be able to change large bills.

• Note another form of transportation: *bemos*, which are small pickup trucks with a row of seats down each side. Fares are calculated on a rather complicated system of zones. Don't get on an empty *bemo*; you may be told that you've just chartered it for yourself.

• When traveling by taxi, always carry some small change with you. Drivers are often short of change.

• For an unusual—and slightly dangerous—form of transportation, ride in a *becak* (bay-tjahk), a bicycle with a carriage for two people in the front and the driver in the rear. Bargain for the fares, which will vary according to distance, weather, and time of day. These vehicles are banned from Jakarta and from the main streets of Javanese cities.

Java: Be aware that rail travel is limited to Java and to local trains on Sumatra. Trains are generally hot, crowded, and uncomfortable; try not to use them except for the single air-conditioned overnight sleeper, which goes from Jakarta to Jogjakarta and Surabaya. Trains usually have dining cars for meals.

Driving

• If at all possible, don't drive. People pay very little attention to traffic regulations. Hire a car and driver instead.

• Be prepared for incredible traffic—and for drivers to beep their horns constantly.

• Note that driving is on the left, as in Japan (and Britain).

• Realize that to drive you must have an International Driver's License.

• Anticipate a problem getting gas. Sometimes gas stations run out, so stop often and keep a full tank.

• Drive very slowly on roads in the countryside.

LEGAL MATTERS, SAFETY, AND HEALTH

• Don't be surprised if Customs officials note cameras and electrical equipment in your passport when you enter Indonesia. They want to be sure that you take the items out.

• Don't try to bring weapons, narcotics, or pornography (a magazine like *Playboy* would be considered pornographic) into Indonesia.

• If you're trying to get something cleared through Customs when coming into Indonesia, be very courteous and say as little as possible.

Should there be any difficulties, act innocent, meek, and friendly. Often Customs officials simply want you to know that they have power. If possible, bypass lower-level officials and go to those in higher places; they are usually more understanding and sophisticated.

• If you're robbed, resign yourself to the stolen object being forever lost, however expensive or important it was to you. Recovering stolen property is *very* difficult in Indonesia.

• Never leave important documents, such as your passport, in your hotel room. Always carry them with you unless you are staying at a large hotel which has safe-deposit boxes. If you have important documents with you, guard them against pickpockets.

• Women should be alert for hassles from men in Java, more than in Bali. Java is a Muslim culture and is less used to tourists. Don't walk the streets late at night. Men and boys may touch single women indecently. The best response is *Kau babi!* (You pig!).

Health: Imported drugs are expensive but available, usually without a prescription. (Keep in mind that drugs have different names in different countries, so it's always wise to have a supply of your prescription drugs.)

• Bring facial tissues to use in public toilets.

• Note that ordinary toiletries, sanitary napkins, and tampons are available.

KEY PHRASES

Note: Although Indonesian is the official language of the country, more than 250 languages and dialects are spoken in the country.

Pronunciation is remarkably similar to Italian pronunciation.

If you learn nothing else in Indonesian (though it is not a very difficult language), learn numbers.

English	*Indonesian*	*Pronunciation*
Good morning	Selamat pagi	Séh-lah-maht páh-geé
Good afternoon	Selamat siang (noon to 4:00 P.M.).	Séh-lah-maht see-áhng
	Selamat sore (4:00 P.M. to sunset)	Séh-lah-maht só-ray
Good evening	Selamat malam	Séh-lah-maht mah-láhm
Good night	Selamat tidur	Séh-lah-maht tee-dúhr
Good-bye	Selamat tinggal	Séh-lah-maht teén-gáhl
Sir	Mas + last name (when man is same age)*	Mahs
	Pak + last name (when man is much older)*	Pahk
	Tik + last name (when man is much younger)*	Teek
Mrs., Miss, Ms	Bu + last name (when woman is much older)*	Boo

	Mpak + last name (when woman is the same age or younger)*	Mpahk
Yes	Ya	Yah
No	Tidak	Tée-dańk
Please	Silakan	See-láh-kahn
Thank you	Terima kasih	Teń-ree-mah cáh-see
Excuse me	Permisi	Pehr-mee-sée
I don't speak Indonesian	Saya tidak bicara bahasa Indonesia	Sań-yah tée-dańk bée-tjáh-ráh bah-háh-sah Een-do-nay-sée-ya
Does anyone speak English?	Apa kamu bicara bahasa inggris?	Ań-pah káh-moo beé-tjáh-ráh bah-háh-sah eén-grées?

* All these greetings may be used without the last name if you don't know the name.

JAPAN

For an insight into Japanese culture, consider two of its products: the very ancient tea ceremony (*cha-no-yu*) and the very modern invention of the Walkman.

The "modern" tea ceremony dates from the 14th century. The ritual of preparing and drinking the tea is really an exercise in discipline, in aesthetics, in attention to process. For the Japanese, *how* something is done is as important as the end product. Anyone can throw a tea bag in a cup, but it takes years of patient study to master the beauty of the tea ceremony ritual. Business visitors to Japan should be especially conscious that to the Japanese it isn't just the result that counts—it's how that result is achieved.

The Walkman with its earplugs allowing users to listen to their personal choice of radio or cassette tape while walking, bicycling, or riding the subway is a reflection of the Japanese ability to create a personal world. Even though 27 million people live in the Greater Tokyo area, there is a sense of each individual moving in a personal orbit—except at subway stops during rush hour. This respect for personal privacy is so great that one of the worst *faux pas* in Japan is to touch another person.

Somehow the ancient and modern mesh in Japan. Next to temples, shrines, and palaces dating from the Middle Ages are recently built office buildings sporting company names that have now become household words around the world.

GREETINGS

• Always address people as "Mr." or "Mrs." Use the Japanese suffix *san* added to the last name.

• For a formal greeting, bow. How long you hold your head down and how low you bow will show the amount of respect you want to show. However, holding your head down for more than about two seconds is excessive, except when paying respect at temples, shrines, or graves, where you should hold your head down as long as prayer continues. Palms should be facing thighs and heels should be together.

• For an informal greeting, use a shorter nod, or lift either hand to the level of your head (as if you were holding your hand up to swear an oath).

• Be aware that there is no physical contact in greeting in public, no matter how close your relationship. Note, however, that younger people often shake hands with Westerners and that more cosmopolitan Japanese often combine a bow and a handshake. Take your cue on whether to bow or shake hands from the Japanese. Never force a handshake on someone who doesn't respond immediately.

• No matter how many times you meet a person in a single day, be sure to bow each time.

• When meeting an older person you know on the street, be sure to stop and bow.

• Note that women call each other by their first names only if they have grown up together or work together in an informal setting, such as a restaurant. Women who have been neighbors for many years still call each other by last names, adding the suffix *san*. Only very close male friends use first names with each other and then only in very informal situations. In offices, use last names even with co-workers. Always use the last name and *san* unless you are talking to young children.

Japanese study English in school, their knowledge of the language is often more academic than conversational. If you're having trouble communicating, write down your question, as people often understand written English better than spoken English.

CONVERSATION

• Good topics for conversation: your ideas about Japan (of great interest to the Japanese); food (assuming that you enjoy Japanese food); sports (especially baseball, a very popular sport in Japan); other countries you have visited; questions you have about Japan (most Japanese view Japan as a very special place and are delighted to share information about their country with visitors).

• Topics to avoid: (unless Japanese bring up the subject) your profession; prices and any other economic questions; families (considered a very personal subject); comparisons of your country and Japan (e.g., how McDonald's operates in Japan and in the U.S.; the Japanese believe they are following the "right" way).

• Remember that, though the

TELEPHONES

• Look for public telephones both indoors and outdoors almost everywhere. The yellow and green telephones accept both ¥10 and ¥100 coins. Red phones accept only ¥10. Green telephones also accept magnetic telephone cards. More and more cities offer gray telephones with monitor screens giving instructions in both Japanese and English.

• Be aware that the charge for a local call is ¥10 per minute. When you hear a warning buzz, deposit an additional ¥10 to avoid being cut off.

• Make direct intercity calls from green, yellow, or red phones.

• To make direct overseas calls, look for an "International and Domestic Card/Coin Telephone." (These words will appear on the phone in both Japanese and English.) Look for such phones at hotels, airports, and major office centers in large cities. Rates and locations will vary, depending on which company owns the phones.

• Purchase telephone cards—in amounts up to ¥1000—at department stores, supermarkets, gift shops, or tobacco shops.

• For police emergencies, dial 110; for fire and ambulance, 119. From a pay phone, press the red button and then make a free emergency call.

• When you answer the phone, say *"Hai* [your name] *desu* (pronounced "dehs" in Tokyo and "deshoo" in Osaka). *Hai* means "yes," and *desu* means "is." For "goodbye," say *"Shitsu rei shimasu"* (pronounced Shee-tsoo ráy shee-máhs).

IN PUBLIC

• Note that the Japanese are very indulgent of *faux pas* made by Westerners, but they are very pleased if they find Western visitors familiar with Japanese customs.

• If you visit a Buddhist temple to observe a ritual, take your shoes off outside and then sit quietly on a tatami mat.

• In a Shinto shrine, stand during the service or sit on one of the benches provided for visitors.

• At any shrine or temple, men should remove their hats, and women should also bare their heads.

• Outside temples, hotels, restaurants, and other public buildings, you'll find umbrella holders. If you have a wet umbrella, leave it there. (It won't be stolen.)

• Whether in public or private, *never* step on tatami mats in shoes or slippers.

• Avoid any display of affection in public.

• Be careful not to touch a Japanese person (a slap on the back, a tug on the sleeve); touching is only for lovers, teenage best friends, babies, and drunks.

• To indicate "No," wave your right hand back and forth in front of your nose, with your palm pointing to the left.

• Expect the Japanese to smile even when discussing sad topics; they consider it rude to express their own sorrow, because it might sadden the listener.

• Don't be surprised if middle-aged or older Japanese look to the side and avoid direct eye contact while talking to you. They may also cover their mouths when they speak or laugh, as it is considered rude to show one's teeth.

• If you pay someone a compliment, expect them to shrug it off. Japanese use this gesture as a way of saying "Thank you." Don't be discouraged or disappointed by this seemingly negative action.

• Avoid eating or drinking on the street. It's considered rude, although young people often do it—probably because of the rise in fast-food restaurants. People buy drinks from a machine and remain there to drink them.

• Women should not sit cross-legged on the floor. Kneel with your legs bent under you for as long as you can stand it and then move your legs to the side, being sure to keep them together.

• Queue for transportation, cinemas, and theaters, but realize that during rush hour people may not queue.

• To attract someone's attention, hold your hand in front of you, palm down, and wave it up and down. Use this gesture only with children, waiters, young clerks, and workmen—never with an older person or a person of rank.

• A more formal way to attract attention: catch the person's eye, and give a quick, shallow bow.

• Counting on the fingers is done on one hand; beginning with the thumb, the Japanese fold the fingers into the palm one by one and reextend them with the little finger as number six.

• Be prepared for Japanese students, eager to practice their English, to strike up a conversation. They will often go out of their way to be helpful to you.

• Don't photograph factories.

• Be prepared to find three types of toilets: a hole over a pit in the ground, a ceramic flush bowl over a pit, or a ceramic flush bowl connected to plumbing. Many toilets are coed. Expect inns, restaurants, and bars to have flush toilets and many private homes to have the non-flush type in rural areas. Almost all private homes in urban areas have flush toilets. At inns, separate toilet slippers of straw are used in the toilet room. In some restrooms in hotels and department stores, there will be one Western-style toilet; it will be marked on the stall door. The Japanese word for "toilet" is pronounced "Oh-toy-ray."

• Be sure to carry tissues and a handkerchief at all times, as many Japanese toilets have no toilet paper and few to none have paper towels for drying hands.

Shopping: Don't expect salespeople in shops to hover over you. In traditional Japanese shops, it's considered rude to approach a customer aggressively. Approach a salesperson when you're ready to make a purchase.

• Never attempt to bargain in a shop.

• Note that Sunday is the major shopping day in Japanese cities (because most people work a six-day week). Shops are often closed one day in midweek.

• Don't expect to have your change counted out as it is in Western countries. In good stores, the full amount will be presented on a small tray. The Japanese consider it insulting to count change in front of you because it insinuates that you think that they might try to cheat you. Don't worry—the Japanese are honest. However, feel free to count the change in front of the sales clerk.

Exercise: Men should feel free to jog wearing shorts, but not women. Try to jog in a park, because the traffic makes jogging very difficult elsewhere.

DRESS

• For business meetings, men should wear a suit and tie in a conservative color, while women should wear a suit or dress, also in a muted, conservative color.

• Since overcoats are considered unclean, don't wear one into an office when making a business call. Remove your coat in the hallway,

carry it, and put it back on after you leave the meeting.

• Avoid loud and flashy styles. To the Japanese, they show a lack of both breeding and seriousness.

• Outside Tokyo, women should not wear sleeveless dresses or blouses.

• For formal wear, men should wear a dark suit and a conservative tie. (Tuxedos are not worn in Japan.) Women should wear a cocktail dress or a dressy dress.

• In assembling a travel wardrobe, women should keep in mind that they will have to sit on the floor in traditional Japanese restaurants and should avoid bringing tight skirts and dresses.

• Many better restaurants require men to wear a jacket and tie and women a skirt or dress. Never wear shorts in a restaurant; if you're under thirty, it's okay to wear designer jeans.

• In fact, neither men nor women should ever wear shorts, except at a resort. Jeans are acceptable—and women can feel free to dress in any style of pants.

• Women should not offend Japanese sensibilities by appearing braless.

• Women should never go topless on the beach. It is against the law.

• Be sure to wear white for playing tennis.

• If you stay at an inn, called *ryokan* in Japanese, expect to be given a *yukata*—a multipurpose cotton robe worn by both men and women. Although intended for use as a bathrobe, it can be worn in the corridors and gardens in the summer. (In winter, the usual kimono is heavy and called a *tanzen*). Never fold the right side of the kimono over the left side; that's a symbol of death. Men should wrap the sash low around the hips and knot it in back. Women should wrap the sash a little higher than men and tie it in back also.

• Other garb at inns include: *geta* (wooden clogs), *zori* (sandals), and *tabi* (ankle socks, which are split for the sandal thong). If you leave your room in your *yukata*, wear clogs. The clothing furnished is for your use only during your stay; if you wish to take it with you, ask to buy it.

• For a winter stay in a Japanese home, bring thermal underwear, turtleneck jerseys, down vests, and thick socks. Japanese homes tend to be cold and drafty.

MEALS

Hours and Foods

Breakfast (Asa-gohan): 7:00 A.M. It consists of a glass of juice, toast, instant coffee, and eggs cooked any way but poached. A traditional Japanese breakfast is very time-consuming to prepare, so most people eat it only on weekends.

Lunch (Hiru-gohan): 12:00 to 1:00 P.M. Most people eat lunch out and tend to make it a very fast meal. Typical fare is English-style sandwiches (e.g., ham, cucumber) or noodles. Soft drinks accompany lunch and tea is served afterwards. At home or on weekends, lunch may be curried rice, rice with fried beef, grilled fish and white rice, or *udon* noodles.

Dinner (Ban-gohan): 6:00 to 8:00 P.M. At an informal meal, rice and soup will be eaten throughout the meal. Likely main courses are roast fish, pork cutlet, or tofu-based dishes.

• At a formal meal, expect many individual serving dishes with a different food in each one.

• Expect rice to be the core of the

meal. All other dishes are to enhance it. *Gohan* means both "rice" and "a meal." In fact, rice is usually eaten three times a day. The rice is kept in a large rice container or wooden keg, which keeps it hot and enhances the flavor.

• If someone has treated you to a meal and invites you again, always say, "Thanks for the last time," when accepting the invitation.

Table Manners

• Recognize that the basis of eating habits in Japan is appearance and elegance, but expect people to make a slurping noise while eating soup or noodles. Note that at the end of a Japanese tea ceremony, the last sip must be accompanied by a slurp to let the hostess know you have finished.

• Note that napkins are not used. You will be offered a hot towel (called an *oshibori*) in an individual basket before the meal. Use it to wipe your hands. When you finish using it, replace the towel in the basket. If the basket isn't removed, use the towel as you would a napkin, but don't use it to wipe your mouth. It's a good idea to carry a supply of tissues, in case the towel is removed.

• Observe that Japanese chopsticks are shorter than the Chinese and are pointed at the end that goes into the mouth. In a home, each member of the family has a set of chopsticks made of ivory, lacquered wood, or bone. A guest in a home or a diner in a restaurant receives a disposable set in a paper wrapper—the chopsticks must be split in two before you can use them. After pulling them apart, some people remove any splinters by rubbing the two sticks together. However, this gesture is not considered elegant. Be careful when manipulating lacquered chopsticks, as they are more slippery than the wooden ones.

• When you have finished, leave the chopsticks on the chopstick rest; if there is no rest, place them horizontally across the top of a bowl. Don't put chopsticks down pointing at the person opposite you. Never place them flat on the table, and never leave them standing in a bowl of rice or other food—that is done only when a person has died.

• Always manipulate both chopsticks with one hand. Never use one chopstick in each hand. If you really can't manipulate chopsticks, request Western utensils; but first try to use chopsticks. It's not only a gesture of friendship, but it also enables you to experience a foreign culture. (Silverware is thought to impart an unpleasant metallic taste to food.) A common mistake is to hold the chopsticks too close to the bottom. They are much easier to manipulate if you hold them half to three-quarters of the way up.

• If you're left-handed, it's permissible to hold your chopsticks in your left hand.

• Don't pick up your chopsticks or begin to eat until those older than you at the table have done so.

• When taking food from a communal serving bowl, turn your chopsticks and use the blunt ends so you won't contaminate the food. (There are no communal serving bowls in restaurants, but you may encounter them in a private home.) You don't need to clean the thick end of the chopsticks because everything you pick up with them is dry, not soupy, and because you won't be holding them at the very top.

• Never transfer a piece of food from one pair of chopsticks to another (as Americans in restaurants sometimes feed one another a sample of a dish) because that is how ashes are transferred in a Buddhist cremation ceremony.

• Don't use your chopsticks to pick at the different items on your tray before choosing one to eat. Know what you want to pick up and take it.

• Follow the Japanese order of eating: eat a chopstickful of rice, then one of the side dishes, and then rice again. To eat just one dish at a time is rude.

• Take small pieces of food with your chopsticks. If a piece is too large to eat in one bite, pinch it with the chopsticks. After its long cooking, the food will be soft enough to break easily.

• While being served a second helping, lay down your chopsticks and stop eating. Never cross chopsticks when they are put down, and remember *never* to leave them stuck into food.

• Note that your host and hostess will sit together at the lower end of the table.

• Before starting to eat, say *"Ita daki masu"* [Eé-tah daĥ-kee mahs] (Now I partake with gratitude); when finished, say *"Gochiso sama deshta"* (Gó-chee-soh śah-mah désh-tah) (It has been a feast).

• Note that the rice bowl is always made of china and the soup bowl of black or red lacquerware.

• Don't take dishes on your right side with your left hand, and vice versa.

• Don't look for serving dishes on the table. The hostess will fill the individual dishes for each person, except for the rice dish. When she extends a tray to you, place your rice bowl on it to be filled. Plan to eat more rice than anything else. If you eat three bowls, you will really please your host, but eating fewer is by no means impolite.

• To begin your meal, lift your soup bowl from the tray, take a sip of soup directly from the bowl, and with your chopsticks pick up one bite of solid food from the soup bowl. (To remove the lid from the soup bowl, squeeze the bottom part slightly; this will prevent soup spilling from the bowl.) Replace the soup bowl and take some rice. Don't finish your soup before eating other dishes; it should accompany the entire meal. Always lift the soup bowl and rice or noodle bowl to drink or eat. Don't lift flat dishes. Taste the various dishes, one at a time, alternating with rice.

• Always leave a little rice in the

bowl. When you finish the rice in your bowl, it signifies that you have finished the meal.

• When receiving a refilled rice bowl, let the bowl touch the surface of the table once before you take any other food.

• Avoid bending over food. Bring rice dishes up to you rather than bending over them. For other dishes, use chopsticks to bring the food to your mouth.

• Eat your food slowly. If you eat rapidly, people will think you haven't been served enough food.

• Anticipate silence during the meal. The talking relates only to the meal and the table: praise of the food, its attractive presentation, the beauty of the china, etc.

• Don't be surprised if there is no dessert, though there may be some fruit. Dessert isn't a course in a Japanese meal.

• Prepare to be offered a shot of *sake*, served in a china cup, before the meal. If you don't care for any, it's acceptable to refuse. Simply put your hand over the cup and say, "None for me." Wait for the host's signal for everyone to drink together.

• When a drink is being poured into your glass, hold the glass up or hold it on the table.

• Don't refill your own cup; guests serve each other. As soon as someone pours a drink for you, take the bottle and fill her or his glass or cup. Hold the *sake* cup with one hand underneath the cup and the

other around it. If you don't want a refill, turn your cup upside down.

• Expect to be offered *sake*, beer, and tea with your meal.

• Note that there are many types of *sake*, though only experts can usually tell the difference. Each restaurant will have its own house brand. *Sake* is served warm all year, but is also available cold in the summer.

• At a banquet, there will be about half an hour of *sake* drinking (with hors d'oeuvres) before the meal is served.

• To toast, say *"Kampai!"* (Kaĥmpíe).

• Expect tea to be served at the end of the meal. There may be green tea, which is believed to counteract acids in meat and fish, or brown tea, which is preroasted.

• Avoid talking with your mouth full.

• Try to finish food. Leaving food is considered rude. If you leave less than half, it's okay, because people will think you're full.

• If you're sitting at a meal and have to blow your nose, get up, excuse yourself, and leave the table.

• Use a toothpick at the table, if you wish, but always cover your mouth with your other hand.

• If you're invited to dinner in a home, don't stay later than 10:00 P.M. The Japanese don't usually stay up late. If they say, "Please stay longer," remain for 10 or 15 more minutes.

• If invited to a tea ceremony, women should avoid wearing perfume, because it interferes with the incense fragrance. The tea will be served without sugar, but sweets are served to enhance the tea. The tea cups won't have handles. Hold the cup with the three middle fingers of your left hand under the cup, and the fingers of the right hand lightly around the cup.

Places to Eat

• Be aware that there are many different types of eating places:

A *koryori-ya* serves seafood, vegetable, and meat dishes à la carte. It's rather like a pub.

A *restoran* is a Western-style restaurant.

A *ryori-ya* is an ordinary Japanese restaurant; it offers alcoholic beverages.

A *soba-ya* specializes in noodles, served either in soup or separately with a soy-based sauce for dipping the noodles into. Drinks are available.

A *ryotei* is a very expensive cabaret, featuring geisha entertainment.

A *sushi-ya* offers raw fish and seafood served on rice; alcoholic drinks are available.

A *shokudo* is a short-order cafeteria. It will probably offer rice served with pork, shrimp, crab, and beef stew. Usually there are no alcoholic drinks.

A *chuka-ryori-ya* is a Chinese restaurant.

A *kissaten* offers sandwiches, coffee, soft drinks, and beer.

A *sushi* bar offers raw fish with vinegared rice and toppings. Don't order hard liquor or ask for hot foods at a *sushi* counter. Any drink other than tea, beer, or *sake* is considered gauche. *Sushi* bars have glass cases displaying the different types of *sushi*. Simply point to what you want.

• To identify the type of restaurant, look at the *noren*—the small, colored canvas curtains hanging above the doorway. Navy-and-white indicates a seafood or noodle restaurant. Black-and-white signifies pork dishes. Red is for a Chinese restaurant. Oval red paper lanterns identify a *yakitori* (kebabs) restaurant. Purple or orange lanterns are for snack bars. If the *noren* are tucked inside, the restaurant is closed.

• If you want a break from Japanese food, try one of Tokyo's many fine French or Chinese restaurants (some of the world's best Chinese chefs are in Japan). There are many pizzerias, but Japanese pizzas are both smaller and more expensive than those in North America.

• The typical meal in a first-class restaurant consists of broiled fish or *sukiyaki* or meat *teriyaki; sashimi* (raw fish) with sauce; salad with vinegar, sugar, salt, and herbs; rice; a boiled dish; and pickled vegetables.

• Dining out can be extremely expensive; try the less expensive restaurants in department stores and office buildings and the small restaurants off the main streets. To save even more, buy food from *yatai* (street vendors). They usually offer *oden* (a clear, soy-based soup with fishcakes). Ordering from street vendors in Japan presents no health hazard.

• Another option: Since most hotel rooms have refrigerators, save on meals by buying food in a supermarket or at the deli counters located in some hotels.

• Even if the menu isn't in English, there will be plastic or wax food models of the various dishes in the restaurant window. If necessary, bring the waiter to the window and point to what you want.

• If the restaurant has tatami mats on the floor, leave your shoes outside.

• Prices are usually given in Arabic numbers.

• Don't be surprised to find many of Tokyo's best restaurants on the second and third stories of office buildings.

• Note that sitting at a counter costs more than sitting at a table, because you have the personal attention of the chef and can watch the food being prepared.

• Remember that beef is very expensive in Japan.

• Be aware that sitting on the floor is extremely difficult for Westerners (and many Japanese admit that it's difficult for them as well). It's acceptable for Westerners to use a sidesaddle position. If you kneel in the traditional Japanese position, put a cushion between your thighs and your calves. If you tire of sitting on the floor, ask for a backrest, called a *zaisu* (záh-ee-sue).

• If you go to a department store cafeteria, expect the waiter or waitress to give you a basket to place next to your chair in which to put your belongings. Put packages on the bottom, and fold your coat over them. In these cafeterias, refills on green tea, brown tea, or water are free, but you pay for each cup of coffee or black tea.

• If cafeteria restaurants are crowded, the host/hostess will ask you to share a table. It's not acceptable to ask to wait for a free table. To be polite, nod to the strangers at the table, and then ignore them.

• If you want water, ask for it. It isn't automatically served.

• When you eat at a restaurant, carry tissues with you, because frequently only the hand towel, called the *oshibori*, is provided.

• Note that not all cooked foods are served very hot, especially in inns. Even in Western-style hotels, your breakfast bacon and eggs may be cool to tepid. It's best to avoid ordering foods you like piping hot.

• Don't tip. If you leave money, the waiter will come after you and return it.

• The person who suggests the meal pays. A foreign woman can pay for a Japanese—male or female— she has invited to dinner.

• Women should have no problems dining alone. Don't, however, order something like *sukiyaki,* which is prepared at the table. The restaurant will not want to tie up a cook for just one person.

• Be aware that Tokyo is an "early" city. Plan to dine no later than 7:00 P.M.

Specialties

• If you can afford it, order beef from the Matsusaka or Kobe districts; the cows are fed special grains and are massaged with beer.

• Try *sashimi*: plain slices of raw fish—which neither smell nor taste "fishy." Pick up the fish slices with chopsticks.

• *Sushi* consists of vinegared rice and other raw or cooked fish with different toppings and fillings, such as omelet, tuna, or caviar—all accompanied by a soy dipping sauce. Eat the sushi with chopsticks. Some garnishes you can pick up with your fingers. Between orders of *sushi*, thin slices of ginger in rice vinegar will be served to freshen your palate.

• If you order *tempura*, you'll receive deep-fried vegetables and seafood in a delicate batter.

• Choose *kakiage* for a deep-fried vegetable and shrimp patty.

• *Sukiyaki* consists of beef and vegetables simmered in a soy sauce and sake.

• Noodles are one of the most popular snack and lunch dishes. *Soba*, made of buckwheat flour, are long and gray, while *udon,* made of wheat flour, are long and white. *Somen* is a fine, white noodle that is eaten cold in summer. Noodles are served in soup and garnished with seafood, meat, and/or vegetables.

• *Yakitori* are kebabs. They may be pork, pork liver, beef, chicken, mushrooms, eggplant, or asparagus. Each small skewer has just one kind of food on it—e.g., two pieces of eggplant, two large mushrooms. There will probably be a ceramic fish in front of you. As you finish a skewer, put it in the fish's mouth. The waiter will charge you by the skewer and its content (some kebabs cost more than others).

• *Tonkatsu* is Japanese breaded pork cutlet. There are three kinds: *rosu*—thickly sliced loin of pork; *hire*—filet; *hitokuchikatsu*—very lean pork.

• *Shabu-shabu* is similar to fondue. Copper pots full of simmering broth are heated from below by gas jets. You are served paper-thin slices of beef, seafood, mushrooms, vermicelli, seaweed, and fish. Put some *ponzu* sauce (made of soy sauce and citrus juices) in your dish. Cook the vegetables briefly in the broth in the copper pot, then cook the meat the same way. When you finish, spoon the broth into your bowl, add the noodles, and eat.

• *Robatayaki* are country grills where you will find a counter and seats surrounding an elevated barbecue. Vegetables, meat, fish, and shellfish are in open baskets, crates, and bowls. Point to those you want. The cook will put your food on a grill and will then serve it on a wooden baker's paddle.

• *Teppanayaki* are steak houses using the best Kobe beef. Customers sit around a grill on which the chef cooks the steak; it is then served with bean sprouts and *ponzu* sauce (made with soy sauce and citrus juice).

• All but the most intrepid risk-takers will want to avoid *fugu*—blowfish or globefish. The liver and ovaries contain a poison which can paralyze and kill humans. A chef who serves *fugu* in a restaurant must be licensed, ensuring that he has passed tests showing that he knows how to clean the fish.

HOTELS

• To assure space in hotels in Tokyo or Osaka, reserve two to three months in advance.

• Note that check-in time at some Tokyo hotels is 1:00 P.M. If you arrive earlier, you will be given a room, if one is available.

• Whenever you leave the hotel, be sure to take with you a card (available at the information desk) with the hotel's name and location written in Japanese characters

(*kanji*). Give this to the taxi driver when you are returning to the hotel or to anyone else who is giving you directions. It's also a good idea to have your destination written in Japanese characters.

• Note that business hotels are the least expensive, and, although tiny, are very good. You'll always find a nice one close to the train station in every city. The rooms are usually singles with a bath. Although there is no room service, there are vending machines on every floor, and most often one restaurant.

• Near train stations, expect to find capsule hotels for men only. They are very cheap. One crawls into the cubicle, which contains a bed—the bath and closet are outside. These hotels are really a convenience for men who have missed the last train.

Ryokans: Although Western-style hotels are plentiful, you can opt to stay in a traditional Japanese inn, a *ryokan* (pronounced ryo-kan). It is usually set in a garden with natural scenery and is designed for relaxation and communication with nature. If you decide to stay at a *ryokan*, bring a phrase book with you. Little English is spoken. You can make reservations for some *ryokans* in advance in the U.S., but you'll have a wider selection if you wait until you arrive in Japan. If you are traveling from Britain by Japan Air Lines, they can make a reservation for you. Most *ryokans* are *extremely* expensive, so be sure to ask the price before making a reservation.

• When you arrive, remove your shoes before you go up the steps, and put on the slippers furnished by the inn. Wear these on wood, stone, or tile surfaces, *never* on the *tatami* mats, the floor covering of pressed straw two inches thick, covered with a mat woven with rush and bordered with linen strips. Leave the slippers in the hallway outside your room. Expect the room to have a low table and a dresser and perhaps a Western-style sitting room. Some rooms have stocked refrigerators. Keep a record of what you eat and drink on the form provided.

• You will have one principal maid assigned to you. She will serve your meals, arrange the bedding, and arrange for your bath. Shortly after you arrive, she will take out *zabuton* (cushions for sitting) from wall closets. She will then serve you tea and sweets. Summon the maid at any time by pressing a button in your room.

• Don't expect a *ryokan* to have a dining room. Both breakfast and dinner (whose cost is included in the room price) will be served in your room.

• At inns in the countryside, there may be no private baths. Be prepared for the bathing facilities to be coeducational—with separate dressing areas—though most inns now have separate bathing for men and women. In cities, Western-style hotels and *ryokans* will have private baths.

• If your room doesn't have a private bath, call the maid and say *"furo"* (bath). She will put you on the list of those awaiting a bath. If possible, arrange for one of the last baths of the night, because by then the incredibly hot water may have cooled down a bit. Place your towel, watch, etc., in a basket in the first room. Move to the second room, and wash and rinse outside the tub. Then soak in the tub. The soaking is for relaxation, not for cleaning.

• Before bedtime, the maid will lay out a *futon*, consisting of quilt, sheets, and a pillow; she will place it on the *tatami* mats. Pillows are usually bags stuffed with husks of grain. They are very hard and difficult for Westerners to get used to.

• Unless you order a Western breakfast the night before, expect a Japanese breakfast, which will probably include soup with bean curd, dried seaweed, hot boiled fish, radish pickles, and green tea.

• Note that there are no locks on room doors in inns because theft is so uncommon. If you're concerned about valuables, leave them with the innkeeper.

• Don't be surprised if the innkeeper or maid opens the unlocked door unannounced.

• Plan to be back at the inn by 10:00 P.M., unless you've made arrangements to get in later. Also plan to check out by 10:00 A.M.

TIPPING

- When in doubt, don't tip. Tipping is virtually unknown in Japan. The only people who should be tipped are drivers of rented cars (not taxi drivers). Give them about 10 percent of the fee.
- In most restaurants, a 10 to 15 percent service charge will be added to your bill.
- If you receive very special service from maids or bellboys, give them at least ¥2000 at the end of your stay. You can buy special envelopes, available at department stores, for money gifts. For a tip, use one of the hotel's envelopes. Write the recipient's name and your name on it. If you wish to tip your maid at a *ryokan*, be sure that the money is in an envelope. Money should never be handed directly to anyone except, of course, merchants.

PRIVATE HOMES

- Don't expect to be invited to the home of a Japanese acquaintance or friend. The Japanese consider their homes private places where others don't intrude; however, Tourist Information Centers in cities can arrange for home visits (usually lasting about two hours in the evening). Apply at least one day in advance for such a visit.
- When visiting, leave your shoes inside the door and take the slippers your host offers. Before stepping on *tatami* remove your slippers. Don't step on the linen bindings of *tatami*, as they wear out quickly. Also avoid stepping on the threshold. Note that the size of a Japanese room is expressed in the number of mats— an 8-*tatami* room, a 10-*tatami* room, etc.
- Expect to spend your visit in a special room reserved for outsiders. You won't be offered (and don't ask for) a tour of the house.
- When visiting in Western dress, men can sit cross-legged on the floor (in a sort of yoga position), while women should sit with their legs folded under their bodies

or with legs together and to one side.

• Even modern apartments have one room with *tatami* and a Japanese-style bath called a *furo*.

• Honored guests are seated in front of the *tokonoma* (alcove). If you visit a home or attend a party in one, don't sit in front of the alcove unless the host insists.

• If you stay in a Japanese home, a *futon* (a thin mattress) will be spread out on the floor wherever there is space. An honored guest is usually put in the room with the *tokonoma*—an alcove for treasured objects. Don't use the shelves for toilet articles, etc.

• Avoid rowdiness or expansive gestures when a guest in a Japanese home. Many walls are flimsy sliding panels, and it's easy to poke a hole in one by accident. Be sure to keep your hands clean so you won't smudge the walls, and keep your elbows close to your body so you won't tear them.

• Don't offer to help with cooking or cleaning up; it isn't customary for guests to help.

• In the winter, join the family at the low table covered with a large quilt and with a box of burning charcoal under it. People sit around the table with their legs under the quilt and study, play games, or watch TV. (More modern homes use an infrared bulb instead of charcoal.)

• When visiting a home with a garden, don't use it for sunbathing or playing games. A garden is considered a work of art.

• Don't wear the special slippers placed in the toilet (and for use there only) in other areas of the house. Leave your own slippers outside the door to show that the toilet is occupied.

• Remember that the bathroom and toilet are separate rooms. The bathroom has a pail of water, a stool, a very deep rectangular tub, and a drain in the floor. Use the pail of water to wash yourself thoroughly. Only go into the tub for relaxing and soaking. Be careful; the water is *extremely* hot. Don't pull the plug; all family members use the same water for soaking (at different times, of course). Always replace the boards on top of the tub to keep water hot for others.

• If you're staying in a home, ask when the bath time is, since everyone soaks in the same water and therefore has to be home at the same time. The Japanese bathe daily, usually after dinner and before bedtime.

• The host will usually invite you to have a bath first. Try to avoid being first, since the water is so hot. When in the tub, don't use the tub's cold tap; that would not be fair to family members, as the water cools off quickly.

Gifts: Bring small gifts. The Japanese are embarrassed to receive large, expensive gifts.

• Bring gifts typical of your area. If you want to give food, bring a special candy from your area, or give chocolates, a Japanese favorite.

• Don't give anything personal, such as a necktie.

• For children and young people, bring candy, dolls, or T-shirts with English slogans (they enjoy English writing as Westerners enjoy Japanese calligraphy, even if they don't know what the characters mean).

• When purchasing a gift in Japan, be sure to tell the salesperson the occasion (e.g., wedding), since certain colors are appropriate for certain occasions. There are also different ways of tying knots for various occasions.

• Be sure to wrap gifts, but don't expect them to be opened in your presence. Waiting shows that it's the act of the gift, not the contents, that is important. Even a gift of money should be wrapped. If you don't have a special money envelope (available in department stores), it's better to wrap the money in a tissue than to present it unwrapped.

• When giving or receiving a gift, hold it with both hands.

• Note that flowers are acceptable gifts from Westerners but are considered a bit ostentatious. The chrysanthemum is the national flower. Don't give camellias, lotus blossoms, or lilies, because they are associated with funerals.

• Never give four of anything because the word for *four* sounds like the word for funerals.

• Don't give white objects or clothing as gifts, since white is the color associated with death.

• While gift-giving is a constant practice in Japan, it is especially important during the summer months—from July to mid-August.

BUSINESS

Hours

Banks: Monday through Friday, 9:00 A.M. to 3:00 P.M., and 9:00 A.M. to noon on Saturday. Due to deregulation, banks are often open later, but there is no uniform time.

Businesses: Monday through Friday, 9:00 A.M. to 5:00 P.M.; they are often open for a half day on Saturday.

Government Offices: Monday through Friday, 9:00 A.M. to 5:00 P.M., and 9:00 A.M. to noon on Saturday.

Shops: Department stores are open from 10:00 A.M. to 7:00 P.M. daily, including Sundays and holidays, with many downtown Tokyo stores open until 8:00 P.M. Most department stores close one day a week, usually Monday or Tuesday. Private shops are open from 10:00 A.M. to 8:00 P.M. daily. However, some private shops are open from 9:00 A.M. to 9:00 P.M. daily.

Money

• The unit of currency is the Japanese yen, symbolized by ¥, which contains coins of ¥1, ¥5, ¥10, ¥50, and ¥100, and banknotes of ¥1000, ¥5000, and ¥10,000.

• Note that major credit cards— American Express, Visa, Barclaycard, MasterCard, Access, Diners Club— are widely accepted at hotels, restaurants, and shops. Most shops don't accept travelers' checks for payment.

• Don't be surprised if a smaller establishment displaying a credit card emblem refuses to let you pay with a credit card. Japan has traditionally been a society in which payment is in cash, and some people have trouble moving into the world of plastic money.

• Don't shop around for a better rate of exchange. The government sets the rate, which is the same everywhere—banks, hotels, etc.

Business Practices

Before the Trip: Prepare carefully before a business trip to Japan. Familiarize yourself with the vocabulary of international business; e.g., such terms as letter of credit. Japanese are often amazed at how little Westerners know of international business.

• Do not attempt to approach a Japanese firm without an introduction from some third party. An ideal introduction would come from someone who knows you, your background, your company, and the Japanese company with which you want to deal; the introduction could be via letter or in person. If you don't know such a person, consider hiring a consulting firm; several, whose names you can get from the U.S. Chamber of Commerce in Tokyo, specialize in bringing two companies together. They solve the language problem and save a great deal of time, a consideration which often makes up for the fee.

• Check carefully the proposed schedule for your trip to Japan before you agree to it. The Japanese tend to overbook visitors and schedules are adhered to slavishly, so make sure you won't need a last-minute change.

• Plan to spend a great deal of time to consolidate a business arrangement in Japan; several trips may in fact be necessary. Never try to rush your Japanese counterparts.

• If possible, prepare visual aids such as charts, drawings, samples, slides, and films for use in your presentation. If you will be using a film, plan to have it narrated in Japanese.

• Arrange for several copies— translated into Japanese—of any written material you plan to use. Each member of the team can then have a copy, which will speed decision-making.

In Japan: Be sure to be prompt for business appointments. In Tokyo, allow considerably more time than you think you'll need if you're going by car or taxi; traffic delays can be lengthy. Also, be sure to allow ample time between appointments.

• Have business cards, called *meishi*, printed in English on one side and Japanese script on the other. Be sure that your card indicates your exact job title, an indication to the Japanese of your rank in your company.

• Hand the business card directly to your host with both hands while facing him. He will read it and nod—a gesture of acknowledgment. Accept your host's business card with both hands and put it in the place in your wallet from which your own card came. Don't put the card in your pocket or briefcase.

• Be conscious that a business relationship is based more on personal relations than on the cost of a product. The Japanese first want to know about you, your age, the university you attended, and your firm (e.g., when it was established, the number of branches and where they're located, the number of employees, and annual sales). Business comes later. Show the same interest in the background of Japanese businesspeople. Too often Westerners are interested only in the end product—the contract. To the Japanese the relationship is most important.

• Begin negotiating by praising the Japanese company and discussing the pleasure of doing business with such a firm. Focus on the advantages of your two companies working together. Don't, however, become overly aggressive; the Japanese do not favor such behavior.

• Be sure that you are negotiating with your counterpart or even a superior in the Japanese company. Your first connection may be with the person whose English is most fluent, but that person may not be your counterpart. If you show willingness to negotiate with that person, you will lose status in the eyes of the Japanese.

• Don't expect a Japanese manager to take the same leadership role as a Western manager—to stand out from other workers. The Japanese manager serves as a mediator or father figure; he is sensitive to the needs of his subordinates and never gives direct orders. If you're meeting with a small group—say, three people—don't be surprised if the subordinates speak little or not at all, even though their English may be superior to that of the highest-ranking person at the meeting.

• Avoid manifesting those qualities Japanese find offensive in many Westerners: speaking loudly; being direct and aggressive; seeking, rather than avoiding, confrontation.

• Don't expect to encounter women in managerial positions (except for the few with American companies and multinationals); however, foreign women are accepted as negotiators by the Japanese. Women must be especially careful to avoid any appearance of aggressiveness. They should appear soft, polite, and self-effacing.

• Always present written material well in advance of discussing a subject. The Japanese don't like surprises.

• Prepare to be very patient. Decisions are made by workers at all levels of a company, not just by the chief executive. This process takes a great deal of time and involves many face-to-face discussions. The contract must be approved at each level of the company. Once a decision is made, however, implementation is immediate.

• If someone laughs during a business meeting, try to find out what is wrong. A laugh usually indicates embarrassment or shock.

• If Japanese are silent at a business meeting, it may indicate that they have not come to a decision. Be patient and allow them to speak first.

• When you reach the point of actually negotiating a contract, employ an interpreter. (If you have employed a consulting firm, they will take care of the hiring.) Consider hiring a translator through Japan Air Lines before your departure or through the Information Desk at your hotel.

• Major Japanese firms have interpreters, but it is better to supply your own. Have your interpreter play a subordinate role to allay any suspicions the Japanese may have. Allow the interpreter representing the Japanese company to do the most translating. Later, meet with your interpreter privately to learn exactly what was said (and what was meant).

• Adhere to Japanese wishes on lucky days—based on astrology—for signing contracts or breaking ground for a building.

Business Entertaining: Note that the Japanese expect to entertain foreign businessmen; they don't expect to be repaid. Anticipate a dinner invitation, rather than a lunch invitation. Don't expect to be invited to your Japanese colleague's home, but prepare for an evening in a restaurant and nightclubs.

• Let the Japanese issue the first invitation to a dinner. Then reciprocate by inviting the most important members of their team to dinner. (Dinner is better than lunch, since many Japanese businesspeople eat at company cafeterias or order take-out food for lunch.) Businesswomen can entertain Japanese businessmen at an expense-account lunch or dinner.

• Expect to be taken to a Western-style restaurant, unless you indicate that you would prefer a Japanese restaurant, which your hosts will regard as a compliment.

• When you're a guest at a restaurant, let the senior-ranking Japanese company official order for you.

• Take your Japanese business guests to a Western-style restaurant, preferably in a large hotel. Don't entertain in a Japanese restaurant, as Westerners don't understand the subtlety and ritual of Japanese dining well enough to act as hosts.

• If you're nervous about entertaining at a meal, hold a cocktail party. It's the form of entertainment involving the least protocol.

• It is very rare for Japanese wives to accompany their husbands for an evening of business entertainment. If the wife is invited, the businessman may well turn up without her and offer an excuse. A Western wife who accompanies her husband may find that she is the only woman in the group; if the evening ends—as it often does—at a geisha house, she and the geishas will be the only women present. (This would also hold true for a businesswoman traveling alone.)

• Japanese businessmen often take visitors for an evening of *hashigo* (ladder drinking), the equivalent of a pub crawl. If you want to drink just a little, take sips and allow your glass to be filled. Sometimes people will suggest that you drink up before they fill your glass; just indicate that they should fill now. By doing this, you can keep your consumption of alcohol to a minimum and still be polite.

• Prepare to be taken to a nightclub called a *karaoke* bar; these bars exist solely for patrons to get drunk. The typical drink, called a *mizuwari*, is Scotch and water. If you don't ask for something else, that's what you'll be served. If you don't wish to drink much, have one drink and then act slightly tipsy. Expect the hostess to bring to your table a tape recorder, tapes, song books, and microphones; everyone at the table must sing a song (many of the songs are American).

• Remember that the Japanese consider frankness a mistake, even when drunk, so be cautious. The following morning, expect people to assume their normal reserve.

• After being invited to a *karaoke* bar, reciprocate by inviting your Japanese colleague to a restaurant. The Japanese don't expect you to take them to *karaoke* bars.

• Realize that no business deal is sealed without dinner in a restaurant or a drink at a bar.

Business Gifts: When you begin a business relationship with a Japanese firm, you will be given a gift. After receiving it, present a group gift—something that represents your company: fine wine, rare Scotch, golf balls, books about your area of the country, or a subscription to a magazine for the whole company.

• Good gifts with your company's logo are pens, appointment books, pocket calculators, digital desk clocks, pocketknives, rulers with calculators. Have the presents gift-wrapped, but don't put bows or ribbons on them, because crossed ribbons mean bad luck. Don't expect to be thanked for the gift.

Note: For advice regarding business greetings, dress, or table manners, see the appropriate sections earlier in this chapter.

HOLIDAYS AND SPECIAL OCCASIONS

• Expect banks, offices, and most shops to be closed on the following national holidays. However, some towns and regions have festivals which are holidays in the area. Check with the tourist office for dates of local festivals.

Holidays: New Year's Day (January 1); Bank Holidays (January 1–3); Adults' Day (January 15); National Foundation Day (February 11); Vernal Equinox Day (date changes from year to year but it usually falls around March 21); Greenery Day (April 29); May Day (May 1—manufacturers are closed but service firms are open); Constitution Memorial Day (May 3); People's Holiday (May 4); Children's Day (May 5); note that some firms stayed closed for the entire week of April 29–May 5; Respect-for-the-Aged Day (September 15); Autumnal Equinox Day (date changes from year to year but it usually falls near September 23); Health and Sports Day (October 10); Culture Day (November 3); Labor Thanksgiving Day (November 23); Emperor's Birthday (December 23); Happy New Year's Holiday (begins December 28 and lasts from 5 to 10 days).

• Note that the period from April 29 through May 5 is known as "Golden Week." Businesses and banks are closed for the entire week, but some shops stay open.

• If a holiday falls on a Sunday, it is observed on Monday.

• If you are invited to celebrate New Year's with a family, bring a small amount of money wrapped in a special envelope for the children. Dress up for visits. Happy New Year visits should be short. You will be served a special liquor, *toso,* a mixture of *sake* and vegetable extract, sweetened with herbs. Even minors drink it.

• For year-end gifts (to thank everyone), look in department stores where assorted gifts are arranged by price; e.g., you might find salami and towels in one box and soap and motor oil in another. If someone has given you a ¥5000 gift in the previous year, return a gift worth the same amount.

• Certain symbolic foods will be served at New Year's: beans for good health; fish roe for prosperity; dried squid for happiness. The New Year's Eve supper of noodles brings the year to a propitious close.

• Vernal Equinox Day in the spring is a Buddhist holiday whose date varies. People visit temples and pray for the souls of the departed.

• If you are invited to a Japanese wedding, be prepared to make a short speech in Japanese. Never use any Japanese word that means repetition, break, or destruction; e.g., never say, "Now you break away from your family and join together." Suitable wedding gifts are money envelopes. Ask a knowledgeable person about the amount you should give, since the sum will depend on your relationship to the bride, the groom, or the parents. Make sure that you purchase the appropriate wedding envelope.

TRANSPORTATION

Public Transportation

• If you need directions, remember that many Japanese can read English better than they can speak or understand it. Try printing your question, and it may be understood.

• Be aware of the police boxes called *koban* at intersections in Japanese cities. Ask policemen there for directions. Many speak a little English, or, if not, will usually call someone who does.

• In tourist areas, subway stops

are clearly marked in Roman characters.

• At most train and subway stations buy tickets from machines. Put in coins, raise the white shield covering buttons with amounts on them, and push the button for the amount of your ticket. You will receive your ticket and your change. Give your ticket to the attendant at the gate. He will punch it and return it to you. Keep the ticket and give it to the attendant when you exit.

• Most urban railway systems are completely automatic. When you enter, insert your ticket in a machine and it will be returned to you. At the exit, put your ticket into another machine. If you have paid too much, the ticket will pop up, and you can use it again. If you have paid too little, the exit gate won't open and a "voice" will tell you to go to the Fare Adjustment window to pay the amount owed.

• Avoid subways and commuter trains during rush hours: 7:00 to 9:30 A.M. and 4:30 to 7:00 P.M. Of the two, the morning rush hour is worse, because everyone has to be at work at the same time, but not everyone leaves for home at the same time.

• Commuter trains and subways run every two to four minutes.

• Note that on public transportation most old people and mothers will let children sit while they stand. If you leave your seat for any reason, leave something on it to show that it is occupied.

• Avoid taking buses, if possible, since all signs and announcements are in Japanese. Most buses have a ticket machine by the entry door. You collect your ticket when you get on and pay when you get off, since fare is determined by distance traveled. If you aren't familiar with the stop at which you want to get off, have its name (and your destination) written on a card in *kanji*— Japanese characters—and ask a passenger to point out the stop to you.

• Note that fares for railroad journeys are calculated by distance and class of service, with additional charges for reservations, sleepers, etc. If you're going to travel by railway in Japan, get a copy of the Japanese National Tourist Office's *Tourist's Handbook* and its *Condensed Railway Timetable*. Both have helpful information in English: the first about buying tickets and the second about schedules. If you plan extensive rail travel, ask your travel agent about a Japan Rail Pass, which must be bought outside Japan. In Japan you can buy excursion tickets (*shu-yuken*), some types of which allow travel over long distances; others are for more limited distances. Note that the JRP and the excursion tickets are valid only on the extensive national railway system, which covers the areas most tourists visit. If you journey includes one of the country's private lines, you will have to pay the fare.

• Be aware that there are several types of intercity service. The most famous is the *Shinkansen*, usually re-ferred to as the "bullet train." Its three lines run from Tokyo to the west (Nagoya, Kyoto, Osaka, Hiroshima, and Hakata); to the northeast (Sendai and Morioka); and north (Niigata). Both regular and first-class service is available. Note: The non-smoking section is very small.

• For long distances it is also possible to take an overnight sleeper from Tokyo or Osaka to distant points. There are many surcharges on such trips depending on the level of comfort and privacy (compartment, lower berth, etc). These surcharges must be paid by holders of the Japan Rail Pass.

• Other types of train service: *tokkyu* (a "limited express," which stops only in major cities); *kyuko* ("ordinary express," which makes a limited number of stops); and *futsu* (local trains, which stop at every station).

• Buy tickets for any destination in Japan at any Japanese Railway (JR) station. Use a vending machine for short distances and a ticket window for long distances.

• Note that seats cannot be reserved on *futsu* trains but can be on all others—from a month to a few minutes ahead of departure. To reserve seats go to an office of Japan Travel Bureau (JTB), Kinki Nippon Tourist Corp., or Nippon Travel Agency. At the railway station, look for a window with green over it, or a glass door surrounded by a green band, for reservations. If you are traveling on JAL, you can make reservations for the bullet train at JAL offices in your own country.

• Arrive at the railway station early to allow enough time to find the correct platform. If you have a reserved seat, note that the place at which each car will stop is marked on the platform.

• Taxis are plentiful in commercial districts and at hotels in major cities. All have meters that operate on distance and time (the time charge can become considerable in Tokyo's traffic). Note that the cab doors are opened and closed electrically by the driver. Don't attempt to open or close the door yourself, and stay clear of the taxi as you approach it; otherwise you could get a nasty smack in the knee. Don't tip taxi drivers except in most unusual circumstances.

• From about 10:45 P.M., you may have difficulty getting a taxi (you will also have problems after the last train in most cities). Drivers are ready to go home and want a last lucrative fare (and reason that tourists are staying in nearby hotels). If you see them holding up two or three fingers, it means they will take you for twice or three times the fare on the meter. If you get desperate, hold up two fingers, which indicates your willingness to pay twice the metered fare.

• Be sure to have your destination written in Japanese characters (*kanji*) for the cab driver. Have a map in Japanese and English with your destination circled and a circle on a nearby landmark. However,

don't be surprised if the driver stops at a *koban* to ask directions. He's not trying to run up the fare. Tokyo is so complicated that even taxi drivers are not familiar with all of it.

Driving

• Keep in mind (both when driving and when crossing streets) that driving is on the left side—as in Britain.

• Don't even consider driving in Tokyo unless you have several years' experience in the Indy 500 and Le Mans. Traffic is many times worse than Midtown Manhattan or the L.A. freeways at their most congested.

• Be aware that streets and highways are extremely crowded and narrow, and that pedestrians often walk down the middle of the street. Road signs (except for some signs on expressways) are only in Japanese characters. If you're driving, try to bring along a Japanese person to translate the road signs.

• Don't assume that other drivers will obey traffic regulations. Truck and taxi drivers tend to ignore anything in their way.

• Be aware that gas is at least as expensive as it is in Europe, far more expensive than it is in North America.

LEGAL MATTERS, SAFETY, AND HEALTH

• Exchange money at banks, in hotels, shopping complexes, or major stores. The government sets the rate, and it is the same everywhere.

• The drinking age is 20, but minors can buy alcoholic beverages in bottles. There are no restrictions on times for buying liquor.

• Remember that, as a visitor, you can buy many items—pearls, cameras, liquor, china, stereo equipment, and coral—tax free, as long as they are taken or sent out of the country within six months. When you arrive in Japan, ask Customs officials to attach a Record of Purchase of Commodities Tax-Exempt to your passport. The shopkeeper will write the purchases on the form. Keep the tax-free items together, as a Customs official will check them against the Record as you leave Japan.

• Look for a sign or a sticker in a shop window indicating that tax-exempt items are for sale there.

• If you mail purchases, get a certificate at the post office to attach to your passport.

• For a complete list of tax-free items, write to the Japan National Tourist Organization (JNTO). There are offices in New York, Chicago, Dallas, Los Angeles, San Francisco, Honolulu, Toronto, and London.

• Women need not fear walking alone at night. Streets are very well patrolled.

• Women riding on commuter trains or subways should avoid wearing high heels or fragile clothing and should hold their purses very tightly in front of them. (This precaution is not to prevent your purse from being stolen, but because something could happen to it in the *huge* crowds on trains and subways.)

• Women should bring a supply of handkerchiefs (or buy a few when you arrive in Japan). There are no paper towels in public restrooms, and tissues aren't adequate for drying your hands.

Health: Bring an adequate supply of any prescription drugs you are taking.

• Note that some antibiotic drugs are available without prescription.

• Ordinary toiletries, tampons, and sanitary napkins are available.

KEY PHRASES

Even experienced travelers are daunted by the language problem in Japan. And there's no doubt that it exists and can prove troublesome. In most tourist areas, however, you will be able to get by with a combination of English, sign language, and a few key phrases in Japanese.

English	Japanese	Pronunciation
Good morning	Ohayo gozaimasu	O-hah-yó go-zyé-mahs
Good evening	Konban wa	Kon-bahn wáh
Please	Dozo	Dó-zo
Thank you	Arigato gozaimasu	Ah-ree-gah-tóh go-zyé-mahs
You're welcome	Doitashi mashite	Dóh-ee-tah-sh' maísh'-te
Yes	Hai	Hi
No	Iie	Eé-yeh
Sir, Mr., Miss, Mrs.	Last name plus San	Sahn
Excuse me	Shitsurei	Sh'-tsoo-ráy
Good-bye	Sayonara	Sah-yóh-nah-rah
I don't speak Japanese	Nihongo Wakarima-sen	Nee-hon-gówah-kah-ree-mah-seń
Does anyone speak English?	Eigo-o hanasu hito imasuka?	Ey-go-wó hah-nah-sue hee-tóe ee-máhs'-kah
I am lost	Michi ni mayoi ma-shita	Mée-chee nee máh-yoy maísh-tah
Where is . . . ?	. . . wa doko desu ka?	. . . wah do-ko dehs kah

MALAYSIA AND SINGAPORE

Fortunately, life provides us with some "10" experiences. One of them has to be sitting in the bar of the legendary Raffles Hotel in Singapore, sipping a cooling drink while gazing at the palm trees that shield the open wall of the bar from the street, and being refreshed by breezes from the ceiling fans, which cool in a gentle way air conditioners can't match.

At such moments, it's easy to forget that modern Singapore is one of Asia's financial centers and one of the world's major ports. Instead, one looks around for ladies with parasols, perhaps sipping tea while some of the great literary people who have stayed at Raffles—Somerset Maugham, for example—drink a Singapore Sling, which was invented in Raffles Bar.

Although Singapore is just off the Malaysian Peninsula and was indeed briefly federated with Malaysia, the two are now separate, despite their many similarities. And both countries have a mix of cultures—Chinese, Indian, and Malay. We have divided each section of this chapter into parts. The first covers those customs that apply to both Malaysia and Singapore. Next comes customs that apply to Malaysia, followed by those that apply only to Singapore. After that come any special customs observed in the Chinese, Indian, or Malay communities. (Note that Malays, the predominant population in Malaysia, are Muslims.)

GREETINGS

• Bow slightly when meeting, leaving, or passing a group of people whom you know.

• Note that the handshake is the most common form of greeting. Men shake hands with both men and women, but not with Muslim women. Women also shake hands; women who are really close friends hold both hands.

• Women should not offer their hands to Muslim men. However, Westernized Muslims may offer to shake hands.

• When greeting people, bow slightly or smile and say "hello."

• When an older person enters the room, both men and women should stand.

• Always use last names when first meeting someone. First names are used only after long acquaintance in Malaysia. Singaporeans are more casual. With Muslim men, however, use "Encik" (ehnchick) followed by the first name. For unmarried Muslim women use "Cik." Refer to married Muslim women as "Puan." Example: Call Ahmed Mustapha (a typical name) "Encik Ahmed." Wait for him to call you by your first name. Then simply call him "Ahmed."

• When attending a party, you may or may not be introduced to each person. Be sure, however, to shake hands with each individual.

• When introducing people, state the name of the older before the younger, the more important before the less important, and a woman before a man (e.g., "Mrs. Smith, this is John").

• If a person has a title—e.g., Professor, Doctor, Architect—use it with the last name.

Singapore: Don't feel obliged to shake hands with everyone at a party. Party guests are usually introduced quickly to everyone. At a large party, however, where people are spread out in small groups, you may be introduced individually with handshakes.

Chinese: Use family names with "Mr.," "Mrs.," etc. Remember that the surname will be the first name you hear (or see). For example, Chen Hua is "Mr. Chen."

• Note that married women are referred to as "Madam" with their birth name. A woman does not take her husband's name when she marries.

Indian: Western women should use the Indian form of greeting when introduced to a man— "*Namaste,*" palms together and a slight bow. Many south Indians, who speak Tamil, will say "Vanakam" (vah-nah-kahm) in greeting. Another appropriate greeting is a nod of the head and a smile.

• Women shake hands with each other but not with men. They may also greet each other with "*Namaste.*"

• Always use last names and "Mr." or "Mrs."

Malay: Extend both hands to other persons and grasp both their hands, a gesture known as *salam.* Use the same gesture when departing. Only members of the same sex use this gesture. A man should not shake hands with a woman unless she offers her hand first.

• In addressing people, use the following guidelines. If a man's name is Isa bin Aman, call him "Mr. Isa" or "Encik Isa." His wife's name might be Zaitun binti Abdullah. Call her "Mrs. Zaitun Isa." ("Bin" means "son of" and "binti" means "daughter of." The name that follows is the father's name.)

• Because of the complexity of names in each ethnic group in Malaysia and Singapore, ask people how they wish to be addressed. If the person replies formally (e.g., "I'm Doctor Smith"), respond in the same way—"I'm Mr. Jones."

CONVERSATION

• Don't be surprised if people ask you personal questions, but it's best if you stick to superficial inquiries about people's families and their personal lives.

• Topics to discuss: sports; travel, if your host has been abroad; your host's success in business and social activities and plans for the future; movies and books.

• Never compare Western standards with those of Malaysia or Singapore.

• Talk about the cuisine and ask for recommendations for places to dine.

• Don't speak about or criticize the bureaucracy, and don't ask a person's views about government policies. Very few people are willing to speak out individually.

• Don't interpret silence or a long pause in conversation as rejection or acceptance of an idea. People are pausing to reflect and don't feel so uncomfortable with silence as many Westerners do.

• Avoid discussing the Israel/Palestine situation and religion.

• Note that a Singaporean sucking air through the teeth means "No."

• Don't tell risqué jokes. In fact, reserve all expressions of humor and jokes until you know a person well.

TELEPHONES

• Look for telephone booths in restaurants, cafés, in shops, and in booths on the street.

• Make long-distance calls from your hotel. Ask if there is a surcharge—often there is a large one on overseas calls. You can avoid the surcharge by calling from a post office. Because of long waits for calls to go through, however, business-people may prefer to pay the surcharge. You can avoid the surcharge by calling collect or arranging to have your office or family call you.

• Note that public phones also accept credit cards for international calls, and most homes have phones with international direct dialing.

Malaysia: Look for orange shelters with orange public telephones. Lift the receiver, and insert a 10, 20, or 50 *sen* coin or a Telecom phone card. Wait until the light goes off, then dial. On most public phones, you must press the release button when your party answers. If you've used coins, a beep after three minutes lets you know that you have 10 seconds to deposit more money, or you'll be cut off.

• Buy telephone cards in Telecom shops, 7–Eleven stores, and Petronas petrol kiosks. There are two types of card phones, and each card can be used in only one type of phone.

• If you have a credit card or phone card, look for a Kadfon, which will accept either card.

• Note that some public telephones have IDD (International Direct Dialing). In major towns make overseas calls from the telephone office.

• In Kuala Lumpur, look for the

International Telephone Exchange, where you can book calls to any country or make a collect call abroad. In major towns make overseas calls from the telephone office (Kedai Telecom).

• For a police emergency, dial 999. For fire, dial 994.

Singapore: Deposit 10 cents Singapore currency or the Telecom phone card. If you use coins, a beep after three minutes signals that you must deposit additional money or you will be cut off.

• Consider buying a telephone card for $2,$5, or $10. They can be purchased at Telecom Customer Service outlets, petrol kiosks, 7–Eleven stores, or post offices. The cards can be used for both local and long-distance calls.

• For police, dial 999. For an ambulance, dial 995.

IN PUBLIC

• Note that older people don't hug or kiss anyone in public; however, many younger people do.

• Show great respect for the elderly. Hold doors open for them and offer them your seat on public transportation.

• Don't cross your legs in front of elders, and don't put your feet on a chair. Sit in such a way that your legs don't show prominently, and be especially careful when with Muslims that the soles of your feet/shoes aren't showing.

• At the entrance to a mosque or a Hindu temple, remove your shoes. Before going into a mosque, if you are not dressed appropriately (e.g., if you're wearing shorts), put on a robe, which will be available at the entrance.

• When with Muslims don't step over the crossed legs of a person seated on the floor.

• Don't pat either a child or an adult on the head because the head is considered the seat of spiritual powers and thus is sacred.

• When gesturing toward a person, use your whole right hand, palm facing upwards. Don't use the right or left forefinger alone. The single forefinger is used to call dogs.

• To beckon someone, extend your arm, palm down, and move your fingers up and down.

• Note that placing the hands on the hips signifies anger.

• Remember that Asians tend to laugh when they are shy or embarrassed, a gesture that often seems inappropriate to Westerners. For example, a saleswoman who has broken a vase a customer has just purchased will probably laugh to cover her distress.

• Be sure to be punctual for all engagements or meetings. If you're going to be late, notify your host.

• Look for Western-style toilets in large hotels and department stores. In smaller shops and other places away from the usual tourist areas, you may find a squat-type toilet. Try to use hotel washrooms, since other public facilities may not be especially pleasant. The usual word for bathroom is *tanda* (tahn-dah). In Malaysia, look for symbols identifying the rest rooms for each sex. In Singapore, signs will be in English.

• Don't forget that if you are caught *not* flushing a public toilet, there is a fine.

Shopping: If you want to try to bargain, begin by offering 50 percent of the quoted price, and settle for a 30-percent reduction.

• If possible, let the merchant be the first to mention a price.

• Remember that if you mention a price in the course of the bargaining (e.g., "Would you consider $75?")—even though it's more than you planned to spend—and the merchant accepts, you are obliged to buy. Don't start the bargaining process unless you are serious about buying.

Malaysia: Realize that bargaining is the normal practice outside of shopping centers or in department stores where prices are fixed.

Singapore: Recall that bargaining is not common, except in open markets or very rural areas.

Chinese: When visiting temples, men should remove their hats. Use the right door for entry and the left door for exit. Ask permission before taking photos.

Indian: Note that when Indians shake their head from side to side, it means "yes."

• Use only the right hand for taking and giving objects on social or business occasions (when you eat, use the right hand; when you shop, handle merchandise and money with the right hand). The left hand is used for cleaning after using the toilet.

• Don't touch statues or religious pictures inside a temple.

• Hindu custom dictates that women not enter a temple when they are menstruating.

Malay: Don't expose the soles of your feet (with or without shoes), and never put your feet on a table in front of another person.

• Ask permission before smoking. Be especially careful to ask when elders are present.

• When visiting mosques, women should have their arms and knees covered. Remove shoes before entering. Women should not shake hands with Muslim men at a mosque because the men will have to wash again before praying.

• In mosques, don't cross in front of people who are praying, and don't touch the Koran. A polite gesture would be to ask permission before taking photographs; the request is seldom, if ever, refused.

• Never sit or stand on a prayer rug.

• Note that Muslims are not allowed to come in contact with dogs. If you have brought one with you, be sure to keep it in another room when a Muslim is visiting.

Exercise: Malaysia: Jog in parks and around large hotels. Women should wear long pants, which may be very uncomfortable because of the humidity. Men can wear shorts. Both men and women would be most comfortable in cotton sportswear.

Singapore: Jogging is very popular. Jog along the roads, in the botanical gardens, in recreational parks (which have jogging trails), and at athletic centers with indoor tracks. Although people jog at any time of day, it becomes hot and humid early, so you may want to exercise in the early morning. Both men and women can wear shorts for jogging.

DRESS

• Don't wear synthetic fabrics; the heat and humidity makes them unbearable. Bring, instead, clothes of natural fabrics such as cotton, linen, or silk. Men should not pack seersucker suits, as seersucker is a synthetic fabric.

• For a business meeting, men should wear a suit and tie, but if the heat makes it seem appropriate, they can remove their jacket. Women should wear a long-sleeved blouse and skirt or a suit.

• Because of the religious beliefs in Malaysia, women must be very careful not to offend by their costume. Women should not wear short skirts, sleeveless dresses or blouses (even sleeves so short they might show the armpits), shorts, halter tops, or bikinis. They should never go braless.

• For casual wear, jeans are acceptable for all. Men may wear open-necked patterned shirts or polo shirts over slacks. Women may wear pants or skirts.

• When invited to a meal in a home, men should wear open-necked shirts, especially those made from local batiks. Never "dress up" beyond a shirt and tie. Women should wear a dress or skirt and blouse.

• Note that some hotels and very elegant restaurants require men to wear jacket and tie at dinner. Check when making a reservation. At many restaurants, however, batik shirts with an open neck are acceptable.

Singapore: Feel free to wear knee-length shorts. They are popular for casual dress.

Malaysia: Remember that yellow is the color of royalty. Don't wear yellow to a formal function or when visiting the palace.

• Don't wear black on a happy occasion.

• Be sure to remove shoes before entering mosques or Hindu or Buddhist temples.

• To a formal dinner, men can wear a long-sleeved batik shirt called a *baju* or a suit. Women should wear dresses (keeping in mind the taboo on yellow).

• Recall that on the east coast bikinis are banned, and topless bathing is forbidden throughout Malaysia.

Indian: To visit temples, women may wear slacks. Legs should be covered, at least to below the knee. Men should not wear hats in a temple.

MEALS

Hours and Foods

Breakfast: Begins between 7:00 and 8:00 A.M. A Malaysian breakfast consists of rice, barbecued meat, and tea. A common breakfast dish—

and one that is very spicy—is *nasi lemak*, rice cooked with coconut milk and fish.

Lunch: Starts between noon and 1:30 P.M. The staple of the meal is rice, accompanied by beef or fish curry, and vegetables, usually spinach or cabbage. The main dishes may be served with cucumbers, hot chili paste, salted eggs, and fried dried fish. All the dishes will be put on the table at once. The Malays and Indians may serve dessert or fruit, such as mangoes, papayas, or pineapple, at simple family dinners. A Chinese banquet always ends with a dessert. Water or tea usually accompany the meal, with coffee—with milk and sugar—served afterwards. In Malaysia never drink the water unless it is bottled or you are sure that it has been boiled. Tap water in Singapore is safe.

Dinner: About 7:00 or 8:00 P.M. Rice is again the staple. Although dinner is a big meal, it is usually made up of leftovers from lunch.

• Note that pre-dinner drinks and appetizers are rare.

• If dessert is served, it will probably be fresh fruit. Don't eat it unless you can peel it.

Chinese: Family meals are seldom accompanied by alcohol. For more formal occasions, expect beer or brandy to accompany dinner.

Indian: Note that most Indians do not eat beef, and many are vegetarians. However, those who are Christian may eat beef.

• Don't look for salad to accompany a meal, since Indians like everything well cooked.

Malay: Since Malays are Muslims, remember that they don't eat pork products or drink alcohol. Many Malays will eat *no* food at all, unless it has been prepared according to Islamic rules.

• Water is the beverage that accompanies meals.

• Look for a wide variety of fresh fruit juices, sodas, mineral water, and some beers.

• Realize that Malaysian coffee is *very* strong and is always served with sweetened condensed milk. If you don't want the milk, state your preference in advance.

Table Manners

• Although most traditional Indians and Muslims usually eat with their hands, expect to be offered forks and spoons. If you aren't given Western-style cutlery and must eat with your hands, be sure to eat only with your right hand; the left hand is considered unclean.

Malay: Expect to see five or six serving dishes in the middle of the table. You will be given a plate with rice already on it. Using the spoon in each serving dish, help yourself to a portion. Combine it with the rice on your plate and eat it with your right hand or with fork and spoon. Holding the spoon in your right hand and the fork in your left, use the fork to push food onto your spoon.

• Never blow your nose, clear your throat loudly, or spit when dining with others.

• If you are having a dinner party, invite an even number of guests to ensure good luck.

Chinese: If the family is very status conscious, expect the host and hostess to sit opposite one another. Guests are seated facing the front entrance, with guests of honor to the left of the host and hostess. Most families are more casual in seating arrangements.

• Don't be surprised if the host apologizes for the inferior quality of the food. It's a custom. Simply reply that the food is good.

• Be aware that before the meal the host will invite guests to drink wine. Even if you don't wish to drink, take a sip or at least pretend to take a sip. Raise the glass with both hands—the left hand should hold the glass, and the right hand should be under the glass.

• At each table setting, expect a rice bowl, a soup bowl, a dish for main courses, a dish for bones, a dish for soy sauce, a cup or glass, chopsticks, a porcelain spoon, and a napkin. The main dish will be in front of you, the bone dish to the side.

• Be aware that fish is often served with its head on. It's considered a delicacy.

• If you have children with you, instruct them not to begin eating until adults have done so.

• When serving yourself, take the pieces closest to you on the serving platter. Be sure that you don't let the serving spoon touch your plate.

• Use the porcelain spoon for soup and chopsticks for other food. The Chinese consider it a compliment if a foreigner tries to eat with chopsticks. If you don't feel comfortable using chopsticks, ask for a fork and spoon. With the spoon in your right hand and the fork in your left, use the fork to push food onto the spoon. If you're left-handed, hold the chopsticks in that hand, or reverse the position of the fork and spoon.

• Never rest chopsticks on your dinner plate or on the rice bowl. Use the chopstick rest, if there is one, or the soy sauce dish or bone plate. When you have finished, place the chopsticks on the rest or on the table.

• Be especially careful not to place your chopsticks upright in your rice bowl; it's considered rude.

• With soup, use chopsticks to eat the chunks of food in it and the porcelain spoon for the liquid part. Tilt the soup bowl toward you.

• Remove bones from your mouth with chopsticks, not with fingers. If there is a bone plate, use it; if not, put the bones on your own plate.

• When eating filled buns, use chopsticks to hold them. If the buns are large, feel free to eat them with your hands.

• If the host places a special bit of food on your plate, realize that he is paying you a great compliment. Return the compliment to her/him at some point in the meal. Use serving chopsticks if they are available or your own chopsticks if you have not yet used them. If no serving implement is at hand, invite the person to help herself/himself.

• Feel free to slurp your soup, and remember that a burp signals appreciation of the food. See if anyone else is slurping, because those of the younger generation may not regard the behavior as polite.

• If you are offered a second helping, refuse it the first and second times. Your hosts will insist, and then you may accept.

• Accept and offer drinks by holding the glass in your right hand with the left hand supporting the right.

• Don't comment if people put ice in their beer or salt on their fruit. It's often done.

• On the other hand, don't be surprised to be served warm water, even on a hot day. Many Chinese believe that iced drinks are bad for the stomach.

• Feel free to stay two hours or more after dinner; Chinese enjoy long after-dinner conversations.

Indian: Always go to the washroom and wash your hands before eating.

• Don't look for a place of honor. The host will tell guests where to sit.

• Note that serving bowls will be placed in the middle of the table, while your plate will be at your place, as will a beverage glass.

• As a Western guest, expect to be given a fork and spoon. There's no knife because the food is already cut into small pieces. When you finish, rest the fork and spoon on your dinner plate.

• Don't touch your own plate with a serving spoon.

• Should you be in a situation where you must eat—as Indians usually do—with your hands, use your right hand. If this hand is soiled, use the left hand to pass plates of food, but remember that your left hand must *never* touch the food. Don't lick or suck your fingers.

• Wait until the host starts eating before you begin.

• Never take food from another person's plate, even your spouse or child.

• Expect to be offered second and third helpings.

• Note that Indian women don't usually drink alcoholic beverages. Western women may be offered drinks and should feel free to accept.

• Don't leave immediately after dinner. Stay for about an hour after the meal for after-dinner conversation in the living room.

Malay: Note that Malays prefer to entertain at home rather than in restaurants.

• Be aware that the meal will probably be ready when you arrive. There are no pre-dinner appetizers.

• If you are visiting in a rural area, realize that men eat first and women later.

• Remember that, on formal occasions, the guest of honor is usually seated at the head of the table or to the right of the host.

• If seating is on the floor, women should tuck their feet to the left, and men should sit cross-legged.

• Anticipate washing before the meal with a small bowl and towel offered by your hostess. (Beware: some travelers have mistaken the bowl's contents for soup.)

• Even if your food is set in front of you, wait to eat until your host asks you to accept it.

• Realize that, when eating, you should use only the first two joints of the finger (up to the knuckle), not the whole hand. (This is a difficult practice for foreigners to master.)

• When passing a heavy serving dish, use your left hand to hold it and support it with your right hand, palm down, under the dish.

• Don't touch a serving spoon to your plate.

• If your host offers you a salt dish, dip your right forefinger into it and then taste. A dish of salt on the table is a symbol of friendship.

• Never refuse any food or drink, whether it's offered in a meal or as a snack. Take it and at least taste a bit; however, to be considered well mannered, you should finish it all. If you must refuse food, give a specific reason—you're allergic, your doctor has forbidden it, etc. If you wish to refuse a second helping, hold your hand over your plate and say, "No, thank you."

• After dinner, stay for about an hour for after-dinner conversation.

Places to Eat

• To sample all the cuisines of Asia, simply try the many restaurants of Singapore and Malaysia. There are northern and southern Indian, Thai, Japanese, Korean, Malay, Indonesian, European, and American restaurants.

• To find the best pastry shops, search on little side streets. Ask acquaintances for the locations of the best ones. You can't eat or drink there, however. If you want to eat the pastry where you buy it, try local coffeehouses, where you can have pastries, local snacks, tea, and coffee. You'll find these coffeehouses mainly in hotels or shopping centers.

• In most restaurants, no matter what type of cuisine, it's possible to order a shared meal with several dishes or an individual meal. Ask your host what the party is doing.

• For an inexpensive meal, look for a snackbar. They serve local dishes, such as curry puffs.

• At most restaurants beer is available. Whiskey and brandy are also available in leading restaurants. Wine is more difficult to obtain.

• Don't anticipate menus being posted outside restaurants.

• If a restaurant is crowded, feel free to join people already seated— but always ask permission first. Don't do this at better restaurants.

• Don't be surprised to be offered a wet paper towel or a cloth towel before a meal. Use it only for your hands.

• As a Westerner, in a Chinese restaurant expect to be offered a spoon and fork rather than chopsticks. If you prefer chopsticks, ask for them.

• Remember to cover your mouth with your other hand if you choose to use a toothpick.

• To call the waiter, make the customary beckoning gesture—the whole hand in motion towards your body. In Chinese restaurants, however, which tend to be very noisy, you'll have to signal very vigorously for attention with both hands raised. Never snap your fingers at a waiter or waitress.

• When eating *satay*, use the stick on which the kebabs come to spear the rice cake and other garnishes.

Singapore: Look for hawker centers, where you'll find many food stalls located under a single roof. Take a table, and then choose food from the Indian, Chinese, or Malay stalls. When the food is ready, a vendor will bring it to you. Pay him. There are rigorously enforced hygiene standards, so the food should be safe to eat.

• You'll find many casual dining places, such as food courts (located in shopping centers and malls) and hawker centers, offering fresh fruit juices made on the spot from a wide range of tropical fruits.

• Avoid sleazy bars. They are usually fronts for prostitution. If drink and conversation are your objective, visit a night spot or a hotel pub.

Specialties

• Be sure to try *satay*, the national dish—kebabs of beef, chicken, or mutton, coated with a spicy sauce, grilled, and eaten with peanut sauce.

• Soups to sample: *soto ayam*, (a chicken soup with chicken pieces, rice, bean sprouts, onion, and celery) and *laksa* (a spicy soup made with fish stock and noodles).

• If you aren't going to Indonesia, eat two of their national dishes in Malaysia/Singapore: *nasi goreng* (rice fried with vegetables) and *nasi padang* (steamed rice served with side dishes of spiced fish, prawns, and vegetables). Other dishes inspired by Indonesia are *rendang* (meats in spices and coconut milk, served with rice) and *gado gado* (salad with peanut dressing).

• Other main dishes from the Malaysia/Singapore area: *panggang golek* (spiced duck with cashews and coconut cream), *dodeng* (ginger beef), *tak otak* (fish mousse in lemon grass and banana leaves), chili crabs cooked in a spicy sauce, *rojak* (a mixture of fruits and vegetables stir-fried in a sweet-and-sour sauce with a shrimp base).

• Noodles are a mainstay of dishes. Sample *mee rebus* (boiled noodles in a rich beef gravy), *mee siam* (spicy Thai-style noodles), and *mee goreng* (fried noodles).

• A sweet specialty is *gula malacca* (a sago pudding made with sago palm sugar).

Malay: Malay cakes, usually made with rice flour and coconut milk, then flavored with special fragrant leaves, are called *kueh*.

Chinese: The Chinese Szechuan restaurants offer a dessert pancake filled with red bean or lotus seed paste.

Indian: Indian sweets usually have milk and sugar as a base.

HOTELS

• Be sure to make reservations well in advance for the better hotels in Kuala Lumpur and other major cities. Good hotels are always in demand.

• If you're traveling off-season, (on the east coast of Malaysia, November to February, when there are heavy rains; on the west coast of Malaysia, December, when there are heavy rains; and in Singapore, January through April), ask if the hotel offers a reduction during that period. Some give 10 to 20 percent discounts.

• Avoid island resorts on the east coast of Malaysia during December. Swimming is dangerous during this stormy monsoon season.

• If you choose a smaller hotel, expect limited facilities—shared bathrooms, inexpensive furniture, and no TV.

PRIVATE HOMES

TIPPING

Malaysia: Expect a 10 percent service charge to be included in your restaurant bill.

• Don't tip taxi drivers; it's not customary.

• Give porters 1 *ringgit* per bag.

• With gas station attendants, round off the cost to the nearest *ringgit*.

• Tip washroom attendants 50 *sen* and for small services (e.g., room-service waiter).

Singapore: Note that tipping is officially discouraged for everyone, including taxi drivers, bellboys, hotel staff, hairdressers, etc..

• Remember that restaurants add a 10 percent service charge to every bill.

• Remove shoes before entering a house. (Be sure to check your socks for holes before you put them on.)

• Don't be surprised to see an altar in a home. The family uses it for prayers. (If you are visiting the home of a Buddhist family, people may stop and say a short prayer each time they pass the altar.)

• When visiting a Muslim family, do not touch the Koran or step on the family prayer rug.

• Be sure to pay for overseas calls, but it isn't necessary to pay for local calls.

• In Malaysian homes, toilets usually have a bucket of water, a scoop, and an extra tap. Malays and Indians wash themselves every time they use the toilet. If you don't want to follow this practice, carry tissues with you. All Singapore homes have flush toilets.

• Recall that in Malaysia there is usually only cold water for bathing. Feel free to bathe daily. Malaysians often bathe three times a day because of the heat and humidity. Most families in Singapore have water heaters and do use them.

• If you are staying with a family with children and you go sightseeing on your own, bring them a treat, such as fruit, when you come home.

Gifts: When invited to a dinner party, bring a bottle of wine, unless your hosts are Muslim. For Muslims, bring pastries or chocolates.

• From abroad, bring items reflecting the culture of your home area.

• For older people, bring fruit or a food basket. Young people may prefer chocolates, a decorative item for the home, or toys for their children.

• Don't wrap your gift in white paper (the color signifies funerals) or in yellow paper (the color of royalty).

Singapore: Note that close friends drop in on one another at any time. If you don't know people well, call ahead. Business associates should call ahead to allow the host time to tidy the house.

• Avoid visiting near or during mealtimes. You might interrupt the family meal, and the host will feel obliged to ask you to join the meal or to stay if a meal is being prepared.

• Ask to help with the washing up after dinner. If it's your first visit, your host will probably decline. Don't press the issue or you might embarrass your host.

• Always offer to pay for your phone calls, especially long-distance calls. Even though local calls from private homes in Malaysia are free,

be sure to ask permission to make the call. Local calls from a Singapore phone are not free.

• If you are a house guest, expect to be deferred to and to receive first choice of food at the dinner table.

• Ask permission to take a shower. Your hosts, however, will expect you to take at least one shower a day. Note that people seldom take long tub baths.

Gifts: Be aware that older Singaporeans don't open gifts in the presence of the giver.

• When invited to a home for a meal, bring chocolates, flowers, or pastries.

• From the U.S., T-shirts are a good gift.

Chinese: Note that some Chinese don't wear shoes in the house. Notice if members of the family have removed their shoes, and follow their lead.

• Expect to be entertained in the living room. Don't expect a house tour, and don't explore the house on your own.

• Never wash your underwear in the bathroom and hang it up there. Ask your hostess' advice about doing laundry.

Gifts: When visiting or when invited to a meal, bring sweets or fruit; if there are children, you might say that they are for them— this indicates that you don't think your hosts are greedy. Your host may return a few pieces of fruit or cake when you leave as a sign of good luck.

• Gifts should always come in

even numbers or pairs when given during the Chinese New Year, a sign of happiness and good luck. Examples: two bags of chocolates, four oranges. Odd numbers are associated with separation and death.

• Good gifts are food hampers, which are available in supermarkets; cakes in reusable tins; chocolates; or cookies.

• Gifts to avoid, especially for older Chinese people: straw sandals, which are worn at funerals; clocks— the Cantonese word for *clock* also means to go to a funeral; knives and scissors or other sharp objects—they indicate the cutting off of a friendship; handkerchiefs, which represent sadness; flowers—they are sent only to sick people or for funerals; white, blue, or black gifts, because they are associated with funerals; wrapping paper with a stork on it, because it symbolizes a woman's death. Young people actually appreciate receiving flowers or watches as gifts.

• Remember that the Chinese give and receive gifts with both hands.

• Do not expect people to open a gift in your presence. If someone gives you a gift, follow this custom.

Indian: Note that many Indians leave their shoes at the door before entering a home. Westernized Indians may not follow this custom. Take your cue from the host.

• Expect to be entertained in the living room. Don't ask to see the rest of the house, and don't investigate other rooms by yourself.

• Be aware that in traditional homes women may not join men for meals. If they do eat at the same time, they usually sit across the room from the men.

• Ask permission before smoking in a home.

• Ask your hostess if you can help with household chores.

• When leaving, remember that it's bad luck for three people to leave at the same time. One person should stay behind for a few seconds.

• Note that there's a ritual exchange when you leave the house. Those in the home will say, "Go and come back." The person leaving says, "I'm going and coming back." Don't say, "Good-bye."

• If you are a houseguest, tell the family your plans for sightseeing, etc.

• In Malaysia, be aware that in some bathrooms you will find a shower but in others only a tap and bucket. Soap yourself and then pour water from the bucket over yourself. Most have a squat-type toilet with a bucket of water used for cleaning, but no toilet paper. Bring your own tissues. In Singapore, expect to find showers everywhere. Many homes have baths and even Jacuzzis.

Gifts: When invited to a meal, bring fruit or sweets for the children in the family.

• Always offer a gift with your right hand.

• Don't give frangipani flowers because they are used for funerals.

• When invited to stay with a family, give a gift for the house, sari material for the wife, and/or gifts for the children.

• When giving a gift of money, be sure the amount is an uneven number. An uneven number is considered luckier than an even number.

• In choosing a gift, avoid the colors black and white. They are regarded as sad colors. Red, yellow, green, and other bright colors are the happy ones.

Malay: Feel free to drop in unannounced. Do, however, avoid the evening prayer time between 6:00 and 7:30 P.M.

• Be aware that some homes have chairs and sofas, but in many homes people sit on mats on the floor. Most Muslims entertain foreigners on chairs and sofas and use mats only for friends and family. Don't step over the crossed legs of anyone seated on the floor. If you sit on a chair, don't cross your legs if older people are present; it's considered disrespectful to elders and dignitaries.

• Always ask permission before leaving the house—e.g., "May I leave now?"

• Never sit or stand on a prayer rug.

• If you're a houseguest, don't sleep late. Get up when the family does.

• Offer to help with household chores.

Gifts: Remember that Malays don't open gifts in the presence of the giver.

• If invited to a meal, bring fruits or cakes.

• When spending a few days with a family, present your gifts when you leave, not when you arrive.

• Good gifts: for women (to be given by women), perfume; for men, cotton shirts with collars (as opposed to T-shirts); for children, toys. Everyone will enjoy souvenirs from your country, such as photographic picture books of your area.

• Don't give pork, liquor, ashtrays, toy dogs (or any item picturing a dog), knives, or personal items to Malays.

BUSINESS

Hours

• Note that in Malaysia, on the heavily Muslim East Coast and in other Muslim states, businesses, banks, etc., are usually closed Thursday afternoon and all day Friday but open Saturday and Sunday.

Businesses—Malaysia: Monday through Friday, 8:00 A.M. to 5:00 P.M.

Singapore: Monday through Friday, 9:00 A.M. to 1:00 P.M., and

2:00 to 5:00 P.M. On Saturday, 9:00 A.M. to 1:00 P.M.

Banks—Malaysia: Monday through Friday, 10:00 A.M. to 3:00 P.M., and Saturday, 9:30 to 11:30 A.M.

Singapore: Monday through Friday, 10:00 A.M. to 3:00 P.M. and on Saturday 9:30 A.M. to 11:30 P.M.

Government Offices—Malaysia: Monday through Friday, 8:00 A.M. to 4:15 P.M. and 8:30 A.M. to 12:45 P.M. on Saturday.

Singapore: Monday through Friday, 9:00 A.M. to 5:00 P.M., and Saturday 9:00 A.M. to noon.

Shops—Malaysia: Department stores and supermarkets are usually open from 10:00 A.M. to 10:00 P.M., Monday through Saturday. Smaller shops are open on the same days from 9:00 A.M. to 7:00 P.M. Some Chinese stores open on Sunday.

Singapore: Monday through Saturday, 9:30 or 10:00 A.M. to 6:30 P.M. Some shops stay open until 9:00 or 10:00 P.M., and some are open on Sunday.

Money

• In Malaysia, the currency is the Malaysian dollar or *ringgit* (M$), which consists of 100 cents or *sen.* Coins are 1, 5, 10, 20, 50 cents and M$1. Banknotes are M$1, M$5, M$10, M$20, M$50, M$100, M$500, and M$1000.

• In Singapore, the currency is the Singapore dollar (S$), made up of 100 cents. Coins are 1, 5, 10, 20, 50 cents and S$1 and S$10. Banknotes are S$1, S$5, S$10, S$20, S$50, S$100, S$500, S$1000, and S$10,000.

• Note that Malaysian dollars and Singapore dollars are *not* interchangeable.

Malaysia: In larger hotels, restaurants, and stores, major credit cards—American Express, Visa, Barclaycard, MasterCard, Access—are accepted. Don't try to pay with travelers' checks anywhere but at well-established hotels for tourists, not in restaurants or shops.

Singapore: The major credit cards mentioned above are accepted. Shops in some tourist areas may accept payment in travelers' checks, but most will not.

Business Practices

• Be aware that the business community is predominantly Chinese, and the foreign businessperson is most likely to be dealing with them. (As a general rule, urban inhabitants are Chinese, and rural inhabitants are Muslims.)

• Try to schedule business trips between March and November. Many businessmen vacation in December, January, and February.

• Avoid the two weeks before and after Christmas, the week before and after Easter, the Chinese New Year—celebrated in January or February—and Ramadan, the Muslim fasting period, which varies according to the lunar calendar.

• Arrange appointments by fax. People travel often and may not be in the office.

• If at all possible, arrange for a letter of introduction before you arrive. Get in touch with the Trade Office for Malaysia/Singapore in your country for help in finding contacts.

• If possible, send your proposal before making a trip. When you arrive, prepare to go over it in great detail.

• For best results, have your company's delegation headed by someone age 50 or over. People are impressed by older people with experience.

• Show deference to the elders and to those senior in rank in the Asian group. Allow them to go through doors first and to be seated first.

• Avoid any physical contact with your business colleagues— e.g., patting someone on the back or putting your arm around their shoulders.

• Bring business cards that indicate your position in your company. Cards in English are acceptable, unless you are dealing with a Chinese company.

• Expect to be offered coffee or tea. Accept, even if you are not thirsty.

• Prepare for a meeting to begin with a period of conversation about you, your family, what you've seen in your host's country, food, travel, or your future plans. At initial business meetings, people want to learn about you and your company. Impress people with the advantages of dealing with your firm and your country. After that, you can go on to negotiations.

• Never criticize anyone directly or show anger.

• Don't talk with your hands.

• Avoid using slang, especially idioms derived from sports (e.g., "I think he can carry the ball"); they won't be understood and will only confuse your Asian counterparts.

Business Entertaining: Be aware that personal contact is essential in doing business. Get acquainted first while dining or during an evening out. Good topics for conversation are local cuisine and vacation travel destinations.

• When reciprocating business entertainment, ask the food preferences of your host, since he may be Hindu, Chinese, or Muslim.

Malaysia: Make an appointment in advance of visiting a factory or office. Make arrangements a week ahead if you're in the country, two months ahead from abroad.

• Exchange business cards at the first meeting. This will ensure that your name is remembered and correctly spelled. Malaysians find Western names difficult.

• Note that both business letters and business discussions are normally in English. Malaysians speak with a British accent and use British pronunciation. Speak slowly and clearly.

• Anticipate dealing with two types of businessmen: those of the older generation and those who were trained abroad. The latter tend to be more open to new ideas. Your potential customers in Malaysia will be hospitable, attentive, polite, and sensitive—but sometimes suspicious.

• Keep in mind that, in the areas where Friday is a work day, Muslims may take a two-hour lunch break to go to the mosque.

• Expect meetings to be held in a conference room.

• When visiting factories, always obey the no-smoking signs. Ask permission before smoking at a business meeting.

Business Entertaining: When a business counterpart invites you to a restaurant, let him do the ordering.

• When you reciprocate—as you certainly should, since entertaining is an important part of business dealings—be sure that all appropriate personnel are invited. Issue invitations either in person or by telephone.

• Remember that their religious beliefs cause Malays who are Muslims to avoid alcoholic beverages both at home and in restaurants.

• Expect business meetings to take place over lunch or dinner. A business breakfast is very rare.

• Realize that you have an advantage if you play golf. The golf course is an excellent place to foster business relationships. Usually, foreign women will be invited to a golf outing only if they are part of a team with men on it.

Gifts: Bring a souvenir from your company: e.g., pens, calendars, or engagement diaries with your company name embossed on them.

Singapore: Plan to make several trips to Singapore to conclude a business deal, and be sure to exercise great patience in negotiation.

• Make appointments to visit business and government offices at least two weeks in advance. Singapore businessmen not only have busy schedules, but they also travel often.

• Be aware that hierarchy is very important. Have a secretary make appointments, rather than making them yourself. To make the call yourself lowers you in the estimation of others.

• Be on time for business appointments, and call if you're going to be late.

• Bring business cards; having your card printed in both English and Chinese is helpful. Exchange cards at the first meeting.

• Present your card with both hands, with the print facing the person to whom you're giving it. Accept business cards in the same way. Don't put them in your back pocket, and don't write on them.

• Wait to be told where to sit. The company may have a hierarchical seating arrangement for meetings that take place in its offices.

• Don't be effusive in compliments. People will think you insincere.

• Be careful not to boast. Singaporeans value humility.

• Try to select a contact in Singapore, since the "network" and "family connection" system is very strong. Foreign businesspeople are at a disadvantage, because they usually aren't related to people in business in Singapore. Even in the large banks, family connections count for a great deal.

• If you are in manufacturing, engineering, or professional services, go to the Economic Development Board, which can help cut red tape. You will be assigned an advocate who will give you information, tell you who's who in the business community, help you meet the right customers, and assist you with documents.

• Consider entering the Singapore market by undertaking a joint venture with a local firm. Be sure that your agreement with them is watertight.

• If you are planning to set up a business, be certain to consult a *feng shui* man. He is a Chinese philosopher who will determine that the building, the windows, the doors, and the furniture are facing in the right direction.

• Remember that Singapore is governed by British law. Use a local lawyer. Consult your embassy or consulate for help in finding legal advice.

• Be aware that Singaporean businessmen may capitalize on your being out of your element. For example, a businessman will probably give a very sketchy version of what he's looking for and will then grill you with very specific questions (e.g., "What's your P and L?").

• Look for giant loopholes in contracts offered by the Chinese.

• Don't be surprised at attempts to negotiate even after the price has been agreed on, a strategy that often surfaces when the last payment on a project is due.

• Women doing business should exercise great tact. Never cause a man to lose face. However, women should feel more comfortable doing business in Singapore than in most other Asian countries. Many women work at all levels of business, and there's little sexual harassment.

Business Entertaining: Always accept a dinner invitation, since personal contact means so much to Singapore businesspeople.

• If you receive a printed invitation to a dinner or party, always respond in writing.

• Don't expect to be invited to a meal immediately after starting to do business. Once your host knows you a bit, he will invite you to a meal. On your side, don't be forward in inviting your host to a meal.

• Anticipate singing a song if you're taken to one of the popular forms of business entertainment, *karaoke*.

• If invited to a Chinese restaurant, for a very, very formal occasion, sit in the chair facing the door (the seat of honor). Do not eat a great deal of any one course. To impress your hosts, eat with chopsticks (practice before you get to Singapore).

• Note that public-sector officials are not permitted to accept social invitations.

• If you invite Singapore businesspeople to dinner in a restaurant, choose a Western-style restaurant.

• Include wives, if you wish, if the meal is not strictly business but a social occasion. Don't discuss business if wives are present. Don't bring your spouse or invite a spouse if the meal is lunch. Lunches are strictly for discussing business. Dinners are more social occasions.

• Never simply assume that your wife is included in an invitation, since most businessmen prefer to keep family apart from their business lives.

Gifts: Don't expect an exchange of gifts on the first meeting. If you give gifts before you know someone well, it would be regarded as a bribe. When you are on more familiar terms with Singapore businesspeople, bring business-related gifts such as pens, or leather cardholders with the businessman's name inscribed.

Note: For advice regarding business greetings, dress, or table manners, see the appropriate sections earlier in this chapter.

HOLIDAYS AND SPECIAL OCCASIONS

• Expect businesses, banks, and most stores to be closed on the national holidays listed below. Some towns and regions in Malaysia have local festivals when everything closes. Check with the tourist office for dates of such festivals.

Holidays—Malaysia:
New Year's Day (January 1); Taipusam, Hindu commemoration of Lord Subramaniam's birthday (January/February, a public holiday in Penang); Chinese Lunar New Year (January/February); Federal Day (February 1); Prophet Mohammed's Birthday (March); Labor Day (May 1); Wesak Day (May/June); Dayak, celebrating the end of a successful rice harvest (June, public holiday in Sarawak); birthday of King Vang di-Pertuan Agong (June 5); National Day (August 31); *Deepavali* (October/November); Christmas (December 25); Hari Raya Haji, a day special to those who have completed the pilgrimage to Mecca (December). Check with the Tourist Office for dates of the Chinese New Year

and for Muslim holidays, which are variable.

Holidays—Singapore:

New Year's Day (January 1); Chinese Lunar New Year (January/February); Good Friday; Labor Day (May 1); Wesak Day, Buddhist holiday in honor of the birth, enlightenment, and death of Lord Buddha (May); National Day (August 9); Hari Raya Puasa, Muslim celebration of the end of Ramadan (August/September); Hari Raya Haji, a day special to those who have made the pilgrimage to Mecca (September/October); *Deepavali*, the Hindu commemoration of Lord Ram's slaying the mythical tyrant Ravana (November); Christmas (December 25). Check with the Singapore Tourist Office for dates of variable holidays.

• If a holiday falls on a Sunday, offices will be closed on Monday.

• If a Muslim holiday falls on a Friday, it is usually celebrated on Saturday.

Chinese: If presenting a gift for the Chinese New Year, give in pairs. Brandy is a popular gift at this time, but make sure it is accompanied by something else, such as a box of sweets. If invited to tea, bring four mandarin oranges for good luck. Don't visit Chinese on the third day of the New Year, because they believe that quarrels will erupt on that day. Don't wear black when visiting during the New Year; it's considered bad luck.

• If you can't visit friends during the first 15 days of the New Year,

call and wish them *"Kong Hee Fat Choy"*—"Good luck and prosperity."

Malay: During Ramadan (the month during which Muslims fast from sunrise to sunset), don't smoke, drink, or eat in front of Muslims, especially during daylight. Hari Raya signifies the end of Ramadan and lasts for two days. People have open house, offering visitors food and drink. It's a good time for visits.

TRANSPORTATION

Public Transportation

• If an empty taxi passes by and the driver waves his hand back and forth, he's indicating that he's changing shifts and won't stop.

• Be aware that trains running through Singapore, Kuala Lumpur, and Penang have first, second, and third classes. First class has air-conditioning and is generally comfortable. Other classes often don't provide pleasant travel. Except for the periods of ethnic New Year's celebrations, seats are usually available. Even so, it's wise to book a week in advance. It's best to book through travel agents, although you can reserve at railroad stations; English is spoken at ticket counters.

• For overnight trips, sleeping berths are available. In first class, there are compartments for two people and bunks have sheets, blankets, and pillows; in second class, the linen is the same but the bunks are open with curtains for privacy.

Malaysia: Don't look for subways. There are none.

• On buses, pay the conductor, not the driver. Exact change is recommended but not required. Note that there are frequent inspections to make sure that you have paid.

• Some local taxis don't have meters. Agree on a fare before you get in. Ask someone what the approximate fare should be. Most local taxis are air-conditioned.

• Keep in mind that there are two types of taxis—local and "out station" (long distance), whose stands are located near major bus stations. The latter, which connect all major towns and cities, are shared taxis and are found at stands located near major bus stations. As soon as they are full, they depart. For comfort, hire the whole taxi for yourself.

• To be sure that you get a ticket on an intercity train, buy it at the railroad station.

• Remember that all first- and second-class trains have sleeping berths on overnight runs. You can make reservations for both classes.

First class is air-conditioned (and *very* cold). Both classes have videos.

• There are air-conditioned long-distance express buses that run throughout the country with all seating reserved. Less expensive, non-air-conditioned buses are also available. Consider bus travel between cities, since Malaysia's roads are among the best in Southeast Asia. However, buses in East Malaysia are less reliable because certain roads become impassable during the rainy season.

Singapore: The subway service in Singapore is called MRT, Mass Rapid Transit. Trains are air-conditioned. No eating or drinking is allowed on board the subway cars. You'll find information booths at every station. Obtain tickets from a vending machine, which will make change, if necessary.

• Consider using the public bus system's island-wide network, with buses running all week from 5:30 A.M. to midnight. Use prepaid fare cards on both buses and the MRT.

• Remember that during business hours you can get a taxi only at taxi stands, which you'll find at hotels and shopping complexes and along major roads. Don't try to hail one on the street. Around 4:00 P.M., drivers change shifts and will refuse to pick up passengers. Radio taxis can be obtained by telephone.

• Be sure that the taxi driver sets the meter as soon as your ride begins. All taxis are metered, and drivers are required to use the meters.

Driving

Malaysia: Expect no problems in renting a car; both major car-rental agencies have outlets in Malaysia. Driving is safer than in many other Asian countries because the roads are good and the traffic patterns easy to follow. Driving can be difficult, however, because there are many, many motorcycles on the roads.

• If you decide to rent a car, keep in mind that you'll need an International Driver's License.

• Avoid driving in Kuala Lumpur, because street names change often, good maps are difficult to find, and traffic is often very congested.

• Realize that most road signs use internationally accepted icons.

• Be aware that driving is on the left, as in Britain and Japan.

• Be sure that occupants of the front seat are wearing seat belts. There are fines if they don't.

Singapore: Bring an International Driver's License if you plan to rent a car.

• Realize that driving is on the left, as in Britain and Japan.

• Be aware that the central business district is restricted to private vehicles and taxis from 7:30 to 10:15 A.M., Monday through Saturday, except for public holidays. Cars and taxis with four or more people, including the driver, are exempt from this restriction. You can buy a daily license for S$4.00 (for

each day) at booths outside the Central Business District.

• Don't worry about reading street signs—they're in English.

LEGAL MATTERS, SAFETY, AND HEALTH

Malaysia: Women traveling alone should feel very safe in cities on the West Coast, but be wary on the East Coast, which is strictly Muslim and where men tend to yell and jeer at women alone.

• Don't try to bribe police. There is a strong movement to wipe out such activity, and you can be arrested for attempting it.

Singapore: Don't try to bring in any reading material that could be considered pornographic. It will be confiscated by Customs agents.

• Males with long hair should be aware that they may be hassled by authorities and served last because they don't conform to Singapore's national values.

• Never drop litter on the street—even cigarette butts. You can be punished by an on-the-spot fine.

• Remember that jaywalking is

an offense for which you can be fined S$50. You won't be exempt just because you're a tourist. Use only designated crossings.

• Look for "No Smoking" signs in public places, and respect them. If you violate the rule, there can be a fine.

• Be aware that possession of and trafficking in drugs are *very* serious offenses, punishable by death.

• If you have a problem with a hotel or shopkeeper, contact the Singapore Tourist Promotion Board. If you have trouble with a taxi driver, report him to the Registrar of Vehicles or to the taxi company.

• Don't send undeveloped rolls of film through the mail. They may be X-rayed.

Health: Toiletries are generally available, as well as tampons and sanitary napkins.

• Don't eat food purchased from a street vendor. Ice cream is especially dangerous, because the milk may not have been pasteurized.

• Note that it's safe to drink the water in Singapore. In other areas, use bottled water.

KEY PHRASES

English	Malay	Pronunciation
Good morning	Selamat pagi	Say-lah-máht páh-ghee
Good afternoon, evening	Selamat petang	Say-lah-máht pay-táhng
Good night	Selamat malam	Say-lah-máht máh-lahm
Sir, Mr.	Tuan *or* Encik	Twan; Én-chick
Madam, Mrs.	Puan *or* Cik	Pwan; Chick
Miss	Cik *or* Saudari	Chick; Sow-dáh-ree
Good-bye	Selamat tinggal	Say-lah-máht téen-gahl
Thank you	Terima kasi	Táy-ree-mah káh-see
You're welcome	Sama sama	Sah-mah sáh-mah
Yes	Ya	Yah
No	Tidak	Teé-dáhk
I don't understand	Saya tidak faham	Sáy-yah tee-dahk fáh-hahm

| I don't speak Malay | Saya tidak boleh ca-
kap Bahasa
Malaysia | Sáh-yah tée-dahk bó-
leh cháh-kaph
Bah-háh-sah
Mah-láy-see-yah |
| Does anyone speak
English? | Ada siapa yang boleh
cakap Bahasa Ing-
geris? | Aȟ-dah see-yáh-pah
yahng bó-leh cháh-
kahp Bah-háh-sah
Eén-geh-rees? |

Note that there are no Malay terms for "Please" and "Excuse me" unless you use them in a sentence.

NEPAL

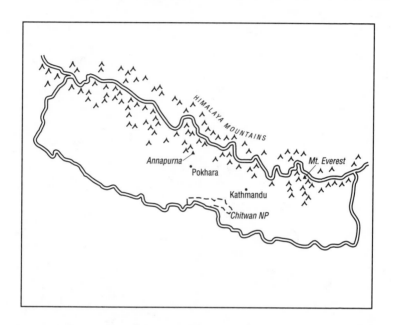

Nepal was all but unknown to the outside world until 1953 when Sir Edmund Hillary and his Sherpa guide, Tenzing Norgay, became the first people to climb Mount Everest and return. Since then, Nepal has been a magnet for mountain climbers and trekkers, with some expeditions ending in triumph and others in tragedy.

One Nepalese Buddhist guide gave a friend advice she considered adopting as a mantra (when the guide saw the friend trying to move swiftly): "Slowly, please, the mountain will wait."

Kathmandu, the country's capital, was founded in 723 A.D. and is in many ways still in the Middle Ages—only two of its hundreds of unpaved streets are named. On the other hand, the city suffers from some of the difficulties found in modern cities—traffic congestion and smog.

Outside Kathmandu and Pokara, expect an adventure. If you visit Chitwan and are near the airport, don't be surprised to hear sirens every 15 minutes. They are set off to clear cows from the fields used for takeoffs and landings.

English	Nepalese	Pronunciation
Elder brother	daai	dye
Elder sister	didi	dee-dee
Younger brother	bhaai	bye
Younger sister	bahini	bah-hee-nee
Father	ba	bah
Mother	ama	ah-ma
Grandfather	baje	bah-jeh
Grandmother	baji	bah-jee

GREETINGS

• When greeting people, press both hands together at chest level and say *"Namaste"* (nah-mahs-táy) or *"Namaskar"* (nah-mahs-káhr). The terms mean, "I salute the god within you." *"Namaskar"* is the appropriate greeting for a person of higher rank. Since this greeting indicates respect and deference, adults usually do not use it with children.

• Note that the higher one's pressed hands are held, the more deference is shown. For a foreigner, chest level should be right.

• Feel free to call people by their first name. To add respect, add *"ji"* (jee)—e.g., John-*ji*.

In a professional setting, add *"ji"* to the last name—e.g., Smith-*ji*.

• Realize that Nepalese refer to each other in family terms even if they aren't related. For example, friends of the same age group may be referred to as brother or sister. Older people will be referred to as mother or father. You may be referred to by one of the family terms, and Nepalese will be pleased if you use the terms, but it isn't necessary to use these forms of address.

• Be aware that handshaking is not common, although the custom is growing more prevalent among men in Kathmandu.

• Never try to shake hands with a woman in a Nepal village.

• If you are an honored guest, don't be surprised if a light, white ceremonial scarf (called a *kata*) is draped around your neck. Leave it on for the duration of your visit.

CONVERSATION

• Realize that more than seventy different languages are spoken in Nepal. Nepali is the national language and is understood almost everywhere. Many people speak English in Kathmandu, but not in other areas.

• Don't share prolonged eye contact with anyone during a conversation.

• As a Westerner, be prepared for *hundreds* of questions about your country and living situation. (One traveler was asked how many helicopters her family had.)

• Bring pictures of your family. Nepalese enjoy talking about their families and will be interested in yours.

• Don't be surprised to be asked very personal questions, even at a first meeting (e.g., about your family—how many children, siblings, what you and they do—where you're from, how old you are, if you're married—and if not, why not). Feel free to ask the same questions of Nepalese, especially about their families.

• Never discuss religion. Proselytizing in any way is illegal.

• Other topics to avoid: anything sexual (not even in joking) and anything negative about Nepal's king and queen.

• Expect Nepalese to offer compliments and to be pleased by receiving them. They are, however, very frank in stating negative opinions—e.g., saying that they don't like your sweater or your hair.

• Try not to be taken aback if a complete stranger asks you to take them back to the U.S. with you. A blunt refusal may be necessary. Simply say, "I can't."

• Men should not be surprised if a Nepalese takes his hand while conversing, as Nepalese men often do.

TELEPHONES

• Don't look for public phones. There aren't any.

• Feel free to ask shopkeepers for the use of their phones. The cost is usually 5 *rupees* for a local call. Pay that sum to the shopkeeper. You can also make international calls from shops. The call will be timed. Pay the shopkeeper on completion of the call.

• Ask at guest houses for the use of a phone to make local calls. The owner will charge a few *rupees* to cover the cost of the call. You need not be staying at the guest house in order to use the telephone.

• If you wish to make calls directly from one of the better hotels, keep in mind that there is a large surcharge.

• Look for telephone offices with the letters ISD/STD/IDD in major towns. Use them for local or long-distance calls. Pay for the call in advance and tell the attendant the phone number. He will direct you to a private booth from which you make the call. If you talked longer than the sum you paid allowed, pay the extra when you have finished. If you talked less time than the sum covered, you will receive a refund.

• Be aware that there are private telecommunications centers in Kathmandu and other tourist areas. These offices offer international direct dialing, fax service, E-mail, and "call back" services. The last allows you to call someone abroad and have them call you back immediately. You'll save money, since calling abroad *from* Nepal is very expensive. Most of these offices accept credit cards.

• Realize that the quality of the telephone system is mediocre. On a long-distance call, there may be such a long pause before your party speaks that you'll think you haven't been connected. Wait. Local service is better, but a storm may cause static or prevent calls from going through.

• When you answer a call, expect the Nepalese person to ask immediately, "Who is speaking?"

• Consider having faxes sent to you at the Kathmandu post office.

• Remember that the emergency number for police is 100 and for an ambulance 102.

IN PUBLIC

• To beckon someone, hold your arm at your side and slightly raised with palm facing you and fingers pointing away from you. Move your fingers toward you in a scratching motion.

• Don't wink, especially at someone of the opposite sex, because it is considered vulgar.

• Expect Nepalese to point with their mouth, by puckering their lips and pointing them in the direction they wish to indicate.

• If you see a Nepalese shake her/his head from side to side, be aware that he/she is indicating affirmation. Don't interpret the gesture as "No." A waiter might use this gesture to mean, "Go on. I'm listening."

• Never step over another person's feet.

• Don't show the bottoms of your feet to anyone.

• Don't point the soles of your feet at anyone—especially a monk or a lama.

• If a Nepalese points to the nose, realize the gesture means "I."

• Do not touch the head of anyone older than you.

- If you see Nepalese dressed in white, do not touch them. They are in mourning.
- Always walk clockwise around *stupas*, Buddhist monuments that are hemispherical mounds topped by conical spires.
- Always remove your shoes before entering a temple.
- Realize that some Hindu temples are exclusive to Nepalese. If someone indicates that you shouldn't enter a certain religious building, don't persist.
- Don't be surprised to see men holding hands and sitting on one another's laps. Such behavior is a normal sign of friendship with no sexual significance.
- Remember that men and women should never demonstrate affection in public. Nepalese husbands and wives don't even walk together.
- Always give or receive objects with both hands.
- Use your right hand whenever possible, since the left hand is used in toilet rooms (called *charpi*).
- Be aware that Nepalese do not usually say "Thank you" to people who are paid for services—e.g., an employee or waiter. "Thank you" is reserved for a person of high rank or for someone who has done something special.
- Never criticize anyone or show anger in public. If you must offer criticism, be sure to do so in private.
- In Kathmandu, be prepared for noise, noise, noise—music coming from windows, taxis, and markets.

- Don't give to children who are begging. You would be encouraging children to leave school to panhandle.
- Expect to see men and women wearing a dot in the middle of their foreheads. Called a *tika*, it's considered a symbol of blessings from the gods. Traditionally, only married women wore *tikas*, but in recent years they have become fashionable, so many people are wearing *tikas* in various colors and shapes.
- Don't be surprised to see topless women bathing at public taps. This action is acceptable for married women who have children with them. However, showing the leg is considered lewd.
- If you see sexually explicit murals on temple walls, do not point or laugh.
- If you're allowed to meet a lama (a Tibetan Buddhist priest who serves as a spiritual guide, orally passing on complex meditations and rituals to disciples) at a Buddhist monastery, give him a *kata*, a white ceremonial scarf, which you'll be able to purchase near the temple.
- Always ask permission before photographing a person, because some people fear that if their photo is taken, their soul will be stolen.
- Never take photos in a temple without asking permission first.
- Never photograph masked festival dancers. They are believed to be the gods whom they represent.
- If you are present when an animal, such as a goat, is sacrificed at a festival and the blood spurts over

people, don't show disgust. If you can sidestep gracefully, do so.

• Be aware that bargaining is very common, especially if you're making a purchase from a street vendor. Bargaining is also common in food shops but not in larger shops.

• If you plan to make a large purchase, be sure to compare quality and price before finally buying the item.

• Remember that the best time to bargain is early in the morning. Shopkeepers are anxious to make the first sale of the day and will be willing to accept a lower price.

• To indicate "No" to a seller, hold one hand in front of you, elbow pointing down, and swivel your wrist.

• Recall that not all areas have public toilets or any toilets at all. You'll find most toilets to be the squat type—i.e., holes in the ground.

• Look for toilets in restaurants and the more expensive hotels in Kathmandu and Pokhara. However, outside of cities, people simply use the outside. Women traveling by bus or car should wear long, full skirts for coverage if they need to use the field.

• Bring toilet paper, because it's not always available. Nepalese use water to wash after using the toilet.

DRESS

• Dress conservatively. Never wear torn or dirty clothing.

• Note that Nepalese appreciate foreigners wearing native dress and will respond enthusiastically if you do. The national dress for men is a long cotton shirt and drawstring pants, although many men in larger cities have adopted Western dress. Women wear traditional saris.

• Women should keep their legs covered in pants or long skirts. Shoulders should be covered. If not, a woman could receive unwanted sexual attention.

• Never wear anything made of leather when visiting a Hindu temple.

• Men should not wear shorts or tank tops (only young boys wear shorts). They should never appear without a shirt.

MEALS

Hours and Foods

Breakfast: Eaten in two parts. At about 6:30 or when the sky turns light, the meal usually consists of sweet milk tea and fried dough, and sometimes eggs. Then at 9:00 A.M. there is a large meal of rice, lentils, and curried vegetables, called *dahl baht.*

Snack: Around 2:00 P.M., Nepalese eat a small snack of bread or noodles or popcorn, and tea.

Dinner: Sometime between 6:00 and 8:00 P.M. The food will be rice (*bhat*), lentils (*dahl*), and vegetable curries (*tarkaari*), which may be accompanied by a pungent pickle (*achaar*). The pickle may be made of tomatoes, coriander, garlic, lemon, and onion. In higher elevations there is no rice, so the meal will center on potatoes and barley.

• Note that the national dish is *dahl bhat*, rice and lentils.

• Realize that Nepalese do not eat beef, because cows are sacred. They eat water buffalo, goat, chicken, and pork instead, but those foods are very expensive. Hence, most Nep-

alese are restricted to vegetarian diets. If people eat meat, it's usually on Saturday, and the meat is goat.

• Be aware that chilies, onions, and garlic are used for flavoring. The food will be spicy, and the relishes and pickles offered will be even more so.

• Don't expect dessert on any but a special occasion.

• Assume that a wide variety of beverages will be available: Coca-Cola, Sprite, Fanta, bottled mango juice (*frooti*), and soy milk in bags. There is no local wine. There are several brands of beer, both imported and domestic. *Chang* is a home-brewed beer (brewed from rice or other grains), but it tastes like hard cider. *Tongba*, a local beer, tastes something like sake.

• Know that coffee is always instant.

• Remember that the national beverage is tea (*chiya*), brewed with milk and a great deal of sugar. You can request milk tea, lemon tea, or black tea.

Table Manners

• Don't expect a Nepalese to invite you to dinner. It is not usual for them to have others to their home for a meal, since people eat with their families.

• Should you receive an invitation, feel free to be a little late.

• Wait to be told where to sit. Your host's caste will determine the seating arrangements. There are also gender issues in seating. Sometimes the seat nearest the fire is reserved for an honored guest or for the head of the family.

• If you are invited to a home, expect to be served by the woman of the house. However, she will eat after the guests and the men of the family. Men and women do not usually eat together. Young children and men (and guests, if there should be any) eat first.

• As a guest, don't be surprised to be served chicken, goat, or yak, none of which is typical family fare. (Most Nepalese are Hindus, but they are not vegetarians by conviction. The role is sometimes forced on them by the cost of food.)

• Even though some Nepalese will find it strange, be sure to bring your own bottled water with you to homes and restaurants for health reasons. Nepalese drink water with meals.

• Wait to be served. Touching cooked food would contaminate it for the others in the group.

• Don't serve yourself. If you want more of any dish, ask for it politely.

• Don't share food from your plate or touch anyone else's food or drink. Be very careful that your fingers don't touch the food on a plate you may be passing to someone else.

• Always eat with your right hand. (The left hand is used for cleaning after using the toilet.)

• Note that food is sometimes served on a metal plate (a *thaali*), which is divided into compart-ments. If the *dahl* (lentils) are in a separate bowl, pour them over the rice, add some vegetable curry and pickle, and squeeze it all together. Then put it into your mouth with your right hand. (It's messy, but everyone will wash up after the meal.)

• Try to finish everything on your plate, since Nepalese do not waste anything.

• When you finish a meal, pour water from a pot on the table over your hand and onto the empty dish.

• Don't expect Nepalese to linger after a meal. They leave to make room for the next group in the family to eat (older children and women).

• If you are out hiking and take a sip from another person's canteen, don't put your lips to it, because once you've touched something to your mouth, you've polluted it for everyone else.

Places to Eat

• Realize that Nepalese rarely go to restaurants for their main meal. Primarily for tourists, restaurants adhere to Western customs.

• Expect to find a wide range of foods available in restaurants in tourist areas—Italian, Chinese, German, etc. Don't expect the food to be authentic, because it's too difficult and expensive for Nepalese to obtain authentic ingredients. Because of these difficulties, stick to eating Indian food, which is usually prepared well, even in the cheapest restaurants.

• Seek out a teahouse for tea and basic snacks.

• Note that taverns of the Kathmandu Valley serve alcoholic beverages and basic Nepalese meals.

• Don't look for either a rating system or for menus posted in windows or on doors of restaurants. Most places serve most types of Western food, except beef, which is forbidden. You won't receive a menu, but the food is often on display, and you can point to what you want.

• Be aware that Tibetan food is commonly offered. *Thukpa* is Tibetan vegetable noodle soup; *momos* (steamed) and *kothe* (fried) are meat or vegetable-stuffed dumplings.

• If you want some of the freshly squeezed fruit juices available at some tourist restaurants, be sure to ask if water has been added (and pass on them if it has). Canned fruit juices and juices in cartons are available in most places. Drink them if you're sure that no water has been added. Most places offer soft drinks such as Coca-Cola and 7-Up.

• When you see "hot lemon" listed under tea, know that it just means lemon and water. If the water has been boiled, it's okay to drink it.

• Don't forget that there is a certain etiquette regarding tea drinking: one person pays for the tea for a friend one day, and the friend pays the next day.

• In sweet shops, expect to find milk and lentil-based desserts, similar to Indian sweets. At some restaurants, a yogurt desert with spices (*sikarni*) is available.

• Don't touch any food in a food stall until you've bought it.

Specialties

• Keep in mind that Nepalese food is very basic. However, in addition to the lentil soup, white rice, and curried vegetables that many people eat every day for every meal, in restaurants you may be offered small dishes of *maasu* (meat marinated in spices and yogurt and then fried in oil or clarified butter [*ghee*]).

• In Tari towns expect to find *roti* (a flatbread) instead of rice.

• In eastern hill areas, try *sokuti* (dried, spiced meat fried in oil).

• For special soups, drink *tama surwa* (made with bamboo shoots) or *thukpa* (a soup made with meat, vegetables, and pasta).

• For main courses, order *sekuwa* (kebabs of marinated spicy meat) or *taareko maachhaa* (fried fish found in the Tari). Another common dish is *dahi chiura* (curd—i.e., yogurt—with beaten rice).

• For dessert, consider ordering *khir* (a sweet rice pudding).

• At a restaurant specializing in Indian food, order *mughlai* (curries) or *tandoori* (meats baked in a clay oven) and various types of flatbread.

HOTELS

• Feel free to try bargaining for the rate at a hotel. Autumn is the heaviest tourist season, so you'll have less leverage then.

• Keep in mind that luxury hotels, offering air-conditioning, heating, pools, restaurants, and business services, are confined to Kathmandu. However, the most expensive hotels are located inside the Tarai wildlife parks.

• If you'll be on a trekking trail, expect to stay in private homes which people open as "teahouses" for extra money.

• Be aware that guesthouses vary in quality, from the primitive to well-maintained small hotels. Most allow you to choose a private bath or shared bath. Expect to pay double for a private bath.

• At simple guesthouses, expect hot running water, which may be turned off at certain times (in some places electricity and hot water are available only from 6:00 to 9:00 P.M.), flush toilets, foam mattresses, clean sheets, and quilts. Although these houses aren't heated and may

be *very* cold in winter, there will be a telephone.

• Note that hot water is not available in village lodges.

• Consider staying at a more upscale guesthouse. It may have a lobby, carpeted rooms, furniture in addition to the basic bed and bureau, sometimes a fan and a telephone. Daily housekeeping service is available. In the winter, portable electric heaters are provided. However, be prepared to find the power and the hot water cut off at times.

TIPPING

• Note that tips are not usually expected, but as Nepalese become more acquainted with Western ways, the custom is becoming more common. Try to set a price beforehand with a porter or taxi driver. If you're satisfied with the service, add a few extra *rupees*.

• Be aware that tipping is expected only in tourist hotels and restaurants.

• Give airport porters *Rs* 20 to *Rs* 25.

• At more expensive hotels, leave the staff *Rs* 5–*Rs* 10 per day.

• Tip waiters—only at restaurants in luxury hotels—10 percent.

• Realize that taxi drivers don't expect tips, but if you wish, give 10 percent.

• Tip trekking staff 10–15 percent at the end of the trip, or better yet, give a practical gift, such as a pair of sturdy shoes.

PRIVATE HOMES

• If you are invited to visit at a specific time, arrive 30 minutes to an hour late.

• Feel free to drop in on a friend, but it's better to arrange a visit in advance via telephone or in person. You can visit any time from early in the morning to before darkness.

• Expect to be offered tea and snacks when you visit.

• Remove your shoes at the entrance to a home and leave them at the doorway.

• Be aware that men usually socialize with men and women with women. As a foreigner, you may join whichever group you wish.

• Never go into a kitchen unless you are invited to do so.

• If you have to make a phone call from a Nepalese's home, offer to pay, since there are charges for local calls.

• If you stay overnight at a friend's house, don't expect to have privacy or time alone. Family members may come in and out of your room without knocking.

• Never throw any garbage into a household cooking fire. Many people consider the flame sacred.

• If you are staying with a family for an extended period of time, help with yard work or light housework. Don't help in the kitchen, because Nepalese are very concerned about who cooks their food. If you're staying for just a few days, don't feel the need to help with chores.

• Feel free to make independent plans, but people may think it odd if you are out much at night. (Families in Nepal are usually home by dark.)

• Don't feel obliged to bring a gift if you are invited to a meal. People are not usually invited to dinner, since the meal is a quick family meal followed by bed. If you are invited to a meal, it will probably be to lunch.

Gifts: Note that people appreciate electronic goods, cosmetics, and clothing from the U.S. For children, bring coloring books, toys, pens, small calculators, or hair clips.

MONEY AND BUSINESS

Hours

Banks: Sunday through Thursday 10:00 A.M. to 2:30 P.M. (winter) and 10:00 A.M. to 3:00 P.M. (rest of year), and Friday 10:00 A.M. to 1:00 P.M.

Businesses and Government Offices: Sunday through Thursday, 10:00 A.M. to 4:00 P.M. (winter) and 10:00 A.M. to 5:00 P.M. (rest of year), and Friday 10:00 A.M. to 3:00 P.M.

Shops: 10:00 A.M. to 7:00 P.M. (Tourist shops may stay open later.) Hours vary, since shops open only when the proprietor arrives.

• Note that many shops and businesses close for an hour at lunch, but government offices don't usually close for lunch.

Money

• The unit of currency is the *rupee*, made up of 100 *paisa*.

• Coins: 25 and 50 *paisa* and 1, 2, 5, and 10 *rupees*. (Smaller aluminum coins are used to give alms to the poor.)

• Notes: *Rs* 1, 2, 5, 10, 20, 50, 100, 500, and 1,000.

• Be sure to handle all money with your right hand. Using your left hand is rude.

• Realize that luxury hotels and some guesthouses accept major credit cards. Many shops accept them but charge 5 percent to cover the commission.

• Be aware that getting change is difficult in non-tourist areas.

• Don't be surprised if shopkeepers refuse to accept old bills, even though they are still valid.

• Keep all receipts when you exchange money, because you'll need them to change back to your own currency when you leave the country.

• Remember that to avoid confusion between Indian and Nepalese currency, Indian *rupees* are referred to as IC and Nepalese as NC.

Business Practices

• Don't forget that most large companies in the public sector are subsidized by the government. Connections are very important.

• Get in touch with the Foreign Investment Promotion Division (FIPD), a section of the Ministry of Industry. It provides foreigners with information on investment opportunities and assists them in identifying local partners. Knowing the "right" people will definitely be of help.

• Realize that outside the Kathmandu Valley, English is not widely spoken. Even if doing business in Kathmandu, have written materials translated to make sure that the documents will be understood.

• Before making a hotel reservation, check to see if such services as fax, Telex, and computers or computer hookups are available. You may find such options in hotels in Kathmandu. Many shops throughout the city have photocopying machines, but the quality varies, so run off a few sample copies before you agree to have a large job done.

• Avoid scheduling trips during mid-April, when the Nepalese New Year begins.

• Try to schedule appointments with the most senior person in an organization. To make an appointment with a high-level official, make arrangements about a week in advance. For an appointment with an official of lower rank, a day or two would probably suffice.

• If possible, schedule appointments between 11:00 A.M. and 1:00 P.M., when the tea break begins.

• Arrive on time for appointments, but be prepared for the meeting to be delayed or canceled.

• Expect to be escorted by a secretary or other office employee to the place for your appointment. Shake hands, or say "Namaste" to that person.

• Don't expect your first meeting to address business issues. Building relationships is vital to doing business in Nepal.

• Anticipate casual conversation at the beginning of meetings. People will discuss such topics as your travels and your positive impressions about the country. Bone up on the culture of Nepal before going there.

• In order not to appear rude, eat the refreshments offered.

• Don't be overly casual with high-level officials. They will only respond to a high degree of formality. Always call such officials "Mr.," "Mrs.," or "Miss" with the last name.

• Expect a great deal of bureaucracy. Be sure to monitor developments in your project closely. If a specific government officer is not available to stamp a document, no one else will have the authority to do it. People also don't want to be held accountable for mistakes. The absence of the right official may cause a delay.

• Realize that there is little or no incentive for many business/government workers to be diligent or on time. Corruption and bribery are a way of life in business.

• Be prepared for accomplishing your objective to take at least three times longer than it would in most Western countries. Adjust your expectations and deadlines accordingly.

• Ask indirect questions, because Nepalese try to avoid saying "No." Don't, for example, ask, "Can you deliver five hundred widgets by January 20?" Ask, "When can you deliver five hundred widgets?" (Even if people do fix a date, the deadline may not be met. Punctuality is not a concept Nepalese easily grasp.)

• Remember that some Nepalese are very fatalistic and believe that if a transaction is meant to be, it will occur. If you ask, "When?" the response may be "Tomorrow or the day after tomorrow."

• Resist any desire to discuss the country's lack of development. People are sensitive to foreigners coming to the country and saying that they can do things better than Nepalese.

• Do not think that a long silence signals boredom. Nepalese are simply ruminating. They are not as uncomfortable with long silences as many Westerners.

• Should your business take an unexpected turn, requiring you to meet a new person, without time to schedule an appointment beforehand, be sure to get a letter of introduction on company letterhead from someone known to the person with whom you're unfamiliar. The letter should explain the reasons you're requesting a meeting and what your needs are. Office personnel will generally bring the letter to the appropriate person, and you will be directed to the place of meeting.

• Don't be surprised if people drop by at your hotel without notice to discuss business or just to socialize. Nepalese don't separate home/ social life and business as many people in the West do.

• Don't expect to see many Nepalese businesswomen. However, foreign businesswomen should have no problems doing business in the country. It's especially important for women to make appointments in advance. Remember that it is inappropriate for men to shake hands with women, even in a business situation.

• If a man is visiting a Nepalese businesswoman, he should keep eye contact to a minimum.

• Anticipate an invitation to a business dinner rather than a business lunch.

• At a formal event, the guest of honor may be adorned with a garland of flowers, called a *mala*. (This gesture may be made at any formal event—e.g., a wedding.)

Gifts: Don't expect to exchange gifts at an early meeting, but feel free to give sample products.

• Don't give business gifts (especially money) in front of a group, because you would appear to be offering a bribe. However, if you give gifts in private, people will accept them readily, and your business goals may be accomplished sooner than they would otherwise.

HOLIDAYS AND SPECIAL OCCASIONS

• Expect everything to be closed on the holidays listed below. Several holidays go by the Gregorian calendar, but religious holidays and New Year's Day are determined by the lunar calendar. Since there are frequent religious festivals, ask in advance if the time you plan to visit Nepal coincides with one of them or if there will be a festival in the area you're visiting.

Holidays: National Unity Day (January 11); Martyrs' Memorial Day (January 30); National Democracy Day (February 19); New Year's Day (mid-April); *Dasain* (September/October); Constitution Day (November 9); King's birthday (December 28).

• Be aware that the most important holiday of the year, *Dasain*, occurs some time in September and October, changing according to the lunar calendar. Lasting eleven days, the holiday celebrates the triumph of good over evil. It includes the sacrifices of animals, such as goats or fowl. Blood is dripped over vehicles to insure the protection of the god-

dess Durga for the coming year. On the tenth day of *Dasain*, Nepalese wear new clothes and visit friends and relatives to exchange greetings.

TRANSPORTATION

Public Transportation

• Look for bicycle rickshaws and auto-rickshaws, which you rent as you would a taxi. The bicycle-drawn taxis are slow and are good for short distances on narrow, winding streets.

• Keep in mind that there are also three-wheeled scooters, called *tempos*. One type has room for two passengers or one person with luggage. The other, which seats six people, has a fixed route and goes only when full.

• In Kathmandu, find taxis at major hotels and around tourist sites. In Pokhara, you'll find taxis at the bus station, in the Lakeside neighborhood, and at the airport when planes are arriving.

• Remember that metered taxis have black license plates. Private cars, which go on long-distance routes, have red license plates.

• If you take a taxi late at night, expect to pay double the meter price, especially if your destination is outside the city.

• On intracity buses, give your money to the fare collector. You don't need exact change, but have some small bills handy.

• If smoking bothers you, avoid buses. It's permitted, and many people smoke.

• Note that the most common—and least expensive—means of getting around the country is via uncomfortable buses, which are *very* overcrowded.

• Go to a bus terminal (sometimes referred to as a "bus park") for intercity buses. Buy a ticket either in advance or just before departure. Remember that tickets have no value if you miss your scheduled bus.

• When traveling a long distance by bus, expect rest stops. Sometimes you'll find a bathroom; other times the "facility" is just a field.

• If you take a long-distance bus trip, be sure to bring your own food and water. Roadside teahouses are usually not very clean.

• When traveling by bus, don't leave anything of value in your luggage, because it will be tied onto the roof.

• If you'll be traveling between Kathmandu and Pokhara, consider taking a deluxe tourist coach. It will be only slightly more expensive than a regular bus. Book a seat in advance at a hotel or tourist agency in either city. These coaches have more leg room, wider seats, and they travel faster than regular buses.

• Note that small airplanes go to a few areas in the country. However, during monsoon season, more flights are canceled than fly.

Driving

• Obtain car rental information at the airport terminal, a travel agency, or your hotel. You can rent a car with or without a driver. If you choose to drive yourself, you will need an International Driver's License. Unless you have some overpowering reason to drive, hire a car and driver.

• Keep in mind that driving is on the left (as in Britain and Japan).

• Be aware that seat belts are not required, and there are no special seating regulations for children.

• Anticipate few street signs. The ones that exist aren't always in English. Ask pedestrians or taxi drivers for directions. Police can be of help, but they aren't always easy to find on the street.

• Except in crowded areas, don't expect to see speed limit signs.

• Everywhere in Nepal, be prepared for the hazard of animals (e.g., cows and dogs) walking in the street, many careless drivers, and *constant* hornblowing.

• Realize there are no penalties for drunken driving, but if you have an accident, you may end up paying large penalties.

• If you are involved in a traffic accident, prepare to be arrested, whether or not the accident was your fault. Police arrest all parties in an accident and then determine who was at fault.

• If you park in the wrong place, expect your car to be towed. Go to the main traffic headquarters and pay a fine to get it back.

• Whether in a rented car or motorcycle, be *very* careful not to hit a cow, because they are scared. People convicted of injuring or killing a cow may have to serve a jail sentence.

LEGAL MATTERS, SAFETY, AND HEALTH

• Remember that only tourists can gamble at the casinos in five-star hotels.

• Recall that there is no age limit for drinking.

• Be sure to insure guides and porters whom you hire against accidental death. You'll find insurance companies in Kathmandu.

• Stay away from drugs, which are sometimes sold on the street.

Sometimes sales are traps; if you fall into them, you could land in jail.

• When you buy a replica of an antique, always request a certificate of *inauthenticity*. Unless Customs knows that you're not trying to take out a *real* antique, you will not be able to take the item out of the country.

• Be aware that pickpocketing is common in Nepal, but violent crime is rare. To protect yourself, carry your money in a money belt.

• Be cautious about walking around at night. You should be okay until 7:00 or 8:00 P.M. if the street is busy, but walking in the dark is somewhat difficult and dangerous. Women should not walk alone at night.

• Bring a flashlight, since power outages are frequent in the Kathmandu Valley.

• Don't wander through the Royal Chitwan National Parks without a guide, since the rhinos there are dangerous.

• Keep in mind that there is a great deal of pollution. More and more people are wearing masks on days when the pollution level is especially high.

• Don't eat raw fruits or vegetables that can't be peeled.

• *Never* drink the water or have a drink with ice in it.

• Don't drink milk, because it may not be pasteurized.

• Women traveling alone should be extra cautious. Don't trust even the most helpful strangers. (One woman was approached on several occasions by single young men who appeared very friendly. Soon after making her acquaintance, they began asking offensive sexual questions.)

• If a man makes an inappropriate advance, make a public scene. This is the tactic Nepalese women use, and the men stop.

• If a woman doesn't have a reserved seat on a bus, she should go to the front of the bus, where women and children receive preference.

• Bring all prescription medications with you. Nepalese pharmacies have a small range of Western drugs—for example, aspirin and cough syrup. Many drugs are available without a prescription. If you buy any, be sure to check the expiration date. Bring your own supply of birth control pills, tampons, toiletries, and cosmetics.

KEY PHRASES

English	Nepali	Pronunciation
Good morning	Shuva Bihan	Shée-vah bee-háhn
Good afternoon	Shuva Din	Shée-vah deen
Good evening	Shuva Ratri	Shée-vah ráh-tree
Sir, Mr.	Mahoday	Mah-háh-day
Mrs., Ms.	Mahodaya	Mah-hah-dáh-yah
Yes	Ho	Ho
No	Hoena	Hóinah
Please and Excuse me	Kripaya	Kree-páh-yah
Thank you	Dhanyabad	Dañn-yah-bahd (only used for something special)
I don't understand	Maile Bujhina	Mahy-láy boo-jée-nah
I don't speak Nepali	Ma Nepali Boldina	Mah neh-páh-lee bol-dée-nah
Does anyone speak English?	Tapaiharu Kohi English Bolnu Huncha	Tah-pie-háh-roo kó-hee english bol-nóo hóon-jah?

PAKISTAN

Pakistan, "The Land of the Pure," was conceived as a separate Muslim state in the vision of the poet Sir Muhammad Iqbal in 1930; it was born in a partition with India in 1947. The country represents a bridge between the worlds of deserts and sheikhs in the Gulf states on one side and the Asia of China and India on the other. It depends on one of the world's largest irrigation systems to raise its crops. In the north three great mountain ranges—best known are the Himalayas—come together, offering some of the world's most spectacular scenery.

Ironically, this most Muslim of countries has twice elected a woman (Benazir Bhutto) prime minister.

by middle- or upper-class people, expect to be introduced by your host to each of the other guests. Acknowledge each person individually and shake hands.

• Never use first names until Pakistanis have invited you to.

GREETINGS

• Remember that men shake hands with men when introduced, and, among the middle class, men and women shake hands. Women and women, however, don't usually shake hands. To be safe, wait until the Pakistani extends a hand, especially if you are a woman.

• Note that, among good friends, men embrace when they haven't seen each other for a long time. Women hug and kiss each other when they meet. But men and women don't show affection to each other in public.

• Realize that Pakistani names are very complicated. Sometimes titles and indications of caste that are really not part of the person's name are attached (e.g., *"khan"* at the end of a name is a title). Use "Mr.," "Mrs.," or "Miss" and the family name, or use the person's academic or job title with the family name. If you don't know a man's name, say *"sahib"* (meaning "sir"); to a woman, say *"begum."* It's also appropriate to ask people how they wish to be addressed.

• If you're entertained at a party

CONVERSATION

• Expect people to ask very personal questions about your family, job, and salary soon after they meet you. If you don't want to discuss such personal items, note that Pakistanis are interested in such topics as handcrafts, folklore, their country, or sightseeing in the city you're visiting.

• Avoid discussing local politics, Pakistan's relations with its neighbors, India, religion, Israel, and Jews. Never discuss sex or joke about it. The subject is taboo, since Pakistan is a Muslim country.

• Never ask a man about his wife.

• Women traveling by themselves should expect to be asked, "Why aren't you married?" and "Why are you alone?" To sidestep such questions, some foreign women "invent" husbands whom they are going to meet later.

TELEPHONES

• Be aware that there are no pay phones. Go to a shop and ask if you can use the phone to make a local call.

• To make a long distance call, seek out a Public Call Office (PCO). The offices stay open long hours and offer both instant international dialing and fax services (in the larger offices). In larger towns, these offices stay open 24 hours.

• If you wish to make a long distance/international call from your hotel, ask about the cost before making the call. Such costs are usually very high.

IN PUBLIC

• Never call Muslims Mohammedans; they believe it makes them sound like followers of a cult figure.

• Be aware that Pakistanis who are religious Muslims stop for prayer five times a day. Be sure to give them privacy while they are at prayer.

• Note that Pakistanis are very protective toward women, even though not many are in *purdah* (seen only by husbands and immediate family members). Expect social occasions to be segregated and women at them to dress very modestly.

• Should you have a dog with you, restrain it and don't let it touch people. Many people consider dogs unclean.

• In banks and post offices, women must be aggressive or men will be waited on first.

• Women should not go out alone at night. When going to the bazaar, women should go in a group or accompanied by a man. If the bazaar is crowded, don't be surprised if men try to rub against you.

• Women should not visit a

mosque during Friday prayers. It's considered in poor taste.

• Women should be careful never to wink.

• If you need to ask directions, avoid asking questions that invite a "Yes" or "No" answer. (For example, don't say "Is the museum that way?" Say "Which way is the museum?) People may not know the answer, but they will feel obliged to appear helpful. Ask several people your question in order to confirm the answer.

• Realize that moving the head slightly from side to side indicates "Yes." A slight backward flick of the head, sometimes accompanied by a "Tsk" or "Tut" means "No." Another gesture meaning "No" is a slight raising of the eyebrows.

• If someone twists the wrist with the fingers outspread, the gesture signals a generalized question, such as "What's going on?"

• Never interrupt or step in front of someone who is praying.

• Be aware that the "thumb's up" sign is obscene.

• Never make a gesture with a closed fist. It's obscene.

• Don't photograph military installations, frontier posts, railway bridges or junctions, and airports.

• Before photographing anyone, ask permission. Most men will quickly agree, but women are often shy. Don't force the issue, because there are social and religious taboos.

• Be aware that men should not photograph women, but women photographers should have no problems.

• Don't give pens or candy to children who have not performed a service for you. You would be encouraging begging.

• Expect to find public bathrooms only in railway stations, airports, hotels, and restaurants. Try to use those in better hotels and restaurants, where you will probably find Western-style toilets. The doors are clearly marked in English for men and women.

Shopping: Bargain everywhere, since there are no fixed prices, except in supermarkets. If you are shopping for jewelry, try to take a Pakistani friend with you to get the best buy. If you are a Westerner by yourself, jewelry merchants may not bargain.

Exercise: Women should not jog outside hotel grounds. Men will be looked on as a curiosity, but they can jog in parks and can dress in shorts.

DRESS

• For business meetings men should wear a suit and tie from November through March. During the rest of the year, a white shirt, tie, and pants are acceptable for business meetings—except when dealing with government officials, in which case a suit coat should be worn.

• Women should wear a long loose top outside a loose skirt that comes below the calves. Although a *kameez* and *salwar* are appropriate dress for women tourists, they should not be worn to business meetings.

• Women should be sure to keep their (upper) arms covered and should *never* wear shorts. To minimize any problems with men, women should dress modestly. Pakistan is a very segregated society, and men aren't used to seeing women traveling alone.

• To avoid hassles, the best outfit for women tourists is loose pants and a long shirt worn outside the pants, or the local dress: a long blouse, called a *kameez* over pants, called *salwar*. They can be bought ready-made in the bazaar or made up quickly by a tailor. (Pakistanis are very pleased if foreign women wear this native costume.)

• Neither women nor men should wear shorts on the street, and women should not wear jeans.

• If invited to a meal in a home, men should wear trousers and a shirt and women should wear a dress with short sleeves (never a sleeveless dress, and never a low-cut top).

• Be careful in paying compliments about someone's jewelry, for example. If you praise something lavishly, the party who owns it will feel obliged to give it to you. (This advice also applies to praising objects in homes.) Don't wear expensive jewelry. If someone admires it, you would be obligated to give it to her/him.

• Remove your shoes before entering a mosque. Women should wear a long-sleeved top with a long skirt or pants. Men should also wear a long-sleeved shirt. With tight jeans, wear your shirt outside, not tucked in.

• Take warm socks with you to visit holy places, because you must take off your shoes, and slippers are not available at the gate.

• For a formal occasion, Western men should wear a dark suit and women should wear a street-length skirt or dress. Tuxedoes aren't worn.

• Be sure to bring waterproof clothing if you will be in Pakistan during the monsoon season (July through September).

MEALS

Hours and Foods

Breakfast: 7:30 to 8:00 A.M. Usual fare is eggs, fried or in omelettes, bread, fruit, milk, and tea.

Lunch: 1:00 to 1:30 P.M. A typical meal is chicken curry and vegetable curry with rice, bread, fruit, and tea. Note that many people go home for lunch and then return to work.

Afternoon Tea: 4:00 P.M. Tea with milk and sugar on the side or *chai*, tea boiled with milk and sugar will be served. Lemon wedges are not traditional, but it's acceptable to ask for them. The tea will be accompanied by fruit salad spiced with coriander, black and red pepper, and lemon juice; *samosas* (triangles of dough filled with meat and vegetables or spiced potatoes and deep fried); *cholas* (chickpeas cooked with lemon juice and green chilies and other spices); and *pakoras* (batter-dipped, shredded vegetables).

Dinner: 8:30 P.M. Appetizers probably won't be served; if they

are, the usual ones are kebabs (skewered meats) or *samosas*. These two items might appear as part of the main meal. Dinner often features fish, chicken, or beef, with curries; *roti* (much like Syrian bread); rice; fruit; and tea. Typical dishes might be *pulao* (rice and meat cooked with spices), *karahi gosht* (meat fried with hot spices, tomatoes, garlic, and green chilies), kebab (grilled minced meat), and *tikka* (meat in a type of tomato/cream [yogurt] spicing sauce).

• Since Pakistanis have Muslim eating habits, don't expect pork products of any kind.

• Remember that Pakistani curries are not so spicy-hot as those in India. Many dishes do not have any chilies in them.

• Note that sweets are not common for dessert, but they may be served after a meal on special occasions.

• If fruit is served, eat it only if you can peel it.

• Before, during, and after meals, people drink Coca-Cola, Pepsi, 7-Up, and lime and soda.

• Water is a common beverage. In middle-class homes it has usually been boiled; before you drink it be sure to ask. Bottled water isn't available except in hotels and modern supermarkets in large cities. If you're going into the countryside, bring water with you, or bring tablets that can be used to purify water (buy them before you leave home).

• Another popular beverage is

nimbu pani—lime, sugar, and water. You may be offered an orange or lemon squash—fruit syrup with water added. Avoid them, however, where the origin of the water is unknown. In the winter, people may serve fresh orange juice. If you know they're preparing a glass for you, ask them not to add salt and pepper (as is customary) to yours, unless, of course, you want to try it that way.

• To be safe, ask for Coca-Cola or Pepsi. Remember that if you ask for "soda," you'll get club soda.

• Another common beverage is *rooh-e-afza*—a syrup-and-water rose-scented drink. It's pink and very sweet.

• In the north, you'll be offered *lassi*, a yogurt drink, which can either be sweet or salted.

• Note that tea is far more popular than coffee. If coffee is available, it is usually of the instant variety.

• Only the Westernized upper classes drink alcohol at home.

• Out of respect, do not drink alcohol in public.

• Keep in mind that non-Muslims can purchase liquor only in hotels. Sign a form saying that you're a non-Muslim and pay a small fee. Both hotel guests and those not staying there must follow this practice. If you have a license (ask at your hotel or a tourism office how to obtain one), you can purchase liquor at government liquor shops in major cities.

Table Manners

• Expect to sit at a table for meals, not on the floor.

• Note that people normally eat with their hands, but when entertaining foreign guests, forks and spoons are frequently used. Keep the fork in your left hand and the spoon in your right. Use the fork to push food onto the spoon, and eat with the spoon. If you do eat with your hands, use only the right hand. The left hand is considered unclean, since it's used for functions connected with the toilet.

• Don't expect napkins in all homes. Even if they are used, wash your hands (in the bathroom) before and after eating. Many families have a small wash basin in the dining room, while in rural areas you may be offered a jar of water, soap, and a towel.

• Look for serving dishes with spoons in the middle of the table. Use the spoons to put food on your plate, even when you eat with your fingers.

• Since hosts will always try to force more food on you, take small portions the first time. Be determined in your refusal when you don't want any more.

• To indicate that you have finished, put the fork and spoon in the middle of the plate. If no utensils have been served, signs that you are finished would be an empty plate, sitting back and withdrawing your hands from the table, or getting up to go and wash your hands.

• If you are a close friend, feel free to stay and chat long after dinner; if you don't know your hosts well, leave about an hour after the meal. However, expect most conversation to take place before the meal.

Places to Eat

• Note that usual restaurant hours are 7:30 to 9:30 A.M., 12:00 to 2:00 P.M., and 7:30 to 10:00 P.M.

• In big cities, look for snackbars, which serve sandwiches, tea, and cold drinks.

• For full meals, seek out international hotel chains, especially if you're looking for Western food. In large cities, you will often find decent Chinese restaurants.

• At restaurants in railroad stations, expect English-style food.

• Note that a café is usually a sleazy tea joint. Most cafés and tearooms are for the working class.

• Don't be surprised to find fast-food places the "in" places for eating.

• Avoid eating in small restaurants. Stick to first-class or hotel restaurants—they're safer bets.

• Be aware that either Wednesday or Thursday is usually meatless, and you'll be able to order only chicken or fish.

• Even if a restaurant is full, don't join people you don't know at their table.

• Women traveling alone should eat in a hotel restaurant. They can expect to be hassled in other eating places.

• To signal the waiter, raise your hand.

• Don't order any food that may have been exposed to flies; e.g., sweets that are not covered or under glass.

• Don't try to have a "Dutch treat" meal. If you ask someone to join you for lunch, you pay.

• Drink milk and eat yogurt only in first-class hotels and restaurants. These places are usually quite clean. Don't, however, drink milk or eat yogurt in family-style or smaller restaurants; their standards of hygiene may be questionable.

Specialities

• Note that Pakistani cooking is similar to that of the Middle East. It features grilled lamb, flatbreads, and yogurt, with milder spices than those used in Indian cooking.

• Try *korma* (meat curry dishes with yogurt and spices); *dahi bindi* (okra with yogurt and spices); *shami kebab* (grilled spiced meatballs); *chapli kebab* (chopped meat patties); *pasandry* (spiced beef strips); *chicken tikka* (grilled boneless chicken marinated in yogurt and herbs); *nargesi kofta* (fried meatballs stuffed with hard-boiled eggs); *biryani* (baked lamb and rice; occasionally the meat is beef or chicken).

• Also sample *khatti dal* (lentils with spices); *chappati* (a pancake-like wheat bread fried on an iron griddle).

• For sweets, eat *firni* (cream of rice pudding) or *jalebi* (pretzel-shaped sweets in sugar syrup).

HOTELS

• In small towns, look for hotels near the train and bus stations.

• Always check your room and bathroom before registering. Be sure that everything works and that locks are secure.

• If you stay in a local inn, expect dormitory-style accommodations with rope beds. Many will not accept foreigners, except in isolated areas where there are no other accommodations.

TIPPING

• Remember that hotels and restaurants include a 10 percent service charge in your bill.

• Note that railway porters charge *Rs* 10 for baggage up to 40 kilograms. At the airport, tip *Rs* 50, regardless of the number of bags. Tip hotel porters *Rs* 20–50.

• When visiting a mosque, give a few *rupees* to the man who looks after your shoes.

• Add 10 percent to your taxi fare for the driver.

PRIVATE HOMES

• If you would like to visit someone you don't know well, call in advance. Good friends drop in on one another.

• Plan visits for Sunday afternoons between 5:00 and 6:00 P.M. Don't stay past 7:00 P.M., because people will feel obliged to invite you to dinner.

• Don't visit anyone between 2:00 and 3:00 P.M. During that hour, women and children nap.

• Remove your shoes before entering a home, unless your host asks you not to.

• Be aware that guests are usually received in special rooms. Don't go wandering around the house.

• Note that traditional homes have areas where men who are not related are not allowed to go. Women guests may be invited to the women's quarters.

• Don't praise an object in the home, as your host will feel obliged to give it to you.

• If you're invited to an urban home with a group, men and women might mingle in the same room, but *never* sit down next to a person of the opposite sex unless explicitly invited to do so.

• Bring photographs of your family. People really enjoy seeing them.

• If you use the telephone, offer to pay for the call, since there is a charge for each call. Your host will probably refuse payment for local calls. Be sure to ask permission, though, to make long-distance calls, and be sure to pay for them.

• Be aware that most people have servants; don't offer to help with the cleaning up and dishes.

• If a business colleague invites you to stay at his home, expect a large, air-conditioned house with four to five bedrooms, each with a bathroom. There is no need to ask permission to take a bath, as there is a constant supply of hot water. Pakistanis bathe several times daily because of the heat. Be aware, however, that there are frequent water shortages. If you turn on a faucet and nothing comes out, the faucet isn't necessarily broken.

• If you take a bath, put only a little water in the tub, and make your shower a quick one so that you don't deprive family members of water.

• You may find a pail of water with a jug in the bathroom and a place similar to a shower stall where you stand to wash yourself. Scoop the water from the pail with the jug and pour it over yourself. If you need hot water, ask in advance so that the hostess or a servant can boil it for you.

• Don't offer to buy groceries for a meal; your hosts will be insulted.

• To please your hosts, tip the servants when you leave. Giving each one 20–25 *rupees* is adequate. You don't need an envelope; simply hand the money to each one.

• If you stay with a family for a few days, invite them out to dinner. They will especially enjoy a Western or Chinese restaurant.

• Realize that modern city homes have flush toilets, but no toilet paper, since people wash themselves after using the toilet, using a round jug filled with water with a long spout (called a *lota*), which is next to the toilet. If you want to use tissues, bring them with you. In towns and villages, you may see a toilet that looks like a stool. Lift the top. There is a seat with a hole cut out and a bucket underneath.

Gifts: Don't feel obliged to bring a gift when invited to a meal. If you really want to bring something, chocolates are an excellent choice. The best source of good chocolates is a large supermarket. Flowers are another good choice, but they are hard to find except in hotel florist shops.

• Bring good-quality chocolates from your country, as well as silk ties and shirts.

• Don't bring liquor unless you are sure that people drink. The upper classes, who are Westernized, often drink and enjoy imported whiskey.

• Bring some postcards with views of your area at home. People enjoy receiving such cards.

• Never give gifts of money, except for weddings and funerals. (People sometimes use the monetary gifts to defray the costs of the funeral.)

MONEY AND BUSINESS

Hours

Business Hours: Monday through Thursday, 7:30 A.M. to 2:30 P.M. (summer), and 9:00 A.M. to 4:00 P.M. (winter), and Friday mornings and Saturday. Many private business offices are open from 9:00 A.M. to 1:00 P.M., and 2:00 or 3:00 P.M. to 5:00, 6:00, or 7:00 P.M. Private offices sometimes close early on Saturday.

Government Offices: Monday through Thursday and Saturday, 8:00 A.M. to 2:30 P.M. (summer), and 8:30 A.M. to 3:00 P.M. (winter). Offices are open for a half day—closing at noon or 12:30 P.M. on Friday.

Banks: Monday through Thursday and Saturday, 9:00 A.M. to 1:00 P.M. Friday 9:00 A.M. to 11:30 A.M.

Shops: Monday through Thursday and Saturday 9:00 or 10:00 A.M. to sometime between 6:00 and 8:00 P.M. Friday 9:00 A.M. to 12:30 P.M.

• Note that all offices and shops have special hours during Ramazan.

• Keep in mind that Pakistan has three seasons: autumn–winter (October through February), spring

(March through June), and summer (July through September). The first is cool, the second hot, and the third wet.

Money

- The currency is the Pakistani *rupee* (singular is abbreviated *Re* and plural *Rs*), which is divided into 100 *paisas*. Coins are 5, 10, 25, and 50 *paisas*, and 100 *paisas*, which equals *Re* 1. Banknotes are *Re* 1, and *Rs* 5, 10, 50, 100, and 5000
- Major credit cards—American Express, Visa, Barclaycard, Master-Card, Access, Diners Club—are accepted in large hotels, restaurants, and shops. Some places will accept payment in travelers' checks, but most will not.

Business Practices

- Try to arrange an introduction from your embassy, a banker, or a lawyer, unless you are representing a large, well-known company.
- Plan business trips between October and April. Most businessmen vacation in the months of May through August, the heavy monsoon season.
- Avoid trips during Ramazan (the Urdu term for Ramadan), since most Pakistanis are Muslim. This holiday occurs at a different time each year according to the lunar calendar. Check with the Pakistani consulate or embassy for its date, as well as for the dates of other Muslim holidays.

- Be sure to make appointments in advance for both business and government calls. If you're dealing with large companies, Telex, fax, or write from your country a month or two in advance to set up appointments. Be sure to confirm your appointments when you arrive in Pakistan. If you're in Pakistan, make arrangements about a week in advance. For meetings with local tradespeople, request an appointment a day or two in advance. The best times for appointments are from 10:00 A.M. to 1:00 P.M.: the best time to find senior government officials in their offices is between 9:30 A.M. and 1:00 P.M.
- Remember that during Ramazan people work only from 7:00 A.M. to 1:00 P.M.
- Realize that many people do not stick to a schedule on Saturday, so avoid making appointments for that day.
- Remember that Pakistanis are not conscious of time, but they expect foreigners to be punctual.
- To avoid humiliating one of your employees and to make sure that your company's message is given proper consideration, don't send a woman to represent the company. She will not be taken seriously.
- Note that the national language is Urdu, but English is widely understood and is the usual language for doing business.
- Always greet the most senior person first.
- Present your business card. Be

sure that your title appears on the card.

• Be sure to accept the tea you will be offered during an office visit. It would be rude to decline. Now is the time to start developing a relationship. At your initial meeting, spend some time chatting about your country, your Pakistani counterpart's trips, your *positive* reactions to Pakistan. (After the initial meeting, feel free to ask about a person's family, but *don't* mention his wife, unless you've known the person for a long time.)

• Don't tell jokes in a formal business setting.

• Expect Pakistani businessmen to be formal, reserved, and very deliberate in business negotiations.

• Don't assume that "Yes" means "I agree." It often means "I see." Pakistanis rarely say "No." Therefore, try to avoid direct questions.

• To earn respect, always remain calm. Never show anger.

• Realize that Pakistanis tend to exaggerate their capabilities. If you hire a local agent, check references. This problem could also crop up in negotiating with businesspeople.

• Be aware that deadlines are rarely met. Allow for that fact in planning. Be very detailed when discussing schedules and plans, and constantly monitor progress. Realize, also, that Pakistani businessmen may exaggerate their ability to deliver a product in the condition agreed upon and on time.

• Keep in mind that final decisions are usually based on the intuition of the seniormost person.

• If your business negotiations require considerable involvement with the government, expect to make several trips to Pakistan. The biggest customer in the country is the Pakistan government, which has many public and semi-public corporations, and which also has a bureaucracy you will have to deal with.

Entertainment: Prepare for a friendly reception from Pakistanis; they are very curious about foreigners. Among the upper classes, the entree to businessmen's families is easy. In the middle class, women will probably not meet a foreign visitor.

• Remember that business dinners are more common than lunches. Conversation will usually be of a social nature, since people want to get to know you.

• Expect to be entertained by a Pakistani businessman at his club rather than at home. There is, however, a great deal of entertaining at home. If you do not see the wife, she may be in *purdah* (i.e., she wears a veil and doesn't associate with men outside her family).

• If you would like to invite the wife of a business counterpart to dinner at a restaurant, ask him discreetly if his wife is in *purdah*.

• Foreign businesswomen should be aware that it will be *very* difficult to pay a restaurant check for entertaining Pakistani businessmen. Ahead of time, stress, "*I'm* inviting *you."* This tactic probably won't work, since local women never pay when they are with a man. One tactic that might work is entertaining in your hotel restaurant and making arrangements beforehand for the meal to be charged to your room.

Gifts: Good business gifts are pens, small transistor radios, watches, Swiss knives, and, in general, any kind of new gadget. If you deal with a person often and know him well, jogging shoes are a welcome gift.

• Be prepared for people to refuse a gift two or three times as a matter of politeness. Persist. Follow this custom when you are offered a gift.

Note: For advice regarding business greetings, dress, or table manners, see the appropriate sections earlier in this chapter.

HOLIDAYS AND SPECIAL OCCASIONS

• On the holidays listed below, banks, offices, and most shops are closed. Some towns and regions have local festivals, which are holidays in the area. Check with the tourist office for dates of local holidays.

Holidays: Pakistan Day (March 23), May Day (May 1), Bank Holiday (July 1—banks only), Independence Day (August 14), Defense Day (September 6), Anniversary of Death of Quaid-e-Azam (September 11), Iqbal Day, honoring the poet who first proposed a Muslim Pakistan in 1930 (November 9), Birthday of Quaid-e-Azam and Christmas (December 25), Bank Holiday (December 31—banks only).

• Islamic holidays, which are moveable: Eid-ul-Fitr, celebrating the end of Ramazan (two days); Eid-ul-Azha, the Day of Sacrifices (during the last month of the Muslim calendar); Muharram (tenth day of the Moslem New Year); Eid-Milad-un-Nabi, birthday of the prophet Mohammed.

• Note that Quaid-e-Azam is the honorific name of Mohammed Ali Jinnah, leader of the separatist Muslim movement which succeeded in establishing Pakistan in 1947. He has an almost saintly status, and visitors should be circumspect when speaking of him.

• Be especially careful to observe appropriate customs if you are in Pakistan during Ramazan. This important religious holiday falls at a different time each year, since it is based on the lunar calendar, and lasts for 30 days. Nothing will be open after 2:00 P.M. (although many places close by 1:00 P.M.). The only restaurants open will be those in large hotels. From sunrise to sundown, people don't eat or smoke. Don't eat, drink, chew gum, or smoke in public during this time.

TRANSPORTATION

Public Transportation

• Don't look for subways. There are none.

• Try not to take buses because they are *very* overcrowded, and men tend to bother women by pinching them, etc. If you decide to take a bus, be aware that women enter from the front and men from the rear. There may be a partition between the two sections. A conductor will collect the fare, which is based on distance traveled.

• Expect to find bus stations near the railway station, or, in smaller towns, near the bazaar. For long trips, take food and drink with you, although buses make scheduled stops for food. It's sometimes not possible to reserve seats in advance. Between major cities, you can take privately operated air-conditioned

luxury buses which feature loud videos.

• Note that there are wagons and minibuses with 15–20 seats. They are slightly more expensive than government buses.

• Look for taxis on the streets. Although many have meters, be sure to discuss the fare in advance. (Ask someone at your hotel what the fare should be.)

• If you have several places to visit, consider hiring a taxi for a day. Drivers are usually only familiar with large hotels and major landmarks; call the office or private home to which you want to go and have them give the directions to the driver.

• Consider traveling by auto-rickshaw—motorcycles with a coach for two people. You'll find them everywhere. Auto-rickshaws and taxis cost about the same, although rickshaws are slightly more dangerous. Rickshaws may be a good choice for two women. They can travel in relative anonymity (e.g., to visit the bazaar and see things without being hassled). As with taxis, bargain for the fare in advance.

• Note that trains have three classes: first, second, and third, with only first air-conditioned. In first class, six people share a compartment with a private bath. Second class is noisy and crowded with no air-conditioning, toilets, or reserved seats. In third class, expect to sit on wooden seats. Trains have dining cars with acceptable food, but it's better to bring your own food and buy a drink on the train. Boys continually come through the cars selling drinks. The drinks are probably safe if they are bottled. Be sure to give the boys small change; don't give a large bill, because they may disappear with it. If you go to the bathroom or the dining car, always take your valuables with you, as there are sometimes robberies on trains.

• Ask a hotel employee or travel agent to obtain your train ticket, because purchasing a ticket on your own is time-consuming and frustrating. If you have no choice, pay the station porter, who will be wearing a red turban and armband, to deal with the purchase for you.

• Note that you must have a reservation for a sleeper.

• Be aware that few people at train stations speak English.

• Be aware that there are special ladies' compartment for women traveling alone. Pakistani women never travel alone; they may travel with other women or with their children. Muslim men may view it offensive if a woman is traveling by herself. If you do travel alone, wear local dress and wrap a large shawl, called a *dupatta* and available everywhere, around you. If possible, buy two seats for yourself on a long-distance bus, minibus, or wagon. Pakistani women always sit in the front or back seats and are often car sick. Two seats will mean that you

won't have to sit next to someone who is car sick.

• Consider that the price of an air-conditioned train and a local flight are usually the same, and thus most people prefer to fly. There are, however, special air-conditioned trains that have no berths. They are less expensive than air travel.

Driving

• Get an International Driver's License if you intend to drive; it's especially important in the event of an accident.

• Don't drive unless it is absolutely necessary. There is tremendous traffic congestion from all types of vehicles—from limousines to donkeys. Most Pakistani drivers usually don't obey signals. It's also difficult to find good road maps.

• Be aware that car rentals are available, but it's much better to hire a car and driver. Driving conditions are bad, and you won't be familiar with areas that are unsafe. Make arrangements at your hotel. You'll pay more than you would for a privately hired taxi, but most drivers speak some English.

• Remember that driving is on the left side of the road (as in Britain or Japan).

• If you commit a minor violation, consider solving the problem with a small "tip" to the policeman.

• Note that only on rare occasions can fines be paid on the spot.

LEGAL MATTERS, SAFETY, AND HEALTH

• Don't try to bring liquor into Pakistan.

• Check with your doctor about shots and antimalarial drugs you should take before visiting Pakistan.

Health: Bring a supply of tissues; they can be used for toilet paper.

• Be sure to bring an ample supply of any prescription drugs you take. Prescription drugs may be unavailable, or they may have different names.

• Never drink tap water or use ice cubes in your drink. This advice is true even in first-class hotels, because parasites are endemic.

• Don't eat buffet meals, even in first-class hotels. Food is kept warm for long periods of time, and bacteria grow.

Safety: Don't go swimming in Karachi between June and August because of the powerful undertow and the prevalence of jellyfish.

• Because of the political violence in some areas, check with your country's state department or foreign office for advisories or warnings before traveling to Pakistan.

• While most ordinary toiletries are available, women should bring a supply of tampons or sanitary napkins.

• Never buy food—especially ice-cream—from a street vendor.

KEY PHRASES

There are no phrase books for Urdu. English is, however, widely spoken.

English	Urdu	Pronunciation
Good morning, afternoon, evening	Salam alai kum	Sah-laĥm ah-lay kóom
Good night	Khuda hafiz	Kóo-dah hah-fiź
Sir, Mr.	Sahib	Sah-híb
Madam, Mrs., Miss	Begum + last name	Bay-góom
Yes	Jee han	Jeé haĥn (nasal "n")
No	Nahin	Nah-hin (nasal "n")
Please	Meherbani	Meh-heĥr-baĥ-nee

Thank you	Shookriya	Shook-ree-yaĥ
You're welcome	Kooyi baat nahin	Kóo-yee báht nah-hín (nasal "n")
Excuse me	Maaf kee-jee-yay	Maĥf kee-jee-yáy
I don't understand	Main nahin samjha (male)	Mehń (nasal "n") nah-héen (nasal "n") sahm-jáh
	Main nahin samjhi (female)	Mehń (nasal "n") nah-héen (nasal "n") sahm-jée

THE PHILIPPINES

SOUTH CHINA SEA

LUZON

PACIFIC OCEAN

Manila • Quezon City

CATANDUANES

MINDORO

MASBATE

SAMAR

PANAY

LEYTE

PALAWAN

NEGROS

BOHOL

SULU SEA

MINDANAO

Davao

SULU ARCHIPELAGO

CELEBES SEA

For trivia fans: What country, composed of 7,107 islands, is the third-largest English-speaking country in the world? Would you have known without the chapter title that it's the Philippines?

Try another: What happened to Ferdinand Magellan when he arrived in the Philippines that *didn't* happen to General Douglas MacArthur? Magellan was killed by the warrior king Lapu-Lapu, while MacArthur returned in triumph.

Visitors to the Philippines encounter a mix of cultures. The islands are the northernmost outpost of the Malay culture. They were controlled by Spain for over 300 years and then occupied by America for more than 40 years. Strains of all three cultures surface in language, customs, and cuisine.

GREETINGS

- Be aware that on first and subsequent meetings the appropriate greeting is a handshake—for men and men, women and men, or women and women. Foreign men should wait for Filipino women to extend their hands.
- Realize that close women friends kiss and embrace, while close male friends shake hands.
- Don't be surprised to see Filipinos greet each other by making eye contact and then quickly raising and lowering their eyebrows.
- To show special honor when greeting older persons, especially relatives, use the terms *lolo* and *lola*. Even greater honor is shown by placing their hand on your forehead—a time-honored gesture of respect.
- At a party, expect to be introduced to each guest individually. Shake hands with each person as you are introduced.
- Address business superiors as "Sir" or "Ma'am," or by their title or profession (e.g., "Congressman," "Attorney"). Use "Mr.," "Mrs.," and "Miss" with business peers.

CONVERSATION

- Speak very slowly and carefully to avoid misunderstandings; Filipinos may have difficulty understanding your accent. English is widely spoken, and some Spanish is used, although the official language is Tagalog (or Pilipino).
- Good topics to discuss: the area you're from, your job, education. Filipinos are very family oriented, so children are a good subject.
- Avoid discussing the political situation in the Philippines and religion.
- Even as a joke, don't criticize a person or his family or an established institution.
- Don't be surprised if people ask you very personal questions—e.g., the price of the clothing you're wearing, whether you're married, your profession—very soon after you meet.
- In conversation, never disagree with elders. If you feel you must offer criticism, be *very* tactful. Filipinos are sensitive and easily offended.
- Keep in mind that Filipinos tend to be shy. Failure to respond may simply mean "No."

• Realize that "Yes" has several connotations. The word may run the gamut from "Maybe" to "No." People are so anxious to please that they have difficulty in saying "No."

• Don't be surprised to find Filipinos constantly interrupting one another and being very noisy when they are in a group.

• Realize that Filipinos are sometimes very direct when criticizing another person.

tory, since phone numbers are always changing.

• Make long-distance calls from your hotel (where there may be a substantial surcharge), or go to post office or a Philippine Long Distance Telephone Company (PLDT) office. To avoid the surcharge, call collect, or arrange to have your office or family phone you.

• Realize that not many Filipinos have telephones in their homes.

TELEPHONES

IN PUBLIC

• Be aware that there are public telephones on street corners and at bus terminals. However, very few are functioning. You'll also find long lines waiting to use the phones. You may also see phones in business districts, but not on residential streets or highways. Often shops will allow you to make local calls without charge. To use a coin telephone, deposit three 25-*centavo* coins, and wait for the dial tone before dialing.

• When you arrive in the Phillippines, obtain a recent phone direc-

• To indicate two of something (e.g., two beers), hold up your forefinger and your middle finger (as in the "peace" sign). The thumb is used to indicate "five" when counting on the fingers.

• Note that someone may touch you lightly on the elbow to gain your attention.

• Don't use your finger to beckon. This gesture is rude. It is used by a master calling a servant, by a person calling dogs, or by a woman trying to seduce a man. Motion to someone with your hand palm down, move your four fingers toward you.

• If you're in a restaurant, be prepared to hear people hissing to gain the waitress's attention.

• Avoid putting your hands on your hips with your elbows out. It's an angry, challenging gesture.

• If you hear a Filipino making a "psstt" sound, he/she is trying to get the attention of someone else.

• Don't be surprised to see women holding hands or men with their arms around one another's shoulders when walking or having their photo taken. The practice has no sexual implications. People who don't know one another don't use these gestures. Be sure, however, to avoid physical contact with members of the opposite sex in public.

• Remember that "ladies first" is very much part of Filipino culture. Men open doors for women, allow them to precede when entering a building, and offer seats to them on public transportation.

• Don't point with your middle finger straight out and your index and little fingers bent. It's obscene.

• Note that one way that Filipinos point is with their mouths—by puckering their lips. Someone may say "Over there" and indicate the direction with his mouth.

• Remember that raising the eyebrows means "No."

• Don't be surprised if a Filipino smiles when upset or embarrassed. It's their way of clearing the air.

• Never show anger in public. It's bad taste to display strong feelings in public. People are expected to control their emotions.

• Remember that Filipinos dislike direct confrontation because it implies loss of face.

• Show respect for older people in emulation of Filipinos, who revere their elders.

• Always ask permission before smoking. Be especially careful not to smoke when visiting a factory.

• Be prepared for people to be very reserved in mixed company. On the other hand, because they are very inquisitive, they may question a great deal. Note that staring is considered rude and aggressive. Even fixed eye contact indicates provocation.

• Don't be surprised if Filipinos are late for social occasions. They are, however, punctual for business meetings.

• Reconfirm any invitation several times, since Filipinos so dislike saying "No" that they may not intend to keep the engagement even if you believe that they've agreed to it.

• Don't be put off if people ask you how much you paid for something purchased in the Philippines. They are probably concerned that you may have been cheated.

• Be prepared for people to decline anything offered at first—for example, food.

• Be aware that food is extremely important to Filipinos. If a clerk in a store you're visiting is having a snack or a coffee break, prepare to wait a long time for service.

• Women should note that Filipino women seldom smoke or drink in public, though foreign women may.

• Before taking pictures, look for signs indicating that photography is forbidden.

• Feel free to photograph people, though it's courteous to ask permission first. Filipinos usually love to have their pictures taken.

• If you're visiting in a rural area, recall that the Angelus bell rings at 6:00 P.M. to announce the correct time and to remind people to pray. Stop when you hear it, and after the bell has stopped ringing, say "Good evening" to anyone near you.

• To find a restroom, ask for a "CR" (comfort room).

• Note that public bathrooms for men are *lalake* (lah-lah-kee) and for women *babae* (bah-bah-ay). Often there are symbols on the doors for the sexes. Toilets in restaurants and bars are usually dirty and without toilet paper. Look for clean toilets in the lobbies of larger, Western-style hotels. Western-style toilets are widely available, even in rural areas.

• Don't be surprised to see public urinals for women. The urinals have raised tiles and slots to stand on. They will be about a foot away from a wall. One squats slightly while facing the wall. Constantly flowing water cleans the urinals.

Shopping: Don't bargain in department stores, but feel free to bargain in markets and small shops.

Start by offering 50 percent of the price, and negotiate from there.

Exercise: Women should jog on the hotel grounds or with someone else near the hotel or in a park. Men should also use the hotel grounds, the area near the hotel, or a park. Both sexes can dress in shorts. It's very hot, so plan to exercise early—6:00 or 7:00 A.M.

DRESS

• For business, men should wear a jacket and tie. Women should wear an elegant dress or a skirt and blouse, and, despite the heat, stockings. People are very fashion conscious; to make a good impression, dress well.

• Men should remember that some restaurants require jackets in the evening. You can substitute a *barong tagalog* (a light-weight, long-sleeved, embroidered shirt, worn outside the trousers).

• Note that there are two kinds of *barongs* for men: the informal one has short sleeves, is made of cotton or polyester, and has little embroidery; the formal one, worn for cocktail parties and semiformal occasions, is made of pineapple fiber and has long sleeves and more embroidery. If you purchase a *barong*, be sure it is an expensive one—to insure the best quality.

• For casual wear, women can wear pants or a skirt but not shorts, and men should wear pants and a shirt. Jeans are acceptable, but the climate is so hot that they will probably be very uncomfortable.

• In Muslim areas (concentrated in the southern part of the Philippines), women should wear knee-length skirts or pants and blouses with sleeves covering the upper arms, especially when visiting a mosque.

• When invited to a meal in someone's home, men should wear a suit and women should wear dressy pants with a top, a dress, or a skirt and blouse. (You probably won't be uncomfortable; most upper-class homes are air-conditioned.)

• For a formal occasion, such as a banquet, men should wear a suit and women a short cocktail dress. Long gowns are worn only for formal diplomatic parties.

• During festivals (fiestas), don't wear anything that can be damaged. People have a custom of throwing water on pedestrians.

• Neither men nor women should wear shorts on the street.

• If you'll be meeting someone you want to impress, don't wear sandals. You will be labeled a "hippie."

MEALS

Hours and Foods

Breakfast: 7:00 to 8:00 A.M. Some traditional Filipinos eat fish and rice. Others have fruits, *ensaimada* (sugary buns), and coffee. Still others eat eggs and sausages, *pan de sal* (sour-dough bread), and hot chocolate. Tea is also a common breakfast drink.

Lunch: 12:00 P.M. or 1:00 P.M. A typical lunch is *sinigang* (a sour soup), cooked pork, *adobo* (a marinated meat stew), rice, and fruit or cakes. Beverages are water and soft drinks.

Merienda: An afternoon snack, retained by Filipinos from Spanish tradition. The meal features sweet fritters, cakes, and tarts. Most sweets are made from coconut milk: *suman* (rice, palm sugar, and coconut milk steamed in banana leaves); *tsampurado* (rice and chocolate); *halohalo* (shaved ice and coconut milk mixed with fried rice grains, corn, or mung bean). The *merienda* is served after *siesta*.

Dinner: 7:00 P.M. Usually there will be a fish or seafood dish, a vegetable dish, rice, fruit, dessert—*sans rival* (made of egg whites, cream, and coconut, with a meringue base), steamed or baked rice cakes with coconut milk and sugar, or *queso puti* (kay-so poot-ee), a white cheese made from water buffalo milk. At an everyday meal, water, soft drinks, and beer will be served. A formal dinner may feature wine.

• Be prepared for families of Spanish ancestry to retain the tradition of dining late (i.e., 9:00 or 10:00 P.M.). Most families, however, eat earlier.

• Realize that rice is the staple and will be served at most meals.

• For Sunday meals a special stew called *pochero* is often served. It has meats and vegetables cut in large chunks, in a sauce of tomatoes, yams, onions, and garlic, and is served with rice.

• Remember that Filipinos almost never cook anything by itself, except for fish, which is broiled or grilled. Chicken, fish, vegetables, and noodles are all combined for soups and stews and then served with rice. The rice and food are mixed together on the plate and *bagoong* or *patis* are added. *Bagoong* is a pungent fish or shrimp paste, and *patis* is an amber-colored liquid fish seasoning. In homes, there will be bottles of these two condiments on the table, while in restaurants they are added to the food in the cooking.

• For beverages, women are usually offered soft drinks: Coca-Cola, orange juice, or *calamansi* (a native drink made of a citrus fruit similar to lemon). Usually only men drink alcohol, principally beer and wine.

• Be aware that people rarely drink tea, and the only coffee is instant. (However, at the best hotels, one can find fresh coffee.)

• Recall that the water in Manila is safe to drink, but bottled water is available. Outside Manila, drink bottled water.

• Note that Filipinos tend to eat three large meals each day.

• The food will seem familiar. From 400 years of Spanish rule and more than 40 years of American occupation, Filipino taste in foods is very compatible with that of Westerners.

Table Manners

• Plan to arrive about 30 minutes late for a dinner party.

• Be prepared to see large numbers of people at a party. Filipinos are very hospitable and invite relatives and friends to parties at home as well as to business functions.

• Don't expect drinks to be served before dinner. However, Filipinos accustomed to entertaining foreigners may serve American-style cocktails.

• Don't leap up when dinner is announced. Wait until Filipino guests have started. It is polite to appear reluctant to go to the table, and customarily the hostess invites people to dinner several times.

• Wait for your host to seat you. The usual seat of honor is at the head of the table. Sometimes the male guest is seated next to the host and the female guest next to the hostess.

• Don't panic if your host or hostess stares at you at the beginning of a meal. He or she is waiting for you to take the first bite.

• At your place, look for a fork and spoon. Some homes put knives on the table, but most don't. Take the spoon in your right hand and the fork in your left. Push food onto the back of the spoon with the fork.

• If there's a lazy Susan or serving dishes in the center of the table, serve yourself. In wealthier families, a maid will bring the food, serving guests first and children last.

• In the countryside, expect village people at home to eat with the right hand, not using forks or spoons. If you're not offered cutlery, you'll have to do the same.

• To emulate Filipinos, when food, drink, or cigarettes are *first* offered, refuse. You can accept the second time, if you wish.

• Never make sounds when eating—e.g., slurping your soup.

• Expect a great deal of talk during meals.

• Try to take small portions, since people will insist that you eat more, and to be polite when dining with a family, you should try to finish everything on your plate.

• Since most upper–middle-class families have cooks, it isn't customary to praise the food. Compliment your hostess on the flower arrangements or the house.

• To indicate that you're finished, place utensils horizontally on your plate.

• Watch your consumption of alcohol, if it's offered. Filipinos rarely become drunk at dinner parties because they believe that drinking too much implies greed.

• Be prepared for a dinner party to end with dancing and drinks after dinner. Men usually drink beer, Scotch, or gin. Women don't usually drink alcohol.

• Realize that it's customary to give people food to take home after a dinner party.

• Plan to leave a dinner party on a weekday about 10:00 P.M. and on a weekend night around midnight.

• If someone drops in while you are eating, or if you bring food onto a train and are eating in front of others, offer to share your food.

Places to Eat

• Note that coffeeshops serve sandwiches, tea, coffee, and soft drinks.

• In hotel restaurants, you can usually choose from Chinese, Filipino, or American dishes.

• The more elegant cafés also serve meals.

• Vendors on the street sell *lechon manok* (barbecued chicken). The chicken will be fresh and safe to eat because there's a rapid turnover.

• Be aware that late dining is possible, as most restaurants are open until midnight.

• Don't expect to find menus posted outside restaurants. Only a few places follow this practice. Reading the menu is easy, since all entries are in English.

• Keep in mind that most restaurants offer à la carte menus. You choose a main dish and its accompaniments—soup, a vegetable, and rice—and each item is priced separately.

• Note that dishes listed on the menu with *ginataan* after them are cooked in coconut milk. *Inihaw* means that the meat or fish are grilled.

• In remote provinces, don't be surprised to see dogs and cats in restaurants.

• Don't be surprised to see a ketchup bottle on the table in a restaurant. It will look like an American ketchup bottle, but it contains banana ketchup, which is actually similar in taste to tomato ketchup.

• Be prepared for everything to arrive whole or on the bone—e.g., fish served with the head, tail, and bones, or chicken with bones in a soup.

• Women eating alone should be aware that Filipino women don't dine alone in restaurants. You will certainly arouse curiosity and possibly unwanted attention (men asking if they may join you). For your comfort, consider eating lunch in a fine restaurant and dinner in your hotel restaurant, where people will be used to foreign women dining alone.

• If you invite Filipinos to dinner, realize that they regard it polite to decline the first time. Press the same invitation; they may decline a second time. Usually they will accept with pleasure the third time.

• Don't be surprised to hear people hiss to gain the waiter or waitress's attention.

• Note that people often have a drink before dinner in a restaurant, even though they don't serve cocktails at home.

• To attract the waiter or waitress's attention for the check, hold your index finger and thumb as though you were holding a pencil, and draw a rectangle in the air. If this simple gesture doesn't work, you may have to jump up and wave your arms.

• When in a restaurant with a group, never try to pay for just your own meal. Pay all or nothing. The custom is that the person who extends the invitation pays the entire bill. Note, however, that Filipinos are so hospitable that it is difficult for a foreigner to pay for a meal. If Filipino friends persist in their offer to pay, let them.

• If you order a soft drink to take out (or from a street vendor), expect the drink to be poured into a small plastic bag. You'll be given a straw. Be sure to tell the waiter or vendor that you don't want ice (except in Manila), since the ice will be made from the local water.

Specialties

• Be sure to sample the Philippine national dish, *adobo*, meat marinated in palm vinegar with bay leaves, salt, garlic, and black peppercorns. The meat is boiled, then fried in lard, and finally simmered in broth.

• To test the Spanish influence in Philippine cooking, try *pochero*—beef, sausage, and pork, with sweet potatoes, tomatoes, cabbage, and chickpeas, cooked in a thick sauce.

• For a typical appetizer, order *lumpia*, which is like an egg roll, filled with pork, vegetables, and chilies.

• For a hearty soup have *sinigang*, made of meat or fish cooked with sour fruits, tomatoes, and vegetables. It appears in many variations.

• Try the country's special main courses: *afritada*, beef in olive oil and tomato paste, served with olives and vegetables; *kari-kari*, beef or oxtail and tripe prepared in a spicy peanut sauce and served with vegetables; *lechon*, barbecued whole pig stuffed with tamarind leaves and accompanied by a vinegar-and-liver dipping sauce. Note that the suckling leftovers are turned into another great dish—*paksiw*.

• Note that Filipino food is typified by the use of lemon, vinegar, *patis* (fish sauce), *bagoong* (shrimp paste), garlic, and onions. Many dishes cooked with vinegar or pulp of unripe tamarind pod produce a distinctive sour taste, which Filipinos enjoy.

• You might want to avoid *balut*, a hard-boiled duck egg containing a partially developed embryo. Filipinos aren't offended if foreigners don't wish to eat it.

HOTELS

• Note that March through May is high season. Hotel prices will be about one-third less from December through February. From June through November expect to pay only half the high-season price.

• Before you check into a hotel, investigate to be sure the shower, electricity, and air-conditioning in the room are functioning.

• Be aware that the top hotels usually have a service fee and tax of 25 percent. Ask for a discount, and the price may be lowered.

• Note that many hotels have fax machines, but it may be *very* expensive to send a fax overseas. (Private telecommunication centers, including Eastern Telecoms and PLDT charge much less.)

• Keep in mind that at beaches there are cottages which vary greatly in price and comfort. Try to inspect them yourself, or have a Filipino friend do so before you agree to rent one.

• In small towns you may have difficulty in finding a hotel. Go to the mayor or the *barrio* captain. He will usually help. You may be invited into a private home. Food and other expenses may cost the family a great deal, but since they want to be hospitable, they may be offended if you offer money. To allow them to accept the money without losing face, tell them, for example, that the money is for the children's education.

• If you leave your valuables in a hotel safe, be sure to get a detailed receipt. Ask whether you can retrieve the valuables at any time: sometimes the night staff doesn't have a key.

• Drivers may try to get you to tip for a short drive by saying that they have no change. If the fare seems accurate, and you wish to offer a tip, round off the fare—e.g., P44 to P50.

• If you stay in a hotel for a few days, give the chambermaid P20.

• Give washroom attendants two *pesos*.

• To young boys who find parking places give one *peso*.

TIPPING

• Expect hotels to include a 10 percent service charge.

• Leave 10 percent at a restaurant if no service charge is included in your bill.

• If the service has been excellent, even if the service charge is included, consider leaving another 5 percent.

• Give porters *p*10 to *p*20.

• Tip taxi drivers 10 percent for a long trip—an hour or more. Taxi drivers don't expect tips for a short trip.

PRIVATE HOMES

• If you're invited to a party, arrive at least 15 to 30 minutes late. To be on time gives the impression that you are anxious and greedy.

• Use the front door when entering a house, never the kitchen door. Filipinos consider the kitchen one of the most private places in the home.

• If you're visiting in a rural area, remove your shoes before you enter a house.

• When entering a home where you'll be keeping your shoes on, be sure to wipe your feet on the mat.

• Phone ahead to make sure a visit is convenient. You don't want to inadvertently drop in on a family at mealtime, because they will feel obliged to ask you to join them. If someone is eating when you arrive and offers to share their food, reply that you have already eaten.

• Always make a special point of greeting and saying good-bye to older people. Filipinos have great respect for their elders.

• In a conversation, direct any questions to the father or husband.

• If children come to greet you, expect them to leave at once. Children don't remain while a guest is being entertained.

• Don't be surprised if a stranger invites you to a meal or to spend the night. Filipinos are very friendly and hospitable.

• When you're visiting, be aware that you'll be entertained in the living room. Don't go into other areas of the house unless you ask permission or are invited.

• All doors in the house are usually kept closed.

• If you're staying with a family, keep in mind that your host and hostess expect to show you around and take you sightseeing. If you want to spend some time sightseeing on your own, be tactful in telling them of your plans.

• Don't be surprised to see even middle-class families with servants. If you need your laundry done, mention it to your hostess, and she will have a servant do your washing.

• If you are staying with Filipinos, expect to be offered the master bedroom.

• If you stay a few days or weeks with a family, tip the servants about 50 *pesos* each.

• Should you be staying with a family that doesn't have a maid, offer to help with such household chores as washing dishes. Your offer will probably be declined.

• Remember that only the very rich have both hot and cold water. In other households, hot water for washing has to be boiled on the stove.

• Expect people to bathe several times a day because of the heat. Few homes have constant hot water; given the climate, it's more refreshing to bathe in cool water. Some homes and many Western-style hotels do have hot-water heaters. If you need hot water, ask your hostess.

Gifts: When invited to a meal, bring cakes or fruits.

• Other good gifts include: T-shirts, cosmetics, good-quality chocolates (a great favorite with all age groups), books with photographs of the country or your region, handcrafted items, and sneakers if you know the recipient's shoe size.

• In choosing a gift, be aware that the Philippines is a very stratified society and people are very oriented to status symbols, such as designer clothes, belts, handbags, etc.

• If you are staying with a family and take a trip and then return, be sure to bring a gift from that other place.

• If you're staying with a family,

present the gifts you've brought from home as soon as you arrive. Don't wait until the end of your stay.

• If you wish, give gifts (e.g., perfume) to the servants at the end of your stay. A gift for servants is not essential, however. You may give both male and female servants money.

• Don't expect a Filipino to open the gifts in your presence.

MONEY AND BUSINESS

Hours

Government and Business Offices: Monday through Friday, 9:00 A.M. to 5:00 P.M., with a two-hour break for lunch. Some offices are open from 8:00 A.M. to noon on Saturday. Offices of some private businesses are open on Saturday from 9:00 A.M. to noon.

Banks: Monday through Friday, 9:00 A.M. to 3:00 or 3:30 P.M. They are closed on Saturday.

Shops: Large businesses, such as department stores and supermarkets, are open from 9:00 or 9:30 A.M. to 7:00 P.M., Monday through Saturday. Smaller shops usually stay open until 10:00 P.M. Many close between noon and 2:00 P.M.

Money

• The monetary unit of the Philippines is the *peso*, which is divided into 100 *centavos*. Coins are issued 1, 5, 10, 25, and 50 *centavos*; and 1 and 5 *pesos*. Banknotes are 5, 10, 20, 50, 100, 500, and 1000 *pesos*.

• Major credit cards are honored in hotels, large restaurants, and tourist shops. Don't try to use travelers' checks for payment anywhere other than hotels.

• Realize that only coins with "Bangko Sentral ng Pilipinas" on them are legal tender.

• Don't change money on the black market. The exchange rate is only slightly better than at banks, and there are many scam artists, so it's not worth the risk.

• When you're buying something or agreeing to a business arrangement, find out if the prices are being offered in U.S. dollars or Filipino *pesos*. Be especially careful with tour offices.

Business Practices

• Get in touch with the American Chamber of Commerce (with three locations in the Philippines) and the Philippine American Chamber of Commerce in New York. They are good resources and fine sources of business contacts.

• Don't plan business trips during the holiday period: June through September.

• Realize the Chinese firms are closed during the entire Chinese New Year period—one week before and after Chinese New Year.

• Realize that you will almost certainly have to make more than one trip to conclude a business deal in the Philippines.

• Women planning to do business in the Philippines should recognize that they will have a harder time than men in establishing credibility and conducting negotiations.

• From abroad, make business appointments about a month in advance.

• If your company isn't well known, bring letters of introduction from mutual friends or business associates.

• When scheduling appointments in urban areas, allow a minimum of 30 minutes between appointments because of the horrendous traffic jams.

• Plan to arrange appointments for morning or late afternoon, since there is a midday siesta break. The siesta is usually from noon to 2:00 P.M. Morning appointments are better, if possible, since the heat makes people lethargic in the afternoon.

• Be aware that English is the usual language of commercial correspondence. Many leading businessmen have studied or traveled in the West.

• Men should remember to wear a coat and tie for business meetings, but after repeated visits to a firm, feel free to wear a *barong*, the national dress shirt.

• Be sure to bring business cards. They can be printed in English.

• If a Filipino businessman gives you his business card with his home telephone number handwritten on it, feel free to call him at home.

• Address business people by their title ("Engineer," "Attorney," etc.) plus their last name.

• When doing business with a governmental organization, try to meet with the top official in the department.

• Realize that Filipinos are more flexible and less formal than other Asians.

• Expect a great deal of small-talk initially. Filipinos want to cultivate a personal relationship before negotiating a business arrangement. Be prepared to talk about your background. Prepare a few questions about Filipino life (avoiding politics) and Filipino food. Don't think you're wasting your time because so much of a meeting is passing in personal conversation.

• Allow plenty of time to conclude a business deal. Business is conducted very slowly, and you'll only make a bad impression if you try to rush things.

• Don't be surprised when Filipinos laugh at a crucial point in a meeting. They tend to laugh the loudest when giving their most important messages.

• At each stage of your negotiations, try to get a written agreement. People may have said "Yes" to save face but not really have meant it, so it's important to have commitments in writing.

• Keep in mind that only the most senior people in an organization have the authority and responsibility for making decisions. Foreigners should try to meet with the heads of divisions.

• Set earlier deadlines that you really want or deadlines for small parts of a project, since Filipinos are rather relaxed about times and deadlines.

• Never smoke when visiting a factory. If you want to smoke during a meeting, be sure to ask permission.

Gifts: Gifts are usually presented at the first meeting. Good business gifts include: a subscription to *Fortune* magazine; a bottle of whiskey (especially Chivas Regal); a desk calendar; a pen-and-pencil set.

• On signing a contract, give a gift more expensive than the first one. A dinner invitation to an expensive restaurant is appropriate or an item (crystal, for example) from an internationally known store.

• Remember that gifts are never opened in front of the giver.

Business Entertainment:

• Note that business breakfasts are now common. They usually take place in hotel coffeeshops.

• If you're dealing with a Western businessman living in the Philippines, he will invite you home to a meal or to an early meal in a restaurant. Filipinos will probably in-

vite you out to dinner. They will invite you to their home only if they feel comfortable with their living conditions. The Chinese rarely entertain at home. They may take you out for an evening (not including wives), which may not end until very late.

• Remember that business lunches are considered more casual than other meals.

• Expect invitations to cocktails or dinner at a later stage of a developing relationship. In a restaurant, prepare to go to the bar for a drink before dinner.

• Keep in mind that sing-along bars (*karaoke*) have become popular entertainment spots. Try to join in the singing—even if you have a hard time carrying a tune.

• If you have negotiated a deal successfully, show your appreciation by inviting your Filipino counterparts and their wives to a restaurant. It's usually best to choose one in a hotel; they are centers for business entertainment.

• Include Filipino wives in dinner invitations but not for lunches, when the conversation tends to be strictly business.

• Businesswomen should be aware that it will be impossible for them to pay the check for entertaining Filipino businessmen. Don't try the time-honored strategy of giving the maître d' your credit card beforehand. That will create *very* bad feelings.

Note: For advice regarding business greetings, dress, or table manners, see the appropriate sections earlier in this chapter.

HOLIDAYS AND SPECIAL OCCASIONS

• Expect banks, offices, and most shops to be closed on the holidays listed below, since they are national holidays. Local towns and regions often have festivals which are holidays—with everything closed—in the area. Check with the tourist office for dates of local holidays.

Holidays: New Year's Day (January 1); Maundy Thursday (three days before Easter); Good Friday (two days before Easter); Labor Day (May 1); Independence Day (June 12); Philippine–American Friendship Day (July 4); Thanksgiving Day (September 21); All Saints' Day (November 1); National Heroes' Day (November 30); Christmas (December 25); Rizal Day (December 30), the anniversary of the death of Dr. José P. Rizal, a Philippine national hero.

• Be aware that during Holy Week (the week before Easter) people do not eat meat or attend parties or sporting events. They stay at home and go to church every day.

TRANSPORTATION

Public Transportation

• Realize that there are no subways.

• If you take a bus, state your destination to the conductor, who will collect your money. The fare is based on distance traveled. Keep your ticket in case an inspector comes aboard. In Manila, the Love Bus, which is blue, is popular. These air-conditioned buses operate on several main routes and charge a flat rate. Have small change ready because drivers can't change large bills.

• For another inexpensive form of transportation, try the jeepneys, converted jeeps used as minibuses that carry eight to ten passengers along the most traveled routes. Destinations are marked on the front and side. The entrance is at the rear, with benches on either side. When you get on, pay the driver according to the distance you are going to travel. When you want to get out, bang on the roof, hiss, or yell *"para"* (páh-rah).

• For long-distance travel, consider one of the large buses or minibuses (called baby buses). Vendors sell food at stops along the way. If buses are full, they will depart earlier than scheduled. Some companies accept reservations; even if you have one, arrive early.

• Look for taxis outside hotels or hail one on the street. Most have meters, and drivers use them. If the cab has no meter, bargain for the fare. Be sure to have lots of small coins for change.

• Make it clear to the driver that you do not want anyone else in the taxi, even the driver's friends.

• Keep in mind that there is an additional 50 percent charge for an air-conditioned taxi.

• Note that the only train service is on the main island of Luzon. The train goes from Manila to Ragay. Typhoons often damage bridges, so train trips can be interrupted. Rail travel is slow and is not recommended; for 25 percent extra you can take an express train. There are three classes, with first class featuring air-conditioning and reclining seats. It is safer (i.e., you're less likely to be robbed) for foreigners to travel first class. Keep your ticket for inspection.

• For short distances, consider a boat. There are outrigger and pump boats. Sit in the front where you'll get the least wet.

• For long trips between islands, consider passenger ships; the large ones are of top quality. There are three classes: first class is air-conditioned; second class is not. (It can be terribly hot in the non-air-conditioned accommodations.) The third is deck class, which means that you sleep on the deck. Ask for a camp bed and linen. Buy tickets a few days before your trip. Note that meals—usually fish and rice—are included in the fare; however, food isn't usually very good, so it's best to bring your own.

Driving

• Note that driving is on the right (as in the United States).

• Remember that traffic is undisciplined and chaotic. It's far better to take taxis or to hire a car and driver.

• If you decide to drive, bring an International Driver's License.

• Be aware that you can rent a car from Avis or Hertz through any five-star hotel or car rental agency.

• Realize that some visitors to the Philippines report that police are willing to make on-the-spot settlements for violations.

LEGAL MATTERS, SAFETY, AND HEALTH

• Be aware that the legal drinking age is 21.

• If you're a gambler, note that there are casinos, and they are only for foreigners. Your passport is necessary for admission.

• Take precautions against theft: To foil pickpockets and thieves, men should keep their wallets in the front trouser pocket, in a pouch around the neck, or in a moneybelt, and women should use a moneybelt, keep shoulder bags and camera bags close to your body, don't pay the taxi fare until all your suitcases have been unloaded from the cab, and deposit valuables in a hotel safe.

• Women should take a taxi if they go out at night and should know something about the area of the city into which they are venturing. There are stark contrasts between the luxurious and poverty-stricken areas, and robberies are possible in both types of neighborhoods.

Health: Western drugs are available, but bring a supply of any prescription drugs you take. The particular drug you need may be difficult to find or may have an unfamiliar name.

• Buy bottled water, because tap water outside Manila is not safe. Be sure to avoid ice in drinks and any drink made with unboiled water.

• Don't buy the sliced pineapples and cut-up coconuts that vendors sell. Buy the fruits whole and cut them up yourself.

• Note that most toiletries, tampons, and sanitary napkins are available.

• Avoid buying food from street vendors, because the conditions are often not hygienic. Ice cream can be especially dangerous, since the milk may not be pasteurized.

KEY PHRASES

Note: You will probably never use key phrases in Tagalog, since English is spoken almost everywhere, but here are some just in case.

English	Tagalog (Manila area)	Pronunciation
Good morning	Magandang umaga po	Ma-gahn-dáhng oo-máh-gah pó

Good afternoon	Magandang hapon po	Ma-gahn-dañg há-poan pó
Good evening	Magandang gabi po	Ma-gahn-dáhng ga-bee pó
Good-bye	Paalam	Pa-añ-lahm
Mrs., Madam	Ginang	Geén-ahng
Mr., Sir	Ginoo	Gee-no-ó
Miss	Binibini	Bee-nee-bée-nee
Yes	Opo	Ó-po
No	Hindi po	Heen-dée po
Please	Paki	Pay-kéy
Thank you	Salamat po	Sah-lañ-maht po
Excuse me	Hindi ko po sinasadya	Heen-dee kó pó see-nah-sahd-ya

SOUTH KOREA

 Although Korea hasn't worked to attract tourists as other Asian nations have, the country's rapid transformation from an agricultural economy to an export-based manufacturing economy has meant that more people from the West are visiting the country.

What greets them is a land of profound contrasts, from flat plains to mountains, from hot, hot summers to *very* cold winters (as fans of *M*A*S*H* will remember), and from Seoul, where people are well acquainted with the ways of the West, to the countryside, where old men often wear a loose jacket and baggy trousers in white—to show that they have retired from activities where they might dirty their hands or their clothing.

GREETINGS

• Make a slight bow when greeting someone. People bow when greeting someone for the first time in a day.

• Note that the younger person greets the elder first when two people meet. Always speak to elders in a group first, because they are highly respected.

• Remember that Koreans have three names. First is the family name, then the clan name, and finally the given name. Confusion can arise since some Koreans put their family names last when writing in the Roman alphabet. Koreans usually address each other by family name or full name followed by the honorific term *songsaengnim* (song-sang-nim), which means "respected person." Feel free to use this title, even when addressing someone in English. You may also use titles alone (e.g., "Doctor," "Professor," "Engineer"), should you not know someone's last name, or you could use titles with the last name.

• Use "Mr.," "Miss," or "Mrs." with the family name. Don't expect to move to a first-name basis. Only closest friends in the same peer group use first names.

• Don't expect husbands and wives to have the same family name. Women don't take their husbands' family name when they marry; therefore Mr. Kong may be married to Mrs. Lee.

• A man introduced to a Korean woman should wait until she extends her hand. If she doesn't, don't shake hands. Korean men and Western men always shake hands. A businesswoman should extend her hand first to Korean men and women.

• Don't be insulted if a friend encounters an acquaintance and doesn't introduce you to her/him. It's not usual to introduce others at a casual encounter.

• At parties, wait to be introduced.

CONVERSATION

• Family is an excellent topic of conversation. Koreans place great importance on family, especially sons. Ask a Korean man if he is the eldest son in his family. If he is, he will be very proud of that prestigious role.

• Other good subjects would be the beauty of Korea, the country's rapid growth in the past 20 years, and Korean food.

• Subjects to avoid: Socialism, Communism, Korea's internal politics, religious persecution. Also avoid discussing unions, uprisings, and criticism of Korea. In mixed company, don't bring up sex-related topics.

• Don't be offended if personal subjects are introduced at a first meeting: "How old are you?" "What degree do you have?" "Are you married?" "How many children do you have?" People ask your age to fit you into a pecking order; the older you are, the higher your rank in it.

• Note that Koreans can be very direct, but they also feel it is important to remain polite and proper, so they sometimes agree simply to preserve harmony.

• When speaking to another person, don't put your hands in your pockets or behind your back.

TELEPHONES

• Be aware that there are three types of public telephones: blue, gray, and card phones. Use the gray or blue telephones for both local and long-distance calls. Pay phones accept 10 *won*, 50 *won*, and 100 *won*. A local call costs 40 *won* for three minutes. When you hear a beep, deposit more money. For long-distance and international calls, use the gray or blue phones.

• If you see a local-call telephone with the phone off the hook, realize that the phone was left that way because there is still credit from the last person's call. To make another call, try pressing the green button. It may or may not work.

• Be aware that there are card-operated pay phones, which may be used to make international calls as well as calls within South Korea. Cards may be purchased at small shops near telephone booths, at banks, or at 24-hour convenience stores.

• Keep in mind that hotel operators usually speak English, so you may make calls from your hotel. Before doing so, inquire about the cost.

• For a police emergency in Seoul, dial 112; for fire 119; for an ambulance 129.

IN PUBLIC

• Don't be shocked to see women walking arm in arm with women, and men with men. However, men and women should avoid physical contact with each other in public.

• Remove your shoes before entering a temple or a home. Before you go out, check your socks. Koreans think it very poor form to appear in socks with holes.

• Treat older persons with the utmost respect. Stand when they enter a room, and greet them with a slight bow.

• Don't sit too close to elders, don't remain standing and looking down on them, don't tap them on the shoulder, and don't touch anyone's head.

• Take off your sunglasses when addressing an elder or a superior.

• To show respect, lower your eyes.

• When handing an object or receiving one, use both hands.

• Don't be demonstrative; e.g., embracing, backslapping, or shouting. Never talk or laugh loudly. However, Koreans are demonstrative and noisy among themselves.

• Don't be put off if people smile and laugh in serious situations. They are probably covering up embarrassment. Korean women hold their hand in front of their mouth when they laugh. Western women should do so if they are laughing heartily or yawning.

• Keep to the left when walking on the street or climbing stairs. Allow people to pass in front of you.

• Realize that Koreans stand, sit, eat, and work very close to one another. Westerners often find it difficult to adapt to this lack of personal space. Even if someone bumps into you or steps on your foot by accident, there will be no apology.

• Don't enter a room without giving notice—e.g., clearing your throat or knocking on the door (even if it is partially open). No one expects you to wait for a response. Walk right in.

• Note that men always enter a door ahead of women.

• Avoid blowing your nose in public. Go to a bathroom or a hallway.

• To beckon someone, hold your arm out, palm down, and wave your fingers up and down. Never use one finger to point at another person.

• Realize that Koreans' social status governs the amount of eye contact that they make. People of higher social status usually keep longer eye contact than people of lower status. Most people make eye contact about half the time during a conversation. When not talking, Koreans look to either side. If a Korean is being reprimanded, he will look down slightly.

• Avoid criticism and public disagreement. Never show anger. It's better to accept an injustice quietly and keep harmony.

• If you offer a compliment, expect it to be graciously denied.

• Koreans don't queue, so don't be surprised if you're pushed out of a line while waiting for a taxi or bus.

• Try not to show—either by expression or joking remarks—any reaction to the countless garlicky breaths you will encounter. Koreans eat a *great* deal of garlic. You may want to chew mints, as many Koreans do.

• Don't eat in the streets.

• Don't bring a loaded camera on a domestic flight. It is not permitted.

• Don't photograph military installations and anywhere near the demilitarized zone.

• Ask permission to photograph older people. Be polite, smile, and bow afterwards.

• Single women traveling alone should expect to be asked why they are alone and if they are married, because it's unusual for Korean women to travel alone. To avoid a long explanation, use a response such as, "My husband will be meeting me soon."

• A foreign woman who smokes on the street, wears rubber thongs, or wears sunglasses should expect to be shouted at. All three actions are considered unladylike.

• Look for public toilets in hotels and restaurants. Those in nicer places may have Western-style toilets.

• Don't be surprised to find a public bathroom being used by both men and women. Women should simply walk past the urinals to the stalls.

• If someone knocks on the bathroom door or a stall door, knock back to indicate that the room or stall is occupied.

• In some places, expect to find squat toilets. If there is no pull cord for flushing, there will be a handle near the floor. Push it with your foot.

Shopping: Expect prices to be fixed in most shops and department stores. You can bargain in markets. Stores in which English is spoken have fixed prices.

Exercise: Joggers should use a park, not city streets. Women should wear pants, but men can wear shorts or sweatpants.

should remove their shoes before entering a temple.

• Keep in mind that Koreans appreciate fashionable dress. When you dress well, you show them that you consider the occasion important.

DRESS

• For business, men should wear a suit with a white shirt and tie. If your Korean counterpart removes his jacket, feel free to do so also. Women should wear a suit in a conservative color and always wear stockings (even in the summer). They should never wear gaudy colors, wild prints, or large pieces of jewelry.

• Don't wear shorts or jeans.

• Women should bring loose skirts or dressy pants to wear for evenings out with Koreans. You may be invited to a restaurant or coffeeshop, where you'll be seated on cushions on the floor and you won't be comfortable in a tight skirt. For dining in a restaurant, men should wear a suit, white shirt, and tie.

• To a meal in someone's home, men should wear a jacket, a tie, and good pants.

• Note that formal dress for men in Korea is a navy or gray Western suit and tie.

• When visiting a temple, women should have their shoulders and legs (to the knee) covered. Both sexes

MEALS

Hours and Foods

Breakfast: 7:00 to 9:00 A.M. Typical fare is vegetables, such as a small dish of spinach or bean sprouts, *kimchi* (pickled vegetables), *kim* (dried seaweed heated in sesame oil and cut in squares), soup, rice, and coffee—instant or drip. In most hotels, Western-style breakfasts are available. There will probably be a coffeeshop.

Lunch: 12:00 to 2:00 P.M. Usual dishes: *Bibimbap* (rice with assorted vegetables, tiny bits of meat, eggs, and tiny dried fish), noodles, omelette on rice, *tonkasu* (pork cutlet), and *kimchi*, or soups or stews with rice and pickles.

Dinner: 6:00 to 8:00 P.M. *Pulgogi* (marinated beef cooked at the table in a stew or on a brazier) is popular but expensive because of the high price of beef. An alternative is *samgyae-tang* (chicken and ginseng stew with rice). *Kimchi* is a common side dish.

• Be aware that rice is the main dish at all Korean meals, accompanied by many side dishes such as *kimchi*, steamed vegetables, and soup made of beef, fish, bean paste, mung bean sprouts, or a combination of items. At times, a meal will feature noodles rather than rice.

• Expect *kimchi* (homemade spicy pickled vegetables) at almost every meal.

• The traditional alcoholic beverages are made from grain or potatoes and are similar to vodka: *takchu, yakchu,* and *soju,* the strongest, which has a chemical taste. Korean beer is very good and is often drunk by men.

• Realize that drinking is very much a part of men's business and social lives. If you don't wish to drink, say that you are taking medication that prevents your drinking.

• Common teas are made of herbs and spices: cinnamon, ginger, ginseng. There's no China tea. Coffee is also available. (If you're offered "American coffee," remember that's another name for weak coffee.)

• *Boricha* (made by throwing cold water onto burned barley or rice and cooking for 20 minutes) is served at most meals. It's safe to drink.

• Other nonalcoholic drinks are *omija-wha-chai,* made—both commercially and at home—from fresh or dried fruits and honey or sugar (it's safe if no water has been used in preparing it); *shik-he,* fermented rice and sugar, flavored with citron.

• Note that breakfast is the main meal in the country, while dinner is usually the main meal in the city.

Table Manners

• Don't be surprised at last-minute invitations. They are typical.

• Feel free to arrive 10 to 15 minutes late to a gathering.

• Don't expect to be offered a cocktail before dinner. People don't serve liquor without food. Appetizers will be served—nuts, strips of dried squid, or fish.

• Usually a fork will be offered; if not, prepare to eat with chopsticks. Brass chopsticks—which look rather like knitting needles—and spoons are used for eating, while ladles made of brass or gourds are used for serving food onto each individual plate. Eat rice, soup, and *kimchi* with a spoon.

• Grasp chopsticks close to the top end, and hold them close to the bowl and to your mouth. Don't make a scratching sound against food bowls with either chopsticks or spoons.

• Between bites, either hold your chopsticks or place them on the chopstick rest. The spoon may be left in your soup. To indicate that you have finished, place your chopsticks flat across your main bowl.

• Don't stick chopsticks upright

into a bowl of rice—a position associated with funeral rites.

• Be prepared to eat a great deal if you are invited to dinner in a private home. Not to do so is an offense to your hostess. If the family is not well off, don't eat everything served, as you will have been given special food, and the children will enjoy the leftovers.

• Try not to be offended by the following Korean practice found in lower-class homes: using the soup spoon to dish things out from common bowls, even after they have eaten soup with the same spoon.

• Remember that the whole meal is served at once, not as a series of courses. A typical family meal will have six to ten small dishes; a banquet may have up to fifty. Hot rice is served in individual bowls to the left of the diner and soup to the right.

• Always take food from the platter and place it in your bowl. Don't eat directly from the platter.

• Never pick up food with your fingers.

• When you pass something, use your left hand to support your right forearm.

• Don't look for napkins. They are never used. No one will be offended if you carry a tissue with you and use it as a napkin. Koreans usually use the little finger to clean the corners of the mouth very discreetly.

• While eating, don't raise dishes and bowls to your mouth. It's considered very low-class to pick them up.

• Don't anticipate lively conversation during the meal. Koreans eat quietly and converse afterwards.

• Expect people to make slurping sounds with their soup (and do likewise if you wish).

• Prepare to be served hot and spicy food. Koreans appreciate it if Westerners try the food, but they are not offended if visitors are not able to eat it.

• When you are asked if you want more food, decline politely twice, then accept. If you are entertaining Koreans, be sure to offer more food three times.

• Don't finish everything on your plate. To do so would imply that there wasn't enough food.

• Don't "save room for dessert." It's not usually served. Fresh fruit often appears at the end of a meal.

• Sweets are usually eaten as snacks. (Don't eat the fruit with your fingers. There will be forks or toothpicks on the table.)

• Feel free to use a toothpick after a meal, but be sure to hold one hand in front of your mouth when doing so. Only men should use toothpicks.

• Don't serve yourself drinks. Pour a drink for your Korean friend and he'll do the same for you.

• Women may pour for men but not for other women. The junior person always pours for the senior (usually age is a mark of senior position).

• Pour a drink with both hands on the bottle or one hand on the bottle and the other hand touching the elbow (a sign of deference).

• If you don't want your glass refilled, leave a little in it. Your glass won't be refilled if there is still some liquid in it.

• Don't drink the water. It's not safe—even Koreans don't drink it. Hot boiled water, which is safe, is often served with lunch in the winter. Bottled water is widely available.

• Try not to show any offense at drunken behavior. Koreans always excuse it and cast no aspersions on the drinker.

• Don't be shocked when you become part of the after-dinner entertainment. Whether in home or restaurant, there's a tradition that *everyone* must sing a solo after the meal. Don't try to get out of it. Do it and get it over with. You don't have to learn a song in Korean; singing in English is perfectly acceptable.

• Note that dinner parties tend to break up early. Many dinner parties take place on weeknights, so people have to get up for work the next day.

Places to Eat

• Two popular kinds of restaurants are the *kalbi* (káh-bee), which specializes in beef ribs, and the *dweji kalbi* (dwáy-jee káh-bee), which features pork ribs.

• *Sul-jip* and *makkolli-jip* are wine houses that serve rice wine (a less expensive drink than beer) and hors d'ouevres called *anju: pindaet-tok* (green bean pancakes), *dotori-mook*

(wild acorn gluten), and *pachon* (fried leeks with clams), for example.

• Beer halls also offer snacks, usually peanuts and dried salted fish. Beer is served *pyong* (bottled) or *saeng* (on tap).

• A *tabang* (tearoom) offers coffee and tea. Feel free to linger over a cup of tea. The *tabang* has become a vital institution in modern Korean culture—a meeting place for young and old, male and female. *Ginseng* is an especially popular tea after meals because it is noted for its medicinal properties. If you are an early customer in the winter, expect to be seated near the fire. Give up your seat after a while so newcomers have a chance to warm up. In the summer *tabang* sometimes serve fresh watermelon, peach, or apple juice. If the juice is just crushed fruit, it's probably safe to drink; if water has been added, don't touch it—ask.

• Note that a café (*kyong-yang shick*) is a more sophisticated place than a tearoom. Cafes serve food and alcohol. Look for them in fashionable shopping areas and near universities.

• If you're seeking a Chinese restaurant, look for a red, swinging sign with Chinese characters.

• Keep in mind that you'll find many Japanese restaurants all over Korea, but they tend to be *very* expensive.

• To save money, eat at a noodle restaurant (*poonsik jip*). Frequented by students, they are inexpensive.

• Don't join strangers at a table

in a restaurant, except in Western-style fast-food places.

• Be prepared to find tables and chairs or cushions on the floor—or sometimes both. If there are cushions, there will be one for each diner at a separate, low table. Sit cross-legged. Be sure that you don't put your feet straight out in front of you under the table. Never stand on the cushions. The same advice applies when dining in a home.

• Expect men to socialize with men and women with women in a restaurant.

• To summon the waitress (there are very few waiters), say *"ajuma"* (ah-joo-máh), which literally means "aunt."

• Ask for a menu in English if you're at a restaurant in or near a Western-style hotel.

• Note that most restaurants' menus are posted on the walls on strips of paper with symbols. Either learn the symbols for your favorite dishes, or look at what other people are eating and simply point to what you want. Another option is to ask for *panchan*, which means "side dishes." You'll get soup, rice, and several side dishes—a filling meal.

• If you invite Koreans to a restaurant, expect them to eat a great deal. It is a sign of respect for the host.

Specialties

• Some specialties to try include *chap chae* (transparent noodles pan-fried with chopped vegetables and meat in a sauce), *san juk* (broiled, marinated cubes of beef, mushrooms, scallions, and green pepper on a skewer), *yook hae* (Korean version of steak tartare), *mandu-kook*, (beef broth with pork and beef dumplings), *kalbi* (broiled or steamed ribs), *kimchi* (hot, spicy pickled turnips, radishes, and cabbage, fermented in a large jar), *tang-su-yook* (sweet-and-sour pork), and *tong-talk* (roast chicken).

• Two very special meals: *pulgogi*, strips of beef marinated in soy sauce, sesame oil, onion, garlic, and spices, and grilled over charcoal (a very expensive dish; if Koreans are going to treat you, they will probably take you to a restaurant where this is served); and *shinsollo*, meat, fish, vegetables, eggs, and nuts, cooked at your table in a "hotpot"—a pot with a chimney heated by charcoal.

• Soups: *kuk-pap* (rice soup with meat and vegetables); *mul-man-du* (soup with dumplings filled with onion, egg, meat, sesame, and chives); *so-long-tang* (beef, chive, and rice soup).

• Rice dishes: *po-keum-pap* (fried rice with vegetables and diced meat) and *bibimpap* (a mixture of boiled rice with vegetables, eggs, and/or fruit and hot sauce—there are regional variations, including one made of vermicelli and grated pear).

• *Myun* (noodles) are considered a lunch dish. *Naing-myun* is a cold plate of buckwheat noodles served with *kimchi*, strips of beef or chicken, sliced hard-boiled eggs, and sliced pear, with a chilled broth poured over it. *Jaing-ban* is a similar dish, but served hot.

• Desserts—served for special guests or on holidays: *chunkwa* (candy coated, thinly sliced fruit), *kai-yut* (sesame-seed candies), *su-jun-wa* (persimmons poached in a syrup and flavored with ginger root), and candied or dried fruits.

• You'll probably want to avoid *pashentang*, which is dog soup, and *san-nakchi* (sahn-nak-jee), which is live octopus.

HOTELS

• While there are many Western-style hotels in the country, you may wish to stay in a *yogwan* (yoh-kwahn), a Korean-style inn. You will find the staff very kind and helpful, although they don't speak English.

Yogwans: Take off your shoes before going into the room.

• Note that there is usually a common washing area in the compound around which the *yogwan* is built.

• Expect the maid to lay out your bed—a thin mattress on the floor, which is heated—with a quilt and sometimes sheets. Pillows made of barley shell or rice husks are very firm.

• When using the toilet, wear the rubber slippers provided by the inn.

• Don't expect a dining room. Some *yogwan* owners will send out for a meal and serve it in your room; others serve simple, inexpensive, home-cooked Korean food.

• Even in winter, always open the window a crack because fumes from the heating system (*ondol*) can be deadly.

• If you'll be staying at a *yogwan* during July or August, bring mosquito repellent in case the inn doesn't provide mosquito netting.

TIPPING

• Expect a 10 percent service charge to be added to your bill in restaurants. If you feel the meal and service were deserving, leave a small additional tip, but doing so is not mandatory and may be insulting.

• Tip porters 500 *won* per bag.

• Note that taxi drivers expect tips from Americans but not from

Koreans. Give between 500 and 1000 *won*.

PRIVATE HOMES

• Be aware that Koreans are very hospitable to foreigners and may (though they probably won't) invite you to a meal or for a visit, but don't expect even a close Korean friend or relative to invite you to stay, because houses are too small. Even in homes of the well-off, at night people use every room for sleeping.

• Never drop in on people. Call people you wish to see and invite them to meet you in a coffeeshop. Don't invite a mixed group, however. Men invite only men and women invite only women.

• Never wear outside shoes in the house. Usually your host will provide a pair of slippers.

• Note that most homes are *ondol* style—underfloor heating. Expect to sit on cushions on the heated floor.

• Never admire anything excessively, or people will feel obliged to give it to you.

• Always wear plastic or rubber thongs to the bathroom, since the floors are often wet.

Gifts: If invited to a meal, bring fresh fruit or flowers.

• Other good gifts: liquor, classical music tapes, pottery, and art objects.

• Don't embarrass Koreans by giving a large or ostentatious gift. People can't afford to reciprocate. Accepting an expensive gift involves an obligation. Someone may return such a gift saying that it is too large. If you are given an expensive gift by a Korean, you might consider whether you wish to accept it, since taking the gift puts you under an obligation to the giver.

• Be sure that a gift of money is in an envelope.

• Always offer and accept a gift with both hands.

• Don't expect the recipient to open the gift in your presence, and don't open a gift you receive in the presence of its giver.

• Don't give liquor to a woman unless you say, "This is for your husband." To give it to her is an affront.

• Never give four of anything. It's bad luck.

MONEY AND BUSINESS

Hours

Government Offices: Monday through Friday, 9:00 A.M. to 6:00 P.M. from March to October, and 9:00 A.M. to 5:00 P.M. from November to February. Saturday, 9:00 A.M. to 1:00 P.M.

Businesses: Monday through Friday, 9:00 A.M. to 6:00 P.M. in the summer, and 9:00 A.M. to 5:00 P.M. (November through March). Some business open on Saturday from 9:00 A.M. to 1:00 P.M.

Banks: Monday through Friday, 9:30 A.M. to 4:30 P.M., and Saturday, 9:30 A.M. to 1:30 P.M.

Stores: Department stores are open 10:00 A.M. to 7:30 P.M., six days a week. The day on which they close varies. Small shops are open from early morning until 9:00 or 10:00 P.M., often seven days a week.

Money

• Note that the unit of currency is the *won*. There are coins of 1, 5, 10, 50, and 100 *won*, and banknotes of 500, 1,000, 5,000, and 10,000 *won*.

• Expect major credit cards—American Express, Visa, Barclaycard, MasterCard, Access, Diners Club—to be accepted at large hotels, restaurants, and shops. You can try to pay in restaurants and shops with travelers' checks, but it's unlikely that they will be accepted.

Business Practices

• Before undertaking a trip, make contact with a Korean in your country who can serve as a reference for you and give you a letter of introduction. Introducing yourself usually doesn't work in Korea. A good source of business contacts is the Korea Trade Promotion Office, an organization with offices in several countries.

• Realize that people prefer to do business in person rather than by fax or telephone. Therefore, you will probably have to make many trips to Korea for a long-term business project.

• Bone up on Korean culture. Businessmen will be impressed if you know something about Korean culture and arts, especially pottery.

• Avoid business trips to Korea from mid-July through mid-August. Korean businessmen vacation then. October is a month filled with holidays when businesses are likely to be closed. Check the calendar of local Korean festivals when scheduling your trip. Businesses may not be closed, but the general holiday atmosphere may make it difficult to get anything significant accomplished. Also avoid the two weeks before and after Christmas.

• If you're dealing with a large firm, expect to be offered a car and driver.

• Don't worry about language problems. English is widely spoken in business circles, and most firms correspond in English. Catalogues and promotional material in English are acceptable. However, you will have an advantage if you have materials translated into Korean.

• Note that the best times for business appointments are between 10:00 and 11:00 A.M., and between 2:00 and 3:00 P.M.

• Be prepared for your meeting to be in a hotel coffeeshop. That's standard Korean business practice, though most offices do have a room with Western furniture for visitors from aboard.

• Arrive no more than a few minutes late for an appointment, but don't expect corresponding punctuality on the part of Koreans. Westerners are expected to be on time.

• Bow when you enter and leave a meeting. Greet the most senior person first. Be aware that Koreans rarely use first names when doing business.

• If the meeting is in the company office, accept the offer of one of the drinks usually served to visitors: coffee, barley tea, or soft drinks. Accept the drink with both hands.

• Bring business cards printed in English on one side and Korean on the other. If you run out of business cards, it's easy to get a new supply printed on short notice. Exchange cards at the beginning of the meeting, using both hands in both giving and accepting. Don't put business cards in your wallet. Put the card on the table in front of you.

• Show respect by using business titles; e.g., "Manager Kim," "Director Lee." It will also help you to keep people straight since over 50 percent of Korea's population is named Park, Lee, or Kim.

• Be prepared for meetings to extend beyond the usual business hours.

• Be formal in manners and behavior until a close working relationship has been established.

• Show both friendliness and frankness in trying to sell your product or services, and be patient— business decisions are not made quickly.

• Be sure to cultivate a harmonious atmosphere and always allow people to save face. Koreans may laugh or smile at difficult moments to hide their true feelings.

• Expect Koreans to be louder and more aggressive than other Asians. This behavior is simply the way people communicate.

• Phrase any question carefully, as Koreans tend to answer "Yes," to everything, since being polite and proper is most important to them. Don't say, for example, "Can the shipment be ready in four weeks?"

A Korean may say "Yes," whether it can be or not. Ask instead, "When can this shipment be ready?"

• Try to establish a personal relationship with someone in the company, especially the person your own age in the highest position. It will be to your advantage, since he will act as your intermediary.

• Expect to do business with individuals rather than at a group business meeting. Further, expect Koreans to be very frank. It wouldn't be uncommon for someone to blurt out "I don't like him" or some other direct comment if you were to mention a mutual acquaintance.

• Note that Koreans are also friendly and proud of their personal achievements.

• Don't be put off if a Korean colleague interrupts you. It's considered a sign of eagerness.

• When passing an item to an older businessman, use your right hand.

• Be aware that some Koreans, usually those connected with smaller companies, may view a contract simply as a guide for doing business. Most people affiliated with large companies understand that contracts are legally binding.

• Never sign a document or write a person's name in red ink, because you would be indicating that the person has died.

• Realize that Korean women hold only low-ranking positions in business. Therefore, only foreign businesswomen who have tremendous expertise, seniority, or rank should be sent to do business in Korea.

• Western businesswomen should realize that Korea is the most difficult country for them to do business in, because Koreans tend to be very sexist. Women must be strong leaders and have a thorough understanding of the business they're trying to accomplish. They must be assertive but not aggressive. They should *never* be loud, but behave in a dignified, refined manner.

• A foreign businesswoman should not offer her hand to a man unless she outranks him.

Business Gifts: Expect to exchange business gifts on your first visit. Wait for Koreans to give you a gift first. Don't open the gift until you have left the group. Bring a gift made in your country, preferably something with your company's emblem, such as a pen. Or bring a bottle of Scotch. Clocks are also good gifts. In Korea, they are considered good luck (a view different from several other countries in Asia). Avoid bringing food gifts, since Korean tastes are very different from Western tastes. An excellent business gift, however, is a large fruit basket, made up in Korea.

Business Entertaining: A man entertaining Korean business colleagues should not include their wives in the invitation, nor should he bring his own wife. Only people directly involved in the business dealings should be included.

• Don't expect to be entertained in a Korean home until you know your colleagues well. You will probably be invited to a bar or restaurant, where you'll be offered many courses which you will serve yourself. (The host does not put food on guests' plates as in China.) Although wives are not included, be prepared for a young Korean lady in costume to help guests with food and drink and to join in the singing, dancing, and even caressing. Businesswomen may choose not to go along, or they might want to suggest an alternative site.

• As a Western businessman, expect to be in a place of honor, with each Korean in your group wanting to pour a drink for you. If you don't take a drink, you haven't allowed each one to play host. If you're unsure of your ability to tolerate liquor, ask for a soft drink.

• Since foreign businesswomen may be invited to a restaurant where they'll have to sit on cushions on the floor, they should avoid wearing tight skirts.

Note: For advice regarding business greetings, dress, or table manners, see the appropriate sections earlier in this chapter.

HOLIDAYS AND SPECIAL OCCASIONS

• Expect banks, businesses, and most shops to be closed on the following national holidays. Towns and regions often have local holidays on which everything in the area is closed. Check with the tourist office for dates of local festivals.

Holidays: New Year's Holidays (January 1–3); Lunar New Year (January/February); Independence Movement Day (March 1); Arbor Day (April 5); Children's Day (May 5); Buddha's Birthday (8th day of the 4th month of the lunar calendar—falls sometime in May); Memorial Day (June 6); Farmers' Day (June 15); Constitution Day (July 17); Liberation Day (August 15); Thanksgiving (late September/early October); Armed Forces Day (October 1); National Foundation Day (October 3); Hangul Day (October 9), celebrates the creation of the Korean alphabet in 1443; Christmas (December 25).

• Note that Chusok, a lunar holiday celebrated during September or early October, is the equivalent of the American and Canadian Thanksgiving and features a feast celebrating the harvest. Don't travel during this period or the few days before and after it. Koreans return to their home towns to visit parents' and relatives' graves. There are many family parties with a great deal of drinking, but foreigners are not entertained during this time. Many shops close the day before Chusok.

TRANSPORTATION

Public Transportation

• Take one of three types of bus: local, express, and highway. Be aware that buses go everywhere—even to the most remote villages—several times a day. Highway buses are air-conditioned and more expensive.

• Look for marked bus stops. The bus number is written on the front, right, and rear window, but the destination is written in Korean.

• To save money, buy tokens ahead of time at cigarette booths, snackshops, or stalls with the sign "Bus Tokens."

• When taking a local bus, don't be surprised when a bus girl literally hoists you onto the bus when you get on. Pay as you enter with exact change or a token.

• If you have a seat, offer to hold packages and handbags for people who are standing. If a person who looks 60 or older gets on the bus, give up your seat immediately. Don't be surprised if people start pulling at your packages without saying anything. They merely want to hold them for you.

• Note that there are subways in Seoul and Pusan, which are fast and efficient. Stops are marked in the Roman alphabet. The subway runs from 5:00 A.M. to 12:30 A.M. After you buy your ticket, insert it into a machine, which will stamp it. Keep it until you complete your journey. It will be collected as you leave the station and you will be told if you owe more money.

• Be aware that there are five types of train service: local, ordinary express (has berths, stops frequently and at night), limited express (which can be reserved in advance), luxury, and new village express. The last, which goes to only a few places, is the most luxurious and the most expensive. To avoid long lines and language problems, buy tickets at Tourist Information Center or Korean Tourist Bureau offices or at automated ticket machines, which require exact change. Signs at stations are written in the Roman alphabet.

• Keep your ticket because you will need it to exit the station.

• Look for regular taxis, which

are usually yellow and green. The "88" taxis, black with gold trim, are more comfortable and more expensive. The "88"'s are found at taxi stands.

• Don't worry abut finding a taxi in Seoul and other cities. It's easy, and the taxis are inexpensive.

• Sometimes people going in the same direction share a taxi (the system is called *hap-song*). If you see a taxi on a street corner, and others are trying to get a cab, shout your destination to the driver. Another option is to queue at a taxi stand, but remember that Koreans do not observe queues and you will have to join the shoving match when a cab appears.

• Be sure to have the address of your destination written down in Korean to show to the driver. It's a good idea to have a card with your hotel's name written in Korean for your return trip.

• If you have U.S. dollars with you, you can try to take a *koax*, a taxi for American service people. They are more expensive, and payment must be made in American dollars.

• Be aware that there are separate cars for women on subways and trains. If you are a woman and feel uncomfortable being pushed and shoved by men, use them.

Driving

• If possible, don't drive. Korean drivers are incredibly aggressive, and traffic is very heavy.

• If you decide to rent a car, get an International Driver's License. Bring a translator with you to the rental agency, since no one there will speak English and the transaction is very complicated.

• Remember that driving is on the right, as in the United States.

• Note that most highway signs are in both English and *hangul* (the Korean alphabet).

• Remember that the driver and front seat passenger must wear seat belts.

• Be aware that there is a very heavy fine for drunken driving.

• Don't expect to find many signs indicating speed limits. The limits are 50–60 km/h (approximately 30–35 mph) in urban areas, 60 km/h (approximately 35 mph) on provincial roads, 80 km/h (approximately 50 mph) on main highways, and 100 km/h (approximately 60 mph) on expressways.

LEGAL MATTERS, SAFETY, AND HEALTH

• Don't bring arms, drugs, pornographic literature, or Marxist literature into the country.

• Don't attempt to import Korean currency. It is forbidden.

• Save the receipts when you change money so that you can reconvert *won* into dollars when you leave the country.

• Don't be surprised to hear air-raid sirens on the fifteenth of the month. On that date every month, there is a 15-minute drill sometime during the day. Get off the streets immediately. Go into a building or a subway. There will be wardens with armbands on the streets, making sure that people get to a shelter. An all-clear siren marks the end of the drill.

• Note that the legal drinking age is 20.

• Don't worry about possible trouble with the police. They are very courteous and helpful to Westerners. If one should approach you, be polite. Apologize for not speaking Korean, and ask for an English speaker.

Health: Be sure to bring an adequate supply of any prescription drugs you are taking, since drugs may be difficult to obtain and may have different names.

• Be aware that most toiletries as well as tampons and sanitary napkins are available.

• Never eat food bought from a sidewalk vendor. Ice cream is especially dangerous, since the milk may not have been pasteurized.

• *Never* drink any water that is not bottled.

• Women should *not* walk alone at night. Korean men tend to drink a great deal, and there are many intoxicated men out after 10:00 P.M.

• Women should not get into a taxi late at night if there are other passengers already inside.

• Women should guard against groping on crowded subways. Some local women carry pins to ward off gropers.

KEY PHRASES

Note: Korean is *not* a tonal language. Its simple phonetic alphabet has 24 phonetic symbols. They can be learned quickly, and it's well worth the small effort to be able to sound out names of places and foods. Korean is not related to other Asian languages but to Finnish and Hungarian. English is widely used in commercial circles.

English	Korean	Pronunciation
Good morning, afternoon, evening, night	Annyong hashimnika	Aňn-yohng háh-shim-nee-kah
Good-bye: person leaving says	Annyong ikeiseyo	Aňn-yohng ee-káy-say-o
Good-bye: person staying says	Annyong kaseyo	Aňn-yohng káh-say-o
Sir, Mr., Ms, Miss, Mrs.	Shi (after last name, as in Kim-shi)	Shee
Yes	Ne	Neh
No	Aniyo	Ah-nee-yó
Thank you	Kamsa hamnida	Kaňm-sah háhm-nee-dah
You're welcome	Ch'onmaneyo	Chón-mahn-ay-yo
Excuse me	Sille hamnida	Sée-lay háhm-nee-dah
I don't understand	Ara ansumnida	Aň-rah aňn-some-nee-dah
I don't speak Korean	Hangungmalul mot hamnida	Haňn-gung-mah-lull mót haňm-nee-dah
Does anyone speak English?	Yongo halsu issumnika?	Yoňn-go háhl-sue eé-some-nee-kah?

SRI LANKA

Jaffna

GULF
OF
MANNAR

Trincomalee •

Batticaloa •

• Colombo

• Galle

INDIAN OCEAN

Centuries ago, Muslim traders referred to the island 30 miles off the coast of India as "Serendib," from which comes the word "serendipity," a pleasant discovery made by accident. Sri Lanka also was visited by traders from ancient Greece and Rome, was ruled successively by Portugal, the Netherlands, and Britain (under its former name, Ceylon), and finally declared itself a republic and took its present name in 1972.

After a visit to the country, British writer George Bernard Shaw observed, "I was convinced that Ceylon is the cradle of the human race because everybody there looks an original. All other nations are obviously mass produced." That the country thinks of itself the same way is evidenced by a Sri Lankan's offer to show writer Paul Theroux the graves of Cain and Abel.

The Sinhalese, the majority of the population, are predominantly Buddhist, while the minority Tamils are mainly Hindu. Some of the Tamils came with invaders from south India centuries ago. Others were imported from India by the British during their colonial dominance because the Sinhalese refused to work on European plantations. Unfortunately, violence between Sinhalese and Tamils in recent years has damaged Sri Lanka's economy badly and played havoc with the country's image with tourists.

GREETINGS

• As a Westerner, shake hands when introduced to a male Sri Lankan. Women do not usually shake hands with men.

• Note that the traditional welcome greeting among the Sinhalese and Tamils is to fold the hands upward in front of the chest while saying "Hello" (see "Key Phrases").

• Don't use first names until you know a person very well.

• If a person is a doctor (M.D.) or professor, be sure to use the title.

• At parties, expect to be introduced to each guest individually. Shake hands with each person.

• Women who are good friends embrace when they meet; men sometimes do also. Foreign men should be sure not to kiss Sinhalese (pronounced "Singhalese") or Tamil women.

• Don't expect a man to greet you if he is smoking; if you are smoking and see someone (e.g., at a party) who will probably approach to greet you, hide your cigarette as well as you can or put it out.

• Don't be surprised to see male youths holding hands. It's simply a sign of friendship.

CONVERSATION

• Topics to bring up: family, where your hosts are from, and schools and colleges they attended. (*Note:* School means elementary school; college is the equivalent of high school from which a student goes on to university, corresponding to a Western college.) Other subjects: sports, hobbies, where people have relatives overseas.

• Try to be relaxed in your conversation. Inquire about others' health and families, and listen to their replies. Sri Lankans think that foreign tourists are too abrupt.

• Don't be surprised when a Sri Lankan uses the expression "What to do?" It's a rhetorical question, simply indicating a pause to think about a problem.

• Do not confuse Sri Lankans with Indians, because they view themselves as culturally distinct. It's difficult to tell the two groups apart by appearance. For example, if you're not sure of a person's identity, don't start talking about an Indian political problem (assuming the person an Indian). It would probably be of no interest to him if he isn't Indian.

• Topics to avoid: Never mention caste. Since caste was originally synonymous with occupation, don't ask a question such as "What does your father do?" Your acquaintance might not want to disclose that his father originally worked with his hands. Don't ask direct questions about a person's religion. You might say, "Are people around here mostly Buddhist?"

• Don't offer your opinion on the problems between Tamils and Sinhalese. Just listen and ask questions.

TELEPHONES

• Look for public telephones in restaurants, cafés, hotels, shops, post offices, and in booths on streets. Deposit 50 cents and dial. At the end of three minutes, there will be a signal; deposit another 50 cents if you wish to continue the call.

• Realize that there is international direct dialing (IDD) to most countries from Colombo and some other communities. If you can't dial direct, book the call (for a minimum of three minutes) through the international operator.

• If you make a long-distance collect call from the post office, expect to wait an hour or more for the call go through.

• Look for three different kinds of card phone (each of which takes a separate card). One called Lanka Pay is yellow and blue; Metrocard is orange and black; a third, Supercard Phone, which is relatively rare, is blue and white. You'll find Lanka Pay card phones at post offices. All three phones allow you to make IDD calls. Buy phone cards in shops that have ads for them in the window.

• Send faxes or Telexes from communications centers.

• For a police emergency, dial 33333. For an ambulance, dial 222222. To reach the tourist police, dial 26941 or 21111.

IN PUBLIC

• Never hand objects to anyone with your left hand, and never receive anything from another person with your left hand. The left hand is to clean oneself after using the toilet and is considered unclean.

• Realize that members of the same sex very often hold hands, but any demonstration of intimacy in public between men and women is totally inappropriate.

• Don't touch a person's head. To Sri Lankans, it's the most sacred part of the body.

• To beckon someone, extend your arm and hand (palm facing down) in front of you, and move your fingers toward your body.

• Note that "yes" is indicated by a cross between a nod and a side-to-side shake of the head.

• When visiting temples, remove shoes and hats before entering. Make sure your arms and legs are covered. These rules hold true even for temples in ruins, for "once a temple always a temple." You may be asked to leave all leather belongings, such as belts and handbags, outside. If so, one person in your group may stay outside to guard them, or if you are persistent, you may be allowed to bring them in.

• Never sit on a statue of Buddha. It is a sacrilege and could lead to your arrest.

• Be very respectful (no loud laughing, fooling around) in a temple, even one that is in ruins. If the idol is present, Sri Lankans still worship there.

• If you meet a Buddhist monk, show respect by raising both hands as in prayer to just below your chin. Don't shake hands. Monks should never be touched. A monk is not allowed to touch money; any donation you wish to leave should be placed in the temple offering box.

• Women should be aware that Sri Lankans regard the smiling behavior of Western women as flirtatiousness. Sri Lankan women smile or appear friendly only with cousins or boys whose parents are close family friends.

• Be on time for social as well as business functions.

• In Kandy, expect elephant owners to ask if you want to sit on an elephant and have your picture taken. Always agree to a price beforehand. They expect you to bargain.

• Be prepared for someone you have photographed to ask for money. Give a *rupee* or two.

• Remember that taking photographs inside museums and caves is usually forbidden. Look for signs.

• Don't photograph in downtown Colombo or at dam sites, military camps, road blocks, airports, or in any military zone.

• Always ask permission before taking photographs in temples. Don't pose or photograph anyone posed next to a statue, because you would be showing a lack of respect.

• If at all possible, send a copy of the photo to people whose picture you have taken. They keep photos forever in albums. Even better is to have an instant camera, so that you can give a copy of the photo immediately.

• To find a public bathroom, look for signs in English or for symbols on the doors. Bathrooms are usually found in hotels, train stations, and other public places. Try to stick to the bathrooms in better restaurants and hotels. Others tend to be dirty. They are merely holes in the floor—with no toilet paper.

Shopping: Bargain except in state shops or department stores. If in doubt, ask, "Is this a one-price shop?"

• In bargaining, never be the first to mention price. Let the seller do that.

• Remember that if you mention a price and the merchant accepts it, you are obliged to buy at that price. Don't, therefore, get into bargain-ing (as opposed to comparison shopping) until you are ready to buy. And don't respond to the merchant with a specific price. Say, for example, "That's more than I intend to spend," until the merchant gets to a price that you are willing to pay.

Exercise: Because of the humidity at sea level and the high altitude of Kandy and the surrounding area, jogging is not a good idea. Even if you confine your jogging to hotel grounds, you may draw a crowd, since jogging isn't the "done" thing. Both men and women should wear T-shirts and Bermuda shorts (not short shorts) made of cotton.

DRESS

• Appropriate casual wear for men is a shirt and trousers; for women, shirt and pants, skirt, or dress.

• Women should not wear revealing tops or dresses and should wear shorts only on the beach.

• If invited to a meal in a home, men should wear slacks and a shirt; they might wish to carry a jacket in case their host is wearing one.

Women should wear a dress or skirt and blouse.

• Note that men are not required to wear jackets or ties except for formal functions. If the invitation specifies formal wear, wear a lightweight or medium-weight dark suit. Women should wear a cocktail dress. Local people will wear native dress, which is considered formal. Most invitations specify the type of clothing to be worn—formal, casual, etc. If you are in doubt as to appropriate dress, ask.

• Wear sandals rather than shoes. They are more comfortable than shoes and if they are slip-on (as are thongs) will be more practical for visiting temples and shrines where shoes must be removed. (Most temples permit people to wear socks, if they don't relish going barefoot.) In summer, the floors can be scorching hot.

• Never wear shorts in a temple (men or women). Some temples will rent you a sarong if you are not dressed properly, but most will simply not allow you enter.

• Never sunbathe in the nude on a beach, an act Sri Lankans find highly offensive.

MEALS

Hours and Foods

Breakfast: 7:00 or 7:30 A.M. It's a hearty meal with eggs, bacon, bread, a meat or fish curry, hoppers (*appa*—waffle-like circles of thin strips of pastry fried in coconut oil), and *sambol*; or string hoppers (*indiappa*) and curry; or milk rice (*kiribath*) and *sambol*. Beverage is tea or coffee.

Lunch: noon to 2:00 P.M. Meat or fish curries, vegetable curries, rice, hoppers, fruit or pudding or ice cream.

Dinner: 8:00 or 9:00 P.M. to 10:00 P.M. Like lunch, it will consist of rice and curries.

• Desserts are usually fresh fruits—most popular are pineapple, papaya, and a variety of bananas.

• Beverages are *thambili,* the liquid of a bright orange coconut, drunk plain or with sugar, lime, and a little salt; "toddy," an alcoholic drink made of coconut sap; *arrack*, a fermented toddy; beer; soft drinks, such as lemonade, orange crush, colas, and ginger beer (the main brand is Elephant House); water. Tea is the national drink; Sri Lanka's tea is considered among the world's finest.

• If you don't know whether water is bottled or has been boiled, ask for a soft drink. (It's rude to ask if the water has been boiled). Usually beer, cola, and other soft drinks are offered with meals.

• Foreign liquors are available in most restaurants.

Table Manners

• Anticipate about two hours of drinking and conversation before dinner. In non-Muslim homes, cocktails—and possibly appetizers—will be served; Muslims will have soft drinks. If you're invited for 6:30 P.M., don't expect to eat before 8:30 P.M. It's a good idea to have a snack before arriving. Common cocktails are *arrack*, which is very strong, and toddy, which is not so strong. Women usually don't drink but may accept a glass of wine. Appetizers such as nuts, cheese pastries, or prawns may be served.

• Always wait for your host to seat you at the table. Seats near the host and hostess (if she's not serving) are the seats of honor.

• In villages, expect food to be served on a plaintain leaf (a fruit similar to a banana) about one foot by two feet in size. Also expect to sit on mats on the floor.

• Though you will almost surely be offered cutlery, realize that eating in Sri Lanka is usually done with the fingers. People use *hoppers, roti,* or rice to scoop up the curries.

• First, put rice on your plate with a serving spoon. Then put various curries on top of it. Mix everything with the fingers of your right hand (up to the second knuckle), making a small ball, and push the mixture into your mouth with your thumb.

• *Never* use your left hand when eating, even with cutlery. The left hand is used for cleaning after going to the toilet. If you're left-handed, practice eating with your right hand before leaving home and think of it as a cultural experience. Be sure not to accept anything with your left hand.

• Expect food to be served family-style and to help yourself from the serving dishes.

• Be aware that rice and curry are the mainstays of Sri Lankan cooking. On your plate of rice, put a spoonful of various curries and *sambol* (grated coconut, lime, salt, red pepper, and Maldive fish—fermented, sun-dried tuna). The curries, cooked in coconut milk, may be made with meat, fish, vegetables, or eggs. The homemade curry powder is prepared from cumin, turmeric, fennel seed, coriander, cardamom, cloves, bay leaves, black and red pepper, mustard, and cinnamon.

• Don't make any comment or try to clean up if someone spills curry on the table while taking it from the serving dish. People have a tendency not to hold their plates near the serving dishes, and curry sauce often drips onto the table.

• If you are invited to a Tamil

home, expect to be served a vegetarian meal.

• Don't be shy about asking for a second helping.

• If you have nearly finished what's on your plate, be aware that turning your head will cause someone to pile a great deal of rice on your plate. To avoid this, fold your hands over your plate so no one can give you more without asking if you want it.

• If you don't care for something, leave it on your plate.

• Push your plate forward gently to indicate that you have finished.

• Use the finger bowls after the meal. If there are no finger bowls, excuse yourself and wash your hands.

• Leave about 30 minutes after the meal has ended, especially if it was served very late. The main socializing takes place before dinner. Take your cue from other guests.

Places to Eat

• Note that a *hotelaya* refers to all kinds of restaurants with both Western and Asian dishes generally available.

• Look for bars serving alcohol only in hotels catering to foreigners.

• In every village, expect to find an eating house called *kade*. The exteriors may be seedy-looking and therefore off-putting to tourists, but the food and tea are often very good (especially at those establishments where long-distance buses and trucks stop).

• If you don't want to be burned by chilies in the food, eat at Chinese restaurants.

• Women should feel free to dine alone in cities. Sri Lanka's middle class is liberated, and women often eat in restaurants alone.

• Note that some restaurants have menus posted in windows. If one doesn't, ask inside what dishes are available. There will usually be someone who speaks English and can explain the dishes to you.

• At smaller resthouses don't expect printed menus, but the waiter will tell you in English what is available.

• At resthouses, be aware that the cook usually has prepared a ready-cooked rice-and-curry meal. If you order this, service will be much faster than if you order other dishes.

• If a restaurant is crowded, feel free to ask others if you may share their table. Sri Lankans are so friendly that they may invite you to sit with them before you ask.

• Remember that rice and curry dishes are often very hot. For medium-spiced dishes, ask for "white curry" called *kiri*. The spiciest curry is called *rathu*.

• Don't suggest a "Dutch treat." There is no such thing. The person who invites always pays. Don't offer to pay if you've been invited; it would be an insult.

Specialties

• Look for several types of special breads: string hopper, waffle-like circles of thin pastry strips fried in coconut oil until crisp, used to eat curry; *indiappa*, string hopper made with rice flour—a popular breakfast dish; egg-hoppers (*bit-hara*): To eat this pancake with a fried egg on top, roll the egg-hopper around the egg (they can also be eaten with jam rolled inside them); *roti*, flatbreads made of flour, coconut, water, and salt, eaten with curries and served as a substitute for rice; *papadums*, crispy fried wafers.

• As condiments, use mango chutney and date-and-lime pickle.

• Another dish to sample is *lamprais*—curries, *sambols*, special prawn paste, and eggplant curry placed around rice, wrapped in a banana leaf and baked.

• Sample *appa*—thin cup-shaped pancakes made from fermented batter of rice flour, coconut milk, and palm toddy. They are crispy on the outside with a soft center. *Appa* is another name for hopper.

• Feed your sweet tooth with *dodols* and *aluwas* (fudge-like sweets), *thalaguli* (sesame balls), or *rasakevilis* (rich, sticky sweetmeats made from rice flour and coconut milk), which are served on special occasions.

HOTELS

• Be very careful to avoid the touts (persuaders) who hang around bus and train stations and in other tourist areas. They hope to entice you to a certain hotel or guest house where they'll get a commission. Though Sri Lankans are usually not intrusive, these touts may be very aggressive. Never trust them. Respond by saying that you already have a reservation.

• Note that there are two types of large hotels: modern, with all types of amenities and facilities, and colonial style, which may offer as many amenities and which also have great charm.

• Realize that hotels near temples can be very noisy during festival times when music blares from loudspeakers.

• Look for inexpensive lodgings in government cottages, bungalows in national parks, and resthouses, but remember that many small snackshops call themselves "hotels," even though they aren't.

• Note that electricity goes off frequently. Many hotels place candles in rooms. It's a good idea to bring along a flashlight.

• If you're visiting the southwest coast during the months of May through October (the low season), ask if your hotel offers a discount during that period.

• Don't expect central air-conditioning except in the larger hotels in Colombo. You may find individual units at other hotels and at beach resorts. Your room will very likely have a ceiling fan.

• If your bed has mosquito netting, be sure to use it. In case it doesn't, it's a good idea to bring some insect repellent with you.

• If there are problems with your room, call the manager, and be calm and reasonable, giving him a chance to right things. Hotels usually back customers, so the manager will probably be cooperative.

• Be aware that hot water is not available in all areas. If you want hot water, ask to have some heated.

• In low-priced hotels, be aware that there may only be a tap and bucket in the bathroom, as well as a squat toilet.

• Never leave valuables in your hotel room, even if it is locked. Hotels usually offer safe-deposit boxes for guests.

• Note that many hotels don't charge for local calls within Colombo.

• Don't expect to be served liquor anywhere but in large hotels. Lodges and small hotels don't offer liquor service.

TIPPING

• At hotels and restaurants, a service charge will be added.

• Tip porters *Rs* 10–20 per bag.

• Give taxi drivers 10 percent of the fare as a tip.

PRIVATE HOMES

• If visiting a traditional home, remove your shoes before entering.

• Remember that hospitality means you will be cared for like a baby. It would be ungracious to resist such care too much. If an offer is *too* generous, you can refuse. But be sure to accept the gestures, which may be costly in time and trouble, and which relatively poor people do for you. To be gracious, follow the motto of the Peace Corps: "Accept, accept, accept."

• When attending a party in someone's home, expect people to break up into two groups: men and women. Western visitors should observe this custom.

• Unless you have made an appointment to visit, feel free to drop in between 4:00 and 7:00 P.M. If possible, call ahead, but spontaneous visits during those hours are okay, since many people don't have telephones.

• Be aware that a *dhobi* (a male servant who collects and returns laundry) will not hesitate to come into your room without knocking (in a private home) to pick up your laundry. If you're embarrassed to be found without clothes on, either lock your door or keep something on at all times.

• Expect a servant to bring you "bed tea/coffee" between 6:00 and 7:30 A.M. unless you ask that he not do so. As a kindness to the servant, ask him to deliver it at a later time. Ask your host when the family eats breakfast—usual times are between 7:30 and 8:30 A.M.

• Offer to pay for phone calls, even though you will probably find phones only in the homes of the wealthy.

• Expect homes of the middle and upper classes to be air-conditioned.

• Note that people normally bathe three times a day because of the heat. In middle- and upper-class homes, there will be hot water, but there won't be in lower-class homes.

• If the family with whom you're staying has servants, give each one 10 to 20 *rupees* when you leave, if you have stayed only a few days. For a longer stay, give 30 to 50 *rupees*. Don't ask your host how much to give, because he will say, "Don't give anything."

• Don't offer to do food shopping. The cook does the shopping in the bazaar. You would only be in the way, and you would be charged more.

• Don't worry about offending your host family if you would like to go sightseeing on your own. Simply tell them in advance that you'll be going off to a certain destination. They may offer you the family car. Tell them that you will get a taxi, but feel free to accept their offer if they persist after you refuse twice.

Gifts: If you are invited to a meal, bring chocolates or a bottle of whiskey (if you know that the family drinks) if you wish; a gift is neither expected nor necessary.

• Give men small electronic gadgets or pens; give women cosmetic cases, perfume, or lipstick; and bring teenagers T-shirts from foreign universities. Children like stamp albums and stamps.

• Don't bring costume jewelry as a gift, since women wear only real gold.

• When presenting a gift, use both hands.

• Don't expect people to open

your gift in your presence. If you receive a gift, put it aside until you are alone.

MONEY AND BUSINESS

Hours

Offices: Monday through Friday, 8:00 A.M. to 4:30 P.M. Some businesses are open on Saturday until 1:00 P.M.

Banks: Monday from 9:00 A.M. to 1:00 P.M., and Tuesday through Friday until 1:30 P.M. (Banks often close early the day before a holiday.)

Shops: Monday through Friday, 9:00 A.M. to 7:00 P.M. and Saturday from 10:00 A.M. until 3:00 P.M. In Colombo, the large department stores often close for lunch at 1:00 or 1:30 P.M. and reopen at 2:30 P.M. Some shops are open until late in the evening.

Money

• The Sri Lanka *rupee* contains 100 cents. Abbreviation for a single

rupee is *Re*; plural is *Rs*. Coins are 5, 10, 25, and 50 cents, and *Rs* 1, 2, 5, and 10. Banknotes are *Rs*, 10, 20, 50, 100, 500, and 1000. (Remember that travelers' checks have a better rate of exchange than cash.)

• Don't accept torn or dirty notes, since merchants, restaurants, etc. will not accept them.

• As a foreigner, be prepared to pay more than Sri Lankans at various tourist sites, such as lodges in national parks and at the zoo.

• Expect major credit cards— American Express, Visa, Barclaycard, MasterCard, Access, Diners Club—to be welcome at major hotels, shops, and restaurants. Be aware, however, that some shops will add a surcharge to credit-card purchases. This is illegal. Before you sign the form for your purchase, check to see that such a surcharge has not been added.

Business Practices

• In planning business trips, avoid the Christmas/New Year period and the April vacation, which falls during the Tamil and Sinhalese New Year and therefore varies from year to year. Most executives take breaks during those times. Remember that many Buddhist holidays are also public holidays, since Buddhism is the country's dominant religion. Check with the embassy or consulates for dates, since the dates of Buddhist holidays change each year.

• Make appointments at least a

week in advance because some offices have flexible hours and many close for lunch. As soon as you arrive in Sri Lanka, reconfirm the appointment. However, if you're in Sri Lanka and want to visit a company, an appointment is usually possible on short notice.

- Try to schedule meetings at the beginning of the day, because people sometimes leave work early.

- When dealing with the government, make *very* sure that you are dealing with the correct ministry and officials. Once again, your country's embassy or consulate may be a source of that information. Most companies are, however, private.

- Anticipate making at least two trips to complete even a simple business deal.

- Bring business cards. It's okay to have them printed in English. Exchange business cards when you are introduced.

- It's acceptable to bring proposals and supporting materials in English.

- Present proposals to the managing director or president of the firm. If you need facts or details checked, approach middle management, since people at the upper echelons will not want to be bothered with such requests.

- Be prepared for a first meeting to be a lunch in a restaurant or even a meal in a home. Sri Lankans want to know you before doing business with you.

- At meetings, expect to be offered tea, the national drink. To be polite, compliment your host on the quality of the tea.

- Don't be surprised if the Sri Lankan belief in astrology affects business decisions. For example, people may want to wait for an auspicious day to conclude an agreement or open a factory.

- Remember that verbal agreements are not considered binding, but written contracts will be strictly adhered to. Nevertheless, leave ample time for delays and include small deadlines, because people are not efficient and deadlines are frequently missed.

- Whatever the provocation, *never* criticize a person in front of others, because maintaining face is very important to Sri Lankans. Don't ever raise your voice in anger, even if a Sri Lankan does.

- If you need secretarial or telecommunications service, ask if your hotel offers such services. Most large hotels do.

- Since Sri Lanka had the world's first woman prime minister, women should anticipate little trouble in being taken seriously in business.

Business Entertaining: Entertain business colleagues at lunch or dinner. Both are equally popular. If you want to discuss business, suggest lunch.

- Feel free to include wives in an invitation to a business dinner.

- Note that Sri Lankan businespeople enjoy being entertained at Western restaurants.

• If you are entertaining Sri Lankans, be sensitive to their food restrictions. Muslims do not eat pork and Hindus do not eat beef (and some are vegetarian).

Note: For advice regarding business greetings, dress, or table manners, see the appropriate sections earlier in this chapter.

HOLIDAYS AND SPECIAL OCCASIONS

• Expect banks, offices, and most shops to be closed on the following national holidays. Some towns and areas have individual festivals, which are holidays in that region. Check with the tourist office for dates of local festivals.

Holidays: Hadji Festival Day, a Muslim holiday celebrating Mohammed's journey to Mecca (December/January); New Year's Day (January 1); Thai Pongal Day, a Hindu festival in honor of the sun god (January 14); Independence Day (February 4); Maha Sivarathri Day, an important Hindu festival, celebrating the marriage of the great god Shiva and his consort (February/ March); Sinhala and Tamil New Year's (April); Good Friday; May Day (May 1); Wesak Poya Day (May); National Heroes Day (May 22); Special Bank Holiday (June 30); Deepavali (October/November/December); Christmas Day (December 25); Special Bank Holiday (December 31).

• Note that Wesak Poya Day commemorates the birth, enlightenment, and death of Buddha. Temple bells announce the dawn, and pilgrims dressed in white spend the day in meditation and listening to monks recite the words of Buddha. At roadside sheds, people give free food to pilgrims. Colombo is especially festive at this time.

• Expect all bars and entertainment centers (except those in tourist hotels) to be closed on Full Moon holidays (called Poya Days), which occur one day each month. They are days of solemn religious observances. In public, never show that you are enjoying yourself.

TRANSPORTATION

Public Transportation

• Keep in mind that there are four types of bus: CTB (formerly government owned but now privately owned), which are red or silver; new and roomy government buses, which are yellow with a blue stripe and a lion logo; other private buses which include modern, large coaches, used for intercity travel; and city or short-term intertown, old minibuses. The modern intercity express coaches are air-conditioned and cost twice as much as ordinary buses.

• Remember that you can reserve seats in advance on CTB buses but not on other private ones. Buses run parallel service with little difference in cost.

• Before you choose bus travel, remember that buses are terribly overcrowded, and drivers are often reckless.

• Be very sure not to sit in one of the first two seats on a bus or train. Those seats are reserved for Buddhist monks, a strict policy. How-ever, people usually ignore the seats allegedly reserved for women.

• To find a taxi, look for yellow tops with red numbers on white license plates. Check for a company name on the side of the taxi, as such taxis are usually safer and have more honest drivers. Ordering a taxi at a hotel, ask for a registered taxi. Many taxis are not metered and can be quite expensive. Settle the fare with the driver before beginning the ride. Almost all drivers speak English.

• As an alternative to taxis (and if you're feeling a bit adventurous), take one of the three-wheeled scooters (like auto-rickshaws). You'll find them everywhere. Negotiate the fare before getting in. Although they have seats and are covered, passengers don't have much protection from falling out.

• Recall that first-class accommodations, offered on overnight trains, have air-conditioning, an observation car, and sleeper berths. It is the only class for which advanced reservations can be made and is offered only on overnight trains. There are also special luxury tourist trains. Second class has cushioned seats, while third offers only hard seats. Both second and third class are crowded, noisy, and stuffy.

• Be aware that there are no second-class sleeping compartments, only fold-down benches, called sleeperettes.

• If you find all seats booked, seek out the station master. He may be able to find a seat for a foreign visitor.

Driving

• Be aware that driving is very dangerous because of the narrow, winding roads with children, bicycles, animals, and trucks. There are no rules of the road and no signs. Drivers care only about what's in front of them and pay no attention to drivers behind them. Drivers don't look in their rearview mirrors and will swerve back and forth, not caring about drivers behind them. Be alert for the constant honking of horns. Pedestrians count on being warned from behind with a horn honk. Driving is on the left, as in Britain and Japan.

• If you want to rent a car, remember that you must obtain a temporary Sri Lankan driver's license. If you have an International Driver's License, you can have it endorsed. The rental agency will obtain the endorsement for a small fee.

• Note that hiring a car and driver costs less than renting a car. Drivers speak English and so can do double duty as guides. Engage a driver through a large hotel, a guest house, a travel agency, or even through a taxi driver.

LEGAL MATTERS, SAFETY, AND HEALTH

• Because of the political violence and civil war in the north and east of Sri Lanka in 1995, be sure to check with your State Department or Foreign Office before leaving for the country to find out which areas to avoid.

• Guard against pickpockets on crowded buses.

• If you stay in a ground floor room in a guest house, don't sleep with the window open because of the danger of thieves entering.

• If you're interested in photographing archeological sites, apply to the Commissioner of Archeology in Colombo to find out if you need a permit—and to get one if you do.

• Keep the form on which you declare all your currency on arrival. You can't exchange money without it. Each time you change money, have the transaction recorded on the form or ask for a receipt. When you leave the country, you must show receipts for money exchanges and for purchases.

• When you leave Sri Lanka, be

sure to change unspent *rupees before* you go through Customs. In purchasing duty-free items in the departure lounge area, you can use only foreign currency.

• Don't try to export antiques—objects more than fifty years old—or birds or animals. All such exports are banned.

Health: Note that imported drugs are very expensive, so bring an adequate supply of both prescription drugs and any nonprescription items (e.g., aspirin, vitamins) you may use.

• Never drink tap water or drinks with ice. Be sure that the bottled water you drink has a seal. Sometimes people put tap water in bottles and use a cork or a cover to close them.

• Only eat vegetables and fruits which can be peeled.

• Be sure that any meat you eat is well cooked.

• Sanitary napkins and tampons are available, but they have different brand names. For example, the main brand of sanitary napkins is called "Filtex."

• Never eat food purchased from a street vendor. Ice cream is especially dangerous as the milk may not have been pasteurized.

KEY PHRASES

Most educated people as well as those involved in the tourist industry speak English.

English	Sinhalese	Pronunciation
Hello, good morning, afternoon, evening, good-bye	Ayubowan	Aĥ-you-bo-wáhng
Mr., Mrs., Miss	Use English forms	
Please	Karunakarala	Kah-roo-naĥ-kah-rah-lah
Thank you very much	Bohoma isthuthi	Bo-hó-ma ees-toó-tee
Yes	Ouv	Ó-oo
No	Natha	Neh
Excuse me	Oben avasarái	Ó-ben-ah-vah-sah-réye
I don't understand	Mata therennay nehe	Maĥ-tah táy-ray-nay néh

I don't speak Sinhalese	Mata Sinhala danne nehe	Mań-tah Seen-háh-lah dań-nay néh
Does anyone speak English?	Kavuruth Ingrisi katakaranavada?	Kau-voo-róot een-grée-see kah-táh-kah-rah-nah-vah-dah?

English	Tamil	Pronunciation
Hello, good morning, good afternoon, good evening	Vanakkam	Vah-nah-kahm
Good-bye	Poyitu varen	Poýit oówa-réhn
Please	Dayavu seydu	Dáhya-voo séh-doo
Thank you	Nandri	Náhn-dree
Excuse me (I'm sorry)	Manniyangai	Mánnee-yángga
Yes	Aamaa	Ań-mah
No	Illai	Íl-lah
I don't understand	Puriyillai	Póorri-ýilla
Is there someone who speaks English?	Inge yaarukaavadu Inglish pesa teriyuma?	Inǵa yańra-kańva-duh Ingglish péh-sa térri-yoo-mah?

There are no Tamil words for the following; Hindi words are used:

Mr.	Sri	Sree
Mrs.	Srimati	Sree-máh-tee
Miss	Kumari	Koo-máh-ree

TAIWAN

In the sixteenth century, Portuguese sailors named it *Ilha Formosa*, "Beautiful Island." Later, the Chinese christened it Taiwan, "Terraced Bay."

Whatever its name, the proximity of Taiwan to China has for centuries made it a place to which people fleeing China have come. As a result, it has become a kind of living museum, with centuries of traditional Chinese culture kept alive in its arts, its entertainments, and its customs.

Despite or because of its adherence to traditional values, Taiwan has prospered and now boasts one of the most affluent lifestyles in Asia.

GREETINGS

• When meeting someone for the first time nod your head and make a slight bow to show respect. Male acquaintances and close friends shake hands. Women greeting other women—even close friends—do not shake hands.

• Note that in names, the family name comes first and the given name last. For example, Chiang Kai-shek's last name was Chiang. Family names are usually one syllable, except for people of Mongolian origin.

• Be aware that husbands and wives don't share the same last name. The wife keeps her family name. When you are introduced to a woman, her husband's last name will usually be stated before the woman's own last name and first name—e.g., Sarah Jones (birth name) Smith (husband's name) becomes Smith Jones Sarah. If you don't know a wife's family name, use "Mrs." and her husband's family name.

• If a person has a title, use it with the family name (e.g., "Professor Chen," "Doctor Lee").

• If you enter a room where there are older people, go to them and greet them first. Shake hands and spend a few minutes talking to them. Never ignore the presence of older people.

• At parties, even large banquets, wait to be introduced.

CONVERSATION

• Good subjects of conversation include family, hobbies, the area you're from, Chinese food.

• Feel free to talk about the People's Republic of China (PRC) and Taiwan's independence. Taiwanese hold a variety of opinions on the issue. Though once the subject was taboo, it's acceptable now.

• Don't be surprised if people ask you very personal questions on short acquaintance. They will often ask you how much your possessions cost. Consider this question a compliment, or a way for people to find out where you purchased an item, so that they can buy one also. If you don't wish to respond, say, "I don't remember" or "Not too much." It's considered a warm gesture to reveal the price.

• When speaking to children, ask them about their schoolwork. When talking with the elderly, it's proper to inquire about their health.

open 24 hours a day, seven days a week.

• Keep in mind that the emergency number for fire and medical assistance is 119, and for police 110.

TELEPHONES

• Look for public telephones in restaurants, cafés, hotels, and in booths on the street. Phones have NT $1, 5, 10, and 50 coin slots. A local three-minute call costs NT $1. Insert more coins if you wish to speak longer.

• Note that some public phones use cards, which can be purchased for NT $100 at bus stop booths, supermarkets, grocery stores, and convenience stores. One special card, with an STD sign on it, allows you to place international calls.

• If you use a phone card, pick up the telephone, insert the card, and then dial the number.

• Make overseas calls from hotels (be sure to ask if they impose a surcharge), post offices, or branches of the International Telecommunications Administration, which are

IN PUBLIC

• Never show affection to a member of the opposite sex in public. No hugging or kissing. Young girls often hold hands, but only good female friends should put their arms around one another's shoulders.

• Don't eat while walking down the street.

• Don't be loud or boisterous; it's considered very poor taste. However, Taiwanese are often loud.

• Avoid being abrupt or very frank, especially when offering criticism. If you must offer criticism, be subtle, and try to inject a little humor into your comment.

• Never touch either adults or children on the head. It's all right to pat children on the shoulder or on the cheek.

• Remember that a modest attitude is very important. If you're complimented, refute the compliment lightly, and expect Taiwanese to do the same.

• Treat elderly persons with respect and deference. For example, always allow them to go through a doorway first.

• While seated, place your hands in your lap. Don't jiggle your legs. Women may cross their legs.

• Don't use your feet to move an object such as a chair or a door. The feet are considered the lowest part of the body. It's rude to touch things with your feet.

• Beckon by moving your fingers toward you with your palm downward.

• Be aware that if you shake your head in the Western gesture of "No," it means "Yes." And note that holding your hand out and shaking it back and forth means "No."

• Prepare to be jostled in crowds. Don't show anger; just push with everyone else.

• If you wish to take pictures in a Buddhist temple, seek out a monk and ask permission.

• Be sure to remove your shoes before entering a temple.

• Don't step on the raised threshold of any doorway.

• Be alert for signs forbidding photography. These are common along the coastline because of concern for military security.

• Don't take photographs of airport military installations or of the ground from an aircraft.

• Look for public bathrooms in parks, main squares, bus and train stations, restaurants, and hotels. Many are identified by the international symbols for men and women. Most have the squat-type Japanese toilet; others have Western-style toilets. Always carry tissues with you, as you won't find toilet paper.

• If your hotel room doesn't come with a bath, which is unlikely, or if you would like to experience another aspect of Chinese life, visit one of the many public bathhouses. The Chinese stress personal hygiene and cleanliness. Almost all public baths have separate sections for men and women. Wash with soap and water before stepping into the bath or whirlpool. Modesty is not a factor, since the Chinese don't regard nudity as obscene.

Shopping: Note that bargaining is fine in some shops but not others. Ask, "Is this your best price?" The response should give you a clue as to whether to bargain. In small shops you may get a discount of as much as one third.

Exercise: You'll see many individuals doing *taiji* in front of their homes early in the morning. Jog in parks or at universities, as many people do around 6:00 A.M. Men and women may wear shorts when it's hot and sweatsuits when it's cold. You may have troubles jogging in Taipei where the air is very polluted. However, Grass Mountain, adjacent to Taipei, is excellent for jogging.

DRESS

• Keep in mind that Taiwanese are very fashion conscious and "dress up" on a daily basis more than most people from Western cultures.

• For business, men should wear a suit and tie. Women should wear suits in conservative colors. Never wear red or gold, because those colors are worn during festivities. Don't wear high-heeled shoes; there's a danger of falling in potholes or cracks in the sidewalks. Make sure that you carry a quality purse.

• For casual dress, teenage girls can wear shorts, but older women should wear slacks or skirts. It's acceptable for men to wear Bermuda shorts but not short shorts.

• Women should never wear low-cut dresses or tops.

• When first going to a home for a meal, men should wear a suit and tie, except in the summer, when a shirt and trousers are acceptable. Women should wear a dress or skirt and blouse. When you've come to know people better, it's fine to dress more casually.

• Be prepared with layers of clothing in winter months. Most homes are not heated.

• Note that tuxedos and long dresses are worn only to diplomatic functions. For other formal occasions, men should wear suits and women dressy street-length dresses or long dresses.

MEALS

Hours and Foods

Breakfast: 7:00 A.M. or earlier. The traditional breakfast is *congee* (a rice gruel), pickled fish, and bread. Or, soybean milk, which is served warm and can be made sweet or salty, with one of the following: sesame-seed buns, rice, *shao bing* (baked pancake with scallions), and *yu tiao* (oil stick—like a fried cruller). Sometimes people breakfast on leftovers from the previous night's dinner. Westernized people usually have eggs, bread, and sweet buns. The beverage is tea.

Lunch: 12:00 P.M. Lunch and dinner are very much the same in content, with fewer dishes served at lunch. A typical lunch might have fried rice with eggs, a meat dish, and a vegetable dish, or it might have noodles with a sauce made with chicken, pork, or beef.

Dinner: 6:00 to 8:00 P.M. There will be rice and three or four dishes, including meat dishes and vegetable dishes. Soup will be on the table with the other dishes; in some restaurants it isn't served as a separate course.

• Note that in homes, rice is usually served with meals. In restaurants, it isn't.

• Fresh fruit—papayas, pineapple, and mangoes—are the most common dessert. Occasionally ice cream is offered.

• Don't expect a beverage to be served with meals. Soup is the liquid with meals. Occasionally, beer or a soft drink will be offered with the meal. Tea is served after meals.

• Beer is a popular beverage. There is only one local brand: Taiwan Beer. (Many restaurants have imported beers.) Other popular drinks are *Shao-Hsing* wine, which is served both hot and cold; hot water, which is considered good for the stomach; cognac, a popular drink for toasting, served in one-ounce liquor glasses; *Mao-tai,* made from sorghum and also used for toasting.

• Tea is a very important drink in Taiwan. Since milk and sugar are never added to it, high-quality tea is essential. The delicate green tea tastes somewhat tangy. Oolong teas, more robust, have a darker color and slightly spicy flavor.

Westerners most commonly drink black tea, which has a very dark color and a very strong taste. It is often mixed with jasmine or orange peel. Tea is usually served tepid, not steaming hot.

• If you attend a banquet, expect tea to be served before anyone sits down at the tables.

• Be aware that rice is the very last course at a banquet. Don't eat it, however. To do so indicates that you haven't had enough. (Odd though it seems, everyone is served rice, but nobody eats it because they are too full.)

Table Manners

• Be especially pleased if people invite you to their home to a meal. It is more usual to take guests to a restaurant.

• Don't anticipate being offered a cocktail before a meal.

• Wait for your host to seat you. The guest of honor is usually seated facing the door.

• In a home, expect each place to be set with one small plate, a rice bowl, a soup bowl, a glass or cup for tea or beer, a small cup for wine, and chopsticks. If there is no soup bowl, and soup is offered, put it in the rice bowl after you finish the rice. There will probably be a plate on the side for bones.

• If you don't feel comfortable managing chopsticks, ask for a fork.

• Wait for the host to serve you from the main serving dishes in the center of the table. Eat what is offered, if possible.

• Remember that a Chinese banquet (the usual way to entertain a guest) can run to twenty courses. Emulate the Chinese and eat sparingly at each course. Try to sample each course, but don't take second helpings, or you'll never finish the meal. If your host presses you to eat, just insist that you are full.

• Note that at a banquet courses are served in sequence, not all at once.

• Don't expect napkins at a meal in a home. Bring a handkerchief or tissues. After the meal, you'll be offered a hot towel. Use it on your hands, not your face.

• If you wish to serve a choice morsel of food to a friend (or to a guest you are entertaining), turn your chopsticks around, pick up the food with the blunt ends of the chopsticks (not the end you put in your mouth), and place the food on your friend's plate.

• When eating rice, hold the bowl close to your mouth and scoop in.

• Place bones and seeds in the special plate provided; if there is no special plate, put them on the table. Don't put them in the rice bowl or on your plate.

• Expect your host to pour *Shao-Hsing* wine, which may be warm or cold. He will then make a toast. If you want more wine, catch someone's eye, raise the glass, and toast. Hold the glass with both hands

when it's being filled and when you're toasting.

• When you are ready to drink wine or brandy, pick up a cup or glass, say a person's name followed by *"Ching"* ("Please"). One toast is *"Gahn bay,"* which means "Dry cup," the equivalent of "Bottoms up!" Drink all the liquid, and then turn the cup upside down. Another toast is *"Sway byen,"* which means "As you wish" or *"Sway yi,"* which means "Drink whatever you wish." If you don't wish to drink much, offer a toast of *"Sway yi"* to those who are drinking." Take a sip, and look at the person you're toasting. If someone toasts you, nod your head as a gesture that you have accepted the toast. Toasting is usually initiated by the host. There is no special order in which people toast, but do offer a toast. Note that you may toast with a soft drink, if you wish.

• Realize that women usually don't drink much. It's acceptable for foreign women to drink beer at a banquet, but not to excess. Women can drink stronger liquors on other occasions.

• If there is a chopstick rest, put your chopsticks on it at the end of the meal. If not, leave them on the plate or on the table. There is no custom as to what direction they should be pointing (as there is in some other Asian countries). Don't put your chopsticks across the bowl; it's considered bad luck.

• When using a toothpick, cover

your mouth with the other hand. However, only use a toothpick at the table if others are also using them. Some people consider using toothpicks rude.

• After a meal in a home, have tea, talk for an hour, and leave. People don't want you to eat and run. At a banquet in a restaurant, leave immediately after tea.

Places to Eat

• Expect to find gourmet Western restaurants in many five-star hotels. Go to Chinese restaurants, which are usually very good and which come in many types: *Szechuan*: Expect hot, spicy dishes with chili pepper and garlic. Ask for *bu la* (boo lah) or *ching hung* (ching hoong) if you want your food less spicy. *Peking*: Anticipate mild dishes combining roast meats, vegetables, and thin pancakes which you fill with food. *Hunan*: Try these restaurants for spicy foods and steamed dishes. *Shanghai*: Expect seafood dishes with salty sauces. *Cantonese*: The Chinese cooking most familiar to Westerners, it relies on steamed and stir-fried dishes with many vegetables. *Taiwanese*: Anticipate seafood with thick sauces. In the North, chefs use garlic; in the South soy sauce. *Mongolian*: There are two major dishes. Hotpot consists of meat, which you cook yourself at the table in a sauce of ginger, bean paste, shrimp oil, and sesame paste. For barbecue, the other major dish, you

choose meat and vegetables, and dip them in sauces. Give them to the chef, who will cook them on a grill next to your table. You'll be offered a sesame bun on which to put the cooked food, but you don't have to use it.

• Be aware of which type of Chinese restaurant you're eating in, so that you won't make the mistake of ordering northern food (e.g., Peking duck) in a Shanghai-style restaurant.

• Plan to dine early. Many restaurants close at 9:00 P.M. and may be out of their best dishes by 7:30 P.M. However, there are soup shops which stay open until late.

• For lunch, try noodle shops. There you can have noodles with soup or with sauces, such as a hot, spicy sesame sauce. An alternative is wonton soup, which has many wontons with a little soup. Some noodle shops have menus with rough translations in English. If they don't, and you aren't with a native speaker, point at dishes others are eating.

• For pastries, ice cream, coffee, or soft drinks, visit a coffeeshop.

• Note that teahouses are for men only. They offer alcoholic beverages, snacks, and light meals. Men often go there to discuss business. Usually there's entertainment by women who sing or play instruments.

• If you're dining with a group of eight or more, plan to reserve a table and arrange the meal ahead of time. The owner or manager will offer set meals in certain price ranges and can be trusted to choose good dishes for you. Be sure to know the regional food the restaurant serves, especially if you want to arrange for a special dish. For popular restaurants, you may have to reserve from a few days to a week in advance.

• Wait for the hostess to seat you. If a restaurant is crowded, you may be asked to share a table with strangers. Don't feel obliged to talk to them.

• At your place, expect a small plate, chopsticks (sometimes with a chopstick rest), a china spoon for soup, a small glass for wine or brandy, and another small glass for beer or soda.

• To order, choose one main dish for each person in the group plus soup and an appetizer. Note that portions tend to be small.

• If there's a lazy Susan in the center of the table, look for the dishes you have ordered to be placed on it so people can serve themselves. Turn it either to the left or right.

• Note that in some restaurants people use the small paper napkin at their place to wipe the chopsticks and bowl before eating (to be sure that they are clean). If you see people doing it, follow their lead. If they aren't, don't do it.

• Be prepared to find Chinese meals boisterous, loud, and chaotic—unlike the quiet atmosphere in elegant Western restaurants outside Taiwan.

• Realize that your Chinese host always expects to pay. People will argue about who is to pay the bill, but the one who issues the invitation pays. There's no such thing as "Dutch treat." The Taiwanese believe that treating people to a meal is a good way to repay favors or to cultivate a business relationship.

• If you go to non-touristy restaurants off the beaten path, expect people to stare at you. Look at them and smile.

• A woman eating alone should not encounter any problems. When you enter the restaurant, have a serious expression, which will convey the message that you don't want to be bothered.

• If you're invited to a banquet, be sure to arrive on time. If you're the guest of honor, realize that you are the first to leave after the meal. Leave about 15 minutes after the meal has concluded.

Specialties

• Some Cantonese specialties are *t'ao jen chi thing* (diced chicken with walnuts), *ku lao ju* (sweet-and-sour pork), and *k'e chia niang tou fu* (Cantonese stuffed bean curd).

• Typical Shanghai dishes are *chih pao chi* (paper-wrapped chicken), *t'ang ts'u pai gu* (sweet-and-sour spareribs), *hsi hu ts'u yu* (West Lake vinegar fish), and *ch'ieh chih ming hsia* (prawns with tomato sauce).

• Sample such Szechuan specialties as *kung pao chi ting* (chicken with peanuts), *chang cha ya* (camphor and tea-smoked duck), *yu hsiang jou szu* (stir-fried pork in hot sauces), *hsia jen kuo pa* (sizzling rice with shrimp), *ma po tou fu* (Ma Po's bean curd), and *yu hsiang ch'iel tzu* (eggplant Szechuan-style).

• From northern China, try *pei ching k'ao ya* (roast Peking duck), *shuan yang jou* (rinsed mutton in hotpot), *meng ku kao pou* (Mongolian barbecue), and *tang tsu chuan yu* (fried whole fish with sweet-and-sour sauce).

HOTELS

• Book far in advance if you're going to Taiwan during October, the busiest period. Many overseas Chinese return for visits during that month.

• At the best hotels (rated four or five plum blossoms rather than stars), expect business centers, meeting facilities, fitness centers, hair salons, and TVs in rooms. Credit cards will be accepted.

• For inexpensive accommodations, check out guesthouses. If your visit is a long one, ask for weekly or monthly rates.

• For those who *really* want budget accommodations, consider the hotels around the island operated by the China Youth Corps (CYC). Accommodations are dormitory-style. They are very popular and are usually full from July through September and January through February. If you haven't made reservations, phone as soon as you arrive in Taiwan.

• Expect the hotel staff to treat you as a personal guest rather than an anonymous visitor. The Taiwanese regard hotel-keeping as an art rather than an industry. However, don't be surprised if a request goes unfulfilled. Most Chinese staff do not understand much English, but they often pretend that they do in order not to lose face. They may pretend to understand a request and then do nothing about it, because they didn't really understand what you wanted. If you have a special request, write it down clearly. People will probably understand written English, but may have difficulty with speaking and listening.

• Look for a carafe of cold, boiled water in your room. Use this for drinking, brushing your teeth, etc. There may also be a thermos of hot water for making tea. Drink only water that is bottled or has been boiled.

• To avoid the possibility of infection, women should take showers rather than baths.

• When you leave the hotel, ask someone to write your destination in Chinese characters, and carry a card with the name and address of the hotel in Chinese characters. Taxi drivers don't speak English.

TIPPING

• Note that tipping is rare and is entirely optional.

• If you wish to tip, a good rule of thumb is to tip only those people who perform direct services: waiters, bar boys, barbers, beauty parlor operators; give them 10 percent of the bill.

• Give porters NT$30 per bag.

• If your room maid at the hotel performs a special service for you, give her NT$100. The same amount would be given to a concierge who has gotten you tickets or performed some other small service.

• Look for a 10 percent service charge to be added to your restaurant bill. If not, leave 10 percent as a tip.

• Don't tip taxi drivers. You can let them keep the small change.

PRIVATE HOMES

• Always make plans before visiting someone. Never drop in. Since many women work, the customary time for visits is in the evening.

• If you are visiting a home and see shoes outside, remove your shoes before entering. Wear the slippers provided by your host.

• If there are elderly persons in the room, greet them first.

• Expect to be offered fruit, a soft drink, candy, or tea. The tea will probably be served in a glass. It may be jasmine or chrysanthemum tea. If you don't care for it, take one or two sips and leave it.

• Don't comment about a particular object (mention that a vase is beautiful) or the host may feel compelled to give it to you.

• Offer to pay for any long-distance calls you make. The offer will probably be refused. If you persist, and the offer is still refused, bring the family a gift.

• When leaving, shake hands with your host. If older people are present, bow to them.

• If the family has servants, don't offer to help. If there are no servants, you can offer to help, but you will probably be refused.

• When you want to take a bath, ask your hostess if it's a convenient time to do so and if the water needs to be heated in advance. All homes have a bathtub, but not all have showers. No one will be surprised if you bathe daily because most Taiwanese do.

Gifts: When invited to a meal bring fruit, cookies, or candy. First-quality tea found in special tea shops is also a popular gift. Someone at the shop will put the tea in a canister and wrap it for you.

• Other good gifts include coffee sets with different varieties of coffee. The family may use it for special occasions or as a treat for guests. Liquor is also welcome.

• Be aware that flowers are usually reserved for weddings and funerals. If you do give them, be sure the arrangement has an even number of flowers.

• Don't give clocks or watches, because the word for those two items is similar to the word for death. Another gift to avoid is handkerchiefs, since they may signify the departure of something or someone.

• Expect people to decline a gift initially. It's a sign of politeness. Persist in offering. If a gift is offered to you, your initial response should be, "I couldn't possibly accept."

• Note that people are very conscious of matching gifts in value. Be sensitive to the financial situation of the person to whom you're giving

the gift. If you give a lavish, expensive gift, the recipient will feel obliged to give you one of similar or greater value.

• Other gifts include cosmetics, chocolates, perfume, picture books of your area, or cassettes or CDs with classical or folk music.

• Present a gift with both hands, but don't expect it to be opened in your presence. If you are given a gift, open it in private.

MONEY AND BUSINESS

Hours

Businesses: Monday through Friday, 9:00 A.M. to noon and 1:00 to 5:00 P.M. Closed some Saturdays. The work week changed on January 1, 1998. Every two weeks, there is a five-day work week. One week people work Monday through Friday; the next week they work Monday through Saturday at noon. Businesses do not usually close for national holidays. If you're planning a meeting on one of those days, be sure to check to learn if the business will be open. Government offices and banks are included in this change.

Government Offices: Monday through Friday, 8:30 A.M. to 12:30 P.M. and 1:30 to 5:30 P.M. Closed some Saturdays.

Banks: Monday through Friday, 9:00 A.M. to 3:30 P.M. Saturday, 9:00 A.M. to noon. Closed some Saturdays.

Shops: Department stores and large shops are open daily, including Sunday, from 10:00 A.M. to 10:00 P.M. Many smaller shops stay open for longer hours, seven days a week.

Money

• The unit of currency is the New Taiwan dollar (NT$), which is divided into 100 cents. Coins are 50 cents and NT$ 1, NT$ 5, NT$ 10, and NT$ 50. Banknotes are NT$ 50, NT$ 100, NT$ 500, and NT$ 1,000.

• Note that major credit cards—American Express, Visa, Barclaycard, MasterCard, Access, Diners Club—are accepted at hotels, major restaurants, and shops catering to tourists. The same places will often accept traveler's checks in payment.

Business Practices

• Try to arrange for a personal introduction or a letter of introduction to the person with whom you wish to do business. It's an advantage if you have a letter from a mutual business friend. However, you could also seek help from the Commerce Department of your country or a bank, preferably one with offices in Taiwan.

• Plan to make several trips to Taiwan to accomplish your business.

• When assembling the group that will visit Taiwan, be sure to include a senior executive from your firm, since age and position are revered.

• Try to send proposals ahead of time. (Have materials translated by a Taiwanese, not by someone from the People's Republic of China.) During your presentation, when you go over what you sent, be prepared to discuss minute details and to allow time for a question period.

• Make sure that you are punctual, but don't be upset if others are late.

• For best results, plan business travel during the months of April through September. Businessmen vacation January through March. Avoid the two weeks before and after the Chinese New Year, which falls in January or February. When making plans, check on dates of other holidays, since they vary according to the lunar calendar.

• Since business entertaining goes on until very late, try to start your round of appointments late in the morning. It would be rude to excuse yourself from the entertainment because of an early appointment.

• To make a favorable impression, learn a few words of Mandarin

Chinese, the official language of Taiwan.

• Remember that personal relationships must be established before business is conducted. Don't feel that you're wasting your time discussing your background, education, etc., and chatting with your Taiwanese counterparts about theirs.

• When scheduling appointments in Taipei, allow at least 30 minutes between meetings (unless they are a very short distance apart and you can go on foot).

• Have business cards printed in English on one side and Mandarin on the other. Many people don't listen to verbal introductions. They wait to see the card. You can have cards printed in Taipei in two days.

• Realize that the Chinese family name usually appears first, but some business people use the Western style of putting their family name last. Be sure to ask, so that you are addressing the person correctly.

• Note that the highest ranking person in the Taiwanese group usually sits in the middle with the second-ranked person at his right and the third-ranked to his left. Knowing the seating arrangement should enable you to determine who is the most senior person in the group.

• When you leave for your appointments, have someone on the hotel staff write the address of your destination in Chinese characters. Take along a card with the name and location of the hotel written in Chinese characters.

• Expect tea or coffee to be served at meetings.

• Don't use your hands when you're speaking. Taiwanese would be distracted.

• Be prepared for Taiwanese businessmen to take a long time to come to a decision. Then—and only then—will they sign a contract.

• Be aware that when people say "Yes," they may just be signifying that they understand you, not necessarily that they agree with you. Avoid saying "No." It's considered rude.

• Never criticize a person in front of others.

• If you are in charge of setting up a subsidiary branch of a company, be sure to consult a *feng-shui* (literally "wind-water") man. He is a geomancer and helps people construct buildings in harmony with elements in the natural environment. He decides the best position for the building entrance, the windows, the gardens, etc. People place great faith in this system. Be sure to take it seriously. Taiwan businessmen can recommend a suitable *feng-shui* man.

• Businesswomen should expect that when dealing with older businesspeople they may have to spend time establishing their credibility. Younger people are used to hiring women and working with Western women. Should a woman be the senior person on the team, she should expect that Taiwanese may address the senior man in the group, unless they are informed otherwise. In fact, some companies may have Western women discuss their business with Taiwanese women of lower rank. Be firm about continuing your discussion with the men.

Business Entertaining: Expect business entertaining to be done in restaurants. You won't be invited to a businessman's home. If you have been treated to a dinner, reciprocate with one of equal value. Bring a small gift for your host.

• Don't discuss business during dinner, unless your host brings up the subject. Stick to chat about families, food, and the culture of Taiwan.

• If you're hosting a banquet, pay ahead of time, or leave the table to pay just before the meal ends.

• Be prepared for business entertaining to be exhausting, because people tend to stay out very late at night.

• If you decide to host a business dinner, feel free to invite the wife of a businessman.

Gifts: Note that popular business gifts are Johnny Walker Red Label Scotch or a subscription to *National Geographic* or *Reader's Digest* or fine pen sets. Give the gift to the person, not the firm.

Note: For advice regarding business greetings, dress, or table manners, see the appropriate sections earlier in this chapter.

HOLIDAYS AND SPECIAL OCCASIONS

• Expect banks, offices, and most shops to be closed on the following national holidays. Some towns and regions have individual festivals, which are holidays in the area. Check with the tourist office for dates of local festivals.

• Note, however, that on many holidays, businesses are open and people don't have the day off from work.

Holidays: Founding of the Republic of China—Foundation Day (January 1); Chinese Lunar New Year (January/February); Youth Day (March 29); Tomb-Sweeping Day and the Death of Chiang Kaishek (April 5); Dragon Boat Festival (late May/mid-June—the fifth day of the fifth lunar month); Confucius' Birthday and Teacher's Day (September 28); Mid-Autumn Moon Festival (September/October); Double-Ten National Day (October 10), commemorating the 1911 beginning of the overthrow of the Manchu Qing dynasty; Taiwan Restoration Day (October 25), honoring the 1945 return of the island province of Taiwan to China; Chiang Kai-shek's Birthday (October 31); Dr. Sun Yat-sen's Birthday (November 12); Constitution Day (December 25—though the government doesn't officially recognize Christmas, Christians observe it).

• Remember that the Chinese New Year is celebrated for at least a week. It's customary to pay visits and give gifts. If you visit a family during this period, give money to the children in a red envelope. (Red is the symbol of good luck and celebration.) Buy the envelopes in bookstores or stationery stores. Give adults gifts of food—canned, smoked ham; dried duck; fruit; nuts.

• If you're in Taiwan for the Dragon Boat Festival, realize that it commemorates the death of Chu-Yuan, a poet who killed himself in a river to protest the corruption of the emperor. People eat dumplings called *dzung-dze* (dzuhng dzi) in his remembrance. The government organizes Dragon Boat races with teams from Taiwan, Hong Kong, Singapore, and the expatriate community competing.

TRANSPORTATION

Public Transportation

• Note that buses provide very frequent and inexpensive transportation. Be sure to avoid the major rush hours, from 7:30 to 9:30 A.M. and from 5:00 to 7:00 P.M. Not only does traffic move very slowly but passengers are packed into the buses.

• On the buses in Taipei, use either exact change, which you put in the box on the bus, or a bus card, which can be purchased at special stores. Bus stops display signs showing the stops along the route. On the bus, you'll find the same display with simple maps. Buses are air-conditioned.

• Note that in the countryside, buses are more expensive and less frequent than in Taipei.

• If you wish to avoid rush hours in Taipei, don't travel between 6:30 and 9:00 A.M. or 5:00 to 7:00 P.M. on weekdays.

• Keep in mind that Taipei and Kaoshung now have metro (subway) systems, but some routes are still under construction. Look for ticket machines at the entrance to the metro. Press the button for your destination; a sign will tell you the fare. If you become confused, find the booths where staff sell tickets. You will find English translations of Chinese signs at each stop. Each stop is announced.

• Realize that there is a surcharge for phoning for a taxi and for luggage service from a driver.

• Hail taxis in the street. Have your destination written out in Chinese before you venture out because most drivers don't speak English. All taxi fares are calculated according to the meter, but some taxi meters don't show current fees— drivers, however, have charts showing the new rates. If you want to go on a long excursion or use a taxi for an entire day, have a hotel clerk or local acquaintance negotiate a set fee.

• In the countryside, negotiate the taxi fare in advance.

• Be prepared for drivers to drive as though they're in a demolition derby. If you can't tolerate the driving techniques of one driver, tell him to pull over, pay, and get out. There is no shortage of taxis.

• Be aware that you can buy round-trip train tickets, but you can't make return reservations until you arrive at your destination. Your hotel can get the reservation for you a day in advance. Trains are extremely clean and comfortable. There are easy-to-follow signs in English in the Taipei Central Railway Station.

• Note that there are express trains with overnight sleepers that run north and south. You'll be offered complimentary tea, magazines, newspapers, and wet hand towels.

Driving

• Take public transportation or taxis in the city. For long journeys, rent a car or hire a chauffeured limousine. Roads are well maintained, but be careful of the careless drivers and the thousands of motorcycles and government vehicles, which have the right of way. On the street in major cities, road signs will be in English. However, in the countryside, signs will be in Chinese. Look for route numbers (which are in Arabic) rather than place names. Don't even try to say place names, since not everyone in the countryside speaks Mandarin. Instead, show them your destination written down, and try to get directions through sign language.

• Be sure to keep your gas tank at least one-third full. Gas stations in the countryside are few and far between, and they often close at night.

LEGAL MATTERS, SAFETY, AND HEALTH

• Realize that you are prohibited from bringing pro-Communist publications into the country and that pornography is also banned.

• When leaving the country, expect to open your suitcases for inspection after checking in for your flight. If you don't agree to this inspection, the bags probably won't be put on the plane.

• Women should take taxis after dark. If you *must* go for a walk at night, ask at your hotel if the area you'll be walking in is considered safe.

Health: Bring an adequate supply of any prescription drugs that you take. Drugs can be difficult to obtain, expensive, and sold under unfamiliar names.

• Note that most ordinary toiletries are available at large department stores, as well as sanitary napkins and tampons.

• Be sure that you don't eat food purchased from a street vendor. Standards of cleanliness may not be high. Ice cream is especially dangerous, since the milk may not have been pasteurized.

KEY PHRASES

Note: Although the official language is Mandarin (*guo-yu*), many people speak Taiwanese (a local dialect). Young people, many people in business, and those in tourism speak English.

English	*Mandarin (Pronunciation)*
Good morning	Zow (rhymes with "cow")-aĥn
Good evening	Wahn-aĥn
Mr., Sir	Shen shung
Mrs., Madame	Tie tie
Miss	Shá-oo jeh
Good-bye	Zigh-jén
Please	Ching

Thank you	Shéh-shéh
Excuse me	Dwáy-buh chee-ee
I don't understand	Woh bun
Do you speak English?	Neé shwo yíng-wen máh?

THAILAND

Chiang Rai

Chiang Mai

• Udon Thani

Ubon Ratchathani

Nakhon Phanom

Bangkok

GULF
OF
THAILAND

Songkhla

Remember the moment in *The King and I* when the king of Siam learns of Abraham Lincoln's beleaguered state and desires to help him out? Suddenly inspired, the king decides to send Lincoln an elephant. The line always gets a laugh in the theater, but the king is simply applying his country's view of political power. In Siam (now Thailand) the person with the most white elephants is the most powerful. This unusual view of politics is only one of the cultural differences Western visitors encounter in Thailand.

Like New York, Thailand provokes strong—and often sharply different—reactions. As with New York City, there's no substitute for a personal judgment.

GREETINGS

• To greet someone in the traditional Thai manner, press your hands together at a level between your chin and the top of your nose, as though in prayer, keeping arms and elbows close to your body, bow your head forward to touch your index fingers. This gesture is known as a *wai* (pronounced "why"). Thais will shake hands with Westerners but will be pleased if you greet them with a *wai*, a salutation that signifies respect. After you have *wai*ed, say "hello" (see Key Phrases). If someone such as a flight attendant or member of a hotel staff makes a *wai* gesture, you can just smile and nod.

• If you are of lower status (e.g., younger, female, with less income), *wai* first. If you are of higher status (e.g., older, male, with higher income), wait for the other person to initiate the greeting.

• Use *wai* both for greeting and departing. It can also be used to say "Thank you" or "I'm sorry."

• If you are younger than the person you're greeting, *wai* first. If you're the older, wait for the younger person to initiate the greeting.

• Note that the lower one's social status, the higher one must raise the hands in *wai*.

• Do not *wai* to children. Simply say "Hello."

• When introduced to a monk, women should *never* shake hands or touch him. Simply say "Hello."

• Expect religious Thai men to kneel before a monk and make the *wai* gesture three times. Foreign men should say "Hello" without shaking hands.

• Address people as Mr., Mrs., or Miss with their first name. Surnames came into existence only about 60 years ago, and people find them difficult to use. On the other hand, introduce yourself as you would in your own country ("Mr. Smith," etc.).

• If someone has a title (e.g., Doctor), be sure to use that with the first name in your greeting (e.g., "Doctor Susan"). Titles are very important to Thais.

• Don't be surprised if Thais give you a nickname, especially if your name is difficult to pronounce. Everyone in Thailand has a nickname.

ommend sights to see and good places to eat. If your impressions of the country are positive, these are good subjects.

• Avoid any reference to sex, as the Thai public attitude is very conservative. Also avoid any criticism of the Buddhist religion.

CONVERSATION

• Feel free to discuss families, children, and people's personal lives. In fact, don't be surprised if someone asks you how much money you earn; it's considered a polite question. If you don't want to answer, say that you make enough to live on. If people persist, try changing the subject. Or you could try saying in a light, humorous tone, "One *baht*."

• Expect Thais to repeat and repeat and repeat a statement. It's their way of getting their point across.

• Expect to be asked how old you are soon after you meet a Thai. In order for a Thai to speak to you correctly, your age must be known.

• Talk about politics and the Thai royal family, but never negatively or humorously—they are an object of adoration and respect in the country. Don't bring up the American musical *The King and I* (wait for a Thai to do so). It has never been presented in the country, because the Thais believe it makes fun of one of their revered monarchs.

• Thais enjoy being asked to rec-

TELEPHONES

• Look for red and blue public telephones. The red are for local calls. The blue are for long distance calls within Thailand. Deposit a one-*baht* coin, which will allow you to speak for three minutes on a local call. (A problem: There are three types of one *baht* coins; only the middle size fits.) After three minutes, there will be a tape recording with the signal that time is running out. Deposit more money to continue the call.

• At some guesthouses and hotels, look for private phones. They require a nine-sided five-*baht* coin for each call.

• For convenience, purchase a phone card at any TOT (telephone office). Many telephones accept them. In airports purchase a card at the information counter or at one of the gift shops.

• Note that TOT telephone offices have fax, Telex, and telegraph service.

• Remember that for a police emergency you should dial 191, 195, or 123. For a fire emergency, dial 199.

• Outside major cities, make calls from the local telephone office or bring a large supply of one-*baht* coins with you.

IN PUBLIC

• Don't be shocked to see women holding hands with other women when walking down the street and men walking with their arms around each other in public, as this is common for friends to do. However, men and women never touch one another in public, and travelers should avoid any public displays of affection between the sexes.

• Be prepared to hear the expression *"Mai pen rai"* (my pen rye), which means "It doesn't matter," and signifies the belief that life should be enjoyed and that problems should not be taken seriously. Expect to be referred to often as *farang*—foreigner. The term is usually not derogatory.

• Don't place your arm over the back of a chair in which another person is sitting.

• Be on time for business functions; Thais regard punctuality as a sign of courtesy, but people are looser about time for social engagements.

• Never touch anyone—especially children—on the head. It is considered to be the dwelling place of the soul.

• Don't point at anyone with your foot. The feet are considered the lowliest part of the body. Don't cross legs with one foot resting on the other knee, and never cross legs in front of an older person. When crossing your legs, cross them at the ankles, not at the knees.

• When handing an object to another person, always use the right hand. Thais often support their right arm with their left hand.

• Emulate the Thais in giving up your seat on a bus or train to a monk who is standing.

• Note that many Thai men smoke, and smoking is permitted almost everywhere.

• Women should not touch a monk or hand an object directly to him.

• Keep a pleasant, smiling attitude. To Thais, criticism of others is in very bad taste. If you have a complaint (e.g., about the service in a hotel or restaurant), be extra calm and polite. To show anger or raise your voice will only ensure that you will lose face, and your request will *not* be granted.

• Women should be especially sure to speak softly to be more easily accepted by Thais.

• Don't be offended if Thais smile or laugh in a sad or tragic situation. They are trying to cover up their sorrow.

• Ask permission to photograph either a monk or a temple. Some temples forbid photography. Be prepared to pay people in hill tribes if you photograph them.

• When visiting a shrine, don't wear shorts or sleeveless tops, remove your hat, and leave your umbrella outside. (Many shrines provide stands for umbrellas outside the entrance.)

• Be very careful to treat any image of Buddha with respect. Don't touch images or statues of Buddha. There is a fine or imprisonment for anyone showing disrespect to Buddha. (An American missionary climbed on a statue of Buddha to have his picture taken and was imprisoned for his act of ridicule.)

• In a temple, don't walk in front of praying Thais; walk around them.

• Remember that, inviting as the beaches in Thai resort areas are, nude sunbathing or nude swimming is both illegal and very offensive to Thais.

• Never throw anything to anyone.

• Don't stand over someone who is older or who has a superior position. If you are taller, slightly lower your head or upper body to show respect. Thais usually show respect for superiors and elders by ducking their head. Don't think that people are cringing.

• Never give a Thai a red pen to sign something, because coffins awaiting cremation have names written in red on their sides.

• When visiting areas with hill tribes, dress modestly, and ask permission before entering a house. Don't touch or photograph spirit shrines or step on the threshold of a door.

• If you venture into remote areas of Thailand, expect to encounter common, outside shower rooms. While showering, women wear a cloth called a *pasin* (pah-sin) and wash under it. A man wears a cloth called a *pakama* (pah-kah-mah). Ask the attendant at the shower room for the appropriate cloth.

• If you need to use a toilet, ask in hotels, restaurants, or stores for *hong nam* (hong nahm), which means "water room." The men's room is *sukha chai* (soo-kah chay) and the ladies' room is *sukha ying* (soo-kah ying). The toilet will usually be the kind over which you have to squat. Pour water from the bucket or jug down the drain when you have finished, and replace the water. Bring tissues or toilet paper with you, as public washrooms often don't have toilet paper.

Shopping: If prices are fixed, a

sign will say so. Always ask, "Is there a discount?" People will never be insulted.

• If you have Thai friends, take one along when you shop. You will probably get a better deal.

• If there is no fixed-price sign, begin by offering 50 percent of the asking price, expecting to achieve a discount of 20 percent.

• Don't expect shopkeepers to refuse your offer directly. Thais always avoid confrontation. If your offer is unacceptable, expect a response such as, "It isn't convenient now." That's a signal to raise your offer if you want the item.

• Remember that if a shopkeeper accepts your price, you are obliged to buy the item. Try to make the seller mention prices, so that you are in a position to accept or reject offers.

• Be aware that there are *no* government gem shops, so don't fall for a scam if someone tells you they exist and offers to take you to one. (The person is trying to steer you to the shop of a friend or an associate.)

Exercise: You might wish to avoid outdoor exercise in Bangkok's polluted air. In any case, joggers should confine themselves to hotel grounds. Shorts are acceptable for jogging.

DRESS

• Be sure to bring clothes in natural fibers, such as cotton and linen, which breathe. Clothes made of synthetic fabrics will be most uncomfortable in the hot, steamy Thai weather. Men should not pack seersucker suits in the mistaken belief that seersucker is a natural fiber.

• Light dresses or skirts and blouses are suitable women's attire for all occasions. Don't plan to wear pants—it's too hot except for nights in November through January. Wear short-sleeved blouses, but never sleeveless ones. If you wear a see-through blouse, wear a camisole underneath. Because of the extreme heat, women are not expected to wear hosiery. Women should not wear black dresses, a color Thais regard as suitable only for funerals or mourning, nor should they wear purple, because that color is associated with the royal family. An exception is formal occasions when black is acceptable if strongly accented with color.

• For men, slacks and shirts—either colored or white, with or without ties, are suitable for almost all nonbusiness functions. For an elegant restaurant a suit and tie are appropriate.

• For business, women should wear plain, conservative dresses—never decolleté or sleeveless or outfits with tight skirts. At the initial business meeting men should wear suits and ties. After that khaki or gray safari suits (which can be made by a local tailor) are appropriate. Thais appreciate your desire to dress like the locals.

• For a formal evening (e.g., a benefit evening or a government-sponsored affair), men should wear traditional summer formal attire—white jacket, black pants, and black tie—and women should wear long dresses.

• Tourists of both sexes are free to wear jeans (though the heat may make them uncomfortable). Knee-length shorts are acceptable on the streets, but never for visiting temples. People in shorts can expect to be stared at, since only Thai schoolchildren wear shorts.

• For visits to temples, women should wear a skirt and blouse or a dress and men should wear long pants.

• Because shoes must be removed outside temples and in Thai homes, bring shoes that slip on and off easily, rather than shoes that must be tied repeatedly in the Thai heat. Wear old or inexpensive shoes outside. Shoes are sometimes stolen from outside temples, and the Bangkok streets often flood and

could ruin your shoes. If slippers are not provided outside a temple or home, go barefoot or in stockinged feet.

• Don't wear rubber thongs on the street; they are considered very low class.

• During the rainy season (June through November), men should bring along extra slacks, as they will probably be splashed constantly around the ankles.

MEALS

Hours and Foods

Breakfast: 7:00 A.M. Thais eat rice soup or poached eggs, and they drink tea or coffee (usually instant). Sometimes raw eggs will be dropped into the hot rice gruel; the eggs will cook in a short time.

Lunch: 12:00 P.M. Expect three or four side dishes, such as curried chicken or sautéed vegetables, with rice or noodles, which may be served in soup or fried.

Dinner: The main meal of the day, served at 7:00 or 7:30 P.M. It is similar to lunch, but there are many more side dishes. Beer will be served with dinner.

Table Manners

• If a Thai invites you to dinner, anticipate being taken to a restaurant. It's more usual than being entertained in a home.

• Note that in some traditional homes, people sit on the floor. Women should tuck their legs to the side. Men should sit cross-legged. Westerners should never stick their legs out in front of them.

• Expect the male guest of honor to sit next to the host and the female guest of honor next to the hostess.

• If you dine in a Thai home, don't wait for your hostess to sit down before beginning to eat. She may not eat or drink with the guests. Begin when your host does.

• Expect to eat with Western-style forks and spoons. Thais use chopsticks only when eating noodles or when eating in a Chinese restaurant. Keep the fork in your left hand and the spoon in your right (in reverse if you are left-handed). Use the fork to push food onto the spoon. Never put the fork in your mouth. That is *very* impolite. If there are no serving spoons, use your spoon to take food from the serving bowls. (Using one's own spoon with a common serving bowl is customary in both homes and restaurants.)

• Expect to be given a plate of rice (or there may be a large bowl of rice). Remember that rice is considered the staple of every meal.

• If noodles are served in a broth, use a spoon for the liquid and chopsticks for the noodles.

• If served sticky rice (*kow neo*), roll a portion into a ball and eat it with your fingers.

• Most food is served finely cut up, so you probably won't need to cut anything, but if you do, cut with the side of the spoon, not the fork.

• Expect soup as the first course for dinner. In a home, your host will serve it from a tureen.

• At dinner in a home, be sure to try a little of everything, even if it doesn't appeal to you, otherwise your host and hostess will be hurt. Don't eat all the food that is served, however, since the servants' meal will consist of the leftovers.

• To eat as the Thais do, take a bite of rice and then a bite of another dish. As in Japan, all the dishes are served at one time.

• Take a very small portion of food, eat it, and then take more. Don't take a large portion the first time.

• Anticipate being served *very* spicy food. Ground chili is frequently used as a seasoning. If you don't care for hot food, remove the torpedo-like red, orange, and green chilies from each spoonful of food, as you would remove bones from a fish. If your dish is still too hot, eat a great deal of rice with it.

• Be aware that some varieties of

bananas have very large, hard seeds. Be careful, or you could break a tooth.

• Never finish the last bit of food in the serving dish. It's considered an honor to have it. Wait until it's offered to you. Refuse it politely, and, when asked again, accept.

• Drink tea or beer (both Thai beers and imported beers are very good) with meals. If ice water is served, don't drink it unless you have seen it being poured from a bottle. More fashionable people favor Scotch whiskey.

• Don't anticipate dessert, except at a formal banquet. Sometimes fruit—usually pineapple, papayas, or oranges—is served at the end of a meal. If you are offered a fruit whose peel is often eaten, be sure to peel it first. At the end of the meal, coffee may be served. If so, it will probably be of the instant variety; there is little freshly brewed coffee.

• Many Thais smoke after dinner, but don't be the first person to light up. Always pass cigarettes around to the men at the table. Traditional Thai women don't usually smoke or drink in public, but Thais expect Western women to do both.

Places to Eat

• If you invite a Thai to dinner, don't be surprised if he turns up with several friends—without advance notice. You must include them in the party and must pay for their meals.

• Note that the word for restaurant is pronounced *ran-ahan.*

• To save money eat at coffeeshops, where tea, coffee, liquor, and Western continental, Chinese, and Thai food is served. Or go to a noodle shop. These are very inexpensive eating places frequented by students. Have noodles in soup or tossed with garlic oil, fermented fish sauce, or meat. Ground peanuts, hot peppers, and vinegar are served as accompaniments.

• Avoid buying food from street vendors, however appetizing the smells. Lack of hygienic conditions make this unwise.

• Don't concern yourself about seating arrangements. Chairs and tables are set up Western style.

• Ask if someone at the restaurant speaks English. If so, they will be pleased to help you.

• Outside moderately priced restaurants, look for samples of the food in the window. You can point out to the waiter what you want.

• Outside of Bangkok, don't expect menus in restaurants. Memorize the names of a few dishes which you enjoy.

• At inexpensive restaurants, feel free to join others at a table if the restaurant is full. At better restaurants, wait to be seated by the maître d'.

• To call the waiter or waitress, say "*Nong*," which means "younger." It's rude to beckon or motion.

• Don't be surprised if, in small, local restaurants, there are different—and higher—prices for foreigners. A restaurant with a menu in Chinese, Thai, and English may have three different prices for the same dish. Food in Thailand is so inexpensive, however, that it isn't worth it to make a fuss or try to bargain. The difference will probably be only a few cents.

• A woman dining alone should not be offended if other diners stare at her. The Thais are simply observing that you are Western and different. Do, however, stick to first-class restaurants when eating alone.

• If you're dining with Thais, order family-style. People usually share dishes; each one is enough for two people. If you are eating alone, be prepared to eat (or leave) a great deal. It's not considered acceptable to ask for a smaller portion.

• If you don't like hot, spicy food, say several times, *"Mai phet"* (my pet).

• When ordering an egg dish, specify that you want chicken eggs by saying *"kye-gye."* Thais do not distinguish between chicken and duck eggs, which have a strong flavor and an off-putting color.

• Be sure to drink only bottled water. The most popular brand is Polaris, which is not sparkling and comes in large bottles.

• *Mehkong* is the local rice whiskey. To try it, seek out local food shops and restaurants; it's not available in tourist spots.

• Be aware that bottles are recycled. If you buy a soda from a vendor, you aren't allowed to take the bottle with you. If you don't want to stand and drink the whole soda so that you can return the bottle to the vendor, have him pour the soda into a plastic bag, which you may take away. Usually, the plastic bag has ice in it. Tell the vendor not to put ice in the bag, since it's not safe to consume unboiled Thai water.

• Remember that you pay if you suggest going to a restaurant with someone. There's no such thing as "Dutch treat," which the Thais call "American share." Say "I'm taking you to dinner." To avoid awkwardness, find the maître d' before the meal, tip him, and tell him that the bill should be brought to you. Don't tell the waiter directly; he won't pay any attention unless the instruction comes from the maître d'.

• If you are part of a group, expect the oldest or wealthiest person to pay. Don't fight over the check.

Specialties

• To sample typical Thai fare, try *kai yang*, barbecued chicken stuffed with grated coconut; *pla kapong*, fish; *poo cha*, crab meat and vegetables deep-fried in a crab shell; *khao pad*, fried rice with pork, crabmeat, garlic, peppers, and fish sauce, accompanied by various chili sauces; *gaeng ped*—one of Thailand's most popular dishes—a beef or chicken curry cooked with coconut milk, chilies, eggplant, and spices; *hommok*, fish steamed with coconut juice, Thai curry spices, coriander, and chilies; and *tom yam gung*, a soup with prawns, chicken or fish, fish-flavored soy sauce, lemon grass, and special leaves called *makroot*.

• To avoid hot, spicy foods, choose one of these mild dishes: *nua phat naman hoi* (noo-ah paht nah-mahn hoy), beef with oyster sauce; *kai yud sai* (ky yet sigh), puffy egg omelettes with stir-fried vegetables; or *gwitio phak thai* (gwee-tyo pahk ty), vegetables and noodles fried together.

• Remember that noodles are described in terms of their width. *Senyai* are wide noodles, and *senlek* are narrow noodles. Either size may be made of rice or wheat. Clear noodles are usually made with rice and opaque noodles with wheat. *Bami* are yellow noodles made of ground rice. Order noodle dishes either wet or dry—with a soupy sauce or without.

• If dessert is available, it will probably be either *foi tong*, an egg yolk and sugar mixture; *salim*, sweet noodles in coconut milk and ice chips; *kow neo mamuang*, sticky rice and mangoes, rice cooked in coconut milk and served with fresh mangoes; or *songkaya*, pudding made of eggs, palm sugar, and coconut milk, served either hot or cold in a coconut shell.

• Think carefully if you are offered a fruit called *durian*. The odor resembles Limburger cheese, but the taste is—according to Asians—delicious. (A common saying is that it "smells like hell and tastes like heaven"). If you try one, eat it outdoors immediately after buying it. To counter its heating effect, drink cool water. The odor will cling to your clothes for days. It is against the law to bring *durians* into hotels or on planes, and they are banned from public places in Thailand, Indonesia, Malaysia, and Singapore. If you eat a great deal of it, prepare for headaches and dizziness.

HOTELS

• If you plan to be in Thailand between November and February, book your hotel room well in advance, since first-class hotels are often full during that period.

• Realize that Thailand has a wide variety of accommodations. For each category, you will find different amenities: L=luxury—a wide range of business services, sports facilities, Western and Asian restaurants, bars, and discotheques; A=first class—business and sports facilities, restaurants, and bars; B=tourist class—air-conditioning and an attached bathroom, restaurants and room service, some TVs showing films on cable; C=economy—probably air-conditioning and an attached bath, and probably a restaurant and room service; D=budget—usually no air-conditioning, probably an attached bathroom, toilets either Western style or "squat" type, toilet paper provided, maybe a restaurant, mostly found outside tourist areas; E=guesthouse—fans, "squat" toilet, no toilet paper, maybe an attached bathroom, maybe no towels; F=guest-house—fans, shared bathroom facilities, "squat" toilets, no toilet paper, some very dirty, others an excellent value.

• If you want a hotel room with a bath tub, be sure to make that request specific. Even in better hotels, some rooms have just a shower.

• Don't expect central heating anywhere in Thailand, even in hotels.

• Be sure to check out your room before registering to make sure that everything—lights, air-conditioning, plumbing, locks—functions properly. If something doesn't, ask for another room—or a discount.

• Note that the hotel rates listed in brochures and rooms have little to do with the actual rates. If you have Thai friends, let them bargain for you; the room may cost 20 to 50 percent less. You can also ask a taxi driver to bargain for you, but you will have to tip him—and you may be beginning a relationship that you don't wish to continue (i.e., he might begin hounding you).

• At standard Thai hotels, try bargaining if there is no posted rate. The hotel may be trying to raise rates for foreigners.

• Don't change money in hotels unless you are desperate. The rate of exchange is very poor. Change money only in banks.

• Note that most hotels provide a safe-deposit box at no charge. Leave your valuables there, including travelers' checks, passport, and credit cards, if you won't be using them (e.g., if you're going to the beach). However, note that in some low-priced hotels, credit cards have been used in the owner's absence.

TIPPING

• Tipping is not usual in Thailand except in places frequented by foreigners. As a general rule, leave loose change, but never just one *baht*. It is better to leave nothing than one *baht*.

• Give a hotel taxi driver 10 percent of the fare as a tip. If you hail a taxi on the street, bargain about the fare before you get in, and don't leave a tip.

• Give porters 10–50 *baht* for three suitcases.

• At airports, there is a fixed fee of two *baht* per bag; at train stations a fixed fee of one *baht* per bag.

• Don't tip in inexpensive restaurants. At better restaurants, a 10 to 15 percent service charge will be added to your bill.

• Thais love Western cigarettes, and a few cigarettes or a package make an excellent tip for people such as taxi drivers or tour guides.

PRIVATE HOMES

• As a Westerner, phone before visiting, although Thais drop in on one another unannounced. There is no "standard" visiting time.

• Be prepared to be invited as a couple or for the male to be invited to a men-only gathering.

• Before you enter a home, look to see if shoes are left outside. Although your host may say you can keep your shoes on, take them off. Slippers are often provided. No one will ever be offended if you remove your shoes. Don't step on the door-sill of a home, because Thais believe that souls reside there.

• Expect to be offered cocktails, soft drinks, tea, and fresh fruit cup when visiting in the afternoon. If you are offered a soft drink in a bottle with a glass that already has ice in it, drink directly from the bottle to avoid using ice possibly made from contaminated water.

• Although Thais might offer one another such snacks as pan-fried clams, squid salad, or a light vegetable salad, prepare to express pleasure when served ham and cheese, a gesture meant to impress Westerners.

• If you visit a family outside Bangkok, expect to find a mat on the floor and a small table with food on it. When you sit, do not cross your legs. Kneel and keep your feet behind you or to the side. Never point your feet at anyone.

• After a visit or a meal, leave by 10:00 P.M. Most Thais get up at 5:30 or 6:00 A.M. to try to avoid traffic jams.

• Most Thai homes visited by Westerners have servants, so don't offer to help in the kitchen. If you can tell that there are no servants, offer to help—though you will probably be refused.

• Offer to pay if you make phone calls in a Thai home. Your offer will probably be refused. It's best, therefore, not to make expensive long-distance calls, since your generous hosts will be stuck with the bill.

• If staying with a Thai family, feel free to be independent about sightseeing alone and spending your day alone. The family will feel flattered if you ask what is important to see and how to get there.

• If you stay overnight in a Thai home, be sure to wear a robe to and from the bathroom (men should not simply wear a towel around the waist). Thais are very modest about the body.

• Realize that many homes now have American-style bathrooms, but don't be surprised if the toilet is in a separate room from the bath or shower.

• Don't be surprised if there is no hot-water heater. The weather is so hot and humid that one isn't necessary.

• Anticipate no surprise from your hosts (as you would encounter in European countries) at taking a daily bath or shower. Thais often bathe two or three times a day because of the hot, humid weather.

Gifts: Although Thais don't usually bring gifts when invited to a meal, as a Westerner, bring flowers, cakes, or fresh fruit. Thais love tulips and roses. Don't bring marigolds or carnations, as both are associated with funerals.

Other Gifts: Women's cosmetics or perfume (especially Clinique brand). Bring men a bottle of liquor, preferably brandy, neckties and tie clips, or cigarettes. Bring teenagers sneakers if you know their sizes; most popular are brands made in the U.S. Also popular are dolls in traditional costumes, as are picture books from your area, stationery, and photo albums.

• If you have stayed with Thai people in the countryside, consider giving money as a gift.

• Don't be offended that your gift isn't opened when you give it. Thais wait until they are alone. If you are given a gift, don't open it in the presence of the giver.

MONEY AND BUSINESS

Hours

Businesses: Monday through Friday, 8:30 A.M. to 5:00 P.M., and sometimes Saturday mornings.

Banks: 8:30 A.M. to 3:30 P.M., Monday through Friday. Saturday, 8:30 A.M. to noon.

Government Offices: 8:30 A.M. to 4:30 P.M., Monday through Friday. Closed for lunch between noon and 1:00 P.M.

Shops: Large shops are open from 10:00 A.M. to 6:30 or 7:00 P.M., Monday through Saturday. Smaller shops open earlier and close later.

Money

• The unit of currency is the *baht*, divided into 100 *satang*. Coins are 25 and 50 *satang* (copper); 1, 2, and 5 *baht* (silver), and 10 *baht* (copper and silver combined). Notes are 10 (brown), 20 (green), 50 (blue), 100 (red), 500 (mauve), and 1000 (khaki) *bahts*. The larger the note, the higher the denomination.

• Note that there are three types of 1 *baht* coins: a small new one, a medium old one, and the largest, the oldest one.

• Use travelers' checks for a better rate of exchange. There are official money exchanges.

• Note that major credit cards— American Express, Visa, Barclaycard, MasterCard, Access, Diners Club—are accepted in hotels, large restaurants, large shops, and souvenir shops. Only hotels will accept payment in travelers' checks (but remember that the rate of exchange given at hotels is often substantially lower than that at a bank).

Business Practices

• The best months for business travel to Thailand are November through March. Most businesspeople vacation during April and May, and May through October is the monsoon season. Avoid the week before and after Christmas and especially the month of April, during which *Songkran*—the Water Festival (the traditional Thai New

Year)—continues for a whole week, and all businesses are closed.

• Arrange for a letter of introduction, and try to have an intermediary. Thais feel more comfortable if they have a mutual acquaintance with a potential business connection.

• Realize that networking with government officials is essential for doing business in Thailand. Therefore, it is important to hire a local agent through your country's Chamber of Commerce or through the commercial section of your embassy.

• To arrange an appointment with a large company, write a month or two in advance. Some small companies will accept visits without an appointment, but large ones won't.

• Try to stay in a luxury hotel. Thais will be impressed because they will believe that you represent a successful firm. Such a hotel will also be a convenience for you because fax machines and other business amenities will be available.

• Try to arrange meetings before 3:30 P.M., because Thais frequently leave their offices at that time to try to beat the heavy rush hour traffic.

• Before leaving your hotel for business meetings, arm yourself with a detailed map of Bangkok, since most taxi drivers know only the main streets, and bring addresses and directions to your appointments—as well as the name and location of your hotel—written in the Thai alphabet.

• If you have several appointments not within a short walk of each other, hire a car and driver rather than taking separate taxis.

• Be assured that English is spoken by people in top management in most businesses; however, if you're dealing with a smaller company or one outside Bangkok, you may need to hire an interpreter.

• Be sure to be on time, but don't be surprised if your Thai counterparts are late.

• Don't be surprised if the initial meeting is held in a restaurant at lunch or over drinks at a club. Thais want to know about you and your interests. Business may never be discussed at a business lunch. However, you may be received in an office and offered coffee and tea. Conversation at the initial meeting should focus on your travels, the beauties of Thailand, and your counterpart's travel overseas.

• Bring business cards, preferably with English on one side and Thai on the other. You can have them printed in Bangkok. Ask at the tourist office (or your hotel information desk) where to find a printer. Thais are impressed by titles, so be sure to use yours on your business card. Also include such details as fax number and home telephone number. Such information will increase your status.

• Dress for success. If you make a lot of money, look the part. Thais are impressed with appearance because it indicates you are of the upper class.

• Businesswomen should always

wear full eye makeup. Hosiery is not necessary, however, because the Thai heat and humidity would make them unbearable.

• Try to learn at least a few words of Thai, difficult as the language is. You will impress Thai businesspeople.

• Be patient and flexible, because business dealings do not move quickly. Thais regard work as a small part of life, and often spend work hours making personal phone calls or running errands. They do not agree with the relentless Western work ethic. Prepare to allow much more time to reach a goal than you would in a Western country.

• Realize that all requests, documents, and correspondence must pass through many layers before they reach top management. Although such a system may seem inefficient to Westerners, Thais see it as deference to rank and authority.

• Never lose control of your emotions, and don't be overly assertive. Anyone who appears impatient, quick-tempered, or impulsive will be looked down on. If an argument appears to be arising, expect Thais to change the subject or make a joke.

• Don't ask a question designed to elicit a value judgment; e.g., "What do you think of this product line?" or "What do you think of Mr. X? Is he someone I can trust?" Any direct confrontation is considered very impolite.

• Realize that Thais will never

say "No." If people start making implausible excuses, or pretending that they don't understand English (if you know they do), be aware that they mean "No." Thais avoid confrontation at all costs. Likewise, they find it difficult to accept a direct negative answer.

• If someone laughs for no apparent reason at a business meeting, change the subject. He or she is embarrassed.

• Don't be surprised if a subordinate refuses to accept any responsibility. Top officials have all responsibility—for minor as well as major decisions. Subordinates act as filters or protectors, so that senior officials aren't suddenly caught with a problem with which they aren't prepared to deal.

• Prepare to have a senior official tell you that he has to check with someone at an even higher level, even when such a person doesn't exist. It's another strategy to avoid confrontation.

• Realize that the key to getting along in Thailand is to be accommodating but not compromise your own values (e.g., if you don't want to go to a "raunchy" nightclub, don't go).

Business Entertaining: If Thai businesspeople invite you to dinner, expect to be taken to a restaurant.

• If you wish to entertain a large number of people, don't stage a Western-style cocktail party. Thais find them boring. Arrange a buffet lunch or supper in a hotel, or a meal in a private room in a restaurant.

• To entertain a small group, take them to a Western restaurant in a large hotel.

• Include Thai wives in entertaining at a business dinner.

• Businessmen need to decide what to do if taken to a brothel or massage parlor, a typical form of business entertaining. Brothels may be like cafés, where women sit with you. When one invites you to her room, you can decline by saying you're married or have a girlfriend.

Gifts: Bring good-quality, brand-name pens as business gifts.

Note: For advice regarding business greetings, dress, or table manners, see the appropriate sections earlier in the chapter.

HOLIDAYS AND SPECIAL OCCASIONS

• Note that banks, offices, and most stores are closed on the national holidays listed below. Towns and regions also have local festivals, which are holidays in the region.

Check with the tourist office for dates of local festivals.

• Be aware that most holidays change annually according to the lunar calendar.

Holidays: New Year's Day (January 1); Chinese New Year (end of January/beginning of February); Magha Puja Day (February), a Buddhist commemoration of Buddha's preaching to 1250 enlightened monks, marked by processions around temples; Chakri Day (April 6), commemorating the founder of the Chakri dynasty; Songkran, the Thai New Year, the Water Festival; Coronation Day (May 5); Visakha Puja (May/June), the most important Buddhist celebration, celebrating the birth, enlightenment, and passing into Nirvana on his death of the Buddha; the Queen's Birthday (August 12); Chulalongkorn Day (October 23), in memory of King Chulalongkorn (the heir to the throne in *The King and I*), who abolished slavery in Thailand; Loy Krathong (October/November), the Festival of Lights; the King's Birthday (December 5); Constitution Day (December 10); Christmas (December 25).

• *Songkran* (Water Festival), the traditional Thai New Year, usually occurs in mid-April, but dates shift according to the lunar calendar. Keep a raincoat handy at all times because water is thrown everywhere to signify the washing away of evil and the bringing of good wishes. Westerners are often the target of water thrown from all directions. The three- to four-day celebration is marked by folk-dancing, processions in the streets, and the sprinkling of water and perfume on the hands of monks, elders, and statues of Buddha.

• Note that in the north *Songkran* may go on for seven days or more. In the southern part of the country, water play is limited to one day.

• Note that for the celebration of the King's birthday, offices close for three days and people usually go away for the weekend.

• Check with the Thailand Tourist Office to be sure of the dates of Buddhist holidays for any given year, since they change with the lunar calendar.

TRANSPORTATION

Public Transportation

• Before starting out on any form of transportation, have your destination and the location of the place you are staying written in Thai.

• Allow considerably more time

than you think you'll need, especially when making connections. Long traffic jams are the norm, and in the rainy season flooding can be a problem, interrupting some intercity services for several days.

• Don't look for a subway in Bangkok. There isn't one.

• Bangkok is built on a series of *klongs* (canals), so some transportation is by water. *Klongs* are *very* polluted. Many have been paved over, so they're not used as much as they once were. The Chao Phya Express is the river bus service. Look for a long boat with a number on its roof. Most stop at the same landings, so you can wait at a wharf for a return boat. Service is most frequent in the early morning or late afternoon.

• For one of the many boats that ferries people back and forth across the river, pay at the entrance to the jetty.

• Note that bus numbers are marked in red. Get on the front or back of a local bus, and state or show your destination to the ticket seller. Keep your ticket until you get off because inspectors sometimes check tickets. Be aware that people are very aggressive at stops and on buses during rush hours, but will usually be kind to a foreigner.

• If you're planning a journey outside Bangkok, remember that long-distance buses have very cold air-conditioning, very loud TVs, and Asian videos.

• Choose train travel over buses if possible. Not only are the trains more spacious—with meals served at your seat—but also they are much safer in terms of accidents and robberies. On either bus or train, be very careful of personal belongings. Take valuables with you if you go to the bathroom or to another car.

• If robbers should board your train, give them whatever they ask. People have been killed for refusing to surrender their possessions.

• Of the three classes of train travel, take either first or second. First class is air-conditioned. Reserve seats in advance through the travel agency in your hotel or at the railroad station. Second class, where you will meet more Thais, has ceiling fans. Sit facing away from the sun.

• Try to book a week in advance for popular destinations outside Bangkok—Chiang Mai and resort areas—especially during holiday periods. Go to the Bangkok train station, where you will find windows for advance booking and same day booking. However, avoid the Bangkok train station if at all possible. There are pickpockets everywhere, and it's hot and crowded. If there's a travel agency in or near your hotel, use it. It will save you from standing in line at the station.

• Remember that buying a return ticket doesn't guarantee you a seat reservation for the return trip. To ensure a seat, buy the return ticket as soon as you arrive at your destination.

• Always take hotel taxis. They are much safer. Taxi fares tend to be so low that the 10 to 15 percent extra for a hotel taxi is well worth it. When you're away from your hotel, phone and have a hotel taxi pick you up.

• Give the taxi driver your destination address written in Thai.

• Before getting into the taxi, bargain for the fare. Ask someone at your hotel what the fare should be. The hotel doorman or a porter may be willing to bargain with the driver for you. Fares differ according to the time of day. (Taxis may have meters, but they are never used.)

• Note that *tuk-tuks*—three-wheeled motorcycles with a passenger seat (pedicabs)—are less expensive than taxis. They go very fast, however, and are rather dangerous, so take a taxi if possible. If you want to signal a *tuk-tuk*, stand at the side of the street, keep your hand at your side, and point your fingers down, then raise them. Be sure to arrange the fare ahead of time.

• For *dire* emergencies, take a motorcycle taxi. Helmets are compulsory, and all drivers have a spare one.

Driving

• Best advice: don't. Thais drive very recklessly, and traffic in Bangkok is a nightmare. Further, most road signs, including warnings, are in Thai. Hiring a car and driver costs only slightly more than renting a car yourself—a small price to pay for "leaving the driving to them."

• If you choose to ignore this

sound advice, get an International Driver's License. You must have one to rent a car. And remember—driving is on the left (as in Japan and Britain).

• If you decide to rent a car, be sure to do so through your hotel or a reputable agency.

• If you rent a motorcycle, you must have an International Driver's License. Tourists are sometimes told that they don't need one, but that's not true. If you are caught by the police without one, you will be charged.

• Note that the speed limit in towns is 60 km/hour (about 36 mph) and in the country it is 100 km/hour (about 60 mph).

LEGAL MATTERS, SAFETY, AND HEALTH

• Don't deal with black market moneychangers. You will get very little extra and could get into trouble.

• Stay in better hotels, which tend to have better security.

• You'll be relatively safe during the day around international hotels and main shopping streets, but be very wary at night, when there is a great deal of street crime, purse snatching, and robbery. Don't roam around at night, especially if you don't speak Thai. Even in the daytime avoid walking in isolated areas. Memorize the word for "Help!" (Shoo-way doo-way) as you will get much quicker results if you ask in Thai.

• Thailand is famous as a center for nightlife—and prostitution. Men can expect to be confronted on the street.

• Avoid the Thieves' Market (as the name implies, a center for the sale of stolen goods) in Bangkok and the Golden Triangle (a center of opium traffic) in northern Thailand. People who "work" in both places do not take kindly to visiting spectators.

• Avoid stray dogs. They may have rabies.

• If you're a woman, and a taxi driver tries to strike up a conversation with you, say that you are married and have children.

• Women should be very careful with handbags on streets and buses. Thieves sometimes slash them and remove wallets, or men on motorcycles may try to grab them.

• Don't wear jewelry—either real or fake—when you go out.

• If at all possible, go out in a group. Women alone who want to sample Thai nightclubs or see the classical dancing should arrange for one of the many available tours.

• A woman traveling alone who arrives in Bangkok at night should take the Thai International bus or public transportation into the city, never an unofficial taxi. Another option is to arrange for your hotel to send a taxi or a limousine for you. It's well worth the extra cost.

• Always take taxis at night, and be sure to use hotel taxis.

• Realize that cars may not stop when they see pedestrians at pedestrian crossings, so be *very* careful

• If you have a problem, seek out the tourist police, a separate group who speak English and other foreign languages. (To find them, you must go to the Tourist Association Center, Tourist Authority of Thailand, at the central office in Bangkok.)

• Don't attempt to take any image of the Buddha out of the country. It is forbidden, and penalties are severe.

Health: Bring an adequate supply of any prescription drugs you are currently taking.

• Drink *only* bottled or boiled water.

• Women should note that ordinary toiletries, sanitary napkins, and tampons are widely available.

• Never eat ice cream purchased from a street vendor.

• It is *impossible* to emphasize too strongly the necessity of *extreme* caution in any sexual matters in Thailand. A few years ago, Thailand, with a population of 58 million, had 800,000 HIV and AIDS cases. One study estimated that 1 in 50 Thais was selling sex, with 800,000 to 2 million women and 800,000 child prostitutes. Many of the prostitutes who come to Bangkok from mountain communities have no notion about STDs (sexually transmitted diseases) or AIDS and thus take no precautions to protect a partner. Despite an effort by the government to introduce the use of condoms into commercial sex, great caution is still necessary.

KEY PHRASES

Note: Thai is a tonal language and is very difficult, but people will be very appreciative if you have learned even a few words, since so few foreigners are acquainted with the language.

There is no accepted Romanization of the Thai language. Some of the sounds cannot be reproduced accurately in Roman script.

English	*Pronunciation*
Good morning, afternoon, evening, hello, good-bye	Sah-waht dee króp (man) Sah-waht dee káh (woman)
Mr.	Coon króp
Mrs., Miss	Coon káh
Please	Dye pród
Thank you	Cop coon króp (man) Cop coon káh (woman)
You're welcome	Yin-dée
Yes	Króp (man) Káh (woman)
No	My króp (man) My káh (woman)
Excuse me	Kor-toht króp (man) Kor-thot káh (woman)
I don't understand	My kowjye
Does anyone speak English?	Kry pud áhn-kleed dye?
Never mind. It doesn't matter. (a common expression)	My pen rye

VIETNAM

After decades of occupation by European/American powers, Vietnam no longer answers to foreign occupants, but it has retained some of the more appealing aspects of colonial society. An inheritance from the French, a thriving café culture flourishes in Ho Chi Minh City (which most residents still refer to as Saigon). A young Vietnamese told writer Laura Delp, "The first things the English built in their colonies were banks. The Spanish built churches. But the French, they opened cafés"—the first in Saigon in the 1860s. A resort area prospers in Nha Trang, where local dishes are served in an outdoor pavilion and local boats can be hired for a floating picnic.

Vietnam has been wary about embracing capitalism, however. Harvard

Economics Professor Dwight Perkins told *Forbes* magazine, "There's a real reluctance to create a friendly investment climate."

There is a hint that inroads are being made: In Saigon/Ho Chi Minh City, there is a California-style restaurant with *designer pizzas*!

GREETINGS

• In greeting, men shake hands and nod slightly when greeting other men. Men and women simply nod and smile. (Vietnamese don't touch members of the opposite sex in public.) However, in cities, Westernized people of both sexes tend to shake hands. People in the countryside, or older, traditional people clasp both hands together above the waist and bow slightly.

• Expect people to use first names right away, but always with the title Mr., Mrs., or Miss. There are only about 100 last names in Vietnamese, and only 20–50 are in widespread use, so it's important that you use the first name. Remember that the last name comes first, middle name second, and first name third. (The last name of 50 percent of the population is Nguyen.) In either oral greeting, or when writing a letter, use the title with the first name. Thus, Pham Thi Mac would be addressed as Miss Mac.

• Call professional people by their first name plus title—e.g., Professor Binh. Even when addressing professionals, such as professors, architects, doctors, or engineers, use the title with their first name. (This is true even if you're addressing the prime minister.)

• When greeting an official or a figure of authority, clasp both the person's hands.

• If you are greeting individuals in a group, always greet older people or those in authority first.

• Make sure that you shake hands gently. Sometimes you pick up a person's hand as though you were going to kiss it and give it a gentle squeeze.

• When addressing people in Vietnamese, use the proper honorific (e.g., the different words for "Mr.," "Mrs.," and "Miss"). Some honorifics mean "older brother," "old sister," "grandfather," "grandmother," and others are used for children. Knowing the correct terms will be a great help when you travel, as correct usage is very important to the Vietnamese. Ask someone who is familiar with the language to teach you the pronunciation of these words. (Since Vietnamese is a tonal language, it's difficult to explain the pronunciation in writing.)

• At parties, if the host doesn't introduce you to others, introduce yourself.

• When leaving someone's company, always shake hands or bow slightly with hands clasped.

CONVERSATION

• Don't be surprised if a Vietnamese asks you *very* personal questions—e.g., "How much did you pay for that?" or "What is your salary?" Try to deflect the salary question by saying something such as, "Enough to live on," since most Vietnamese make about $200 a year. People often say things that Westerners find inappropriate. A Vietnamese might say, "You're fat. You should lose weight." Don't show offense.

• Don't ask people what their political views are and avoid discussing the current political situation.

• Good topics for initial conversation include health, profession, family (e.g., "Are you married?"

"How many children do you have?" "What do they do?").

• Never brag about your accomplishments, and don't underestimate a person's status if he/she seems shy, reserved, or self-effacing.

• Don't be surprised to see people hold their hand or something else over their mouth when they speak. This gesture is a cultural tradition and not a sign of nervousness.

• Learn to ask open-ended questions, because people don't like to say "No." When faced with a direct question, people tend to change the subject or just smile and nod.

• Note that Vietnamese love joking, and their humor can be sarcastic, in contrast to the humor of other Asian countries. However, jokes in a foreign language are usually difficult to understand, so avoid telling them.

• Never joke about "Uncle Ho" or "Mr. Ho" (Ho Chi Minh). He is regarded as the father of his country and is a venerated figure.

• Realize that Americans are more sensitive about the Vietnam War than the Vietnamese are. If you wish to discuss the war, speak in general terms about the sacrifices people had to make. However, note that people are upset with Americans who come searching for MIAs, because many Vietnamese soldiers are also MIAs. According to the Buddhist religion, if there are no graves for these people, their spirits wander the country restlessly and don't reincarnate. This subject is one best avoided. Keep in mind that

Vietnam has experienced five wars in its recent history. The war with America was only one of them.

• Be aware that the most common foreign language spoken is English. (One lawyer remarked that a Vietnamese to whom he was speaking on the phone had such impeccable English that he sounded like a native English speaker.) You may hear people singing lyrics from American popular songs. One of the ways for people to learn English was to buy music tapes on the black market or to listen to the Voice of America (which uses a special 3,000-word vocabulary).

• Expect middle-aged people who are better educated to speak Russian, because many studied in the former Soviet Union. However, most don't wish to speak the language because of their dislike of the Russians.

• Note that older, educated people tend to speak French, as a result of the French colonial period in Vietnam.

• Don't speak quickly or loudly. If you're in a rush and speak very quickly, people may think that you are angry with them.

• Never lose your temper.

• Prepare to find people very self-effacing. Give compliments when they are due—e.g., tell people if their English is good. (Until five or six years ago, it was illegal to study English or to read English books.) Don't expect compliments from the Vietnamese. They are not in the habit of offering them.

• Don't refer to any of the minorities as Vietnamese. They have experienced discrimination but have been forced to integrate. You will be able to identify minorities by their dress—homespun hemp clothing in very bright colors, a great deal of embroidery, headdresses, silver bangles, and heavy jewelry.

• Especially with the Hmong and other minorities, don't compliment a child, because they believe it might attract the attention of evil spirits, and her/his soul may be stolen.

TELEPHONES

• Note that Vietnam has a new and excellent phone system. However, many people do not have telephones.

• Don't anticipate difficulty in finding operators who speak English.

• Expect people to answer the phone *"allo"* (ah-lo), a custom adopted from the French.

• Make local calls from any hotel or restaurant phone. They are free. However, if you find a phone with a box next to it, put in 2000 *dong* for three minutes. If you talk longer, there will be additional charges.

• To make a long-distance call, go to the post office. Give the phone number at the central counter. You usually prepay. In cities, you pay for one minute initially. In the countryside you pay for three minutes, even if you only speak for one minute. You'll be directed to a booth (which will probably be incredibly hot). You'll find a clock in the booth, so you can keep track of your time. For even one second over a minute, you must pay for the full minute. If you haven't used all the time for which you paid, you'll receive a refund.

• Consider buying a phone card at the post office. Use them at public phones, which are found on street corners in towns and cities.

• Remember that it's incredibly expensive to telephone abroad. The best strategy is to call your party, pay for one minute, and have her/him call you back.

• For emergency numbers, check in each area you visit. There is no universal number for emergencies. For Ho Chi Minh City and Hanoi, the emergency numbers are police, dial 13; fire, dial 14; ambulance, dial 15.

IN PUBLIC

• Avoid eye contact when first meeting people. This action is especially important when girls or young women meet someone. In fact, it's best not to make eye contact at all, since it is considered a sign of aggression. Do remember to smile a great deal.

• Don't be surprised if people stare at you, a foreigner. Don't stare back. If you venture off the beaten path, people will stare at you endlessly. Children may touch your arms, because they've never before seen hair on people's arms.

• Realize that as a foreigner, you'll pay more for everything than locals do.

• Don't pat another person on the head, because it is considered the most spiritual part of the body. Be especially careful not to touch the head of a baby, because people believe that the baby may get sick.

• Refrain from touching anyone on the shoulder or slapping another person on the back.

• Be sure that you don't use your index finger to beckon another person, because that's the way animals are summoned. Hold your palm down and wave the fingers back and forth (as though you were sweeping) at the person you wish to signal. The same gesture is used for hitch-hiking.

• Avoid touching a person of the opposite sex in public. Even husbands and wives don't touch. However, members of the same sex often do. It is common to see two men or two women walk down the street holding hands.

• Note that even close relatives who have not seen another for a long time will not hug and kiss in public. The most affectionate display would be to touch one another's arm.

• Never assume an aggressive stance, such as putting your hands on your hips or crossing your arms.

• Don't point the soles of your feet at another person.

• Note that if a person is nodding as you are speaking to her/him it does not necessarily mean that the person agrees. It simply means that he/she is listening and understands you.

• Expect actions to be performed gently, never abruptly. A Vietnamese would not bang a glass or a plate on the table.

• Never display anger. Doing so is considered a weakness. People will usually react by smiling. Showing anger causes the other person to lose face. Instead of showing anger, try chatting with the person. A calm demeanor will make it easier to obtain what you want. In Vietnam,

only people of the lower classes show rage.

• Realize that most Vietnamese, no matter what their religion, believe in spirits. Many ceremonies and superstititions have evolved from these beliefs. A few examples: breaking a bottle of fish sauce is bad luck; children should not eat eggs or bananas on the day of an exam; passing a funeral is good luck. Many Vietnamese also believe in astrology.

• If you visit a Buddhist pagoda (an excellent idea), find the monk (called a *bonze*) and ask permission to enter. Always remove your shoes before entering. Leave 5000 *dong* (the equivalent of 50 cents) in the donation box.

• Expect people to be punctual, except for government officials—especially ones who are in powerful positions.

• Be prepared for a great deal of noise. Vietnamese feel that the more noise there is, the more people are enjoying themselves.

• Feel free to give money to old people and children. They will not accost you. Children sometimes come into restaurants to try to eat people's leftovers. If you wish, you may buy the child a meal there. If you're on the street near a stand that sells food, you may buy a meal or several dishes for a child. The children will not eat in front of you. They will take the food home to share with others.

• Be aware that the government is still wary of and suspicious of

Americans. Local authorities may try to confine you to certain areas.

• Note that the Vietnamese enjoy posing for photos. If possible, take their address and send them a print. Especially in rural areas, people will cherish the pictures. (One woman who traveled extensively in the countryside reported that very poor people often pulled out a twenty-year-old letter and photo from abroad to show her.) When people die, a photo is needed for the altar. People often can't afford one, so the photo you send would be a good deed.

• Don't photograph military installations, harbors, airports, or government buildings.

• When you go to the post office, buy stamps, stick them on with glue, and immediately return to the counter to have the stamps cancelled. Otherwise, they will be taken off for resale.

• Be sure to treat religious statues and portraits of revered political figures with respect—e.g., don't hang anything on a statue of Ho Chi Minh. At his mausoleum in Hanoi, don't honk your horn or drive on the road around it. This area is the only place in Vietnam that is quiet. There are no repercussions for making noise, but silence is a sign of respect.

• If you visit Ho Chi Minh's mausoleum, be sure to wear sturdy shoes; you can't wear shorts or carry any bags with you. Hold your hands straight down by your sides. Soldiers will physically move your arms if your elbows are bent or if your hands are behind your back. (Interesting note: Every year his body is sent to Russia for two months for "maintenance.")

• If you will be encountering people from one of Vietnam's 54 ethnic groups, dress modestly, ask permission before photographing them, and avoid sitting on doorsteps or going into a home unless you are invited. Be sure not to photograph or touch village shrines.

• Remember that shopkeepers sometimes believe that if the day's or month's first customer makes a purchase, then the remainder of the day or month will be lucky. If you are the first customer, you may be pushed *very* hard to buy something. The shop owner may, in fact, become bullying and rude.

• Keep in mind that the most important rule in bargaining is not to become angry or annoyed or to let the transaction become overly important. For Vietnamese, bargaining is a method of establishing a relationship, not ruining it.

• In cities, look for public restrooms in restaurants and hotels. There will be toilet paper available.

• Don't be surprised to see people urinating on the streets in cities. In the countryside, where there are no public toilets, people say they're "going to the field."

DRESS

• When meeting a person in authority, dress your best. Your costume will indicate that you're aware the person is important and will show your respect.

• Women should wear skirts below the knee.

• Pay someone to wash and iron your clothes so that they are always spotlessly clean (the cost will be minimal). Vietnamese manage to have very clean clothes, even when working in muddy rice paddies.

• If you see people wearing white headbands, realize that they are going to or coming from a funeral.

• At beach resorts, you will see foreigners in bikinis, but such dress is not appropriate. Vietnam has no nude beaches. At the beaches, you'll find changing rooms for which there is a fee.

• Wear shorts only if you're playing a sport. Neither men nor women should wear them on the street.

• If you're wearing a shirt and pants, keep your shirt tucked in. Otherwise, people will associate you with workers, who leave their shirts out to keep cool.

• You may see local women wearing a high-necked, fitted, long tunic with slits, called *ao dai*. The tunics are worn over very long, wide pants. Women of social standing usually wear this outfit. Since the Vietnamese think the Western figure isn't built to wear such a costume, don't consider buying one.

• Women should not wear revealing or off-the-shoulder clothing during the day.

• For business, men should wear a suit and tie, and women should wear dresses or skirts.

• If you're invited to an evening affair, keep in mind that the Vietnamese dress very elegantly. Women should wear a conservative dress or a blouse and skirt. Men should wear a tie and jacket. No one wears tuxedos, however, except when getting married or playing in a band.

• If you decide to visit the *cu chi* tunnels, wear long pants; otherwise you will scrape your knees. The interiors are very hot and humid. Don't go into the tunnels if you're claustrophobic or if you don't like the dark. (The tunnels were used by the Viet Cong to disappear and reappear quickly. They contain storage rooms, tactical quarters, kitchens, and surgical centers.)

MEALS

Hours and Food

Breakfast: Before 7:00 A.M. People rise early, because work begins early due to the heat. Expect a large variety of noodle soups with seafood or meat, along with rice (called *xoi*), which may be sticky. The beverage will be strong tea or strong coffee (if any milk is added, it will be sweetened, condensed milk). Coffee is French-style, very strong and poured through a filter at the table.

Lunch: 11:00 or 11:30 A.M. Lunch consists of meat and rice with pickled vegetables or noodle soup.

Dinner: In cities, about 7:00 or 8:00 P.M.; earlier in the countryside, where people eat early and go to bed at dusk. Dishes will be similar to those at lunch: soup with vegetables and a little meat. There may be fish or eggs or meat and rice. Wealthier people will serve more dishes, all of which are served simultaneously. In the countryside, fewer dishes will be served.

• Note that noodle soup is eaten three times a day. Most popular is beef noodle; there is also pork or chicken noodle soup. You'll find a tremendous amount of salt or monosodium glutamate (MSG) in soups.

• Realize soup is so popular because the heat requires the consumption of large quantities of liquid. Because they perspire so much in the heat, the Vietnamese use a great deal of salt in their cooking.

• Know that rice is the staple of the Vietnamese diet and appears at almost every meal. If you're in the countryside, be careful when eating rice. Sometimes there are small stones, which can break your teeth.

• Remember that the Vietnamese do not usually eat dessert, but you may find crème caramel on the menu in restaurants.

• Expect fruits and sweets to be eaten as snacks after naps or when guests visit in the afternoon.

• If you eat the *durian* fruit, *never* have alcohol with it. The combination can be lethal.

• Remember that strict Buddhists are vegetarians.

• Prepare for dishes in the South to be spicier than those in the North.

• Note that tea is the most common beverage and is drunk throughout the day. In Vietnamese homes, a pot of tea is made in the morning and is kept warm with a tea cozy or in a thermos. If visitors come, hot water may be added to the cup to heat the tea. Vietnam has many different types of tea: green, black, artichoke, jasmine, lotus, hibiscus, and rose.

• Hold the teacup with the thumb and index finger, using the middle finger for support, if necessary.

• Don't drink the tea leaves in the bottom of the cup.

• When asked what you'd like to drink, request water (if you are able to verify that it's bottled water), coffee, or tea. If a family doesn't have what you want, they'll be embarrassed. Most people don't keep a supply of soft drinks in their home. Alcoholic drinks are served often—beer (local and imported), rice wine, and for special occasions imported whiskey or brandy.

• Expect beer to be available in the homes of wealthier families.

• In the countryside, you'll find homemade rice whiskey. After work or at lunch, men in the country drink this whiskey. Sometimes, there is only one small glass, which is passed from person to person.

• Look for bottled mineral water called *nuoc suoi*.

• When you purchase bottled water, *make sure* that the bottle is sealed. If the bottle is just closed, it's probably been refilled with unclean water.

• Since you can't drink tap water, a good substitute to buy on the street is fresh coconut juice, a drink that is supposed to settle your stomach. Ask the seller to cut off the top of the coconut, and drink directly

from it. Don't allow the seller to pour the juice into a glass, which may not be clean.

• Women should be aware that Vietnamese believe only prostitutes smoke and drink. They are, however, forgiving of Western women, particularly in business settings. People in the countryside tend to be more traditional. A woman who drinks will not "fit in."

Table Manners

• In the North, refuse the offer of a meal several times. This is polite since, in the past, people did not have enough food and offered it out of courtesy. If you are pressed four or five times, accept.

• If invited to a dinner in a home, feel free to be a little early or a little late. People will begin eating appetizers while waiting for late guests.

• Expect the following table setting: a bowl on a small plate (use the plate for discarded bones, shrimp shells, etc.), a soup spoon on the left, chopsticks on the right on top of a napkin (if there is one), sometimes chopstick rests, a small bowl at the top right for dipping sauces, a glass, sometimes salt and pepper and lime. If you see a shaker or small dish, don't assume it contains salt or sugar. It may be MSG. If there is whole shrimp or crab with shell, feel free to use your fingers to eat it. Sometimes you'll find a finger bowl with lemon and water or tea in which to clean your hands.

Western guests may find a French-style formal table setting with cutlery, plates, and several wineglasses.

• In the countryside, prepare to find tables about twelve inches off the ground and the seats about three inches off the ground. You'll be more comfortable with this low seating, since smoke will rise from the fires of the stoves, and there are no chimneys.

• Expect your host to seat you. Usually, the ends of the table are reserved for the oldest or most respected men and women.

• Let your host sit down first at the table, and wait for his signal to start eating.

• Don't be surprised if your host takes pieces of food from each platter and puts them in your bowl. If your host serves you a taste of a dish you don't want, it's acceptable to decline. However, if the food is already in your bowl, take a small taste to be polite.

• Remember that the custom is for rice to be placed in the eating bowl with bites of different dishes taken from the platters and eaten with the rice. If rice remains in your bowl at the end of the meal, soup will be poured over it.

• If a serving spoon is available, use it to take food from the platters so that your chopsticks don't come into contact with the communal food. Otherwise, turn your chopsticks around so that only the clean ends touch the food.

• Don't take huge portions of meat. You're supposed to add a little bit to your rice bowl for flavoring.

• Bring the rice bowl close to your mouth, and use the chopsticks to "shovel" the rice into your mouth. Slurp as much as possible when eating noodles or soup, as it is polite to do so.

• When you are finished or pausing, place your chopsticks across the bowl, or if one is available, use the chopstick rest. Don't stick the chopsticks into the bowl.

• In the South, expect grilled food to be served with lettuce and herbs. Avoid eating the lettuce, since it has probably been washed in unsanitary water.

• Note that if you finish all your food, you have signaled that you want more. Leave something in your bowl. The exception, however, is rice. Never leave rice in your bowl. Doing so is rude.

• Remember that soup may be served last to clean out the rice bowls. Remember, it's okay to slurp as you drink the soup.

• At some time during the meal, make a short speech, thanking your host for the meal.

• Recall that it is common for Vietnamese to take a toothpick from a container and clean their teeth after a meal. They will cup their other hand over their mouth to be discreet.

• Don't smoke between courses. It's fine to smoke after the meal, but it is polite to request permission to smoke anytime you're indoors.

• Feel free to stay and chat after dinner. Young people tend to stay longer than married people with children.

Places to Eat

• Expect to find Chinese, French, and Thai restaurants, most of which—along with coffeeshops and food stands—stay open until midnight. (Vietnamese enjoying going out in the evening for coffee, tea, Coca-Cola, or a beer.) Probably because Vietnam has a large number of Buddhists, there are many good vegetarian restaurants. You'll also find restaurants specializing in exotic animals—e.g., bear, monkey, or snake. People eat these creatures for their alleged medicinal qualities.

• Note that people in the South are more likely to go out to eat. In the North, people tend to go out only for a special occasion.

• Don't make a reservation unless your party is a large one.

• If you go to a Chinese restaurant, don't be surprised if you are asked to join others at a very large table if no small tables are available.

• If you purchase food on the street, check to see how clean the area is and whether there are insects around. It's not a bad idea to check out a restaurant's kitchen for evidence of dirt, cockroaches, etc. You may also go into the kitchen if no menu has been posted, so that you can point to what you want.

• In a tourist area, look for menus posted in English. Often there will be a price next to the item. If there isn't, and you don't ask the cost in advance, you'll have to pay whatever you are charged.

• Note that a soup restaurant offers a limited selection. The basic Vietnamese soup with chicken, beef, or shrimp is called *pho*. A fried noodle place will offer choices: *banh pho* (white rice noodles), *mien* (clear noodles made from rice mixed with manioc powder), and *mi* (yellow wheat noodles). Point to your choice.

• Some restaurants in Hanoi specialize in *pho bo* (a soup described in "Specialties").

• To summon the waiter, say "*Ahn*" (ahn), which means "older brother." To call the waitress, say "*Chi*" (chee), which means "older sister." Never use the terms "Garçon," or "Boy."

• Expect to see two bottles on the table, one with *nuoc mam*, a spicy fish sauce made from the liquid of salted, fermented fish. It is lighter in color than the other sauce, a hot soy sauce.

• Note that a Vietnamese delicacy is snake. When served, it is brought to the table alive. Then it's killed, and the blood is served as a drink. If this doesn't appeal to you, tell your host that you don't want it when he invites you, *not* when you're entering the restaurant. (On the other hand, if you're feeling adventurous, go for it!)

• Don't eat lettuce or rice paper. Rice paper is left to dry in the sun, exposed to flies and other insects. Lettuce is washed in unsanitary water.

- Don't be surprised to see diners eating a baked turtle.

- Control your shock if you find the innards of chickens or pigs in soups or a hard-boiled fertilized egg, which is cooked just before the chick is to hatch.

- Don't expect dishes to arrive at the table in a prescribed order. Hide your disappointment if, for example, you wanted the rice with the main course and it arrived earlier or later.

- Be aware that snacks, such as nuts, may be brought to your table. The restaurant may try to charge you, even if the package isn't opened. Check your bill carefully to avoid a charge.

- Remember that the person who issues the invitation is the one who pays. If you say, "Let's go out to dinner," you pay. (This rule also applies to movies.) Younger people are more open to splitting the bill. In a family, the oldest person pays.

Specialties

- The national dish, *pho* (pronounced "fir" without the "r"), is based on beef stock with a variety of ingredients, including ginger, lemon, garlic, chilies, onion, beansprouts, coriander, and noodles. Some people add pork, others chicken or fish.

- In the North, the most popular dish is *pho bo*: hot beef stock poured over paper-thin slices of raw beef and rice noodles with lemon juice, mint, coriander, onion, and green chili peppers. The dish is eaten at breakfast, lunch, or dinner.

- In the North, the food is similar to Chinese and is less spicy than food in the rest of the country.

- In the middle of the country, food is spicy, with a great deal of chili.

- The South has a great variety of fruits, vegetables, and herbs, with an Indian influence found in some dishes—e.g., curries.

- A specialty in Hanoi is *che*, a sweet snack made with coconut milk and sweetened, cooked green beans. There are many varieties: One is like pudding and eaten with a spoon, while another is dry and eaten by hand. *Che* might also contain dried coconut flakes, dried bananas, peanuts, dried lotus seeds, or *agar-agar* (a jellylike substance); some have all the above ingredients. You can buy *che* in almost every market and on every street in Hanoi.

- *Banh xeo* (pancakes filled with shrimp, pork, bean sprouts, mushrooms, and garlic, served with lettuce and a dipping sauce); *bi cuon* (a transparent spring roll made with a type of rice noodle, filled with prawns, bean sprouts, and assorted vegetables); *bo vien* (beef balls—beef marinated in *nuoc mam*, sugar, and oil, processed into a paste, and then boiled and served with soup); *cha ca Hanoi* (fish marinated in *nuoc mam*, fried in butter and dill, and served with white noodles and condiments); *cha gio* (deep-fried spring rolls—made of rice flour—served with lettuce, herbs, and dipping sauce); *gio lua* (finely ground pork boiled inside a banana leaf); *tom vo vien chien* (shrimp made into paste and deep fried, served with rice).

• During Tet (the New Year), a traditional dish called *banh chung* is served. It's a square cake made of sticky rice and filled with pork, beans, and onions, then wrapped in banana leaves.

• Another delicacy is a fertilized egg, which is hard-boiled the day before it hatches.

• Note that French bread (*baguette*) is sold everywhere.

not have hot water and air-conditioning. Don't accept a room until you have run the air conditioner and checked the hot water.

• Expect most hotels to include breakfast in the cost of the room. The meals are often abundant.

• Vietnamese who have lived abroad (referred to as *Viet-Kieu*) should realize that they will be charged the same price as foreigners for a hotel room (about three times the price for native Vietnamese).

• Leave your valuables in the hotel safe and be sure to get a receipt for them.

• Don't let a Vietnamese woman stay in your hotel room overnight. It's illegal.

• If you find mosquito netting, be sure to use it. Mosquitoes can infiltrate even air-conditioned rooms, and you don't want to risk malaria.

• In most hotel rooms, expect to find a can of tea and a thermos with hot water in it.

HOTELS

• The most popular hotels are those from the Colonial period which have been modernized. They have a certain charm, and offer private baths and air-conditioning.

• Keep in mind that the five-star hotels, where business people tend to stay, have all the amenities of five-star hotels worldwide.

• Many inexpensive hotels do

TIPPING

- A waiter would consider a tip of 10 percent of the bill very generous
- Don't feel obliged to tip taxi drivers, but you may wish to give up to 10 percent.
- Give hotel maids the equivalent of US $1 per day.
- For the washroom attendants you'll find in large hotels or nightclubs, leave the equivalent of US 50 cents or US $1.
- Give tour guides the equivalent of US $10–20 per week. It's considered polite for all the members of the tour group to put their tips into a single envelope.
- Don't expect to find porters. People don't trust others to carry their bags. A taxi driver or tour guide may help if you ask.

PRIVATE HOMES

- Don't drop in on people, because they may be embarrassed if their house isn't clean, or if they have nothing to offer. If the Vietnamese don't have a telephone, send a note via a cyclo (see "Transportation"), rather than just showing up at their door. Sending a message will cost less than US $1.
- Anticipate being served a drink or offered fruit when you arrive for a visit. Vietnamese don't usually ask first what you would like. Don't feel obliged to finish a drink; if you do, your host will refill your glass.
- Be respectful of the ancestral shrines you will find in homes.
- Don't be surprised if Vietnamese invite you to stay with them. Refuse at least three or four times. They may be very poor and are offering just to be nice. If they *really* persist, feel free to accept the invitation.
- Be aware that apartments may be small, and houses may hold many members of an extended family, so privacy is almost nonexistent.
- If water has to be heated, ask if it's convenient for you to take a hot

shower. In the very hot weather, consider taking a cold shower.

• Remember that bathrooms sometimes have cauldrons of water with a dipper. Wash yourself and shampoo your hair *outside* the cauldron. Don't bathe in the cauldron, because the water is for everyone in the household.

• Note that food is often cooked over a charcoal stove in the kitchen.

• If you're staying with a family, make your bed and ask if you can help with chores.

• If you're staying with a family during Tet, don't expect hot food. No cooking is allowed, so people have cold foods. Housework also is forbidden. Lights must be left on in the house, and people make lots of noise to frighten away bad spirits.

• Since Tet is really a family holiday, try to be sure that people aren't just being polite if they invite you to visit. On the third day, people honor the dead. Don't visit if you are pregnant or if you've had a recent death in your family, since people believe that you will bring bad luck.

Gifts: When invited to someone's home to a meal, bring one or two bottles of wine, a cake, or toys for the family's children.

• Consider giving the popular gifts of imported foods and chocolates.

• For men, bring whiskey and cognac (cognac has a somewhat higher status), ties, tiepins, and pens.

• Keep some balloons and pens with you. They are good gifts to hand out to children. At Tet, children receive gifts or coins wrapped in red paper. Lotus seeds and sugared winter melons are popular candies.

• Don't wrap your gifts in white paper or with white ribbon, since the color is associated with funerals. It is also associated with purity. White narcissus is a good gift, because it symbolizes prosperity.

• Don't give handkerchiefs, because the Vietnamese word for handkerchief is associated with the word for difficulty.

• Flowers to avoid: chrysanthemums, because they are reserved for funeral wreaths; *hue*, a flower with tall stems and many tiny white flowers, used at altars; pink roses, which are for lovers; any yellow flowers, because they are associated with betrayal.

• Expect Vietnamese to put aside your gift and open it later. Don't expect people to thank you after they've opened the package.

• Note that auspicious gifts for Tet are tea, candied ginger, crystallized coconut, peach and apricot tree branches, and live kumquat trees. Try to present the gift a few days before or during Tet, when the recipient will not feel obliged to buy you a gift, since it will be too late.

MONEY AND BUSINESS

Hours

Businesses and Government Offices: 7:30 to 11:30 A.M., and 1:00 or 1:30 P.M. to 5:00 or 5:30 P.M.

Banks: In most places, Monday through Friday, 9:00 to 11:30 A.M. and 1:30 to 3:30 P.M., and Saturday, 9:00 A.M. to noon.

Shops: Some stay open very late, as do food markets.

• For the most part, people begin work very early because of the heat. After a meal and a nap, beginning at 1:00 P.M., they return to work.

• During Tet, whose dates, based on the lunar calendar, usually fall between late January and mid-February, shops and businesses are closed. The festival lasts for somewhere between three days and one week.

Money

• The unit of currency is the *dong*. There are no coins. Bills come in the following denominations: 500; 1,000; 2,000; 5,000; 10,000; 20,000; 50,000; 100,000; and 500,000 *dong*.

• Note that the 5,000 and 20,000 *dong* notes are similar in color. Check carefully when using one of the bills.

• Be aware that American Express, MasterCard, and Visa credit cards are accepted in some of the main hotels, restaurants, and airlines in Hanoi and Ho Chi Minh City. Travelers' checks are beginning to be accepted.

• Remember that in cities you can pay for almost anything with U.S. dollars, but it's better to have some *dong* to pay for such small expenses as pedicabs, food markets, etc. You can't, however, use U.S. dollars in rural or remote areas.

• In the countryside, realize that travelers' checks will be useless. People in rural areas may not even recognize bills over 5,000 *dong*; they will think that they're fake.

• Keep in mind that the commission you pay when you exchange travelers' checks is higher than the commission when you exchange cash.

• Don't forget that black market rates and official rates for the exchange of money are almost the same. It's not worth risking the possibility of being cheated to exchange on the black market.

• Prepare to pay more than the Vietnamese for hotels and transportation. (Train travel costs are three times greater for foreigners than for Vietnamese.)

• Recall that all official business transactions must be in *dong*.

• When you receive change, check the bills. Dirty or torn *foreign* notes will probably be rejected. However, the same is not true for *dong* notes.

Business Practices

• Note that business contacts are essential. Seek them through an overseas accounting firm with an office in Vietnam, lawyers, banks, your embassy, or the Chamber of Commerce. Accounting firms are especially good sources because they find overseas investors for Vietnamese partners.

• Since personal contacts are so important, try to obtain an introduction to the people with whom you wish to do business. An alternative is a letter of introduction.

• Set up meetings before you go to Vietnam. Often many phone calls, faxes, and E-mails may be necessary before you receive a response. Since people don't like to make appointments long in advance, make the appointment two to three weeks in advance, reconfirm a few days before you leave for the country, and telephone just before you leave to make sure that the time is still all right with the Vietnamese.

• Avoid going to Vietnam during Tet (see "Holidays and Special Occasions"), when all business and shops are closed from three days to a week. It might, however, be a good time for a trip to become acquainted with business contacts in a relaxed atmosphere (e.g., the tennis courts). Ask your business contacts if they would be able to meet with you during Tet, and make your plans according to their response.

• Find out from your embassy when the Communist Party Congress is to be held, because it will be difficult to meet with people during that time.

• Note that many businesses choose an auspicious day on the lunar calendar to start a business or to have important business functions. Consider buying a calendar that indicates auspicious days and times. These calendars are widely available.

• When planning your wardrobe, remember that the North is cooler and more formal. Men wear suits and ties. The South is so hot that jackets are seldom worn. Dark pants, a shirt of a conservative color, and a tie are acceptable. Women should wear clothes that cover the shoulders and the knees.

• Because the business community is small, consider meeting people at social functions and sports clubs.

• Don't choose a Vietnamese who emigrated to another country (referred to in Vietnam as *Viet Kieu—Kieu* is pronounced "Q") as part of your group going to Vietnam. These people are not trusted, especially by the government.

• Remember that in Communist societies there are very few national business laws, and people are now trying to codify a body of laws so that they can start doing business overseas. There is a consensus in the country that foreign investment is essential for economic advancement. However, progress is *very* slow.

• Note that many Vietnamese executives work at odd hours, so be prepared to meet one colleague at 6:00 A.M. and another at 10:00 P.M. Most meetings are held in the morning, however. Meetings often take a long time, so don't schedule appointments close together.

• Recognize that English has become the language of business.

• Be prepared for congestion and construction to make trips between appointments take a very long time.

• Plan on prolonged business negotiations. Learn to avoid saying "No" by telling a white lie (e.g., that you're under pressure to leave the country). Vietnamese often use this strategy.

• If you hear references to the "great gray middle," a person is referring to the legion of bureaucrats who have the power to sign or not sign documents. Dozens of permits are required at the local and national level. The bureaucrats' procrastination often causes huge problems in doing business. Some people use a Vietnamese "fixer," who will endure the waiting for you and will grease the appropriate palms.

• Be *very* affable in dealing with government officials. They have a great deal of leverage over foreign business.

• Be sure to hire your own translator, because the translator's allegiance is to the person who hired her/him. In a meeting, don't address the translator. Look at the people to whom you are speaking.

• Have major proposals translated into Vietnamese, but present them in English as well. When dealing with government ministries, you need not have materials translated; however, you do need Vietnamese translations when dealing with local officials.

• When greeting a Vietnamese associate, shake hands or bow. If you bow, stand about three feet from the person and nod your head slightly.

• After the initial greeting, present your business card, offering it first to the most senior person and then to others, according to their rank in the hierarchy. Give and receive cards with both hands. As a sign of respect, read each card as you receive it, otherwise, you may alienate the person with whom you wish to do business. It's fine to have your cards printed in English, but you'll make an excellent impression if you have them in English on one side and Vietnamese on the other.

• Bring twice as many business cards as you think you'll need.

• If you're bringing a laptop computer, use batteries to run it. The electrical current in Vietnam is 220AC.

• Look for fax facilities at post offices, business centers, and major hotels.

• If you're dealing with government officials, give them a gift immediately. Within the private sector, give a gift when you've come to know people. There is a fine line between bribery, which is illegal, and a gift. If possible, ask a Vietnamese colleague what an appropriate gift would be.

• Before starting a discussion of business, it's polite to talk about your families, your stay in Vietnam, and where you're from. If you know the person well, be sure to ask about each of his children, beginning with the eldest son and concluding with the youngest daughter. The better your personal relations, the more time people will be willing to spend with you. Even after several meetings, it's important to ask about people's families. Don't bring up recent events in Vietnam, because people may be sensitive. Listen attentively if a Vietnamese brings the subject up and try to remain noncommittal.

• Try not to be impatient. Developing trust is crucial to doing business, and it may take *many* meetings to establish it.

• Expect to be offered tea, and sometimes fruit. Wait until the most senior person has sipped his tea before drinking yours.

• When the parties are ready to discuss business, talk about your approach to your project and what it involves. Don't bring up the issue of contracts right away.

• Explain *honestly* and in detail the consequences of your proposal.

• If you ask a direct question, and the answer is "Yes," realize that the meaning is "Maybe" and that

"Maybe" means "No." However, you will receive a clear signal that consensus has been reached in your favor.

• Be prepared for decisions to be made by consensus, rather than by a single person.

• Allow much more time than you think you'll need for a contract to be fulfilled or a delivery to be made. Deadlines are frequently ignored.

• Note that in cities people may remain in their offices or go to cafés at lunchtime, while in the countryside, people usually go home to lunch with their family.

• Realize that there is great respect for women, since originally Vietnam was a matriarchy. It is almost easier for foreign businesswomen to accomplish their goals than it is for men. Women should remember that they will be treated with more respect if they don't smoke or drink. Foreign businesswomen won't be pressed to go out for an evening's drinking.

Entertainment: Expect to be invited to a business dinner after people have come to know you. The dinners are social occasions—a time to ask people about their interests.

• Before a dinner in a restaurant, make a short, formal speech (in English), offering a toast in which you express your pleasure at working with the Vietnamese. It is polite to applaud your own speech along with the members of your party.

• If the Vietnamese are entertaining you, don't be surprised if they choose a restaurant that serves snake or other animals. They may just want to watch your reaction. Feel free to refuse the exotic foods.

• When people are celebrating, realize that they expect you to drink many, many glasses of liquor—one for each person's toast. To deal with this issue, you could take one drink and say that it's for everyone, or take only a sip with each person's toast.

• Don't leave a business dinner until the person in the most senior position departs.

HOLIDAYS AND SPECIAL OCCASIONS

Holidays with fixed dates:
January 1 (New Year's Day); April 7 (in honor of the emperor-founder Hung Vuong); April 30 (liberation of Saigon from U.S. control in 1975—government offices are closed); May 1 (Labor Day); September 2 (National Day—commemorates the founding of the Democratic Republic of Vietnam in 1945 on the day of Japan's surrender).

Holidays with variable dates:
Tet, between late January and mid-February, dates based on the lunar calendar. The festival lasts from three days to a week.

• Note that January 1 is celebrated as a public holiday, in accordance with the Gregorian calendar. Tet is the Vietnamese New Year, celebrated according to the lunar calendar.

• Tet is an abbreviation of *Tet Nhat*, meaning the first day of spring between harvest and planting time. Although it's officially a three-day holiday, celebrations often last a week, with dragon dances, fireworks, and flowers everywhere. Tet is everyone's birthday. Everyone becomes a year older. The first person to enter a house in the New Year brings either good or bad luck. If a respected person is the first to enter the house, the year will bring good luck. If someone who isn't respected enters first, luck will be bad.

• Realize that it's difficult to find a place to eat or to find transportation during Tet.

• Be sure to dress well during Tet.

• Expect prices to skyrocket during Tet. Vietnamese believe that if they are very free with money during Tet, they will get more in the coming year.

• During the first day of Tet, shopkeepers are very aware of the first person who crosses his threshold, because he/she gives an indication of success or failure for the rest of the year.

TRANSPORTATION

Public Transportation

• Remember that to communicate a street name or an address to a driver, taxi driver, etc., you should have it written down. Often people will not understand spoken instructions because of your accent.

• Note that *cyclos* are three-wheeled bicycle rickshaws. The passenger sits in front of the driver. Cyclos are available by the hour or by the trip.

• Taxis are very inexpensive. You can phone for one or find one on main streets in Ho Chi Minh City or Hanoi. Outside those cities, taxis are rare. Taxis have meters, which drivers always turn on.

• At the airport, be prepared for taxi drivers to swarm around you. Once you select one, however, the others will leave you alone.

• Women should note that if they take a motorcycle taxi, they should not put their arms around the driver's waist, or he will assume that they are interested in him sexually. Be careful of your handbag. Someone driving by may snatch it.

• Men should know that if they accept a ride on the back of a woman's motor scooter, they should be prepared for *more* than just a ride. Indeed, the woman may turn out to be a man.

• If you take a motorcycle taxi or a pedicab, determine the price in advance.

• Don't use a pedicab unless a hotel or restaurant operates it.

• Should you have a motorbike and a helmet, never leave the helmet strapped to your motorbike. It will be stolen.

• During Tet, expect planes and buses to be packed with people traveling to be with their families.

• Realize that buses are extremely crowded, only have limited routes, and are frequented by pickpockets.

• Note that intercity buses exist, but they are very crowded and not air-conditioned. It's much better to take a plane. After three to four hours on a bus, people are usually draped over one another. (This is the exception to the Vietnamese rule that people never touch one another in public.)

• Be aware that sometimes it's possible to purchase a ticket on an air-conditioned intercity mail bus. The price is slightly higher than that on a regular bus, but the comfort will justify the additional expense.

• Rise very early to take a long-distance bus. Buses usually leave at 4:00 or 5:00 A.M.

• Realize that trains have three kinds of seats: hard seat, soft seat, and sleeper. A sleeper may or may not have a foam mattress. There are six berths to a compartment, and each berth has a different price (top, middle, lower). The air-conditioning rarely works.

• If you plan to take a train between Ho Chi Minh City and Hanoi, expect to spend 40–44 hours en route.

• When taking a train, keep in mind that each station is assigned a certain number of seats per compartment. For example, should you be taking a sleeper (which holds up to six), only two people of your group may be able to stay in the same compartment if you all get on at Ho Chi Minh City. Stations that are still coming up "own" the other seats. To get around this problem, buy a hard seat or a soft seat. When you get on the train, pay the conductor, and you can have a sleeper, usually for 110 percent to 120 percent of the fare at the station. Sleeper compartments must be booked at least three days in advance. Bring your passport when you make the reservation, which you can do through a tourist agency.

• Expect trains to be like those of the nineteenth century, moving at about 30 miles an hour. If time isn't important, the slow trip can be interesting.

• Train windows have grates on the outside, which make it difficult for passengers to see out or to take pictures. The grates are essential, however, because children throw stones at the train windows. Do *not* lift the grates.

• Don't expect a dining car on most trains. The dining car on the Hanoi–Ho Chi Minh City train serves simple food; the fare for first class on a long-distance train includes the price of meals. If you buy a sleeper, food will arrive on trays, but it isn't tasty.

• Bring your own food to be safe when you travel by train if there is no dining car. If you don't, food is sold at the windows at every stop, but its cleanliness may be suspect.

Driving

• Remember that foreigners are not allowed to drive. However, it is possible to hire a car and driver.

• Don't have your driver go long distances at night because of the high number of accidents.

LEGAL MATTERS, SAFETY, AND HEALTH

• Note that there is no minimum age for drinking.

• Bring extra visa photos to present to immigration when you arrive. If you don't have them, you'll have to wait a long time to have your photo taken on the spot.

• Be very careful about what you bring into Vietnam. Don't bring any religious or political literature. Don't bring any anti-Vietnam literature or pornography. Don't be surprised to have CDs and videotapes such as *Rambo* confiscated.

• Don't be surprised if Customs confiscates videos you have taken with your video camera, since they don't know what you've photographed.

• If you want to take antiques out of the country, go to the Department of Information and Culture to have your purchases approved before you leave. The items are inspected and sealed. (Tour guides can arrange this transaction for you.) Luggage is X-rayed when you leave the country, and Customs may confiscate antiques that haven't been approved.

• Have film checked by hand at the airport, because the antique X-ray machines might damage it.

• If you go into the countryside, bring toilet paper, soap, and medicine. Medicine that you purchase in the country may be out of date. Do *not* trust pharmacists. They can't read English writing on packages and go by guessing and hearsay. (One woman was given vaginal cream instead of antibiotic ointment for a cut.) If you go to a pharmacy, ask if you can go behind the counter and find the medicine yourself.

• If there's an emergency, don't use the medical system in Vietnam. If at all possible go to Singapore or Bangkok.

• Realize that malaria is a real threat. Take an antimalaria drug before and during your trip.

• Check with the Centers for Disease Control in Atlanta, Georgia, (USA) to learn which vaccinations are recommended.

• Keep in mind that the condoms available in Vietnam are of poor quality. Bring your own to prevent sexually transmitted diseases (STDs), including AIDS (called SIDA [see-dah], the French word used locally).

• Be sure to use insect repellent.

• Don't drink tap water or use ice cubes made from tap water.

• Don't drink milk. It hasn't been pasteurized.

• Always carry a photocopy of your passport. If the police want to confiscate your passport, give them a copy and say that you don't have the original.

• Be very careful when crossing the street because of the erratic traffic—bicycles, scooters, pedicabs, cars, buses, and trucks. There are very few stop signs or crosswalks.

• Stick to beaten paths. If you wander, you may step on a leftover grenade, shell, or land mine. Don't be tempted to touch a mine, leftover shell, or grenade.

• If you are the victim of a crime, don't bother going to the police. It's a waste of time.

• Although Vietnam is a relatively safe country, guard against pickpockets around major hotels and bars, especially at night. Don't carry large amounts of cash or wear expensive jewelry. Street crime is less common in Hanoi than in Ho Chi Minh City.

• Be wary of children selling maps on the street. Some are pickpockets.

• Be especially careful if you are in Vietnam during Tet, when there are even more thieves and pickpockets around. Avoid crowded areas.

• Especially in Ho Chi Minh City, be aware that pickpockets want eyeglasses. They will steal them right off your nose. Bring an extra pair of glasses and your prescription.

• Women should expect to be treated with a great deal of respect.

• A woman should not, however, wear high heels and should not go into a bar, get drunk, and stagger around, or she'll be a target of unwanted attentions.

• Women won't necessarily be the victims of violent crime, since no one wants to ignite strong reactions from national or international security forces.

KEY PHRASES

Vietnamese is a tonal language, and the meaning of a word changes completely with a different inflection. In giving the transliteration of Vietnamese words, we can only be approximate. We have used the following accent marks to indicate the appropriate tone:

No marking signifies an even tone

´ above a letter means a rising tone

` above a letter means a falling tone

'means a tone similar to the one used when questioning in English

~ means a high broken tone, which dips a little and then rises rapidly

. under a letter means a low tone that falls and ends abruptly

English	Vietnamese (transliteration)	Pronounciation
Hello	Xin chào	Seen chow
Good-bye	Chào tạmbiệt	Chow tahm byet
Mr.	Ông	Ohm
Mrs.	Bà	Bah
Miss	Cô	Co
Please	Xin vui lòng	Seen voo-ee lahm

Thank you	Ca'm o'n	Cahm euhn
You're welcome	Không có chi	Chahm (ch as in Bach) co chee
Yes	Ph'ai	Fie
No	Không	Chahm (ch as in Bach)
Excuse me	Tôi xin lỗi	Toy seen lo-ee
I don't understand	Tôi không hiêu'	Toy chahm hee-oo
Does anyone speak English?	Ai n'oi du'o'c tiếng Anh	Aye no-ee deuk teen ahn?

AUSTRALIA

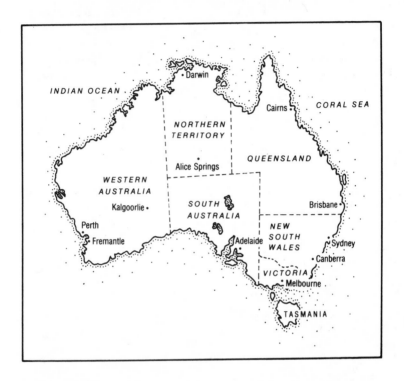

For years we knew little about Australia. Then Qantas Airlines raised our consciousness with its symbol, the cuddly koala, and Australia opened up in earnest.

Westerners have begun visiting Australia in record numbers and have encountered a people of incomparable friendliness. One visitor returned and said, "We Americans have always had a reputation as very friendly people. We look like a crowd of misanthropes next to the Australians. They must be the world's nicest people." Australians say that visitors often remark, "If I were younger, I'd move here."

GREETINGS

- Note that men shake hands with men and with women in greeting and departing, but women usually don't shake hands with other women. With very good friends, males pat each other on the shoulder, women kiss one another, and sometimes good male and female friends kiss in greeting.
- From a distance, greet a friend or acquaintance with a wave.
- Listen for "Good day" (pronounced "g'day" or "g'die"), words used widely as a greeting (though not by the upper classes). The informal, rural good-bye is "Hoo-roo."
- Expect first names to be used frequently, but wait until you're invited to use them.
- Don't be surprised to hear children address their teachers, and sometimes their parents, by first names.
- If you're invited to a party, expect the host or hostess to introduce you to each person.

CONVERSATION

- Good topics of conversation: sports (cricket, tennis, golf, swimming, sailing, soccer, rugby), travel, jobs, and hobbies. Cricket and rugby are very popular topics of conversation. If you don't understand these sports, people are pleased if you ask to have them explained to you.
- Note that it's fine to ask people what sort of work they do, but don't ask about finances—salaries, profits—or religion, etc.
- Avoid any comparisons indicating that your country is superior to Australia in any way.
- To make a hit, praise Australia and its beauty.
- Note that in Australia accent is more an indication of class rather than of region.
- If you're interested in someone's view on the relations between Australia and the United Kingdom, be very diplomatic in your questions. There is a strong movement for Australia to become a republic, but some people have strong feelings that the country should retain its relationship to Britain.

TELEPHONES

• Look for public telephones in pubs or in glass booths by the road-sides. Some stores also have public phones.

• For local calls, deposit 40 cents for an unlimited amount of time.

• Phone cards are widely available and are a great convenience when using public phones.

• For long-distance calls within Australia, look for gray-green STD (Subscriber Trunk Dialing) telephones. Dial your number directly and pay for the time you actually use.

• If you wish to make overseas calls, inquire if your hotel has ISD (International Subscriber Dialing) telephones; they allow you to dial international calls directly. Also ask if there is a surcharge. If it is too high, use the ISD telephones at a post office.

IN PUBLIC

• Men should avoid any demonstrative behavior with other men; e.g., hugging. It's considered unmanly. Demonstrative behavior between the sexes is tolerated.

• Don't behave in any way which could be interpreted as "putting on airs." Australians are very down-to-earth, straightforward people and are offended at insincerity. Genuine friendliness will impress them. If you hear the expression "cutting the tall poppy," it means that someone has gotten above herself/himself and needs to be brought back to earth.

• Avoid "blowing your own horn." Always be modest about your achievements. Australian experts always pretend that they don't know much. Never say, "I happen to know a great deal about X" (sailing, computers, etc.). Instead say, "I've had a little experience with X." Underplay your expertise.

• Men should never wink at women. It's considered improper.

• Don't make the thumb gesture used by hitchhikers in the United States. In Australia, it means "Get lost." Also, the "V" sign with the palm held toward you is obscene.

• As in Britain, you'll find public toilets everywhere. More modern toilets have two little moon buttons on the flush bar. The one that's half-colored is for a "half flush." The one fully colored in is for a "full flush." We leave it to your judgment which to use.

Shopping: Possibly due to the influx of Asians (from an area where bargaining is ubiquitous), Australians are now sometimes bargaining, even in better stores. It's not common, but it does happen. Whether you wish to try is a personal choice. Ask in discount stores if the price is lower if you pay cash. Feel free to try bargaining in "trash or treasure" places.

• To get a bargain, shop around. Prices vary considerably between stores.

• Note that sizes are metric, as in Europe.

Exercise: The Australians are great joggers. You'll feel comfortable jogging anywhere and can wear shorts.

DRESS

• Note that Australians dress very informally. Follow their lead, but don't wear flamboyant clothes.

• For business, men should wear a jacket in a conservative shade—gray, blue, or brown—and a tie. In hot weather, remove the jacket when invited to do so. If you will be visiting during Australia's summer (the Northern Hemisphere's winter), bring a lightweight jacket or suit for business wear. Women should wear a dress or skirt and blouse for business.

• In warm weather, expect to see many Australians in shorts of a solid color (usually khaki), high socks, and a short-sleeved shirt with or without a tie. However, since Australia has one of the highest rates of skin cancer in the world, many people have taken to covering up and wearing wide-brimmed hats during the sunny months to protect themselves from the sun.

• In northern and rural areas, men usually wear short shorts—never Bermuda shorts—and long white socks. Men who decide to wear shorts should be sure that they aren't plaid or patterned—unless they want to be identified as Americans immediately.

• Men may wear shorts or jeans in the city. Women may wear jeans, but not shorts. However, don't call attention to yourself by wearing *very* short shorts.

• Women who want to fit in should follow the custom of Australian women in wearing skirts more often than pants.

• If invited to a meal in a home, men should wear a jacket and tie—except in summer when a tie isn't necessary—and women should wear a dress, skirt and blouse, or dressy pants and blouse.

• To dinner in a restaurant, men should wear a jacket and tie, and women a dress, skirt and blouse, or dressy pants and blouse.

• For a formal reception or a dinner dance, men should wear black tie and women cocktail dresses.

• If you're visiting the outback, wear jeans, T-shirt, and thongs. Bring a hat and a handkerchief to brush off flies. There is really no protection against the flies in the outback. Waving the hand to keep them off is known as the "Australian salute."

• Note that clothing policies at beaches are extremely liberal; there are even some topless beaches. Both men and women usually wear bikinis. Bring a hat to the beach because of the intensity of the sun.

MEALS

Hours and Foods

• Since Australia has the highest percentage of foreign-born residents of any country in the world, meal times tend to vary, so the following are general guidelines only.

Breakfast: 7:30 to 8:30 A.M. A typical breakfast might be bacon and eggs or steak and eggs with bread, jam, honey, and coffee or tea. Other popular breakfasts are spaghetti on toast or baked beans on toast.

Lunch: noon to 2:00 P.M. At home, people usually have thin sandwiches in the English style—a thin slice of meat or cheese between two slices of bread. In a restaurant, choose from pizza, fish dishes, and a variety of ethnic dishes.

Afternoon Tea: A cup of tea, taken around 4:30 P.M. If you're invited to "tea"—not "afternoon tea"—expect dinner. You can tell by the time of the invitation. An invitation to tea for 6:30 P.M. during the week, or 7:00 P.M. or later on the weekend, means dinner.

Dinner/Tea: 6:00 or 6:30 P.M.

Expect meat—usually either beef or lamb—grilled, roasted, or broiled, and accompanied by boiled peas, green beans, or squash and potatoes. European migrants introduced salads about 15 years ago, so one might be served at a dinner. Desserts tend to be heavy cakes and puddings. Somewhat lighter is Pavlova (a meringue shell filled with fruit and whipped cream).

• The water in Australia is safe for drinking.

• If you're invited to drinks, even at what seems to be dinner hour, don't expect a meal. Having people for drinks is a fairly common method of entertaining.

• If you're invited to a meal, don't expect cocktails unless your hosts know Americans well. Usually beer and wine are served before dinner, accompanied by tiny pies and nuts.

• Expect beer (always served well chilled) to be drunk with the meal, although more and more families are serving wine (Australian wine is both good and inexpensive). Very few Australians drink hard liquor.

• In recent years, liquor licensing laws have become more liberal. Laws vary from state to state, so you'll have to check the regulations for the area you're in. After hours, you can get a drink in a large hotel. Theoretically, hotels are supposed to serve guests only, but at the larger ones, it would be difficult for the staff to separate guests from nonguests.

• Be aware that the names for sizes of beer glasses vary from state to state. In some a seven-ounce glass is called a "glass"; the next size up is a "pot"; larger than that is "jug"— usually enough for a few people or one drunkard. In New South Wales, a 10-ounce glass is called a "middie" and a 15-ounce glass a "schooner."

• Remember that Australian beer is stronger than British or American beer.

• Realize that every member of a group of men seated together *must* pay for a round of drinks in turn. This is called "shouting" a round.

Table Manners

• If you are guest of honor, expect to sit to the right of the host or hostess.

• Look for the table to be set in familiar fashion, with fork on the left and knife on the right. Start with the outside silverware, and work in. If you're unsure, watch your hostess.

• To eat Australian-style, hold the knife in your right hand and fork in your left hand. Use the knife to push food onto the fork. If you're left-handed, reverse the utensils. When you finish eating, place the knife and fork on your plate, side by side, diagonally.

• Spoon soup away from you, not toward you.

• When not eating, keep your wrists on the table. Don't put your hands in your lap.

• Expect food to be served family-style or brought in on individual plates.

• Women should never say, "I'm stuffed" after a meal because it means that they are pregnant.

Places to Eat

• Remember that traditional Australian cooking is very simple. For sophisticated, international cuisine, try an Italian, French, or Asian restaurant. There are also many small, family-run foreign restaurants, featuring the foods of India, Italy, Poland, and the Middle East.

• To save money, look for delicatessens, which feature inexpensive and cosmopolitan foods; you can buy cold cuts, salads, and sandwiches to eat there or take out.

• Note that pub hours are usually from 10:00 A.M. to 10:00 P.M. Hours are longer in summer months. After 10:00 P.M., you can drink in a restaurant, but you *must* order food with the drink.

• Remember that many restaurants have BYO (Bring Your Own) wine licenses. Such restaurants are popular and economical for informal occasions.

• Look for menus posted in restaurant windows. Many places have adopted this custom.

• At an informal restaurant, if no table is vacant, feel free to ask others if you may join them at their table.

• Realize that chicken and turkey are more expensive than beef, pork, lamb, or veal—and are considered luxuries.

• If you want coffee with milk, ask for white coffee.

• If you dine with a group of friends, plan to pay for your own meal.

• Ask the waiter if you should pay him or at the cash register. Even in better restaurants, you sometimes pay at the cash register.

Specialties

• Barbecues are an Australian favorite. Popular dishes are steaks, grilled prawns, and fish roasted in foil. Sometimes the dishes are garnished with pineapple and bananas.

• A very popular meat dish is carpetbagger steak—beef tenderloin stuffed with raw oysters, sautéed or grilled over charcoal. Another popular meat dish is rabbit pie.

• For fish, try Victorian yabbies, a small type of lobster; John Dory, a fish unique to Australia that tastes somewhat like halibut or swordfish; barramundi, a gamefish from the north; or Moreton Bay bugs, an outrageously named small crustacean.

• In Queensland, try mud crab and banana prawns (which are huge) and the local snapper.

• Other specialties: kangaroo-tail soup (now difficult to obtain), and damper, a sour-dough-type bread.

• Beets—called beetroot—will appear in many sandwiches and on hamburgers.

• If you wish to share an Australian addiction, try Vegemite, a strong-smelling yeast spread used on bread or toast that is a British "delicacy." It looks somewhat like axle grease and tastes like salty axle grease to most North Americans.

HOTELS

• Recall that "hotel" can mean a place for accommodations or just a drinking establishment. The word "pub" covers the same two types of establishment. There's only one way to find out which a place is: Ask.

• Note that you can rent flats of one to three rooms, equipped with kitchen utensils, for just a few days— or longer. Serviced flats are excellent alternatives to hotels, especially if you're traveling with a family. They are considerably cheaper than hotels, and shopping for groceries, which is a chore at home, becomes an adventure. (It's especially fun to see the different names under which products are marketed in another country.)

• If you choose a farmhouse holiday, expect accommodations and prices to vary considerably. Some have private cottages, while in others, you stay with the family and share their bathroom. Be prepared to be treated as a member of the family. Often you *can* join in the farming activities, but you don't have to.

• Remember that a private hotel does not have a license to sell liquor, but it does accept guests. Often it does not serve meals. A guesthouse, however, usually serves breakfast.

• If a hotel clerk or travel agent tells you that a hotel has fans, that means it isn't air-conditioned.

• If you use a washcloth, bring one with you, as most hotels won't have them.

• If you're told that your room has a "jug," look for an electric tea-kettle for making tea or coffee. Hotels usually provide tea bags, instant coffee, milk, and sugar in your room.

• If the hotel offers continental breakfast, expect fruit or juice, cereal, toast with butter and jam, and coffee or tea. A "cooked breakfast" includes all the above, plus eggs, bacon, and sausage.

• Note that an offer of "morning tea" means that someone will deliver tea and cookies (called "biscuits") to your room before 7:00 A.M.

• Should you want a drink after pubs close at 10:00 P.M., try a hotel bar, though they are supposed to serve only guests. If the bartender agrees to serve you, leave a generous tip.

TIPPING

• Note that tipping is not customary in Australia, but in elegant hotels and expensive restaurants near such hotels, people have become used to receiving tips.

• Be aware that hotels and restaurants do not add service charges. In elegant restaurants, leave 10 percent of the check.

• Tip hotel porters $1 per bag.

PRIVATE HOMES

• Don't expect Australians you meet in the country to invite you to visit them after a short acquaintance. They want to know you fairly well before welcoming you into their homes. If you're a friend of a friend, however, and call someone while you're in Australia, anticipate an invitation to "tea"—usually meaning dinner (see "Meals")

• Never drop in, except on very close friends. Always telephone in advance to ask if it would be convenient for you to visit.

• Don't expect to be offered a tour of your host's house. Australians regard such tours as showing off.

• When you visit someone at home, expect to be offered beer, tea, or coffee—usually served without an accompanying snack.

• Offer to pay for any phone calls you make from a private home.

• If you stay with a family for a while, offer to help with cleaning up after dinner, food shopping, and other chores.

• Note that the sink and bathtub are often located in the bathroom, while the toilet is often in a separate room (informally referred to as "the loo"). If you want to use the toilet, ask for "the toilet," not the bathroom.

• Note that "On" and "Off" switches, and faucets, are opposite to the way that they are north of the equator.

• Be reassured that homes have constant hot water. No one will be surprised if you take a bath daily.

Gifts: If invited to a meal in a home, bring flowers, chocolates, or a bottle of wine.

• As a foreigner visiting for the

first time, bring a picture book of your local area, or food specialties from your area. Bring only canned or preserved foods, since fresh foods will be confiscated at Customs.

• If you're visiting a family from the Middle East, don't bring liquor as they may be Muslim.

MONEY AND BUSINESS

Hours

Businesses: 9:00 A.M. to 5:00 P.M., Monday through Friday.

Government Offices: 9:00 A.M. to 4:30 P.M., Monday through Friday.

Banks: 9:30 A.M. to 4:00 P.M., Monday through Thursday, and to 5:00 P.M. on Friday. Some banks—especially those in city centers—open earlier and stay open later.

Shops: 9:00 A.M. to 5:00 or 6:00 P.M., Monday through Wednesday, and until 9:00 P.M. on Thursday and Friday; 9:00 A.M. to noon on Saturday. Many supermarkets stay open late, and some city shops are open on Sunday.

Money

• Remember that the currency is the Australian dollar, divided into 100 cents. Coins: 5 cents, 10 cents, 20 cents, 50 cents, $1, and $2. Notes: $5, $10, $20, $50, and $100.

• You'll be able to use your credit cards almost everywhere. American Express, Visa, Barclaycard, Master-Card, Access, and Diners Club are accepted in hotels, restaurants, and shops.

Business Practices

• Try to schedule business trips to Australia during the months between March and November. Avoid December through February, popular vacation months. Avoid the week before and the two weeks after Christmas and the week before and after Easter.

• Be sure to make business appointments about a month in advance of your visit.

• To make a good impression, take some time to learn about Australia and its cultural background before you go there. Australians will delight in discussing their country with you.

• Australians are not at all class conscious and can be approached very easily, no matter what their position. They will almost always make time to give a visitor an appointment.

• Bring business cards, although not all Australians use them.

• Be sure to be on time for your appointments.

• Be prepared to find most businesspeople easy-going and amiable. Recall that personal relationships are just as important to Australians as productivity. Try to develop a friendly relationship, especially by partying with people in the evening (but never discuss business while partying).

• Be aware that Australians also tend to be cynical, laconic, and understated in thir conversation. They also feel free to express negative opinions about people and situations. Don't be put off by such directness.

• To gain Australians' respect, don't try to avoid taking a position on an issue. Take a definite stand. But don't take a position in which you don't believe just because you think it will please others and make them more likely to accept your company. Be sincere. Australians see through—and dislike—any display of phoniness.

• Never behave in any way that could be interpreted as patronizing.

• Don't expect compliments on a good presentation or a job well done. Australians don't usually give such positive reinforcement.

• Expect Australians to be more interested in major issues than in fine points and miniscule details.

• Never give orders to an Australian. Always negotiate.

Entertaining: Expect to do business over drinks. Be sure to buy your round of drinks in turn. Don't, however, use entertainment as an opportunity to talk business. During their free time, Australians want recreation. If an Australian brings up business, you can feel free to discuss it.

• You will have a bit of an advantage if you play golf, since most Australian businessmen do. However, as a rule, business is not discussed until after the golf game is over.

Note: For advice regarding business greetings, dress, or table manners, see the appropriate sections earlier in the chapter.

HOLIDAYS AND SPECIAL OCCASIONS

Holidays: New Year's Day (January 1); Australia Day (January 26), commemorating the first European settlement of Australia; Good Friday; Easter; Easter Monday; ANZAC or Veterans' Day (April 25), honoring Australia's war heroes' tragic loss in the Dardanelles in 1915; Queen's Birthday (second

Monday in June); Christmas (December 25); Boxing Day (December 26).

• Note that Labor Day and bank holidays vary from state to state. In New South Wales, Labor Day is the first Monday in October; in South Australia, the second Monday in October; in Western Australia, the first Monday in March; in Victoria, the second Monday in March; in Queensland, the second Monday in May.

• Be aware that holidays in Australia are usually spent escaping to the beach or countryside. Few are celebrated with festivals except ANZAC Day, when there are ceremonies at war memorials, parades (and a great deal of drinking).

• Should you be invited to an Australia Day celebration, expect a barbecue of beef or lamb, salads, and a favorite Australian dessert, a Pavlova—meringue filled with whipped cream and fruit.

• Note that the businesses which do not close all day on Melbourne Cup Day come to a halt at 2:30 P.M., when the 2½-minute horse race is run. If you're invited to join someone at the track, expect a lunch of champagne and chicken, and the company of racing fans in outrageous fashions.

TRANSPORTATION

Public Transportation

• On local buses, tell the conductor or driver your destination, and he will tell you the fare, which is based on the distance to be traveled. You don't need exact change. Keep your ticket, as inspectors sometimes get on to make sure everyone has a ticket.

• Be aware that bus terminals are clean and cheerful. The buses are air-conditioned, and overnight buses have washrooms and toilets.

• If you take one of the world's most charming forms of public transportation, the trams in Melbourne, be *extremely* cautious when getting off. Look both ways for cars (remember that traffic is on the left side of the road, as in Britain). In central Melbourne, look out for approaching trams, as well.

• Hail taxis on the streets or look for taxi ranks at hotels and in downtown areas. You can also call taxis; look in the Yellow Pages for numbers. Taxis have meters and are both clean and safe.

• A male taking a taxi alone may

observe the Australian custom of siting in the front seat. Australians would find it odd if a man sat by himself in the backseat—a reflection of the country's lack of social distinctions. Women alone should sit in the backseat, as should couples.

• Buy tickets for local trains— suburban trains—from an attendant at the station or at automatic ticket machines and some shop outlets.

• For unlimited first-class train travel, buy an Austrailpass before you leave home. The only extra charges are for sleeping berths and meals.

Driving

• Note that an American driver's license can be used in Australia for a year.

• Remember that driving is on the left, as in Britain.

• Be aware that seat belts are compulsory. There is a fine for not wearing them, except for passengers sitting in rear seats if the rear seats aren't equipped with belts.

• Remember that children are not allowed to sit in the front seat. They must sit in a car seat in the back and must be restrained, either in a car seat or with a seat belt.

• At intersections, give way to cars coming from the right, unless traffic at the intersection is controlled by stop signs or traffic lights.

• If you rent a mobile phone with your car, remember that it's illegal to drive and talk on the phone at the same time. There will be a fine if you're caught.

• Don't drink and drive. You may be stopped for a random breath test. Consequences are serious if you fail it.

• If you are planning to rent a car and drive to the Outback, realize that car-rental companies will let you take four-wheel drive cars *or* they will charge enormous amounts for insurance for other cars. Don't even consider taking a car that isn't four-wheel drive into the Outback; you'll never make it on the unpaved roads. The best course is to take a plane, train, or bus to the Outback and rent a four-wheel drive car there.

• Before driving in the Outback, consider the road conditions, which are *very* bad. In addition, distances between towns can be enormous, and there aren't many service stations in between. An additional hazard is that people who drive regularly in the bush often speed from dirt roads onto highways.

LEGAL MATTERS, SAFETY, AND HEALTH

• Remember that visitors staying less than six months may take out currency only up to the value declared on entry.

• Don't bring in food, seeds, feathers, leather skins, plants, or fruits. If discovered, they will be confiscated, and you will have to pay a *very* large fine.

• If you bring in a TV set—even for your personal use—you will have to pay duty on it.

• Be sure to be cooperative and polite when dealing with the police.

• Women traveling alone should take taxis after dark. Street crime is rare, but don't walk around late at night in parks or lonely places.

Health: Even though prescription drugs are widely available, bring an adequate supply of any drugs you may take, since drug names differ from country to country.

• Women will find most toiletries, sanitary napkins, and tampons available.

KEY PHRASES

Australian	*North American English*
G'day	Hello
Are you right?	Are you okay?
How're you going?	How are you doing?
Ta	Thank you
No worries	You're welcome
Aussie (pronounced Ozzie)	An Australian
Oz	Australia
Pom or Pommy	Englishman
Sheila	A young woman
Bloke	A guy
Arvo	Afternoon
Lemonade	7-Up
Biscuit	Cookie
Milk bar	Soda fountain

Stone	14 pounds
Bonnet	Hood of a car
Boot	Trunk of a car
Torch	Flashlight
Footie	Australian rules football
Chrissie	Christmas
Loo	Room with toilet (informal)

NEW ZEALAND

What do a kiwi, a Kiwi, and a Kiri have in common? New Zealand, of course. A kiwi is a flightless bird native to the country, and from it New Zealanders have derived their nickname for themselves, "Kiwis." And a Kiri is Dame Kiri Te Kanawa, whose glorious voice has taken the international opera world by storm.

Visitors to New Zealand have found more than kiwis, Kiwis, and Kiris. They have encountered more sheep than people and have found on the country's two islands—North Island and South Island—a wide range of environments, with high mountain ranges and glaciers, hot springs, lakes, dense forests, great rivers, and rolling grasslands.

New Zealand is a paradise for those who love to birdwatch and those who love to fish. Because there are no predatory animals, birds abound, and because warm and cold currents meet near the country, fish in many varieties are found in the country's waters.

GREETINGS

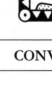

CONVERSATION

• With new acquaintances, always shake hands when greeting and leaving. Wait for women to extend their hands.

• Don't shake hands with people you see frequently.

• Expect New Zealanders to greet you by saying "Gidday" (Good day)—with the accent on the last syllable—or "Hi." Visitors should simply say "Hello."

• Start out by addressing people as "Mr.," "Mrs.," etc., but expect New Zealanders to switch to first names very soon. After the first meeting or two, doctors and professors don't expect you to use their titles.

• The traditional greeting among Maori tribes people is to rub noses.

• Good subjects include national and international politics; weather; sports, especially rugby, cricket, fishing, and hunting; and what you have been doing and plan to do in New Zealand.

• Subjects to avoid: racial issues; personal questions, such as job and schooling; nuclear arms.

• Because there is a great deal of rivalry between New Zealanders and Australians, don't praise Australians to New Zealanders.

• Note that the term "kiwi" refers to any New Zealander, but it is not usually applied to the Maoris (the original natives of the country).

TELEPHONES

IN PUBLIC

• Public telephones are located on streets, in shopping malls, and in post offices. Credit card phones are yellow; card phones are green; coin phones are blue.

• Purchase telephone cards at gas stations, post offices, or any shop displaying the lime-green "phone cards are available" sign. They are available in denominations of NZ $5, $10, $20, or $50.

• A local call from a public phone costs 20 cents a minute. International calls have a minimum charge of NZ $3.

• For all emergencies dial 111 and state whether you need police, an ambulance, or the fire brigade. There is no charge.

• Know that people are very friendly and willing to help if you have a problem, such as a broken-down car or being lost.

• Speak quietly and keep your voice down. New Zealanders are quiet and mellow.

• Never hold your index finger and middle finger up straight (as in the "V" for "Victory" sign), with your palm facing inward. It's an obscene gesture.

• Be sure to ask before you photograph Maoris. They sometimes don't want to have their pictures taken. (There may also be signs in some places forbidding photography.)

• Look for public bathrooms in restaurants, gas stations, and some shops. There are also some public facilities on the streets. Public bathrooms are very clean. Local "Plunket Rooms" are a real boon to mothers traveling with small children—they come with a room where you can tidy up and change diapers. The Plunket Society is a state-subsized organization providing free baby care.

• Don't try to bargain in any store.

Exercise: Feel free to jog in urban and rural areas. Both men and women can wear shorts.

MEALS

Hours and Foods

Breakfast 8:00 A.M. In winter, breakfast begins with porridge with brown sugar and cream, followed by boiled or scrambled eggs and bacon. In summer, cereal is usual, such as Wheetabix, which is a type of shredded wheat.

Lunch: Noon. Usually a light meal of bread and butter, cheeses, and salads. Note that "chicken salad" means a piece of chicken and a salad on the side.

Dinner (called "tea"): 6:00 P.M. A typical "tea" would be lamb, potatoes, cabbage, and dessert—in winter, steamed puddings, and in summer, fruit or custard.

DRESS

• For business, men should wear a suit and tie during the week. During the weekends, for a business dinner, a jacket and tie would be acceptable.

• For evening business entertainment, wear a business suit, but not the same one you've worn during the day.

• Women should wear a suit, skirt and blouse, or a dress for business meetings.

• When invited to a home for dinner for the first time, men should wear a jacket and tie, and women a dress or skirt.

• Don't expect restaurants to have a dress code. Most do not require a jacket and tie.

• If you like lamb, prepare to feast in New Zealand. Lamb is the principal meat, usually served with mint sauce or an orange-juice sauce.

• As beverages, men traditionally drink beer (most frequently served chilled) and women gin-and-tonic. In recent years, wine has become increasingly popular. For a nonalcoholic drink, ask for a fruit cordial, a fruit syrup mixed with water, or tea, the most popular beverage at every meal, served with milk and sugar.

Table Manners

• When invited to a meal, don't expect cocktails and appetizers. The meal will be served as soon as you arrive.

• Don't be surprised if there is no conversation during meals. People tend to concentrate on eating.

• Expect food to be served either in individual serving bowls and dishes or to have your plate come with food already on it.

• Although people usually finish everything on their plates, if you really don't care for something and leave it, your hostess won't be offended.

• Feel free to smoke between courses, but take your cue from your host or from other smokers in the group.

• When invited to a meal, stay for coffee or tea, and then leave. New Zealanders are "early to bed and early to rise."

Places to Eat

• Tea shops usually serve lunch, cakes, buns, coffee, and tea. In smaller towns, some serve all three meals.

• In cities, look for delicatessen-like shops for take-out ("takeaway") food or for regular sit-down meals. They offer meat pies, sausage rolls, sandwiches, cakes, coffee, and tea.

• Be aware that restaurants in the countryside are few and far between. In the countryside most serve only fish and chips, a few meat dishes, and cakes.

• Try pubs. Serving both hot and cold food, they are generally good places to eat. Pubs are open from 11:00 A.M. to 11:00 P.M., Monday through Saturday. They are closed on Sunday.

• Note that "entree" does not mean main course. It means a small serving of a hot dish before the main course.

• Note that most hotel bars are open from 11:00 A.M. to 10:00 P.M. Realize that bottles of liquor can be bought only at the bottle department of pubs or at bottle stores. There are also wine shops, which sell only wine.

• If you are in a group wanting to drink beer, save money by ordering a "jug of draft." It holds five eight-ounce glasses worth of beer.

• Remember that licensed restaurants can serve drinks only with meals.

• Be prepared for toast to be served room temperature, with the crusts cut off.

• Note that some fish-and-chips shops sell shark, often called "flake" or "lemon fish."

• Be aware that it is illegal for a restaurant to serve trout, but if you catch your own, you can ask your hotel restaurant to prepare it for you.

Specialties

• To "taste New Zealand," try: *tamarillo* (sometimes called tree tomatoes), an egg-shaped red or yellow fruit eaten as a fruit or served as a vegetable; *kumara*, a kind a yam, a staple of the Maoris, served roasted as an accompaniment to roast meat; *babaco*, a yellow fruit that tastes like a banana and looks like a papaya; *feijoa*, a round fruit, somewhat like a guava.

• In elegant restaurants, try some of the following dishes: boiled crayfish with melted butter; whitebait (a fish) fritters; muttonbird, a salty, gamey bird; Pavlova, a dessert of meringue and whipped cream with passionfruit or kiwi fruit.

• For a true New Zealand feast, go to a *baangi*, an outdoor steam roast, derived from a Maori custom. In a shallow pit large stones are covered with firewood. On top of the wood go beef, chicken, corn, potatoes, *kumaras*, shellfish, and eels. The food is then covered with sacks and earth and cooked for an hour and a half.

• Try "hogget" instead of lamb. It's an older lamb, with more flavor.

• In eating places of all types—pubs, take-away shops, railway station restaurants, etc.—look for meat pies, and try them if there is a sign saying "homemade." Varieties include minced beef, bacon and egg, and beef and kidney.

• For a typical New Zealand dessert, order Dundee cake, which is much like fruitcake, or Pavlova, the "national" dessert—meringue, whipped cream, and kiwi or strawberries.

• At tea time, eat scones and piklets, pancakes served cold with butter and jam or whipped cream.

HOTELS

• Make hotel reservations well in advance if you plan to be in New Zealand during its main holiday season, from mid-December through the end of January. Don't look for government ratings for hotels, as there are in some European countries. New Zealand doesn't offer such rankings.

• If you're staying for just one night, don't be surprised if there is an extra charge of NZ $1.

• Ask about reductions if you're staying in off-peak season (May through September) or if you are traveling with children.

• In even the least expensive hotels, expect an electric kettle (called a "jug") and tea, coffee, sugar, and milk either in your room or in a centrally located room. When you finish using the kettle, be sure to switch it off, so the heating element doesn't burn out.

• Inquire at your hotel about laundry facilities on the premises where you can do your own laundry. There is rarely a charge.

• Should you want bed-and-breakfast accommodations, look for guesthouses or private hotels. In both you'll have hot and cold water, a shared bath, and a large breakfast. Guesthouses sometimes serve dinner—but only to guests—while private hotels serve all meals both to residents and non-residents. Neither serves liquor. Ask if you need to reserve for dinner when you check in.

• For another way to meet native New Zealanders, stay in motel flats, which are usually operated by owners. Usually the flats consist of a lounge with sofa beds, one or two bedrooms, a kitchen, and a bathroom. Expect to make your own beds and do your own dishes.

• Note that licensed hotels serve drinks from 11:00 A.M. to 10:00 P.M. (until 11:00 P.M. on Saturdays) in bars, but you can order a drink at any time with a meal, and registered guests will be served at any time.

• If you decide on a farmhouse holiday, you'll have your own room but will usually share a bathroom with the family. Included in the cost will be two meals a day, taken with the family. You needn't help with the farm chores, but if you want to, just ask the family.

• In planning your schedule, re-member that check-in time at most hotels is 2:00 P.M., and check-out time is 10:00 A.M.

• If you use a washcloth, bring one with you, as they are sometimes not furnished in New Zealand accommodations.

TIPPING

• Be aware that tipping is not widespread. Neither service charges nor taxes are added to restaurant or hotel bills, since employed people don't depend on tips for their income.

• Don't tip taxi drivers unless they carry several bags for you.

• Give porters at airports, train stations, and hotels NZ$1 to $3 per bag.

PRIVATE HOMES

• Feel free to drop in on friends without making advance plans. A good time for visiting is about 3:00 P.M.—weekdays or weekends—near teatime.

• Remember that usually only women do the dishes. (Men retire to the living room for a beer.) A woman should ask the hostess if she can help with the dishes. The offer may or may not be accepted.

• If you make long-distance calls from a home, offer to pay. Local calls are free.

• Remember that New Zealanders do not necessarily bathe fully every day. If you're staying with a family, ask the hostess if it's convenient for you to have a bath. Water may have to be heated in advance.

Gifts: If invited to a meal, bring chocolates or whiskey.

• Other gifts include university T-shirts and sweatshirts for teenagers; good-quality leather items, such as handbags and belts; sets of sheets with fitted bottoms (if you know the bed size) and towels; chewing gum for children.

• Avoid giving clothing with designer labels on the outside.

MONEY AND BUSINESS

Hours

Business Offices: Monday through Friday, 9:00 A.M. to 5:00 P.M.

Government Offices: Monday through Friday, 8:30 A.M. to 4:30 P.M.

Banks: Monday through Friday, 9:00 A.M. to 4:30 P.M.

Shops: Monday through Friday, 9:00 A.M. to 5:00 P.M., and Saturday, 9:30 A.M. to 12:30 P.M. One night a week, usually Thursday or Friday, shops are open until 9:00 P.M.

Money

• The New Zealand dollar is divided into 100 cents. Coins: 5, 10, 20, and 50 cents, NZ $1, and $2. Banknotes: $5, $10, $20, $50, and $100.

• Be assured that you will be able to use credit cards. Hotels, restaurants, and shops usually welcome

American Express, Visa, Barclaycard, MasterCard, Access, and Diners Club.

Business Practices

• If your business relates to manufacturing, do some research before attempting to do business in New Zealand. The country's industry is protected by very strict regulations. If an item can be manufactured locally, it can't be imported.

• Be sure to make an appointment three to four weeks in advance with business and government offices.

• Avoid business trips during December and January, the most popular holiday period. The best times are February through May and October and November.

• Be five minutes early for appointments. Punctuality is very important.

• Expect the first meeting to be either lunch at a restaurant or hotel or a meeting in the New Zealand company's office. At an office meeting, you'll be offered coffee, or tea, with sugar. If you don't want either, it's acceptable to refuse.

• Be prepared for the pace of business to be less intense than in Western countries. New Zealanders don't believe that "time is money."

• Be aware that New Zealand businessmen are more conservative than their Australian counterparts. The atmosphere is similar to the business climate of London.

• Fax machines are very common

and can be found in many hotels and motels.

• To impress New Zealand businessmen, bone up on sports, especially trout fishing and rugby. New Zealanders will be pleased if you show an interest in the country's sports, as they are very proud of their accomplishments.

• Never assert authority in a heavy-handed way. Be polite in asking subordinates to do something.

Business Entertaining: Note that wives are included in invitations for evening entertainment, since business won't be discussed.

HOLIDAYS AND SPECIAL OCCASIONS

Holidays: New Year's Day and next day (January 1 and 2); Watangi Day (commemorating the treaty of Watangi between the Maori chieftains and the British— February 6); Good Friday; Easter Monday; ANZAC (Australia New Zealand Army Corps) and Memorial Day (April 25); Queen's Birthday (first Monday in June); Labor Day (last Monday in October); Christmas (December 25); Boxing Day (December 26).

• Note that in Wellingon, Anniversary Day (January 21) is a holiday; Anniversary Day is celebrated in Auckland on January 29.

• Be aware that New Zealand comes to a halt on Melbourne Cup Day in Australia (first Tuesday in November). The day is devoted to betting and keeping track of the race events by radio.

TRANSPORTATION

Public Transportation

• Look for taxis at stands or phone for one. If you call, there will be an additional charge of NZ $1 to $1.50. In larger cities, taxis have meters; in smaller places, drivers will quote a flat fee. It isn't necessary to tip taxi drivers unless they perform a special service, such as carrying several pieces of luggage.

• Don't use buses for long-distance travel. They go over winding roads, make many rest and refreshment stops, and often stop so that the driver can deliver packages en route. If you can't take a train to your destination, it's better to rent a car than to go by bus. However, if you're on a strict budget and have a good deal of time, buses are the cheapest way to travel.

• If possible, use trains—they are clean and comfortable—for long trips. Be aware, however, that trains don't go everywhere. Although trains don't have classes, some have twinette sleeper cars and a section of seats, as well as a buffet car for food and drink. Trains without buffet cars make refreshment stops of 15 minutes, allowing time for a visit to the station snackbar where you can get sausage rolls, hot meat pies, or sandwiches.

• Ask your travel agent at home about buying a Travelpass, which allows travel for about half the normal fare. Also ask about the types of trains which will go to your destination. Book train travel in advance through travel agents or at the train station, if possible.

• Be sure to book in advance for inter-island steamers. There are no classes and no overnight accommodations. Trips take about 3½ hours. The steamers have bars, cafeterias, TV rooms, information bureaus, and shops.

Driving

• Remember that driving is on the left, as in Britain.

• Expect roads to be good, except in remote areas.

• Bring your current driver's li-

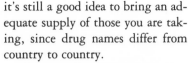

cense or an International Driver's License to rent a car.

• Wear your seat belts. It's illegal not to.

• Note that some rental agencies offer visitors the same no-fault accident compensation as New Zealanders do. Shop around for one that does.

• Keep in mind that the speed limit on the open road is 100 kilometers per hour and in cities and towns 50 kilometers per hour. When an area is sign-posted LSZ, that identifies a Limited Speed Zone and means that you must drive *very* cautiously.

it's still a good idea to bring an adequate supply of those you are taking, since drug names differ from country to country.

• Women should note that most toiletries, sanitary napkins, and tampons are available.

• The major health hazard is sunburn or sunstroke. Be sure to use sunscreen and wear a hat and long sleeved shirt.

LEGAL MATTERS, SAFETY, AND HEALTH

• Don't try to bring New Zealand currency into the country; it's prohibited.

• Don't try to take Maori artifacts out of the country.

• Remember that only those over age 20 are allowed in pubs, and in some pubs women are not welcome. Look for signs to that effect.

Health: Be assured that prescription drugs are widely available;

KEY PHRASES

New Zealand	*North American English*
Sheila	Girl
Tucker	Food
Kai (Kye)	Food
Bach	Summer cottage
Pudding	Dessert
Dag	A good guy
Hard case	A character, a funny guy
Mate	Male friend
Poms, pommies	The English
Kiwi (with a capital "K")	A native New Zealander
Ta-ta (tah-tah)	Good-bye
Chemist	Pharmacist
Lorry	Truck
Krook	Sick

Although you probably won't hear Maori spoken, some Maori words turn up in place names. Among them:

Nui	Big, plenty of
Roto	Lake
Rua	Cave, hollow, or two
Tahi	One, single
Wai	Water
Whanga	Bay, inlet, or stretch of water

ABOUT THE AUTHORS

Our collaboration on *The Travelers' Guide to European Customs and Manners* has led to four more books on customs and manners around the world: *The Travelers' Guide to Asian Customs and Manners, The Travelers' Guide to Latin American Customs and Manners, The Travelers' Guide to Middle Eastern and North African Customs and Manners*, and *The Travelers' Guide to African Customs and Manners*. In our research and travel, we've discovered the infinite diversity of the world's cultures.

We brought to this book our love of travel and our curiosity about the daily lives of people in other countries. (Before collaborating, Elizabeth Devine had written books and numerous travel articles, and Nancy Braganti had taught foreign languages in America, Europe, and Israel.) Between us, we have visited about half the countries in this book.

Revising this book involved hours of personal interviews, reading, and traveling—to verify that information in the first edition was still valid and to find out how the cultures had changed since our first edition.

We interviewed dozens of people from the Asian countries covered, as well as Westerners who have lived there. For the greatest breadth of coverage, we interviewed people in a wide range of occupations: entrepreneurs, journalists, teachers, dentists, anthropologists, secretaries, newspaper editors, hotel managers, etc. We checked and rechecked information with our sources and with people at various embassies and consulates.

ELIZABETH DEVINE
NANCY L. BRAGANTI

Additional copies of *The Travelers' Guide to Asian Customs and Manners* may be ordered by returning the coupon below with a check or money order to Publishers Book and Audio, P. O. Box 070059, 5446 Arthur Kill Road, Staten Island, NY 10307; for credit card orders, call (800) 288-2131. For information on quantity orders and discounts, call the St. Martin's Press Special Markets Department at (800) 221-7945 or (212) 674-5151, extension 645.

Also available in this series are *The Travelers' Guide to Latin American Customs and Manners*, *The Travelers' Guide to Middle Eastern and North African Customs and Manners*, and *The Travelers' Guide to African Customs and Manners*.

Please send me _____ copy(ies) of *The Travelers' Guide to Asian Customs and Manners*
(ISBN 0-312-1953-1) @ $16.95 per book $_____
Please send me _____ copy(ies) of *The Travelers' Guide to Latin American Customs and Manners*
(ISBN 0-312-02303-0) @ $13.95 per book $_____
Please send me _____ copy(ies) of *The Travelers' Guide to Middle Eastern and North African Customs and Manners*
(ISBN 0-312-05523-4) @ $13.95 per book $_____
Please send me _____ copy(ies) of *The Travelers' Guide to African Customs and Manners*
(ISBN 0-312-11909-7) @ $14.95 per book $_____
Postage and handling
($2.00 for the first copy + $1.00 for each additional book) $_____
Amount enclosed $_____

Name_____
Address_____
City_____ State_____ Zip_____